NTA UGC NET/JRF/SET ECONOMICS

Dr. Simranjit Kaur

Published By

Invincible Publication Pvt. Ltd.

Published by

Invincible Publication Pvt. Ltd.

201A, SAS Tower, Sector 38, Gurugram – 122003
www.invinciblepublishers.com

NTA UGC NET/JRF/SET ECONOMICS BY Dr. Simranjit Kaur

Updated Edition 2025-26

This edition can be exported from India only by Invincible Publication.

ISBN: 978-93-90767-20-5

Invincible Publication Pvt. Ltd.

Sales Office: 4760-61/23, Basement, Pratap Street, Ansari Road,

Daryaganj, New Delhi - 110002
Email: invinciblepublishers@gmail.com

Preface

Welcome Future Professors and Research Scholars!

This book is designed to be a valuable companion for aspirants preparing for **UGC NET/JRF, SET, PGT**, and other **state-level Assistant Professor examinations in Economics**. It offers **unit-wise summarized notes** for all ten units, presented in a **lucid and easy-to-understand language** helpful for quick revision. The content is tailored to the **objective-type exam pattern**, and every effort has been made to simplify complex concepts in a learner-friendly manner. Each unit covers key concepts and frequently asked topics. Instead of blindly following just syllabus, this book helps students focus on what truly matters for cracking the exam. We truly hope it proves to be an essential resource on your journey toward success in the teaching field.

For detailed conceptual classes and lectures, kindly follow the Course Classes, available on MS STUDY GURU application. Stay connected for regular updates, lectures and guidance through the online platforms of Dr. Simranjit Kaur.

Telegram Channel: MS Study Guru

YouTube Channel: MS Study Guru

Android App: MS Study Guru (Available on Play Store)

*For Previous Year Questions (MCQs practice), you may refer to our **UGC NET Economics previous year questions book**, which provides questions with explanations by Simranjit Kaur.*

Content

Note: The book is revision notes. For detailed syllabus and explanations kindly rely on course classes of MS Study Guru by Simranjit Kaur.

Microeconomics

Concept Of Demand

The concept of demand was given by Alfred Marshall in 1890's in his book "Principles of Economics".

Law of demand: It was given by 'Alfred Marshall.' It states that there is an inverse relationship between price of the commodity and the quantity demanded of it, other things remaining constant.
In case of normal goods, the demand curve slopes downward from left to right.

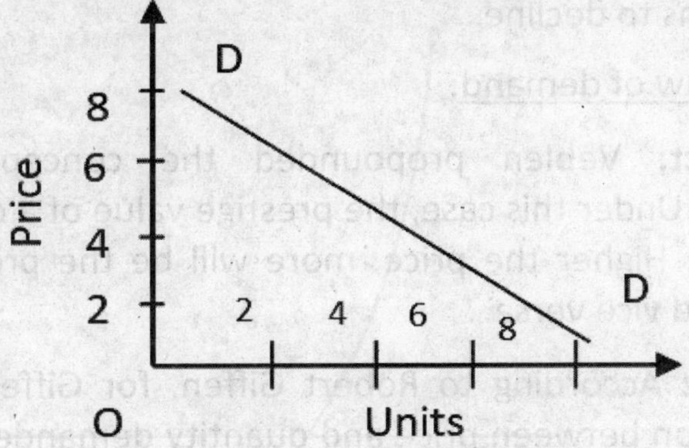

Reasons for downward sloping demand curve –

1. **Income effect:**

Price decrease
↓
Real income increases
↓
Purchasing power increases
↓
Increase in demand

2. Substitution Effect:

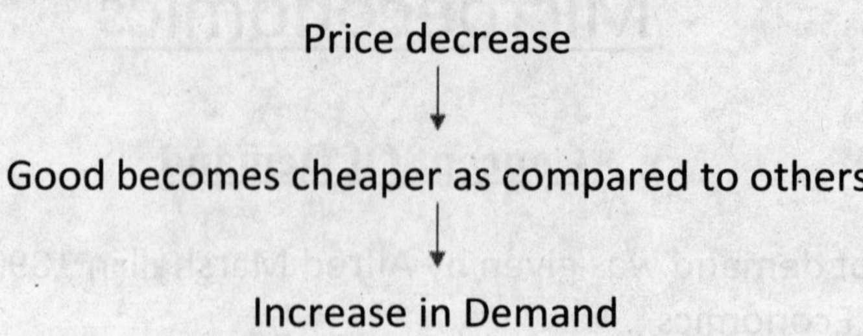

3. Law of diminishing marginal utility:

According to this principle, as consumer buy more units of a commodity, the marginal utility of that commodity continues to decline. Therefore, consumer will buy more units of commodity only when price of that product begins to decline.

Exceptions to the law of demand:

1. **Veblen Effect:** Veblen propounded the concept of Conspicuous consumption. Under this case, the prestige value of a commodity is linked with its price. Higher the price, more will be the prestige and quantity demanded and vice versa.

2. **Giffen Goods:** According to Robert Giffen, for Giffen goods there is a positive relation between price and quantity demanded. Giffen goods are low priced goods having only few substitutes i.e. bread and rice. For example: rise in the price of bread make drain on the resources of poor families that they forced to curtail the consumption of meat and more expensive foods and will consume more of bread.

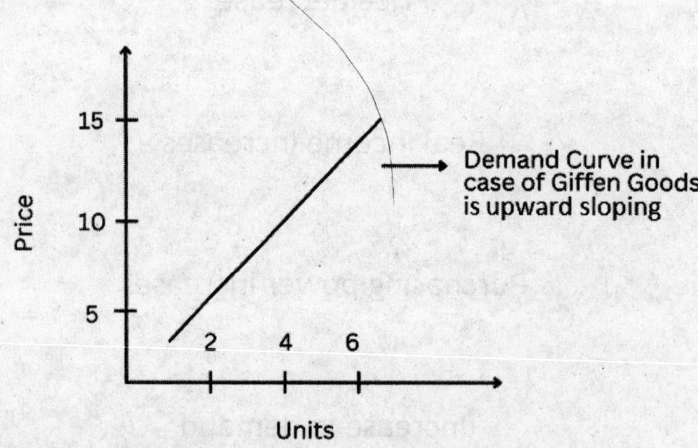

3. **Bandwagon effect:** Individual demand commodities because others are doing so. So, demand for a product can increase even when its price rises. Example: Many people buy the latest iPhone just because everyone else is buying it, not necessarily due to its technical superiority.

4. **Snob Effect:** Individuals demand commodities because others are not demanding them because commodities have prestige value or exclusive than others. Examples: People buy Luxury Watches (Rolex, Patek Philippe) not just for timekeeping but because they are expensive and exclusive.

Inferior Goods And Giffen Goods

Giffen Goods	Inferior Goods
1. Giffen goods are special type of inferior goods whose demand increases when price increases, violating the law of demand.	1. Inferior goods are those goods whose demand decreases as a consumer's income increases.
2. Violates law of demand (upward sloping demand curve).	2. Follows law of demand (downward sloping demand curve).
3. Substitution effect is weaker than negative income effect, as total demand increases when price increases.	3. Substitution effect is stronger than negative income effect, so when price rises, consumer buys less of the good & switches to substitutes.

*All these effects are explained in detail in the upcoming sections

Demand Function

Factor Determining Demand	Relation with Demand
1.Taste and preference of demand	+
2.Income of the People	+
3.Change in the price of related goods	Substitutes (+) Complements (-)
4.Advertising	+

5.Future expectation about the price	+

Increase or Decrease in Demand

- Leads to shift in demand curve.
- Caused by factors other than price of that commodity.

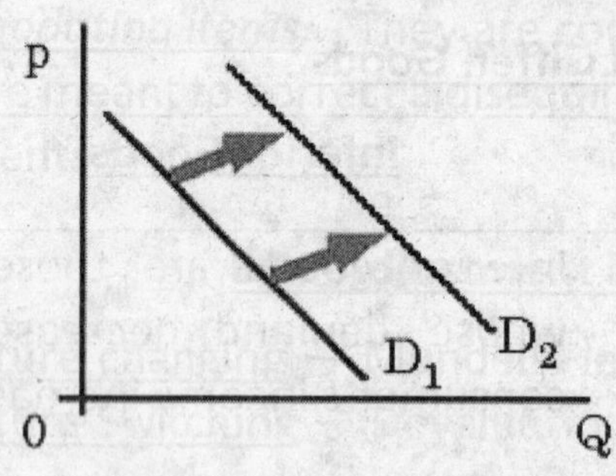

An increase in demand

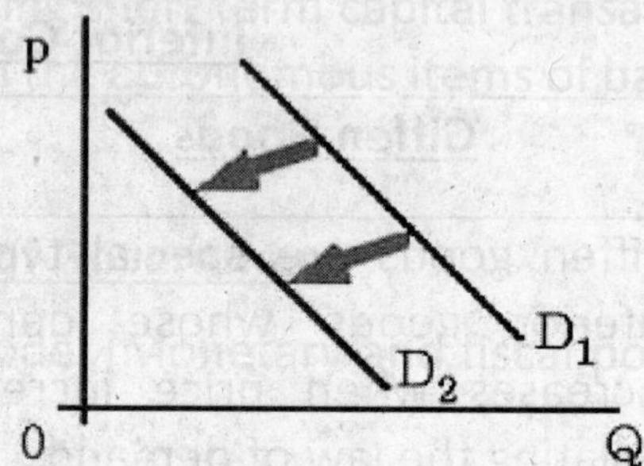

A decrease in demand

Expansion or Contraction of Demand

- Leads to movement along the demand curve.
- Caused due to increase or decrease in price.

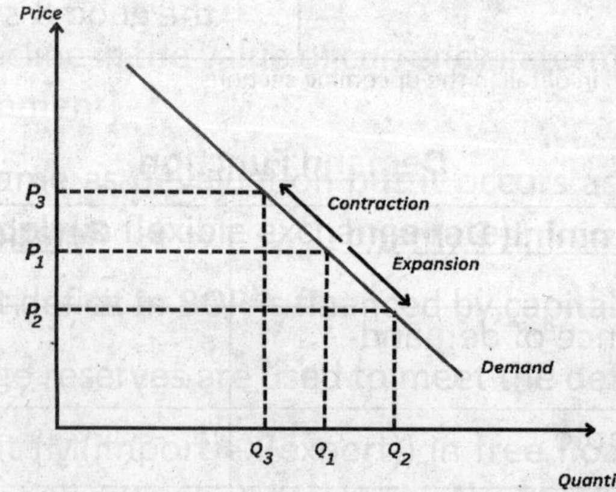

Miscellaneous

Durable Goods	Perishable Goods
➢ They can be stored	➢ They cannot be stored
➢ Prices are not volatile	➢ Their prices are volatile

Derived Demand: It is the demand for goods which are used to produce other goods. Example labour.

Demand Function: D = f(p), i.e., demand is function of price

Inverse Demand Function: p = f(D), i.e. price is function of demand

Substitution Good	Complementary Goods
Substitute goods are independent to each other i.e. tea and coffee.	Complementary goods are interdependent i.e. car and petroleum.
If the price of one good increase the demand of a substitute increases.	If the price of good increases the demand of its complementary decreases.
Cross elasticity of substitute goods will be positive.	Cross elasticity of complementary goods is negative.

Law of Supply

The law of supply is a fundamental principle of economic theory which states that, keeping other factors constant, an increase in sales price results in an increase in quantity supplied. In other words, there is a direct relationship between price and quantity supplied; quantities respond in the same direction as price changes.

Elasticity of Demand

- Concept was given by Marshall.
- Elasticity of demand measures the responsiveness or change in demand due to factors like price, income, price of related goods etc.

Price Elasticity

Price elasticity is the proportional change in quantity demanded divided by the proportionate change in price. Formulae for elasticity:

$$\text{Price Elasticity of Demand} = \frac{\%\ \text{Change in the Quantity Demanded}\ (\Delta Q)}{\%\ \text{Change in the Price}\ (\Delta P)}$$

$$\text{Price Elasticity of Supply} = \frac{\%\ \text{Change in the Quantity Supplied}\ (\Delta Q)}{\%\ \text{Change in the Price}\ (\Delta P)}$$

Degrees of Price Elasticity of Demand:

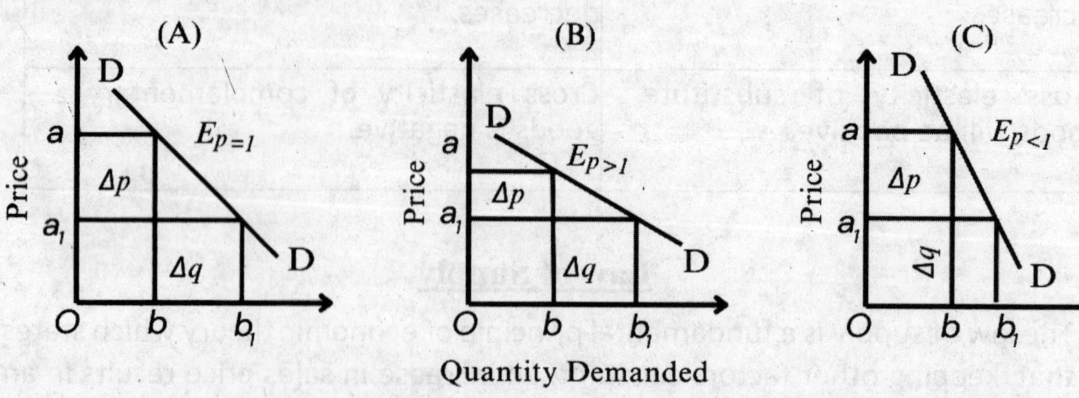

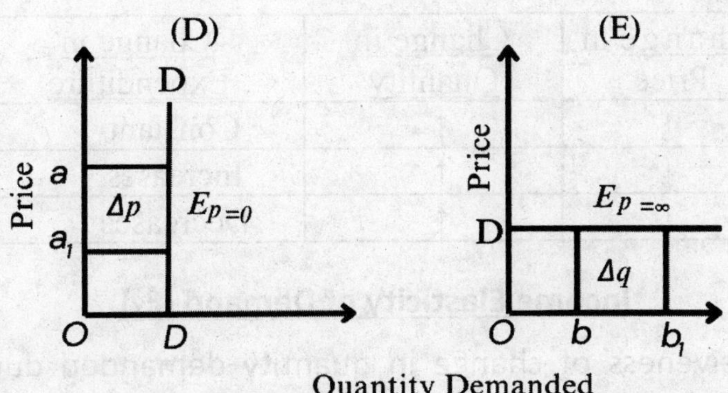

Measurement of Price Elasticity of Demand:

a) Proportionate Method:

$$E_p = \frac{\%\ change\ in\ q}{\%\ change\ in\ p} = (-)\frac{\Delta Q}{Q}\ x\ \frac{P}{\Delta P}$$

b) Point elasticity method:

$$E_p at\ any\ point = \frac{Lower\ Segment}{Upper\ Segment}$$

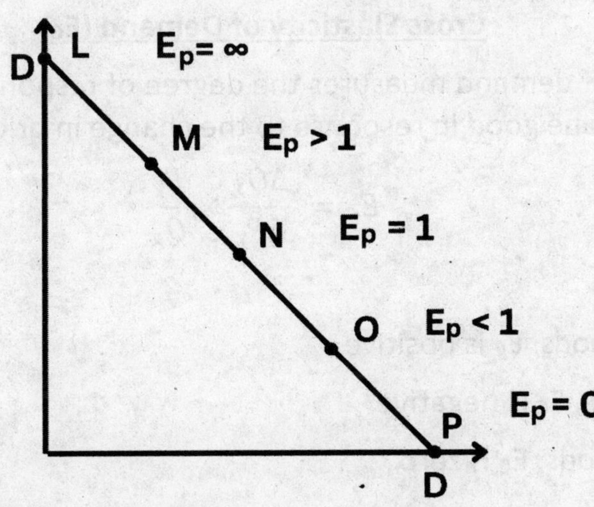

c) Revenue method:

$$E_p = \frac{AR}{AR - MR}$$

d) Total Expenditure Method: Propounded by Marshall

Situation	Change in Price	Change in Quantity	Change in Expenditure	Ed
A	↓	↑	Constant	Ed = 1
B	↓	↑	Increases	Ed > 1
C	↓	↑	Decreases	Ed< 1

Income Elasticity of Demand (E_Y)

It is the responsiveness of change in quantity demanded due to change in income levels.

$$E_Y = \frac{\Delta Q}{\Delta Y} \times \frac{Y}{Q}$$

For Normal Good, $E_Y > 0$

For Inferior Good, $E_Y < 0$

For Luxury Good, $E_Y > 1$

For Necessary Good, $0 < E_Y < 1$

Cross Elasticity of Demand (E_C)

Cross elasticity of demand measures the degree of responsiveness of change in the demand for one good in response to the change in price of another good.

$$E_C = \frac{\Delta Q_X}{\Delta P_Y} \times \frac{P_Y}{Q_X}$$

For substitute goods, E_C is positive

For complements, E_C is negative

For unrelated goods, E_C is zero

Elasticity of Substitution (E_S)

$$E_S = \frac{\Delta\left(\frac{Q_X}{Q_Y}\right)}{\frac{Q_X}{Q_Y}} \times \frac{MRS_{XY}}{\Delta MRS_{XY}}$$

Numerical Problems

Question 1. Match the following

List I	**List II**
Two-Variable Linear Regression Model	**Elasticity**
A. $Y = \beta_1 + \beta_2 X$	I. $\beta_2 X$
B. $\ln Y = \beta_1 + \beta_2 X$	II. β_2
C. $Y = \beta_1 + \beta_2 \ln X$	III. $\beta_2 (X/Y)$
D. $\ln Y = \beta_1 + \beta_2 \ln X$	IV. $\beta_2 (1/Y)$

A. $E_d = \frac{dY}{dX}\frac{X}{Y} = \beta_2 \frac{X}{Y}$

Answer: A-III, B-I, C-IV, D-II

Question 2. For the demand function $P = 16 - q - 0.5q^2$, find the price elasticity of demand at q=4.

$$P = 16 - q - 0.5q^2$$
$$P = 16 - 4 - 0.5(4)^2$$
$$P = 4$$
$$\frac{d_p}{d_q} = -1 - q$$
$$q = 4$$
$$\frac{d_p}{d_q} = -1 - 4 = -5$$
$$E_d = -\frac{d_q}{d_p} \times \frac{p}{q} = -\left(\frac{-1}{5}\right) \times \frac{4}{4} = 0.2$$

Question 3. For a demand function $p = 10 - 2x - 0.5x^2$, what is the price elasticity of demand at $x = 2$.

$$p = 10 - 2x - 0.5x^2$$
$$p = 10 - 2(2) - 0.5(2)^2$$
$$p = 4$$

Also,

$$\frac{dp}{dx} = -2 - x = -2 - 2 = -4$$

Now,

$$E_p = -\frac{dq}{dp} \times \frac{p}{q} = -\frac{-1}{4} \times \frac{4}{2} = 0.5$$

Question 4. The demand function for Good A is given by $Q_A = 100 - 2P_A + 0.2Y + 0.3P_B$, Find the cross-price elasticities of demand at $P_A = 6$, $Y = 500$, $P_B = 10$.

$$Q_A = 100 - 2P_A + 0.2Y + 0.3P_B$$

$$\frac{\Delta Q_A}{\Delta P_B} = 0.3$$

Now put values of

$$Q_A = 100 - 2(6) + 0.2(500) + 0.3(100)$$
$$= 100 - 12 + 100 + 3$$
$$= 191$$
$$Now, \xi = 0.3 \times \frac{10}{191}$$
$$= 0.016$$

Utility Analysis

Cardinal or Marshallian Approach: Utility is the power of a good to satisfy human wants.

Cardinal Utility Analysis

Assumptions:

a) Utility is cardinal [It can be measured]

b) Consumer is rational

c) Marginal utility of money is constant

d) Utilities are independent

e) Law of diminishing marginal utility is based on introspection.

Total utility (TU)

Total satisfaction achieved after consuming all the units of a particular commodity.

$TU = \Sigma MU_X$

Marginal Utility (MU)

Additional utility achieved after consuming additional unit of a commodity. Marginal utility curve is the slope of the total utility curve.

$$\text{MU} = \frac{\Delta TU}{\Delta Q} \qquad MU_n = TU_n - TU_{n-1}$$

Law of Diminishing Marginal Utility:

This law was first put by Gossen in 1854. It states that as the consumer consumes more and more of a commodity, the marginal utility derived on consuming each additional unit keeps on declining.

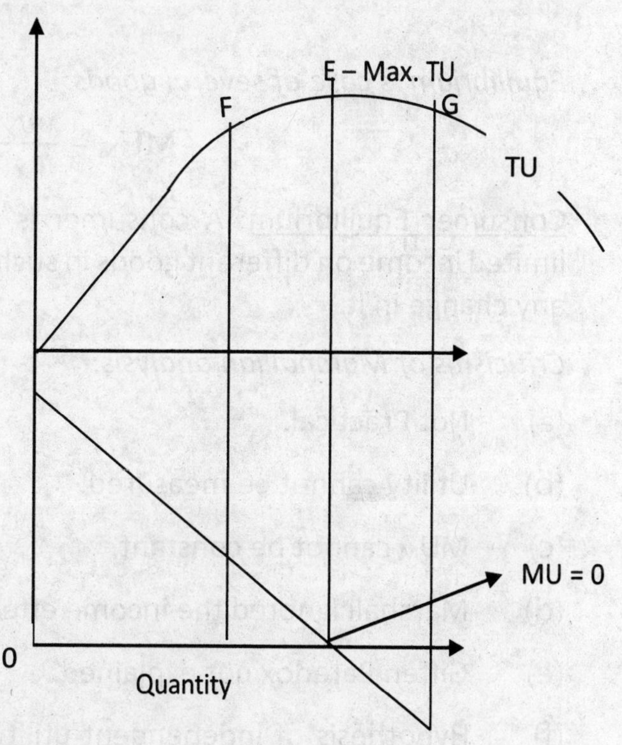

Relation between TU & MU:

- When TU is increasing, MU is decreasing.
- When TU is maximum, MU is zero.
- When TU starts declining, MU become negative.

Law of Diminishing Marginal Utility depends on the following factors:

- Goods are not perfect substitutes for each other.
- Marginal utility of money is constant.

Law of Equi-Marginal Utility

It is known as Gossen's second law. The law states that a consumer should spend his limited income on different commodities in such a way that the last Rupee spend on each commodity yield him equal marginal utility in order to get maximum satisfaction.

Equilibrium is case of single good:

$$MU_x = P_x \cdot MU_m$$

But if we **assume:**

$$MU_m = 1$$

Then it simplifies to:

$$MU_x = P_x$$

Equilibrium is case of several goods:

$$\mathrm{MU_M} = \frac{MU_X}{P_X} = \frac{MU_Y}{P_Y} \text{----}$$

Consumer Equilibrium: A consumer is in equilibrium when he has spent his limited income on different goods in such a way that he has no tendency to make any change in it.

Criticisms of Marshallian analysis:

(a) Not Practical.

(b) Utility cannot be measured.

(c) MU_M cannot be constant.

(d) Marshall ignored the income effect.

(e) Giffen Paradox not explained.

(f) Hypothesis of independent utility is wrong. For Ex. - utility from a pen depends upon its ink also. So, it is not independent.

Ordinal Utility

The theory of ordinal utility was developed in 1934 by British economists John Hicks and Roy Allen. The main ordinal utility theories are Indifference curve analysis and revealed preference theory. J.R. Hicks published his theory of indifference curves in his 1939 book, Value and Capital. Paul Samuelson first introduced the theory of revealed preference in 1938.

Indifference Curve (IC):

An IC is the locus of points which yield same utility to the consumer.

Assumptions:

(a) Utilities cannot be measured. They can be ranked.

(b) Consumer is rational.

(c) Diminishing Marginal Rate of substitution.

$$MRS_{XY} = \Delta Y/\Delta X = MU_X/MU_Y$$

(d) Based on weak ordering.

(e) Preferences of a consumer are consistent and transitive. In the indifference curve approach, if a consumer is indifferent between bundles A and B at one point in time, they should also be indifferent between A and B at another time. Transitivity in IC approach depicts that if the consumer is indifferent between A and B and also between B and C; then it is assumed that he will be indifferent between A and C too.

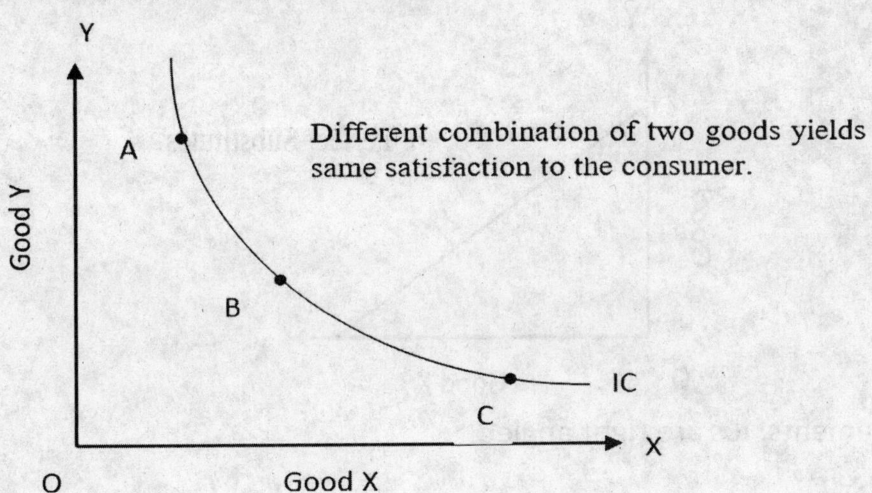

Indifference Map: Indifference map shows all indifference curves which rank preferences of consumer (set of ICs').

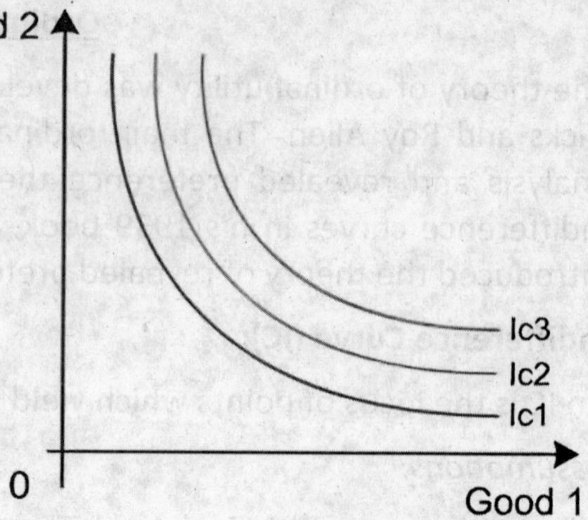

Properties of IC:

- Downward sloping.
- Two ICs never intersect.
- Higher IC means higher satisfaction
- Convex to the origin.
  - The convex shape of IC shows diminishing MRS.
  - MRS_{XY} is the amount of Y that will be given up to obtain each additional unit of X.
  - MRS is decreasing because want of the Good is satiable. Goods are imperfect substitutes of each other.

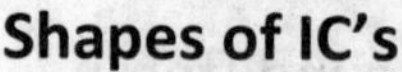

Shapes of IC's

For perfect substitutes, MRS_{XY} = Constant and $E_s = \infty$ [infinity]

For perfect complements, the Marginal Rate of Substitution (MRS_{xy}) is either 0 or ∞ (infinity) and $E_s = 0$

(a)Substitutes: IC is downward sloping straight line.

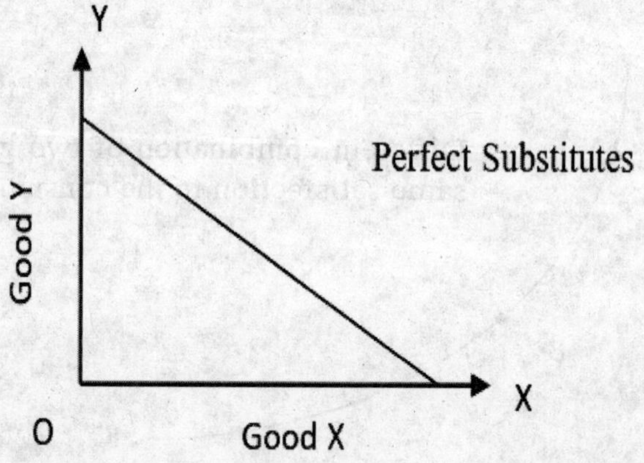

(b)Complements: ICs are right angled.

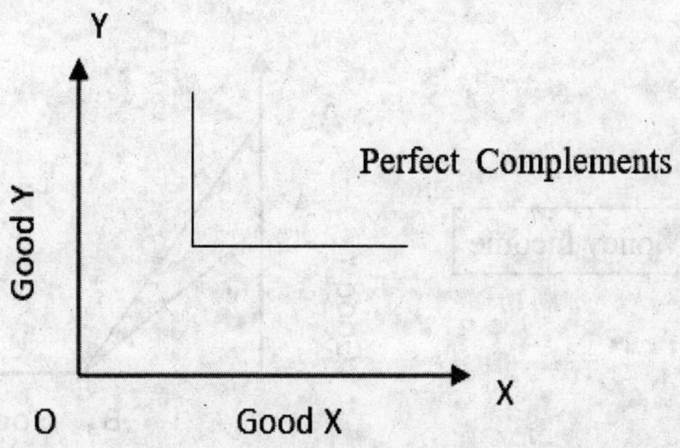

Budget Constraint/ Budget Line/Price Line:

It shows the combinations of goods that can be purchased if the entire money income is spent.

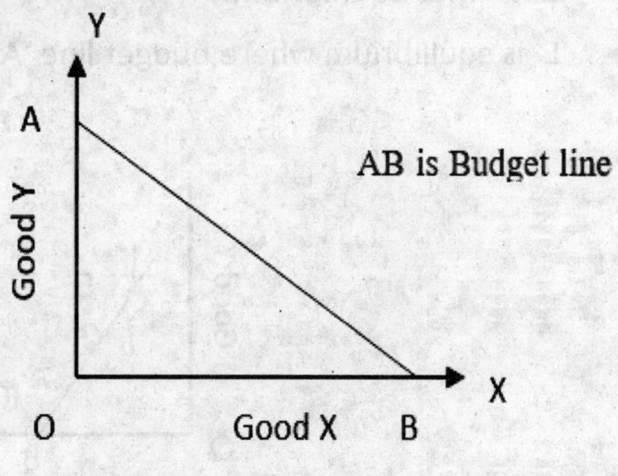

- With change in income levels, budget line shifts.
- With change in prices, budget line moves. With decrease in price, budget line moves forward. As a result of decrease in price of 'X', budget line moves from AB to AB_1.

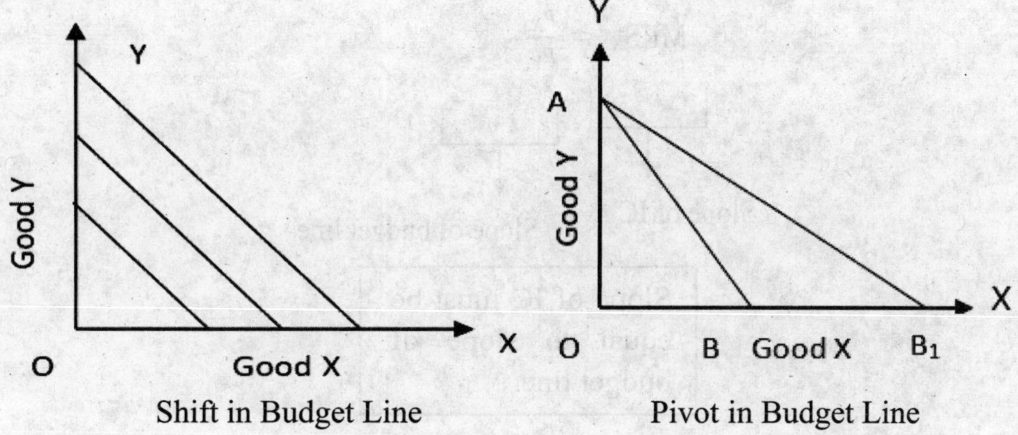

Shift in Budget Line

Pivot in Budget Line

- As a result of decrease in price of 'Y', budget line moves from BA to BA_1

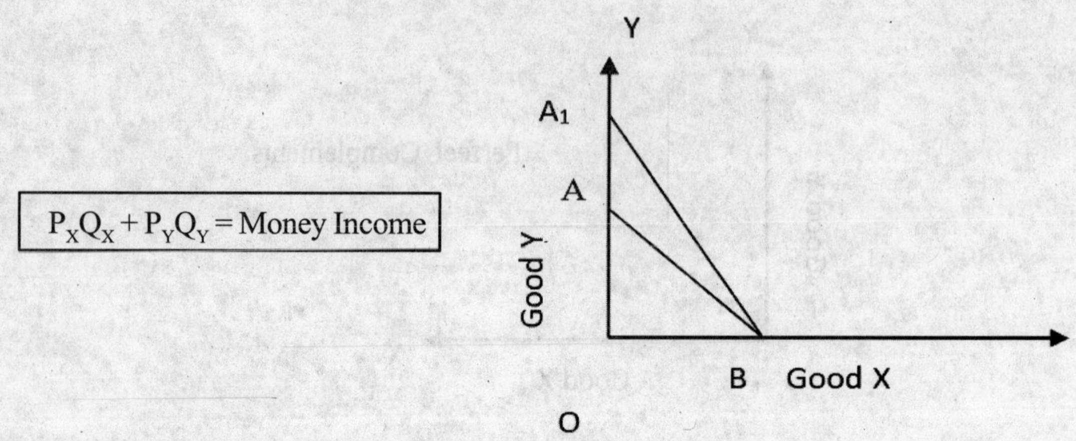

Consumer Equilibrium:

'E' is equilibrium where budget line 'AB' and Indifference Curve 'IC' touches.

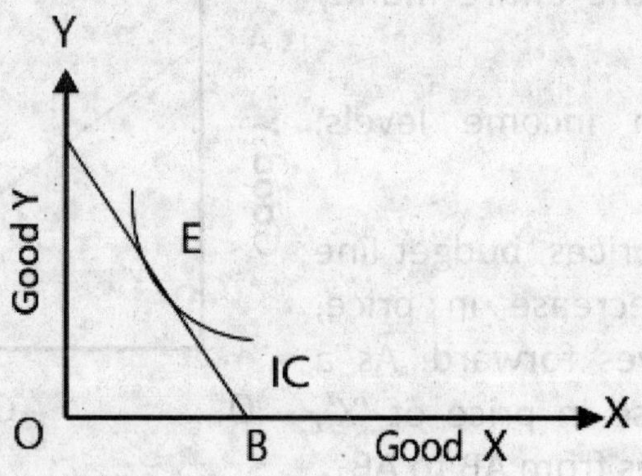

First Order Condition:

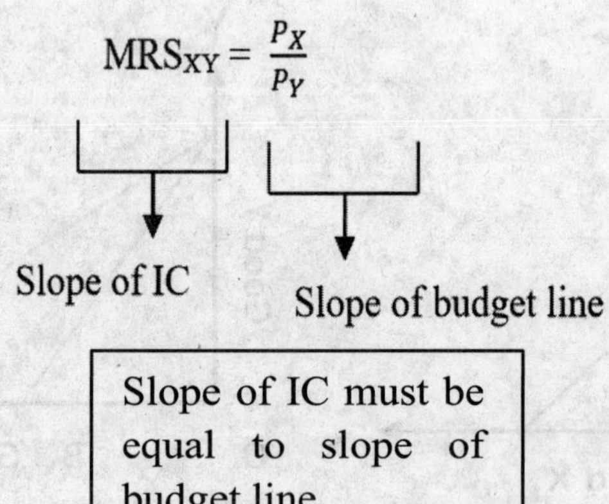

Second order condition:

At the point of tangency, IC should be convex to the origin.

In other words, MRS_{XY} must be falling at the point of equilibrium.

Corner Solution:

In case of corner equilibrium for convex IC's, consumer buy only one commodity

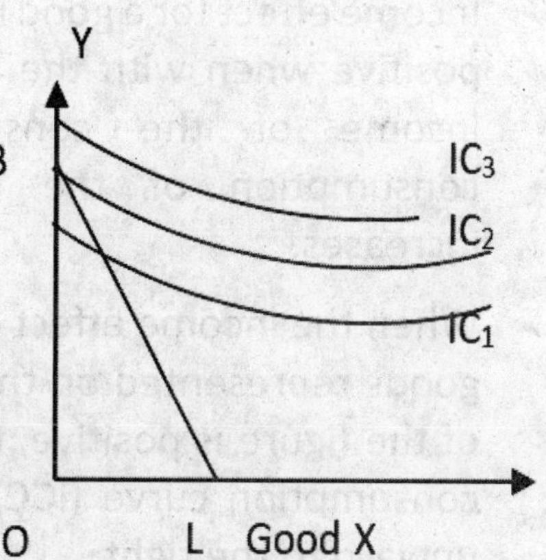

Monotonic preferences:

Consumer prefer a particular bundle over another bundle if the former consists of at least more of one good and no less of other. If A (3,5) and B (3,2) are available to consumer then he will prefer A over B as A consists of more units of second commodity.

Diamond-Water Paradox by Adam Smith

He observed that water that is essential for life has very low price, whereas diamonds which have little practical use, are very expensive. Few economists, solved the diamond-water paradox by introducing the concept of Marginal Utility. Water is available in abundant quantity so that its relative Marginal Utility is low. Thus, its price is low. Diamonds are scarce, their relative Marginal Utility is quite high and thus their price is high.

Income Effect: Income Consumption Curve

The income effect means the change in the consumer's purchases of goods as a result of a change in his money income.

- Income consumption curve is thus the locus of equilibrium points at various levels of consumer's income.
- Income consumption curve traces out the income effect on the quantity consumed of the goods.

- Income effect can either be positive or negative.
- Income effect for a good is said to be positive when with the increase in income of the consumer, his consumption of the good also increases.
- When the income effect of both the goods represented on the two axes of the figure is positive, the income consumption curve (ICC) will slope upward to the right.
- Income effect for a good is said to be negative when with the increases in his income, the consumer reduces his consumption of the good. Such goods for which income effect is negative are called Inferior Goods.

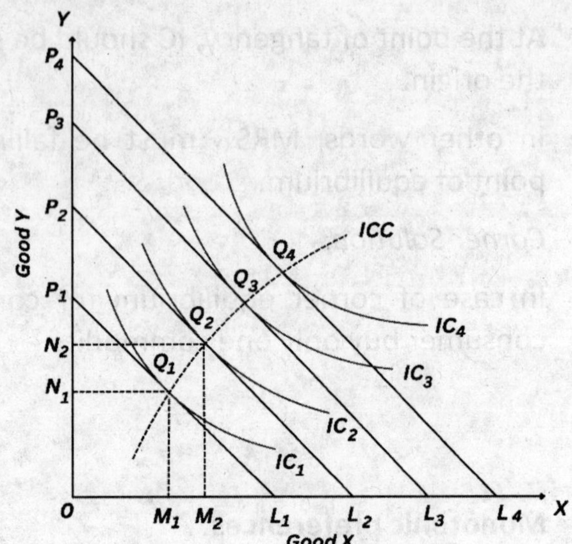

ICC in Case of Normal Good

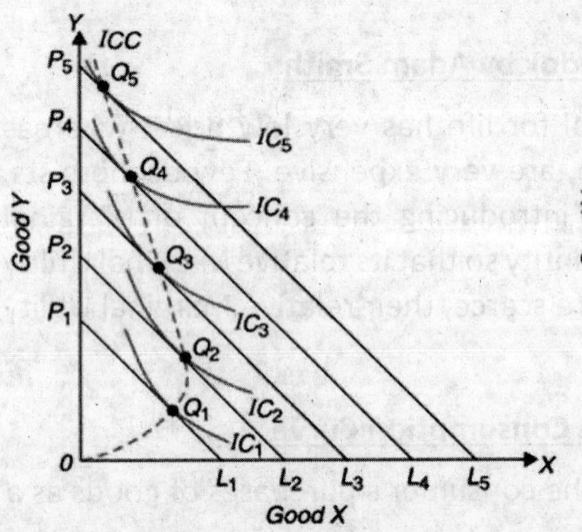

Income Consumption Curve in Case of Good X being Inferior Good

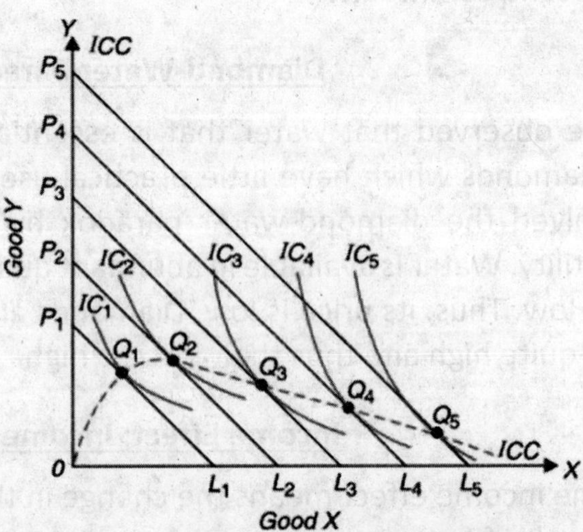

Income Consumption Curve in Case of Good Y being Inferior Good

Income Consumption Curve and Engle Curve

(Given by Ernet Engel (1821-1896)

- As the income of a family increases, the proportion of its income spent on necessities such as food falls and that spent on luxuries (consisting of industrial goods and services) increases.
- The poor families spend relatively large proportion of their income on necessities, whereas rich families spend a relatively a large part of their income on luxuries.
- This change in the pattern of consumption expenditure (that is, decline in the proportion of income spent on food and other necessities and an increase in the proportion of income spent on luxuries) with the rise in income of the families has been called **Engel's law.**
- It explains the relationship between income and quantities purchased of goods.
- The curve showing the relationship between the levels of income and quantity purchased of particular commodities has therefore been called Engel curve.
- Engel curve for normal goods is upward-sloping which shows that as income increases, consumer buys more of a commodity.

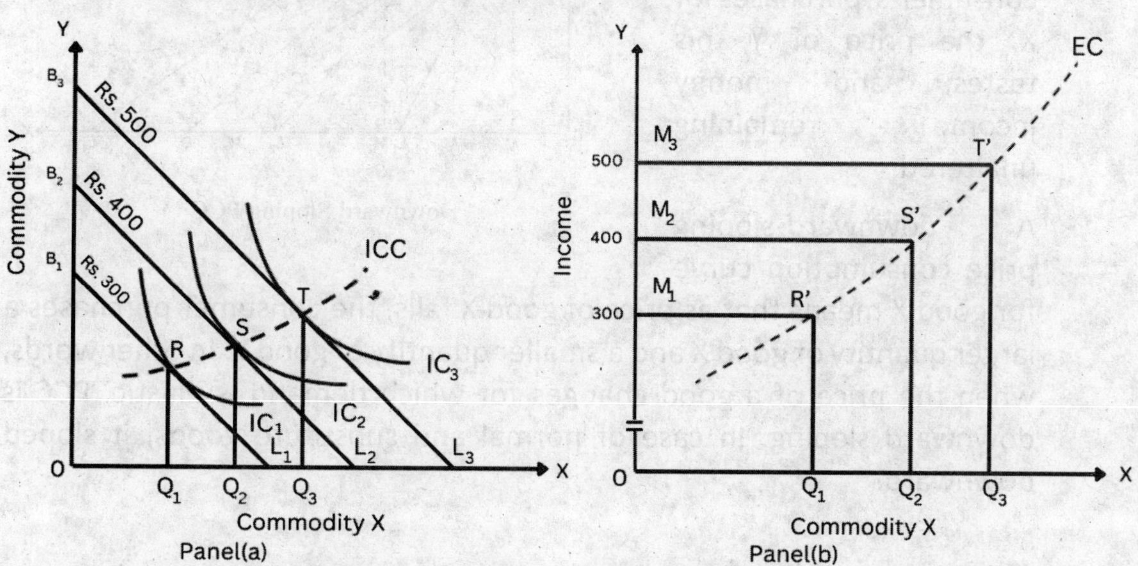

Deriving Engel curve from Income Consumption Curve in case of Necessities

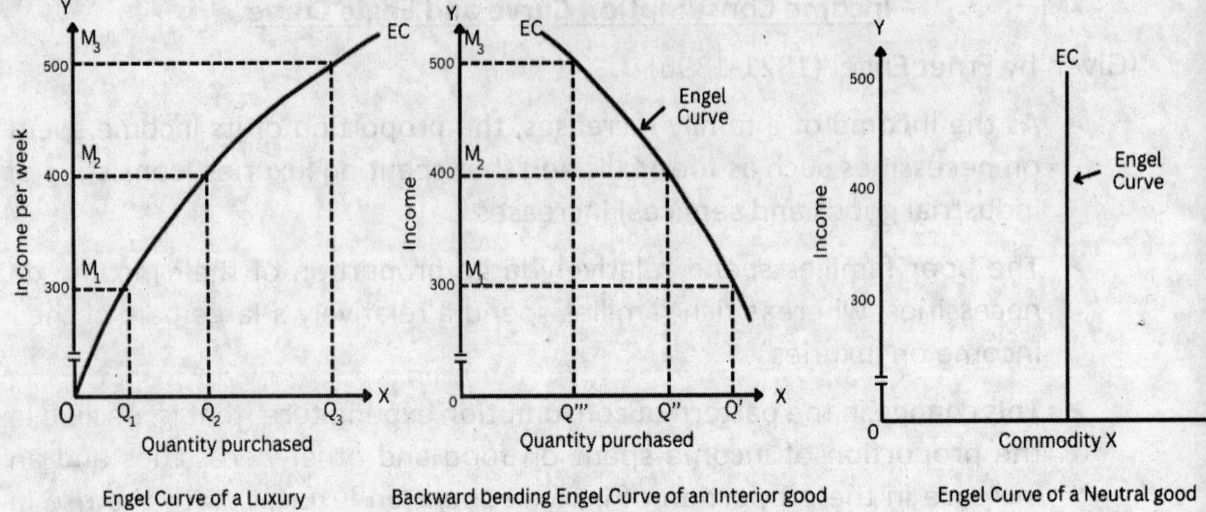

Engel Curve of a Luxury

Backward bending Engel Curve of an Interior good

Engel Curve of a Neutral good

Price Effect: Price Consumption Curve

- Price consumption curve traces out the price effect. It shows how the changes in the price of good X will affect the consumer's purchases of X, the price of Y, his tastes, and money income remaining unaltered.

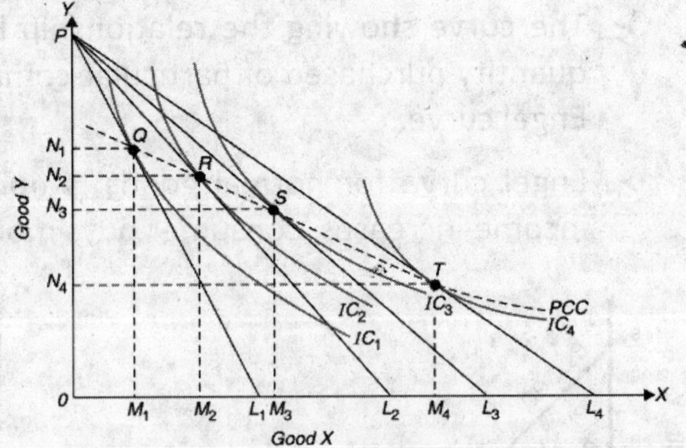

Downward Sloping PCC

- A downward-sloping price consumption curve for good X means that as price of good X falls, the consumer purchases a larger quantity of good X and a smaller quantity of good Y. In other words, when the price of a good changes for which demand is elastic, PCC is downward sloping. In case of normal and substitute goods, it sloped downward.

- Upward-sloping price consumption curve for X means that when the price of good X falls, the quantity demanded of both goods X and Y rises. We obtain the upward-sloping price consumption curve for good X when the demand for good is inelastic, (i.e., price elasticity is less than one) for normal or complementary goods, it is upward sloping.

Upward-Sloping Price Consumption Curve

- The price consumption curve for a good can take a horizontal shape too. It means that when the price of the good X declines, its quantity purchased increases proportionately but the quantity purchased of good Y remains the same.

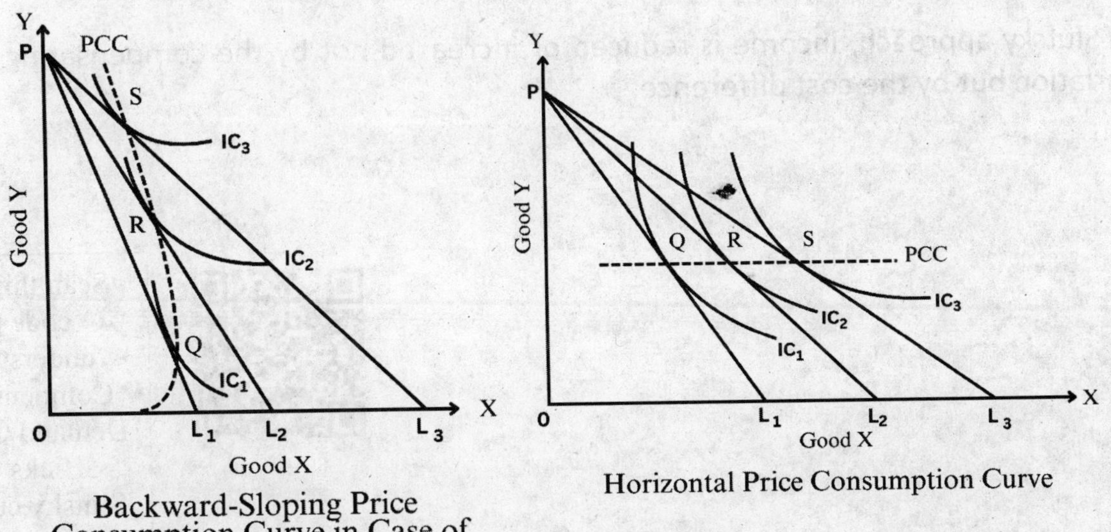

Backward-Sloping Price Consumption Curve in Case of Giffen Goods

Horizontal Price Consumption Curve

Compensated Demand Curve

Demand curve which incorporates the effects of changes in price of a commodity, real income remaining constant is called income compensated demand curve or simply compensated demand curve.

Thus, whereas ordinary demand curve describes the effects of both the substitution and income effects of the changes in price of a commodity, compensated demand curve includes the effect of only substitution effect.

1) Real income remains constant.

2)Considers only substitution effect.

3) Compensated demand curve is better while studying consumer surplus.

There are two approaches of compensated demand curve: Compensating variation in income (given by Hicks) and cost difference approach (Slutsky).

Compensating Variation in Income

Compensation variation, or CV, is the adjustment in income that brings the consumer back to the original utility after an economic change has occurred. This concept is given by Hicks. Consumer remains on the same Indifference curve.

Cost difference approach

In Slutsky approach, income is reduced or increased not by the compensating variation but by the cost difference.

Scan this QR code to understand Compensated Demand Curve, Hicks & Slutsky curves, price, income & substitution effect

Substitution Effect

Substitution effect means the change in the quantity purchased of a good as a consequence of a change in its relative price alone, real income or level of satisfaction remaining constant.

The substitution effect which is propounded by Hicks and Allen is called the **Hicksian Substitution Effect** and that developed by E. Slutsky is known as **Slutsky Substitution Effect**.

The two concepts differ in regard to the magnitude of the change in money income which should be affected so as to neutralize the change in real income of the consumer which results from a change in the price.

Hicksian Substitution Effect:

In the **Hicksian substitution effect** price change is accompanied by a so much change in money income that the consumer is neither better off nor worse off than before, that is, he is brought to the original level of satisfaction.

The money income of the consumer is changed by an amount which keeps the consumer on the same indifference curve on which he was before the change in the price.

The amount by which the money income of the consumer is changed so that the consumer is neither better off nor worse off than before is called **compensating variation in income**. Compensation variation, or CV, is the adjustment in income that brings the consumer back to the original utility after an economic change has occurred. This concept is given by Hicks. A fall in the relative price of a commodity always leads to an increase in its quantity demanded due to the substitution effect, the consumer's satisfaction or indifference curve remaining the same. Thus, the Substitution effect moves quantity in the opposite direction of price change.

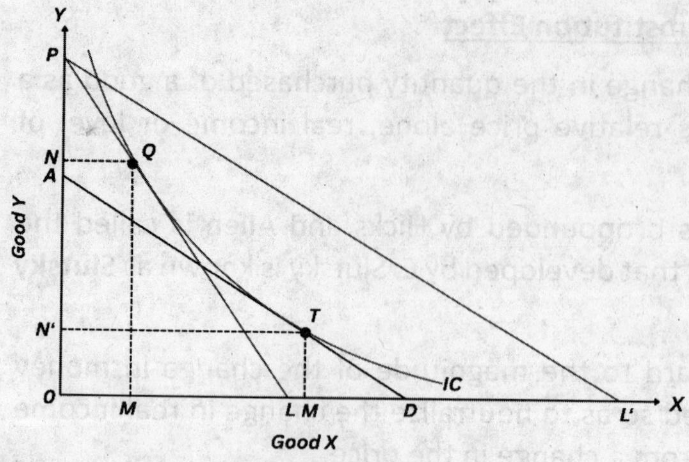

Hicksian Substitution Effect

Slutsky Substitution Effect and Cost Difference:

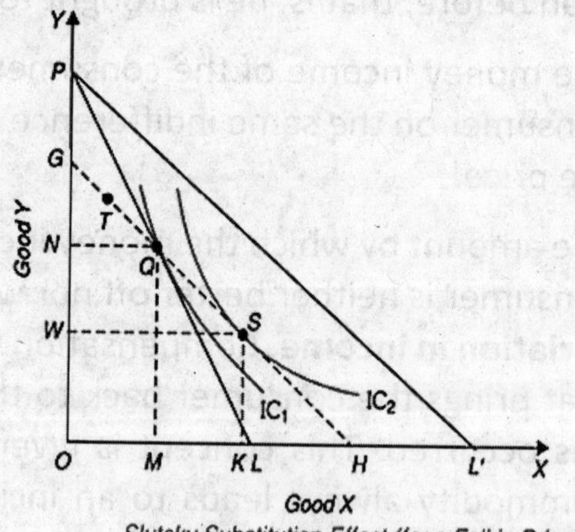

Slutsky Substitution Effect (for a Fall in Price)

- When the price of a good changes and the consumer's real income or purchasing power increases, the income of the consumer is changed by the amount equal to the change in its purchasing power which occurs as a result of the price change.
- In Slutsky's approach, income is reduced or increased (as the case may be) by the amount which leaves the consumer to be just able to purchase the same combination of goods, if he so desires, which he was having at the old price. Consumer moves on a higher indifference curve i.e. have increases satisfaction.
- Slutsky substitution effect, income is reduced or increased not by the compensating variation but by the cost difference.

Price Demand Relationship:

$$\textit{Price Effect } (PE) = \textit{Income Effect } (IE) + \textit{Substitution Effect } (SE)$$

Goods	PE	IE	SE
Normal	Negative.	Positive	Negative
Inferior	Negative. (IE<SE)	Negative	Negative
Giffen	Positive. (IE>SE)	Negative	Negative

Note: Watch this video lecture

Normal Goods: The income effect and substitution effect in case of normal goods work in the same direction and will lead to the increase in quantity demanded of the good whose price has fallen.

Inferior Goods and Giffen Goods: In case of giffen and inferior goods, Income and substitution effect goes in opposite direction. But income effect in case of giffen goods is much stronger than in case of inferior goods, which makes total price effect positive for giffen goods. In other words, in case of giffen goods, the quantity demanded of a Giffen good varies directly with price.

1. In Case of Normal Goods

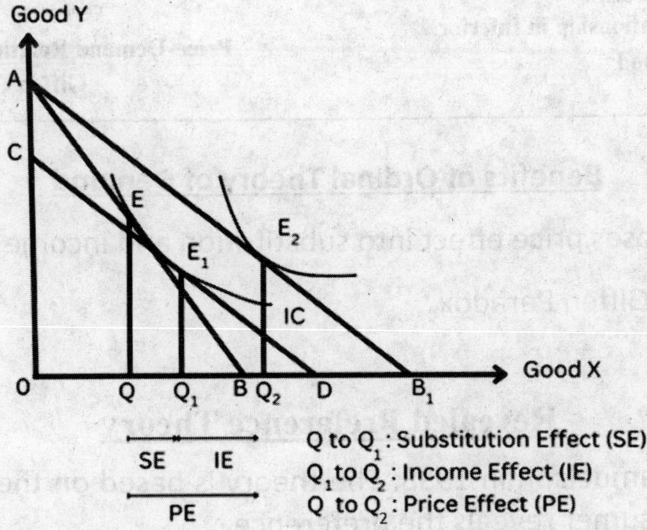

In the given diagram, AB is the price line. Consumer equilibrium is at E. When the price of X reduces, price line shifts ahead to AB_1. New consumer equilibrium is at E_2. Because of price reduction, consumer real income increases. Increase in real income is compensated by parallel shifting of price line from AB_1 to CD. By doing so, we can eliminate income effect. So, new equilibrium is at E_1. The shift from E to E_1 denotes substitution effect. Further, the shift from E_1 to E_2 denotes income effect which is the increase in the consumption solely due to increase in income. As we can see in diagram, all effects go in same direction.

2. In Case of Inferior and Giffen Goods

We can see from following diagrams that income effect and substitution effect go in opposite direction.

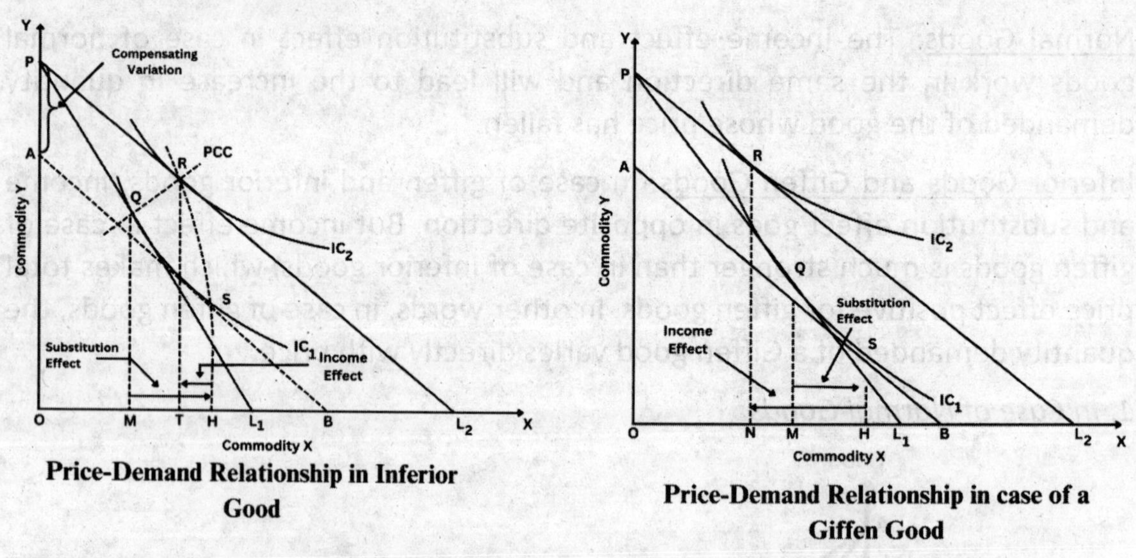

Price-Demand Relationship in Inferior Good

Price-Demand Relationship in case of a Giffen Good

Benefits of Ordinal Theory of Demand

1) Decomposes price effect into substitution and income effect.
2) Explains Giffen Paradox.

Revealed Preference Theory

It was given by Samuelson in 1938. The theory is based on the hypothesis that choice of the consumer reveals the preference.

Assumptions:

1) Consistency (If A is preferred to B in one particular instance, then he cannot choose B rather than A in any other instance when both are available to the consumer.
2) Transitivity (If A > B and B > C, then A > C).
3) Strong ordering (Relation of indifference between various alternative combinations is ruled out).

Revealed Preference Theory cannot explain Giffen goods, as it assumes that price and quantity demanded move in opposite directions — thereby excluding the Giffen case

Weak Axiom of Revealed Preference (WARP): This axiom states that given incomes and prices, if one product or service is purchased instead of another, then, as consumers, we will always make the same choice. The weak axiom also states that if we buy one particular product, then we will never buy a different product or brand unless it is cheaper, offers increased convenience, or is of better quality (i.e., unless it provides more benefits). As consumers, we will buy what we prefer and our choices will be consistent, so suggests the weak axiom.

The Strong Axiom of Revealed Preference (SARP) is a fundamental concept in consumer theory that extends the Weak Axiom of Revealed Preference (WARP) to ensure consistency in consumer choices across multiple goods and varying budget constraints. While WARP addresses direct choices between two bundles, SARP accounts for indirect preferences, ensuring transitivity. SARP states that if a consumer chooses bundle A over bundle B when both are affordable, and subsequently chooses bundle B over bundle C under a different budget set, then the consumer should not choose bundle C over bundle A in any budget set where both are affordable. This transitivity ensures that if A is revealed preferred to B, and B to C, then A must be revealed preferred to C.

Miscellaneous

Utility function: Utility depends on quantity of goods and services consumed. It denotes as $U = f(x_1, x_2, ..., x_n)$

Indirect utility function: Utility depends on prices and incomes. It denotes as U = f (M, P) where M is budget constraint and P are prices. It measures maximum attainable utility given budget constraint whereas utility function measures actual level of utility.

Hicksian demand function: Hicksian demand is function of prices and utility. Hicksian demand function is compensated demand function. We have to minimize expenditure given utility to find Hicksian demand function.

Marshallian demand function: Marshallian demand is a function of prices and budget. We have to maximize utility given budget to find Marshallian demand function.

Hicks Logical Ordering Theory of Demand: In 1956, Hicks published a book titled *"A Revision of Demand Theory"*, in which he revised the demand theory he had originally presented in his earlier work *"Value and Capital."*

Consumer Behaviour Under Uncertainty

Theory was propounded by 'Neumann and Morgenstern'

Risk: More than one possible outcome but probability of each possible outcome is known.

Uncertainty: More than one possible outcome but probability of each outcome is not known.

For a Risk Averse, Marginal utility of Money diminishes as he has more money.

For a Risk seeker, MU_M increases as money increases with him.

For a risk neutral, MU_M remains constant as money increases.

Different individuals will have different indifference curves between expected return and degree of risk depending upon their risk aversion. The individuals who are highly risk averse have more steep indifference curves because when curves are steeper Standard Deviation requires a large increase in income to maintain satisfaction. Deviations are higher in expected income and Marginal utility of money diminishes. Those who are less risk-averse they have flatter indifference curves.

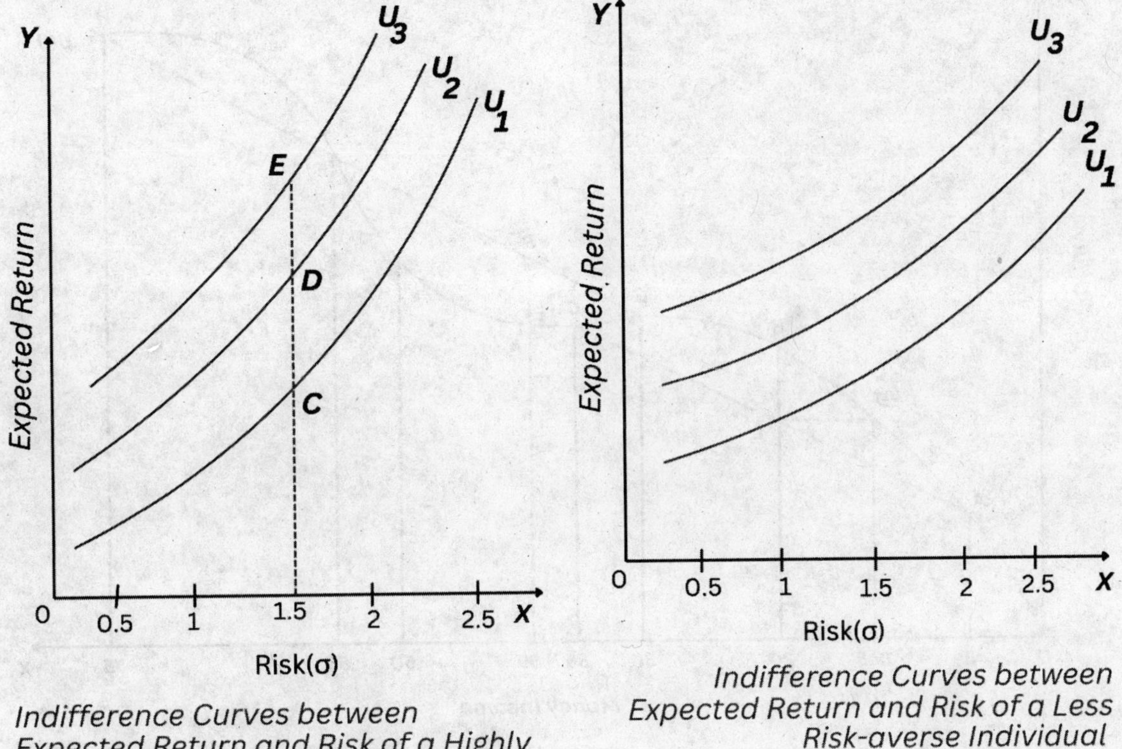

Indifference Curves between Expected Return and Risk of a Highly Risk-averse Individual

Indifference Curves between Expected Return and Risk of a Less Risk-averse Individual

Friedman Savage Hypothesis:

For most people, MU_M diminishes up to a certain level of money income. It increases from middle level to a certain higher level of money and at very high levels of income and eventually it again diminishes.

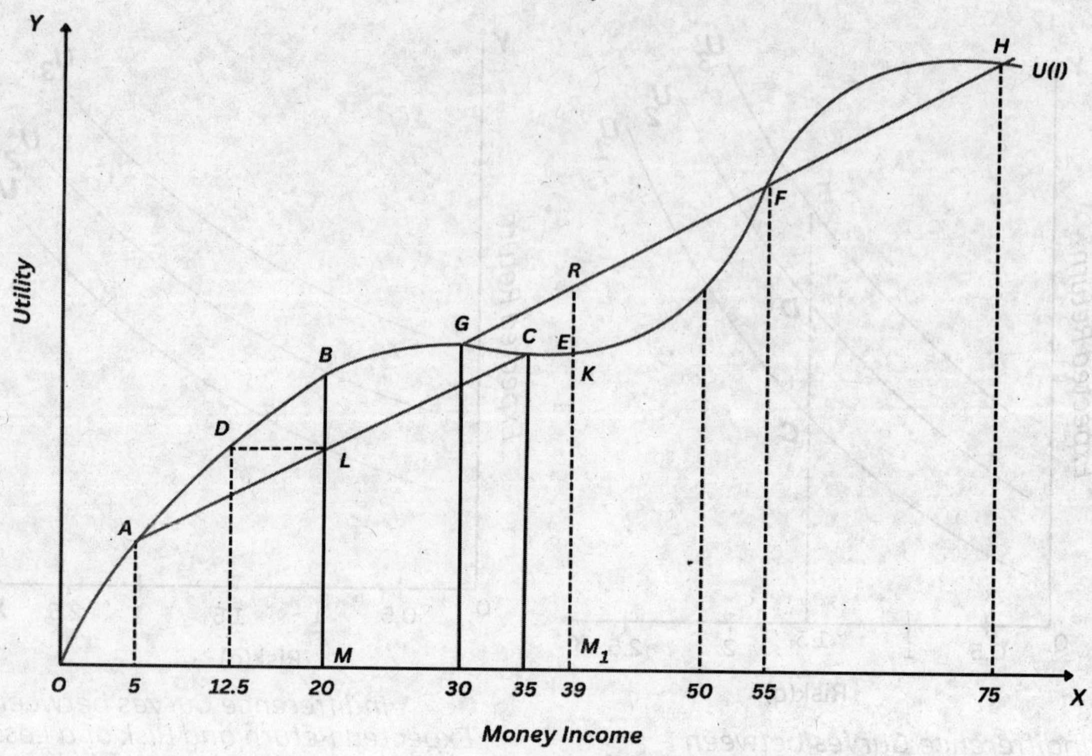

Friedman Savage Hypothesis

Numerical Problems

The utility function of a consumer is given by U = ƒ (q_1, q_2) = $q_1.q_2$, suppose the price of q_1 is p q_1 =1 and price of q_2 is p_2 = 2. The consumer wants to spend amount of k units only what will be his demand for q_1 and q_2? **(JUNE 2023)**

1. $(q_1, q_2) = \left(k, \frac{k}{2}\right)$

2. $(q_1, q_2) = \left(\frac{k}{4}, \frac{k}{6}\right)$

3. $(q_1, q_2) = \left(\frac{k}{2}, \frac{k}{4}\right)$

4. $(q_1, q_2) = \left(\frac{k}{2}, \frac{k}{3}\right)$

Solution:

$$L = (q_1, q_2) - \lambda(q_1p_1 + q_2p_2 - k)$$

$$L = (q_1, q_2) - \lambda(q_1 + 2q_2 - k)$$

$$\frac{\partial L}{\partial q_1} = q_2 - \lambda$$

$$\frac{\partial L}{\partial q_2} = q_1 - 2\lambda$$

$$\frac{\partial L}{\partial \lambda} = -q_1 - 2q_2 + k$$

$$q_2 - \lambda = 0$$

$$\lambda = q_2$$

$$-q_1 - 2q_2 + k = 0$$

$$-2\lambda - 2\lambda + k = 0$$

$$-4\lambda = -k$$

$$\lambda = \frac{k}{4}$$

$$q - 2\lambda = 0$$

$$2\lambda = q_1$$

$$q_2 = k/4$$

$$\boxed{q_1 = \frac{2k}{4} = \frac{k}{2}}$$

Production Theory

Production function is technical relationship between the inputs and the outputs.

Q = f (L, K) (Output is a function of labour and capital).

Total Product (TP): The total product of a variable factor is the amount of total output produced by a given quantity of the variable factor, keeping the quantity of other factors such as capital, fixed. As the amount of the variable increases, the total output increases. But the rate of increase in total output varies at different levels of employment of the variable factor.

Average Product (AP): Average product of a variable factor (labour) is the total output (Q) divided by the amount of labour employed with a given quantity of capital (the fixed factor) used to produce a commodity.

$$AP = \frac{TP}{L}$$

Marginal Product (MP): Marginal product of a variable factor is the addition made to the total production by the employment of an extra unit of a factor.

$$MP = \frac{\Delta TP}{\Delta L}$$

Short run production function: When quantities of some factors are fixed, while varying the number of other factors.

The study of short-run production function when at least one factor is kept fixed forms the subject of law of diminishing returns which is also known as **law of variable proportions.**

Long Run production function: When all factors are variable is called the long run. The length of the long run, that is, the time period required for changes in all inputs depends on the industry. The behavior of production when all factors are varied proportionately is the subject matter of **returns to scale.**

Production Function

Law of Variable Proportion	Law of Returns to scale
[Short Run Law]	[Long Run Law]
[1 factor Variable, others fixed]	[All factors Variable]

Law of Variable Proportion or Law of Diminishing Marginal Product

In the short run, the producer can change the quantity of output only by changing the quantity of variable factors. If we increase the employment of an input, keeping other inputs constant, eventually, a point will be reached after which the resulting marginal product starts falling. This is called the law of diminishing marginal product or returns to a factor.

The law of variable Proportion states that when more and more units of a variable factor are added with fixed factors, initially TP increases at an increasing rate, then increases at a diminishing rate, and finally starts to decline. If we express in terms of MP, the law states that when the quantities of variable factors are added with fixed factors, initially MP increases, then falls, and finally becomes negative.

Assumptions:

1. The state of technology is assumed to be given and unchanged.
2. There must be some other inputs such as capital must be kept fixed.

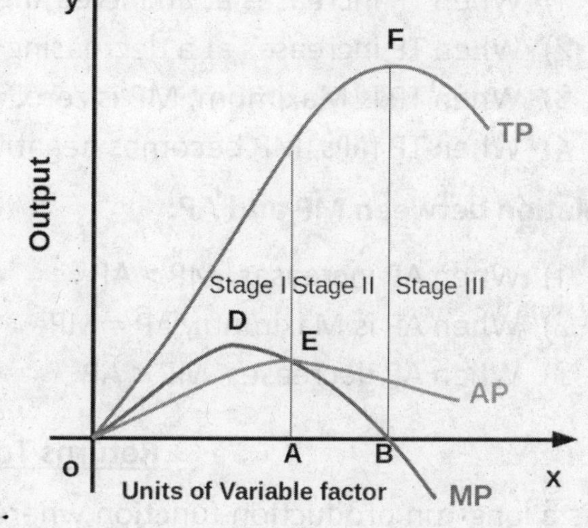

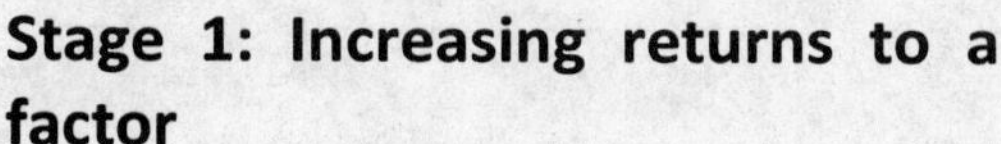

Stage 1: Increasing returns to a factor

Under this stage the MP increases, reaches maximum and starts decreasing. TP is increasing at increasing rate. This stage ends where the AP reaches maximum.

Reasons:

1) Indivisibility of factors.
2) Specialisation increases.
3) Fixed factor is effectively utilised.

Stage 2: Diminishing returns to a factor

Under the stage, MP and AP decrease. TP is increasing at decreasing rate. Stage ends where MP becomes zero.

Reasons:

1) Scarcity and indivisibility of a fixed factor.
2) Imperfect substitutability of factors.

Stage 3: Negative returns to a factor MP become negative TP starts falling.

Reasons:

1) Variable factor is in excess of fixed factor.

2) Most optimal stage of production is stage 2 where Total product is Maximum.

Relation between TP and MP:

1) When TP increases at an increasing rate, MP also increases.
2) When TP increases at a decreasing rate, MP falls
3) When TP is Maximum, MP is zero.
4) When TP falls, MP becomes negative.

Relation between MP and AP:

1) When AP increases, MP > AP
2) When AP is Maximum, AP = MP
3) When AP decreases, MP < AP

Returns To Scale:

It is a long-run production function where factors of production are variable. It refers to the change in output caused by proportionate change in all inputs.

It also has 3 stages:

1. Increasing Returns to Scale: The % change in output is more than % change in inputs that means one percentage increase in inputs result in more than one percentage increase in output.
2. Constant Returns to Scale: -: The % change in output is equal to % change in inputs which means one percentage increase in inputs results in equal percentage increase in output.
3. Decreasing Returns to Scale: The % change in output is less than % change in inputs that means one percentage increase in inputs result in less than one percentage increase in output.

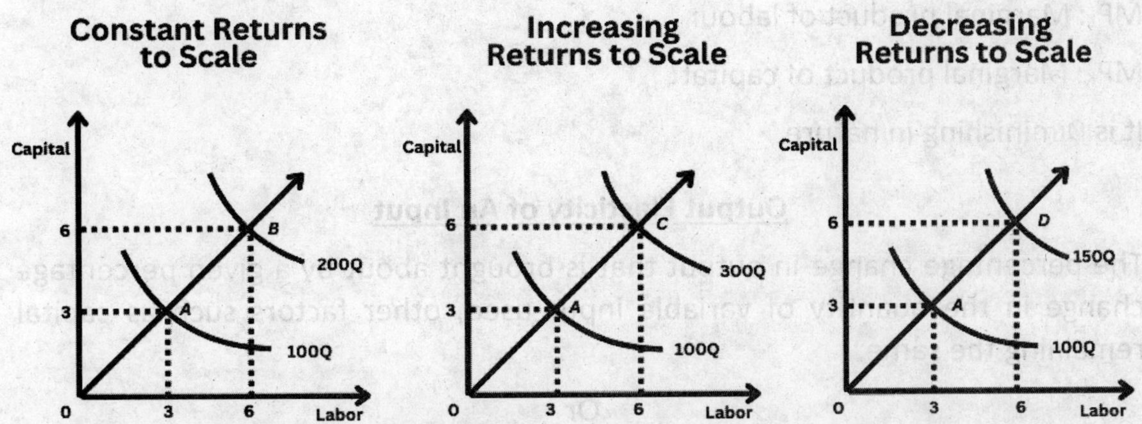

Reason of increasing returns to scale is economies of scale and of decreasing returns to scale are diseconomies of scale.

<u>Economies of Scale</u>: Advantages due to expansion of output.

<u>Diseconomies of Scale</u>: Disadvantages due to expansion of output.

Isoquants / Equal-Product Curves / Iso-Product Curves

Isoquant are the locus of various combinations of inputs producing the same level of output.

Capital

O

Labour

Properties:

1) Downward sloping
2) Convex to origin
3) Two isoquants never intersect.
4) Higher isoquant means higher level of production.

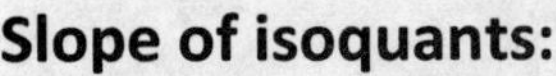

Slope of isoquants:

Marginal rate of technical substitution [MRTS] (No. of units of capital sacrificed to get one unit of labour).

$$MRTS_{LK} = \frac{MP_L}{MP_K}$$

OR

$$MRTS_{LK} = -\frac{dK}{dL}$$

MP_L: Marginal product of labour

MP_K: Marginal product of capital

It is Diminishing in nature.

Output Elasticity of An Input

The percentage change in output that is brought about by a given percentage change in the quantity of variable input used, other factors such as capital remaining the same.

Or

Output elasticity of labour is the ratio of marginal product of labour to its average product.

$$Output\ Elasticity\ of\ an\ Input = \frac{MP_L}{AP_L}$$

Homogenous Production Function

A homogeneous function is a function of many variables such that if all the variables of a function are multiplied by a scaler, then the value of the function multiply by some power of the same scaler. For e.g.,

$$Y(X, Z) = X^2 + Z^2$$

Multiplying each variable with scaler λ

$$Y(\lambda X, \lambda Y) = (\lambda X)^2 + (\lambda Z)^2$$

$$Y(\lambda X, \lambda Y) = \lambda^2(X^2 + Z^2)$$

$$Y(\lambda X, \lambda Y) = \lambda^2 Y$$

Thus, the degree of homogeneity is 2.

A function with any degree n is called a homogeneous function. In other words, if Q is a homogenous function, then anything raises to power 'm' gives us the degree of homogeneity. Now let us consider the following example:

$$Q(x, y) = f(x, y)$$

Multiplying m we get,

$$Q(mx, my) = f\ (mx, my)$$

$$Q(mx, my) = m^k f(x, y)$$

If K = 1 -> Constant Returns to scale (CRS)

If K > 1 -> Increasing Returns to scale (IRS)

If K < 1 -> Decreasing Returns to scale (DRS)

Important points about homogenous and homothetic function:

1. Homogeneous functions are a subset of set of **homothetic functions.**
2. All homogeneous functions are homothetic but not all homothetic functions are homogeneous.
3. Homogeneity of degrees 1, more than 1 and less than 1 means constant returns to scale, increasing returns to scale, and decreasing returns to scale respectively.
4. Let $H = e^Q$ where $Q = Ax^\alpha Y^\beta$

Thus, $Q = Ax^\alpha Y^\beta$ is homogeneous function and $H = e^Q$ is homothetic function H.

5. *Linearly Homogenous Production function means homogeneity of degree one* i.e. Constant Returns to Scale.

Cobb Douglas (CD) Production Function (1928)

It was proposed by Knut Wicksell (1851-1926), and tested statically evidence by Charles Cobb and Paul Douglas. The Cobb-Douglas production function can be given as

Scan here to watch a full video on Cobb Douglas & CES Production Function

$$Q = AL^\propto K^\beta$$

where Q = Output
A: It represents Total factor productivity that is the result of an improvement in efficiency or technology.
L: Labour
K: Capital
$\propto$: tells output elasticity of labour or share of labour in production

β: tells output elasticity of capital or share of capital in production.

Properties:

1. Homogenous of degree ∝+ β. In special case when ∝+ β is 1, it is linear homogenous of degree 1.

$\propto + \beta = 1$	CRS
$\propto + \beta > 1$	IRS
$\propto + \beta < 1$	DRS

2. Elasticity of substitution is unity, i.e., $E_S = 1$
3. Diminishing returns to each factor.
4. Coefficients of it represent output elasticity of input. Elasticity of output in relation to labour is '∝' and in relation to capital is 'β'. In other words, share of labour in National Income = ∝, share of capital in National Income= β

Output Elasticity of Labour

$$E_L = \frac{MP_L}{AP_L} = \frac{A\alpha L^{\alpha-1}K^{\beta}}{AL^{\alpha-1}K^{\beta}} = \alpha$$

Output Elasticity of Capital

$$E_K = \frac{\beta AL^{\alpha}K^{\beta-1}}{AL^{\alpha}K^{\beta-1}} = \beta$$

5. AP and MP are functions of ratio of factors.

Illustration. Let the production function be $Q = AL^{\alpha}K^{1-\alpha}$

Marginal Product of labour is given by

$$\frac{dQ}{dL} = A\alpha L^{\alpha-1}K^{1-\alpha}$$

$$= \frac{A\alpha L^{\alpha}K^{1-\alpha}}{L}$$

$$= \frac{A\alpha L^{\alpha-\alpha}k^{1-\alpha}}{L^{1-\alpha}} = \frac{A\alpha K^{1-\alpha}}{L^{1-\alpha}}$$

$$= A\alpha\left(\frac{K}{L}\right)^{1-\alpha}$$

Average Product of labour is given by

$$= \frac{AL^{\alpha}K^{1-\alpha}}{L} = \frac{AK^{1-\alpha}}{L^{1-\alpha}}$$

$$= A\left(\frac{K}{L}\right)^{1-\alpha}$$

6. The expansion path is linear, homogenous and passes through origin.
7. Proves Euler theorem

$$Q = MP_K \times K + MP_L \times L$$

8. Negative slope isoquants and strict convexity.

Euler Theorem/Product Exhaustion Theorem:

If the factors are paid according to their Marginal productivity, then total output will be exhausted. It holds true in linearly homogenous production function.

$$\boxed{Q = MP_K \times K + MP_L \times L}$$

But Wicksteed, Clark and Walras show that assumption of homogenous production function is not necessary. It holds for all types of production function.

Constant Elasticity of Substitution (CES) Production Function (1961)

It was given by Arrow, Minhas, Chenery & Solow. The function is given as

$$Q = \gamma\left[\alpha L^{-\beta} + (1-\alpha)K^{-\beta}\right]^{-\frac{1}{\beta}}$$

γ = Coeff. Of Technical Efficiency

α = Distribution Parameter

β = Substitution Parameter

$$E_s = \frac{1}{1+\beta}$$

Elasticity of substitution (Es) varies between 0 and infinity.

If β is 0, it leads to unitary Elasticity of substitution

If β is infinity, Elasticity of substitution will be zero

If β is -1, Elasticity of substitution will be infinity.

CD is a Special case of CES

If β is 0, it leads to unitary Elasticity of substitution, which is a special case of linearly homogenous characteristic of Cobb Douglas production function. Thus, Cobb Douglas production function is special case of CES production function.

Ridge Lines

Ridge lines are the locus of points of isoquants where the marginal product of one of the factors is zero. Production outside the ridge lines is inefficient. Regions outside the ridge lines are called regions of economic nonsense. The optimum stage of production is the region between the two ridge lines and hence called the region of Economic Production.

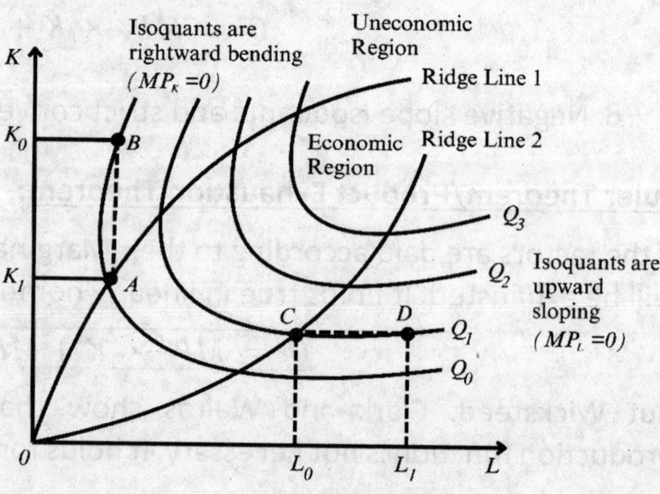

Elasticity of Technical Substitution

It shows the percentage change in the capital-labor ratio (K/L) resulting from a percentage change in the marginal rate of technical substitution (MRTS).

$$\sigma_{Lk} = \frac{\Delta\left(\frac{K}{L}\right)}{\frac{K}{L}} \cdot \frac{MRTS_{LK}}{\Delta(MRTS)_{LK}}$$

Iso-Cost Line

An iso cost line is defined as the locus of various combinations of factors which a firm can buy with a constant outlay.

The Equation of the Iso-Cost Line is the total cost incurred on the factors of production for production of a commodity is equal to the sum of the payments made for labour and capital. The payment for the labour used is equal to the wage rate (w) multiplied by the amount of labour used (L).

Total payment made for labour is W.L

The total payment made for capital is r.K

where r is the price per unit of capital and K is the quantity of capital used.

The total cost equation can be C = w.L + rK

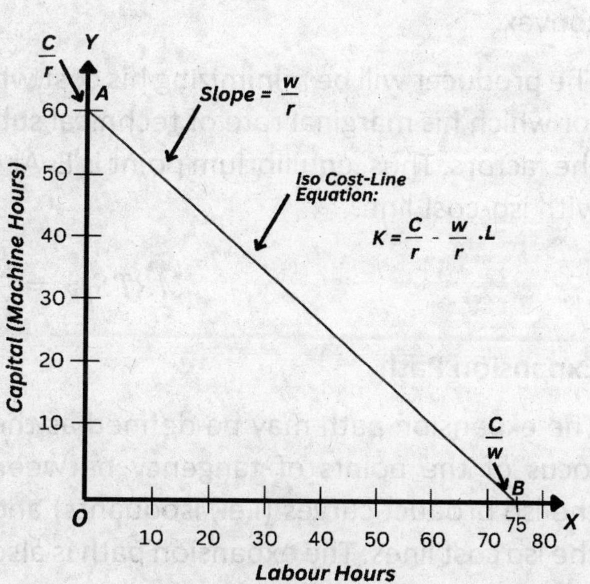

Least Cost Combination

An isoquant map represents the technical conditions of production for a product and a family of iso-cost line represents the various levels of total cost outlay, given the prices of two factors. To produce a given level of output, the entrepreneur will choose the combination of factors which minimizes his cost of production, for only in this way he will be maximizing his profits. Thus, a producer will try to produce a given level of output with the **least-cost combination of factors.**

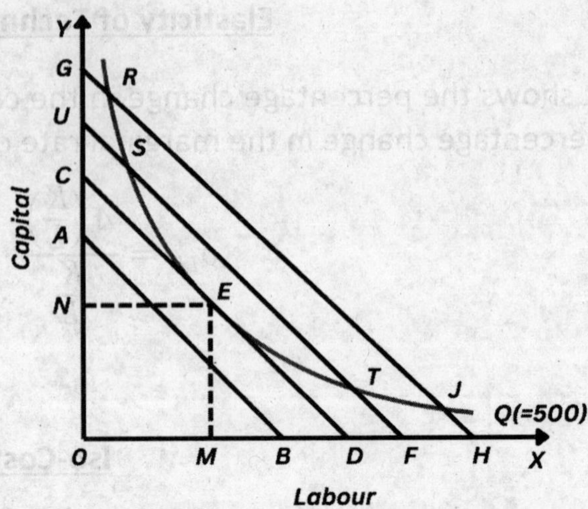

Minimizing Cost for a Given Level of Output

The marginal rate of technical substitution (MRTS) is given by the slope of the isoquant at its various points. On the other hand, the price ratio of the factors is given by the slope of the iso-cost line.

Definition of MRTS: It is the rate at which one input can be substituted for another input, keeping the output constant. It is diminishing as isoquant are convex.

The producer will be minimizing his cost when he is using the factor combination for which his marginal rate of technical substitution is equal to the price ratio of the factors. Thus, equilibrium point is E. At equilibrium, isoquant curve is tangent with iso-cost line.

$$MRTS_{LK} = \frac{P_L}{P_K} \text{ or } \frac{w}{r}$$

Expansion Path

The expansion path may be defined as the locus of the points of tangency between the iso product curves (i.e., isoquants) and the iso cost lines. The expansion path is also known as scale-line because it shows how the entrepreneur will change the quantities of the two factors when it increases the level of output. It may be also defined as locus of points of revenue maximization.

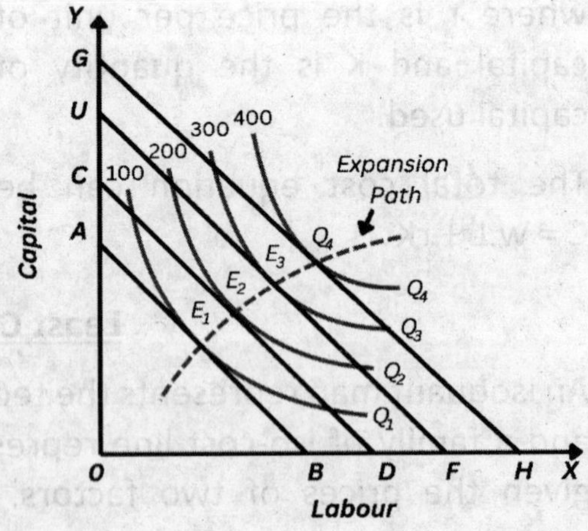

Production Possibility Curve (PPC)/ Production Possibility Frontiers (PPF): Combination of two goods which can be produced given the technology.

ISO – Revenue Line: It is the locus of points of Combination of two goods produced which generate equal revenue

Producer Equilibrium in Case of Multi-product Firm:

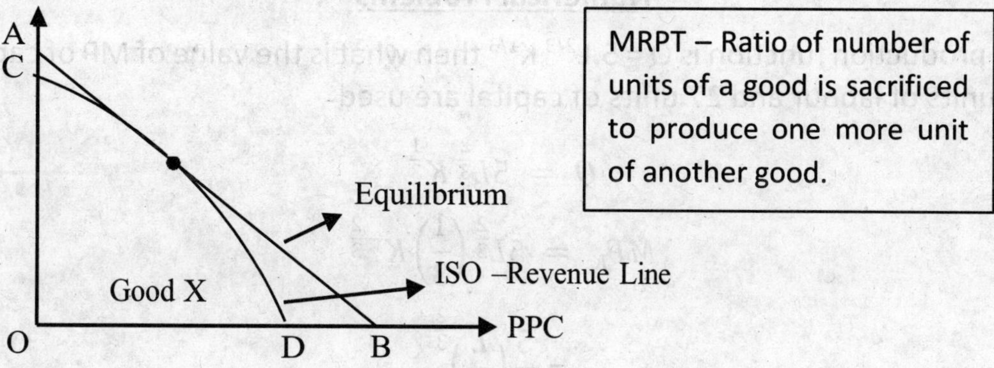

Marginal Rate of Product Transformation: It is the slope of PPC which is increasing due to which PPC is concave.

$$MRPT_{XY} = \frac{MC_X}{MC_Y}$$

where MC_X & MC_Y are marginal cost of X and marginal cost of Y respectively.

At equilibrium,

$$MRPT_{XY} = \frac{P_X}{P_Y}$$

PPC is concave in shape as more and more of one good is produced, factors producing it become less and less productive. Hence more units are sacrificed. Therefore, MRPT is increasing.

Economic Efficiency: Resources are distributed in a way that generates greatest benefit to consumers and producers. Economic efficiency is divided into technical and allocative efficiency.

Technical Efficiency: Maximizing the output with given inputs is called output oriented technical efficiency.

Minimizing inputs to produce given output is called input oriented technical efficiency.

<u>Allocative Efficiency:</u> When it is impossible to make someone better off without making some other worse off, then it is called allocative efficiency.

Numerical Problems

If the production function is $Q = 5.L^{2/3} K^{1/3}$ then what is the value of MP of capital, if 64 units of labour and 27 units of capital are used

$$Q = 5L^{\frac{2}{3}} K^{\frac{1}{3}}$$

$$MP_K = 5L^{\frac{2}{3}}\left(\frac{1}{3}\right)K^{-\frac{2}{3}}$$

$$= \frac{5}{3}\left(\frac{L}{K}\right)^{\frac{2}{3}}$$

$$= \frac{5}{3}\left(\frac{64}{27}\right)^{\frac{2}{3}}$$

$$= \frac{5}{3}\left[\left(\frac{64}{27}\right)^{\frac{1}{3}}\right]^2$$

$$= \frac{5}{3}\left(\frac{4}{3}\right)^2$$

$$= \frac{5}{3} \times \frac{16}{9}$$

$$= \frac{80}{27}$$

Cost Theory

Cost of production consists of all the payments that necessary to obtain the factors of land, labour, capital and management required to produce a commodity.

Cost = f (Output)

Explicit Cost: These costs are out of the firm or cost of having a Factor of production.

Implicit Cost: These are the prices of owned goods and services and are included in average cost. Also called imputed cost.

$$Economic\ Cost = Explicit\ Cost + Implicit\ Cost$$

Opportunity Cost: Cost of next best alternative. Also called transferred earnings.

Historical Cost: Original price of Factor of Production when bought in the past.

Sunk Cost: It is a kind of historical cost which cannot be recovered.

Traditional Theory of Costs

Total Fixed and Variable Cost in Short Run

TFC: Fixed costs are those which are independent of output, that is, they do not change with changes in output. These costs are a 'fixed' amount which must be incurred by a firm in the short run, whether the output is small or large.

Fixed costs are also known as overhead costs and include charges such as contractual rent, insurance fee, maintenance costs, property taxes, interest on the borrowed funds, minimum administrative expenses such as manager's salary, watchman's wages etc.

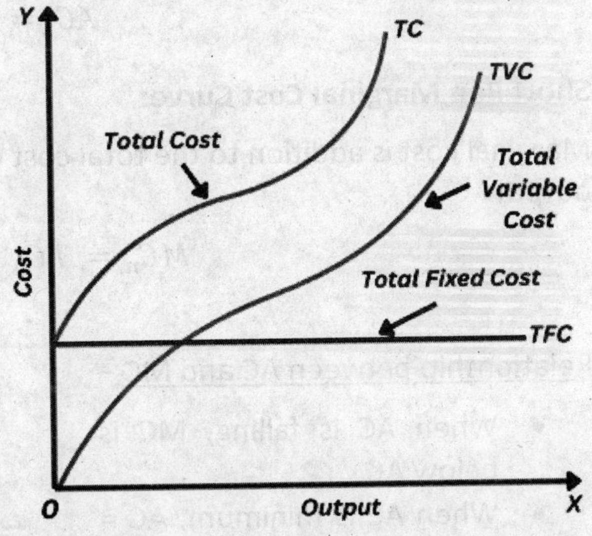

TVC: Total variable costs change with changes in output in the short run, i.e., they increase or decrease when output rises or falls. These costs include payments to labour employed, the prices of the raw materials, fuel and power used, the expenses incurred on transportation and the like.

$$Total\ Costs = Total\ Fixed\ Cost + Total\ Variable\ Cost$$

The Short Run Average and Marginal Cost Curves

Average Fixed Cost: The average fixed cost can be obtained from dividing the total fixed cost by the level of output. This curve is called rectangular hyperbola (decreases but never touch axis).

$$AFC = \frac{TFC}{Q}$$

where Q represents the number of units of output produced.

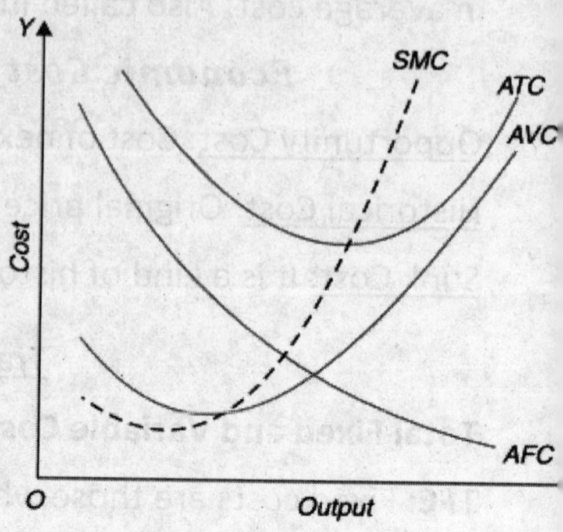

Short-run Average and Marginal C Curves

Average Variable Cost: Average variable cost is the total variable cost divided by the number of units of output produced.

$$AVC = \frac{TVC}{Q}$$

$$Average\ Total\ Cost\ (ATC) = AVC + AFC$$

$$AC = \frac{TC}{Q}$$

Short Run Marginal Cost Curve:

Marginal cost is addition to the total cost caused by producing one more unit of output.

$$MC_n = TC_n - TC_{n-1}$$

Relationship between AC and MC –

- When AC is falling, MC is below AC.
- When AC is minimum, AC = MC
- When AC is rising, MC is above AC.

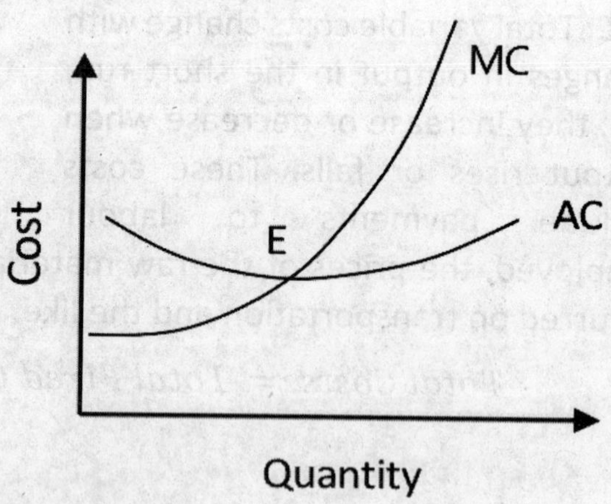

Long Run Cost

Long run cost curves are flatter as compared to short run costs.

Short run period: At least one factor is fixed, and others are variable.	Long run period: All factors are variable.

(LRAC) Long Run Average Cost Curve is also known as planning curve. Plants are used at less than full capacity at point left to the minimum point and are used more than full capacity at point's right to the minimum point. The optimum plant size is when it operates at minimum LAC.

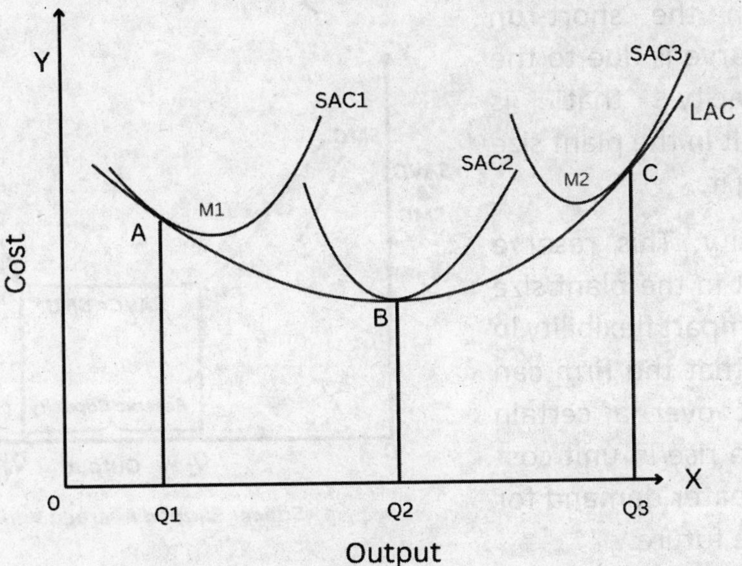

Reasons for the U-Shaped LAC Curves

The relevant principle governing the shape of the long-run average cost curve is that of returns to scale.

Economies and Diseconomies

Economies of scale: Advantages due to expansion of output.

Diseconomies of scale: Disadvantages due to expansion of output.

Economies of Scope: Economies of scope refer to the reduction in costs that occur when a firm produces two or more commodities together rather than a single one. In other words, Joint production of a good is more efficient than the separate production.

Diseconomies of Scope: Joint production is less efficient than the individual production.

Modern Theory of Costs

Cost curves are not U shaped due to reserve capacity.

Saucer- shaped short run average variable cost curves (SAVC)

The saucer type shape of the average variable cost curve implies that there is a flat stretch over a certain range of output in it. It has been pointed out that this flat stretch in the short-run average cost curve is due to the reserve capacity that is consciously built in the plant size while designing it.

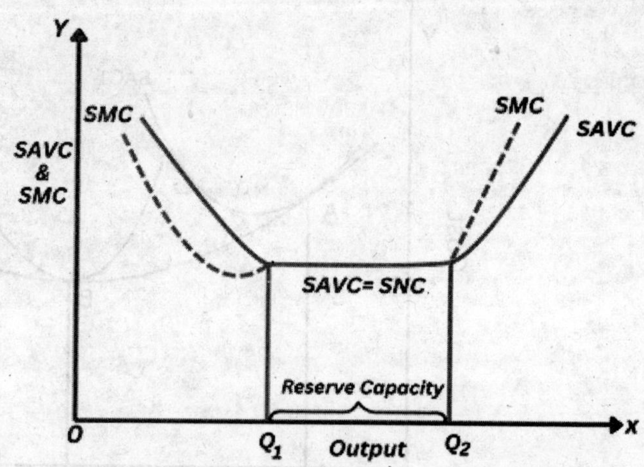

Saucer Shaped Average Variable Cost Curve

Reserve Capacity: This reserve capacity is built in the plant size with a view to impart flexibility in production so that the firm can expand output over a certain range without a rise in unit cost to meet any greater demand for its output in the future.

L – Shaped Long Run Average Cost Curve

At a very large scale of production, the managerial cost per unit of output may rise, but the technical or production economies more than offset the managerial diseconomies so that the total long-run average cost does not rise or even falls continuously though at a very small rate. The L-shape of the long-run average cost curve implies that in the beginning when output is expanded through increase in plant size and associated variable factors, cost per unit falls rapidly due to economies of scale.

Reasons:

1. Economies of Scale

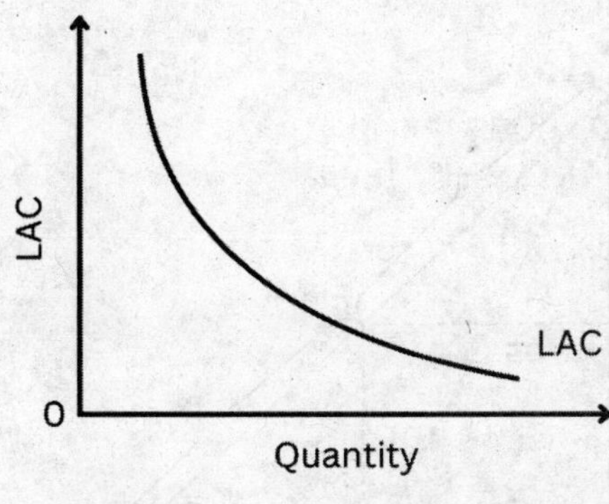

2. Learning Effect
3. Technological Progress

Learning Curve (By Kenneth Arrow)

It states that the increase in cumulative output leads to decline in per unit cost due to learning by doing.

Revenue

Total Revenue: Total revenue from the production and sale of a product of a firm is the total quantity of the product produced and sold multiplied by price of the product.

$$TR = PQ$$

where TR stands for total revenue, P for price and Q for quantity of the product produced and sold.

Average Revenue: Average revenue is the revenue earned per unit of output produced and sold. Average revenue (AR) is equal to price when a firm sells all units of output produced at the same price (that is, when it is not discriminating prices).

$$AR = \frac{TR}{Q}$$

Marginal Revenue: Marginal is defined as the extra revenue earned by producing and selling an extra unit of output.

$$MR_n = TR_n - TR_{n-1}$$

$$MR = \frac{\Delta TR}{\Delta Q}$$

Marginal revenue is given by the slope of the total revenue curve. The slope of a marginal revenue curve is twice that of the average revenue curve.

Relation between TR, MR and AR –

When Ed = 1, TR = Max., MR = 0

When Ed > 1, TR increasing, MR is decreasing

When Ed < 1, TR decreasing, MR becomes negative

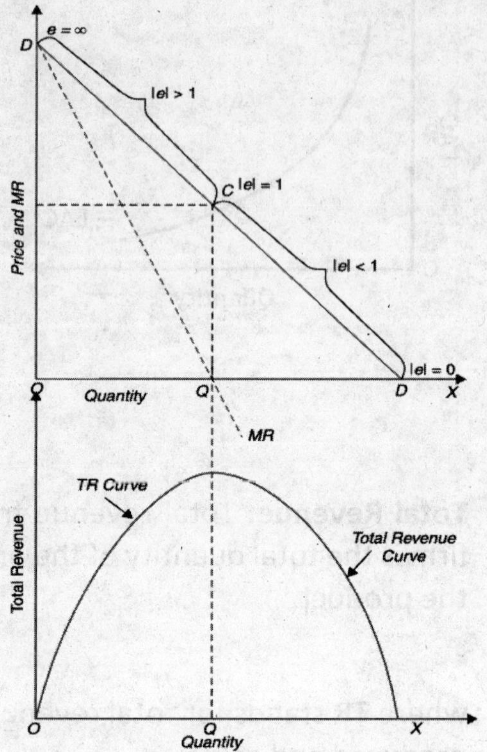

Relationship between Price Elasticity of Demand, Total Revenue and Marginal Revenue

Elasticity formula

$$e = \frac{AR}{AR - MR} \; or \; MR = AR\left(\frac{e-1}{e}\right) \; or \; AR = MR\left(\frac{e}{e-1}\right)$$

Market

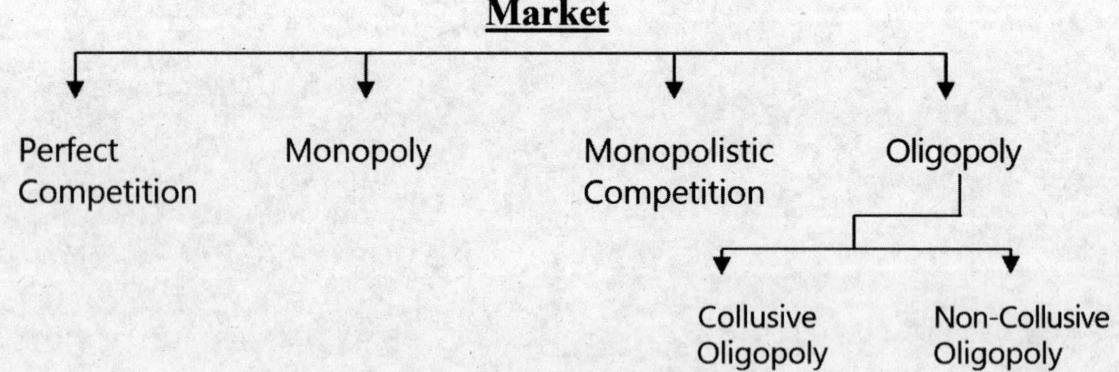

Form of market	No. of Firms	Nature of product	Price Elasticity	Price Control	Ease of Entry
Perfect	Large	Homogenous	Infinity	Zero	Free
Monopolistic	Large	Differentiated	Large	Some	Free
Pure Oligopoly	Few	Homogenous	Small	Some	Limited
Differentiated Oligopoly	Few	Differentiated	Small	Large	Limited
Monopoly	One	Unique	Very Small	Very Large	Strong Barriers to entry

Scan here to watch video lecture on Perfect Competition, Monopoly & Monopolistic Competition.

Perfect Competition

Short Run Equilibrium of Perfect Competition

Conditions

(1) MC = MR

(2) MC should cut MR from below

A firm can have:

- Super normal profit when AR > AC
- Normal profits when AR = AC
- Minimum Loss AR < AC

Super Normal Profit

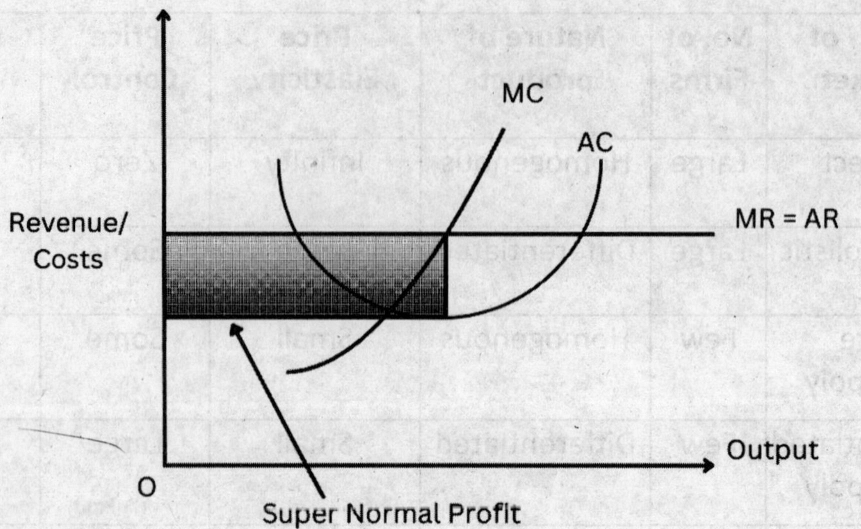

Normal Profits

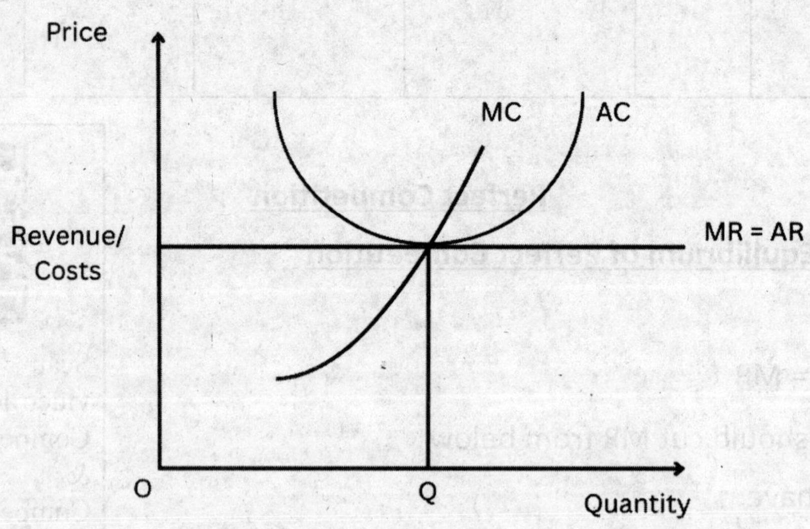

Minimum Loss

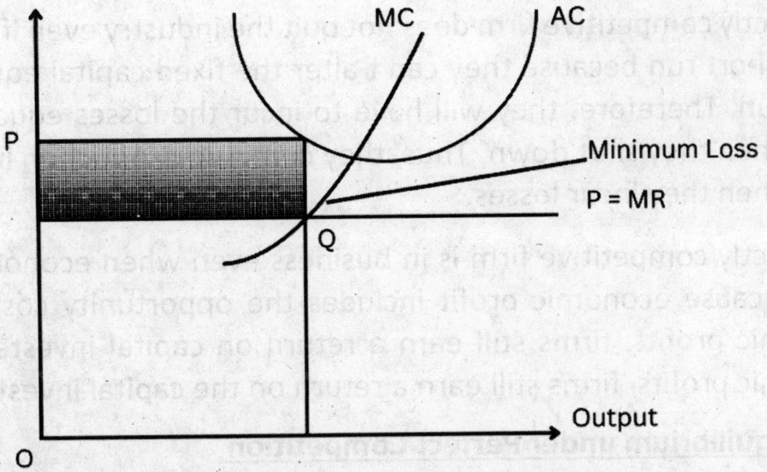

Supply Curve

Supply curve under perfect competition is upward sloping part of MC above the minimum point of AVC

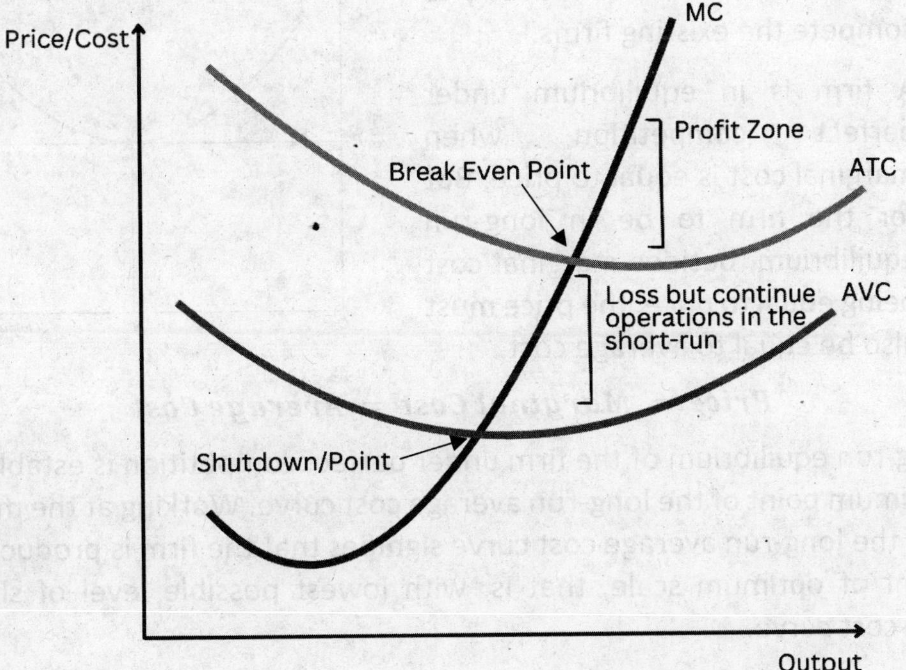

Shut Down Point : P≤ AVC

Points of Remember: -

(1) A perfectly competitive firm does not quit the industry even if it incurs losses in the short run because they can't alter the fixed capital equipment in the short run. Therefore, they will have to incur the losses equal to fixed cost even when they shut down. Thus, they continue production in the short run even when they incur losses.

(2) A perfectly competitive firm is in business even when economic profits are zero because economic profit includes the opportunity costs. So, at zero economic profits, firms still earn a return on capital invested. So, at zero economic profits, firms still earn a return on the capital invested.

Long-run Equilibrium under Perfect Competition

- The firms, in the long run, can increase their output by changing their capital equipment;
- New firms can enter the industry or old firms can leave the industry to compete the existing firms.
- A firm is in equilibrium under perfect competition when marginal cost is equal to price. But for the firm to be in long-run equilibrium, besides marginal cost being equal to price, the price must also be equal to average cost.

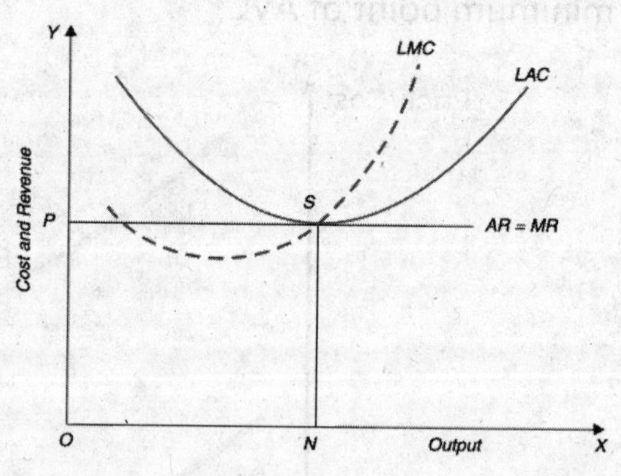

$$\textbf{Price} = \textbf{Marginal Cost} = \textbf{Average Cost}$$

The long-run equilibrium of the firm under perfect competition is established at the minimum point of the long-run average cost curve. Working at the minimum point of the long-run average cost curve signifies that the firm is producing with the plant of optimum scale, that is, with lowest possible level of short-run average cost curve.

The perfectly competitive firm by producing at the minimum point of the long-run average curve LAC is enjoying all possible economies of scale i.e., it has exhausted the economies of scale and has no incentive to move to any other point on the long-run average cost curve LAC.

Long-Run Supply Curve Under Perfect Competition

1. **Increasing Cost Industry:** The long-run supply curve LRS slopes upward to the right
2. **Constant Cost Industry:** While the long-run marginal cost curve of the firm will be sloping upward in its relevant part, the long-run supply curve of the industry in this case is a horizontal straight line.
3. **Decreasing Cost Industry:** Long-run supply curve of a decreasing-cost industry slopes downward from left to right.

Economic Efficiency [Perfect Competitive Market]

Under perfect competitive market, resources are used efficiently and maximizes satisfaction.

Optimum Resource Allocation: Optimality is shown by following conditions which prevail in the long run equilibrium of industry.

1) Output is produced at minimum feasible cost.

2) Consumer pays minimum possible price which just covers marginal cost.

3) Plants used in full capacity in long run so there is no wastage of resources

4) Firm earns normal profits.

5) It is achieved when Production possibility curve is tangent with highest possible indifference curve.

Consumer Surplus (CS): Price consumers are willing to pay – what they actual pay.

Producer's Surplus (PS): Market price at which sellers sell -(minus) minimum price they are willing to sell.

Criticism of perfect Competition

Maximizing total economic surplus is not a good measure of equity. It may not be fair/equitable.

Monopoly

Causes/Sources: Patents or copy rights controls our essential raw materials.

Natural Monopoly: Experiences economies of scale and the AC is diminishing in nature.

Legal /Statutory Monopoly: The Government provides the legal status through patents or copy rights.

There is no supply curve in monopoly because there is No unique price – quantity relationship. Firms does not equate price with marginal cost. It equates with MR with MC. Supply curve is relevant when firm exercises no control over price and take it as a given.

Conditions of Equilibrium:

- MR = MC
- MC should cut MR curve from below

Super Normal Profit

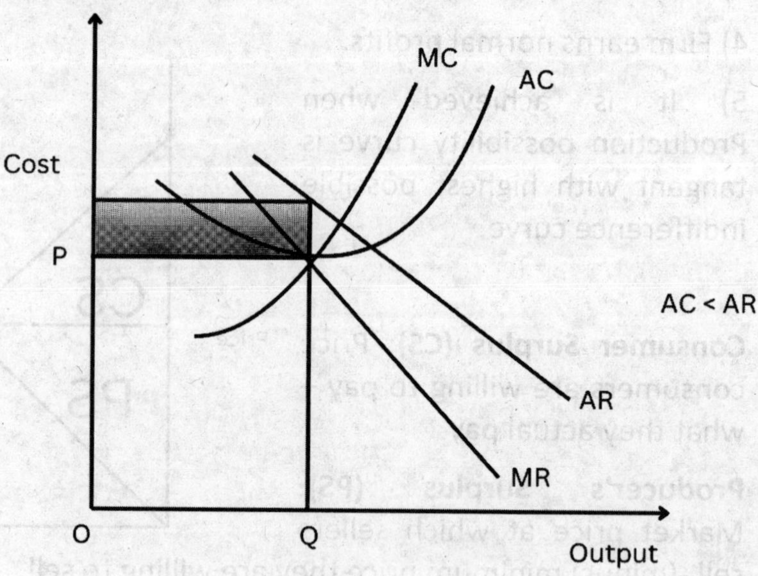

Normal Profit

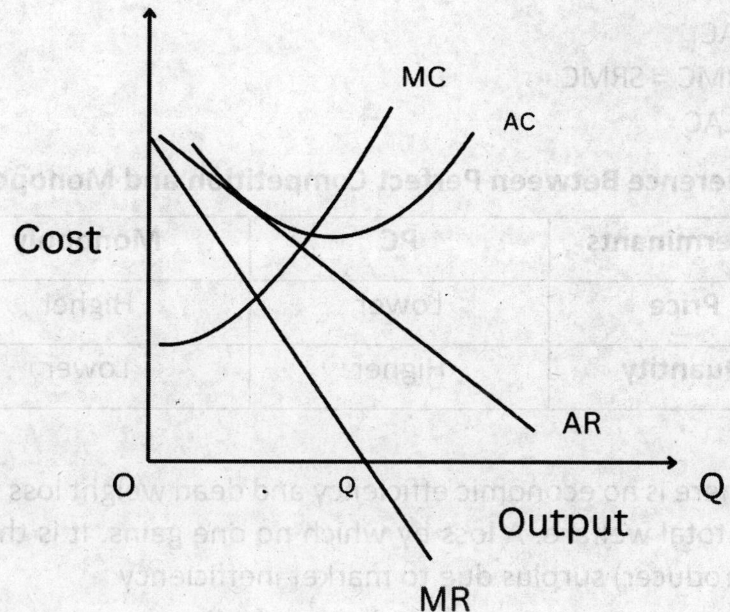

Losses

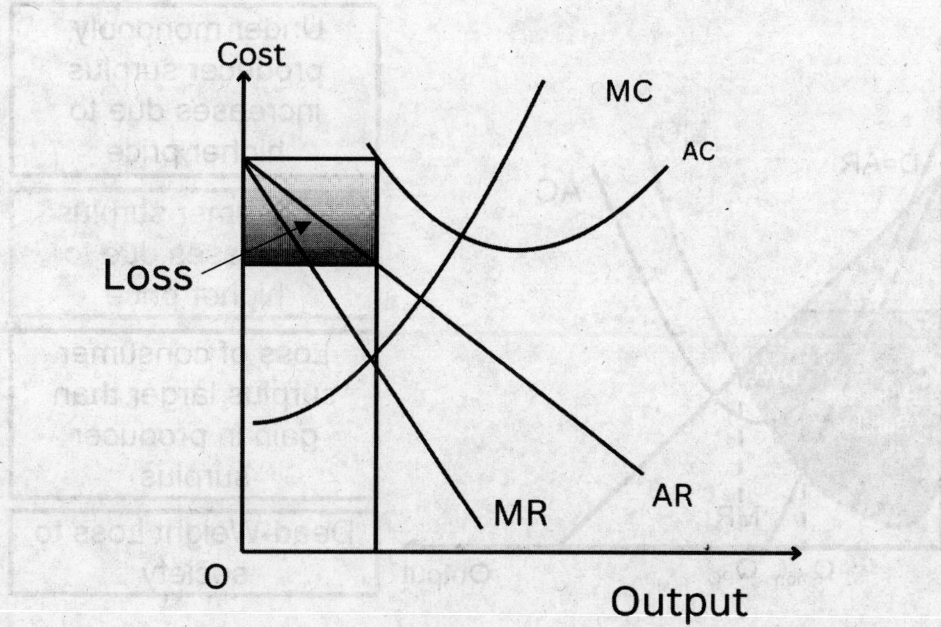

<u>Long Run</u>

The monopolist earns only super normal profit because there are barriers to entry.

Conditions:

- SAC = LAC
- MR = LRMC = SRMC
- Price > LAC

Difference Between Perfect Competition and Monopoly

Determinants	PC	Monopoly
Price	Lower	Higher
Quantity	Higher	Lower

In Monopoly there is no economic efficiency and dead weight loss (DWL) occurs. DWL is loss of total welfare. A loss by which no one gains. It is the loss in total (consumer + producer) surplus due to market inefficiency.

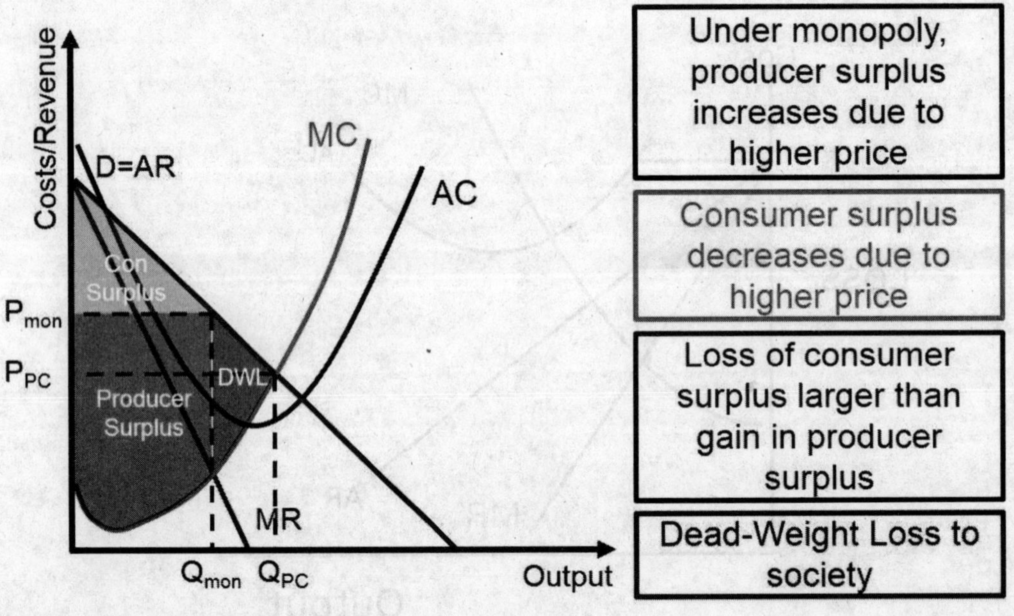

Price Discrimination

Charging different prices from different consumers for the same good. It can either be systematic or unsystematic.

Conditions: No interaction between the two markets. Goods cannot be commuted between the two markets.

Degrees of Price Discrimination

First degree price discrimination (Reservation price): Extracts entire consumer surplus. Monopoly is able to sell each separate unit of the product at a different price.

Second degree price discrimination: Monopolist is able to charge separate price for different quantities or blocks of a commodity from buyers. Note that some consumer surplus is left with the buyers.

Third degree price Discrimination: Different prices are charged in different markets depending on the elasticities.

E.g.- Dumping [electric company sells electric power at a lower price to the households, at higher price to the manufacturers.]

If E_P is low, price charged will be higher.

If E_P is quit elastic, price charged will be lower.

Price Discrimination is possible in case of Monopoly, possible to some extent in case of monopolistic and not possible in case of perfect competition.

Conditions for equilibrium for a discriminant monopolist $MR_A = MR_B = MC$

Inter Temporal Price Discrimination: Separating customers with different demand functions into different groups which leads to charging different prices at different points of time.

Peak Load Pricing: Charging high prices at peak times and lower price during off peak time periods.

Degree of Monopoly Power:

$$M_P = \frac{1}{E_d}$$

Extent to which a monopoly has control over either price or quantities.

Learner's measure

$$\frac{P - MC}{P} or \frac{P - MR}{P}$$

Cross E_P or Triffin's measure

$$\frac{1}{e_C}$$

Bain's measure

$$\frac{P - LAC}{P}$$

Higher the difference b/w price and LAC, higher will be the Monopoly power.

Concentration Ratio: It measures the extent to which the large firms control the output.

Gini Coefficient: It is a measure of inequality in a distribution and is measured with the help of Lorenz curve.

Gini Coefficient = 1 (In case of Monopoly)
= 0 (In case of perfect competition)

Monopolistic Competition

In monopolistic competition there are large no. of firms and product differentiation.

Condition of Equilibrium:

(1) MR = MC

(2) MC should be rising under short run, in Monopolistic Competition.

Firm can earn super normal, normal profits or minimum loss. But in long run, firm earns only Normal Profits; Demand curve in Monopolistic Competition is more elastic than in case of Monopoly.

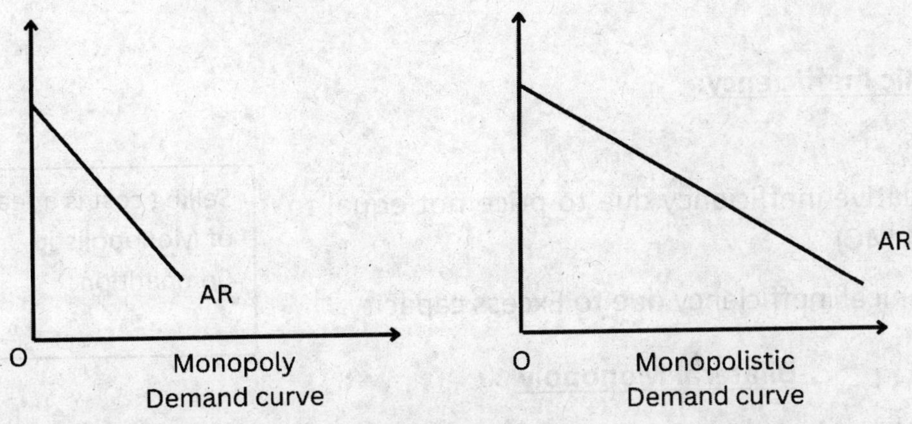

Price is greater than marginal cost under monopolistic competition.

Excess Capacity

Extent to which the long run output is falling short of ideal output/ socially optimum output is called excess capacity. [Excess capacity is a long run concept]

Reasons:

1) Downward sloping demand curve
2) Product differentiation
3) Entry of a very large number of firms

Small demand left to each firm, as a result of which firms are made to produce less than the optimum capacity.

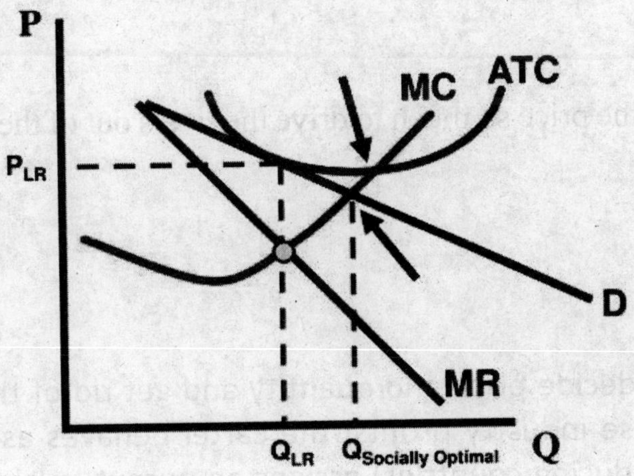

Economic Inefficiency:

Reasons:

(1) Allocative inefficiency due to price not equal to MC. (P > MC)

(2) Technical inefficiency due to Excess capacity

Selling cost is a feature of Monopolistic Competition

Bilateral Monopoly

Monopoly + Monopsony

In monopoly there is single seller & in monopsony there is single buyer.

Oligopoly

Competition among the few.

Causes for existence of oligopolies.

1) Economies of scale

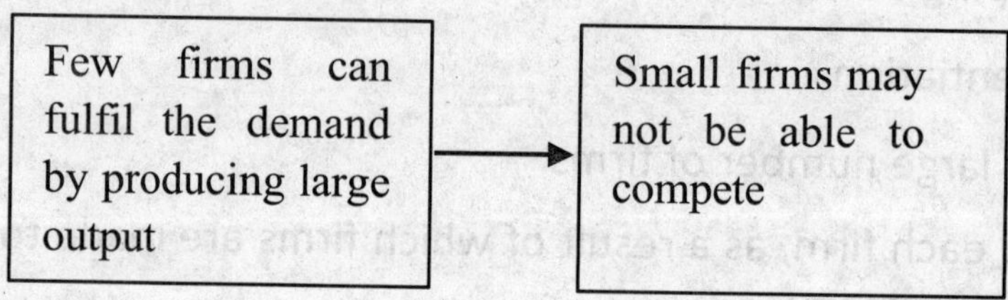

2) Barriers to entry.
3) Product differentiation.
4) Predatory pricing: lowering the price so much to drive the rivals out of the market.

Collusive Oligopoly

Firms have tacit agreement.

a) Cartel: Group of firms mutually decide price and quantity and get rid of the uncertainty. The goal is to maximise industry profits: the cartel behaves as a monopoly i.e. the OPEC (13 oil producing countries) assigns an output level to each member

Cartels are of two types

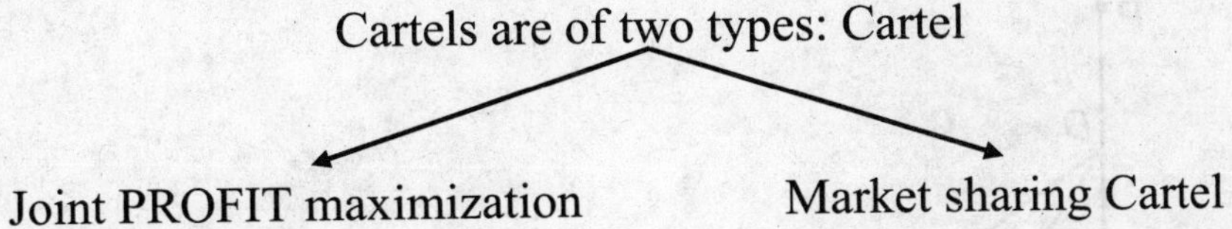

b) Price Leadership: Under this one firm will set its price which will be followed by other firms.

Price Leadership

Low cost firm set a low price which is to be followed by high cost firms.	Dominant Price Leadership firm with maximum market share leads.	Barometric Price Leadership firm which is oldest and most experienced.

Non-Collusive Oligopoly

Firms have not tacit agreement.

Cournot Model (1838 by Augustine Cournot)

- Two firms.
- Firms produce homogeneous goods.
- Firms assume that other firm will keep its output constant.
- Marginal cost of producing a good is zero.
- The firms simultaneously take the decision.
- The output produced by other firm is the 1/2 of the remainder.
- At the end, both forms produce 1/3rd of the total output.
- Cournot price is between Monopoly price and Competitive price.
- Cournot price is the 2/3rd of the most profitable price.
- Cournot output is the 2/3rd of the Maximum output or Perfectly Competitive Output.

- Firms maximized individual profits but not joint profits

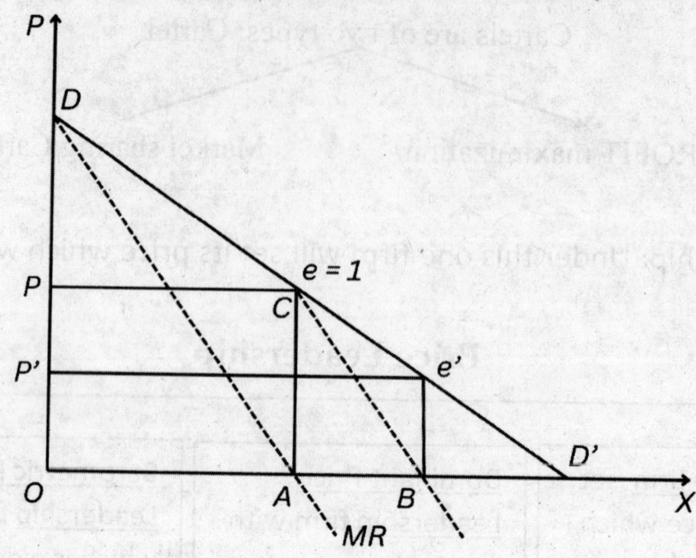

1. A produce quantity A at price P and maximise individual profits.

2. B assumes A will keep output constant (OA), considers its demand CD' and produce half of remaining output.

3. This is naïve behaviour of firm of never learning from past pattern of reaction of rival. Firm keep adjusting the output assuming that the rival's output will remain constant each time.

4. After repeated reactions, finally each firm produce 1/3 of total output and together (1/3+1/3) = 2/3 of total output.

5. Maximise individual profit but not industry profit as price is less than monopoly price.

Bertrand Model (1883)

- Firm assume that other firm will keep the price constant.
- Unlimited productive capacity.
- By undercutting the price, the firm can capture the entire output.
- Concluding result Price= AC
- Total output produced by the two firms is perfectly competitive output.

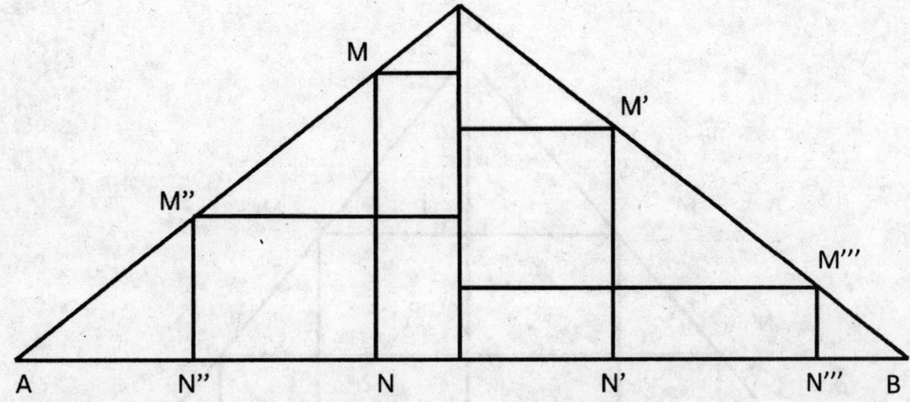

Firm A set price MN. B sets slightly lower from it (M'N') to increase its demand assuming firm A will not change its price. Then A again lowers it to M''N'' assuming firm B will not change its price. At the end both will charge perfectly competitive price.

Edgeworth Model [1897] (Modification of Bertrand model)

- Firms have limited capacity.
- Firms do not get any determinate solution.
- Both firms share the market equally.

Firms under cut the price and reach perfectly competitive prices. Later the firms start increasing the price and reach monopoly price. As a result, the price keeps oscillating between monopoly and perfectly competitive price.

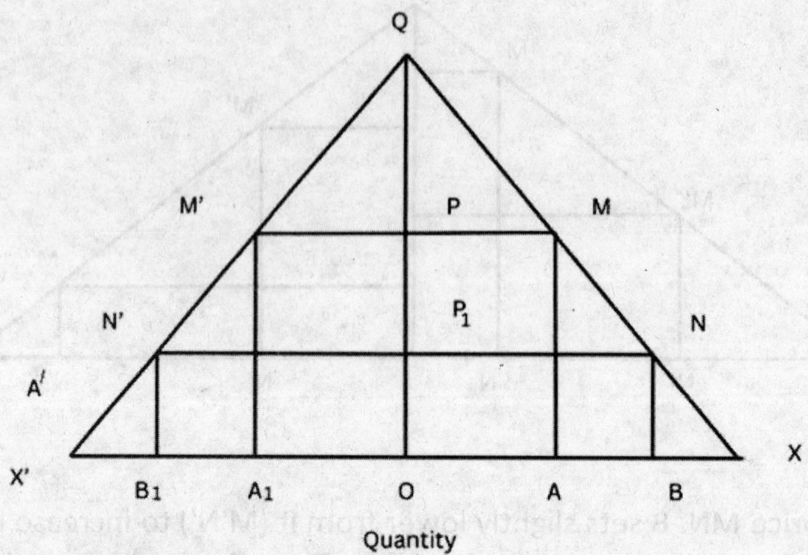

- Let us suppose that there are two firms 1 and 2 in the market. The size of the entire market is B_1B.
- It can be observed from the figure the firm 1 has the maximum capacity of OB amount of output and firm 2 has the maximum capacity of output OB_1.
- Let us imagine that there is a single firm, the firm 1 in the market. Being the only firm, the firm will behave as a monopoly. The firm will therefore sell OA amount of output and charge a price equal to OP.
- Let us suppose that at this point the the firm 2 enters the market and assumes that the firm 1 will not change its price as the firm 1 is enjoying maximum profit and thereby firm 2 sets its price slightly below firm1's price (OP).
- Now as the firm 1 realizes the reduction in its sale, it will set its price slightly below the price of firm 2 in order to regain the lost market.
- This will ensue a price war between the firms. The price war takes the form of price cutting which continues until the price reaches OP_1. At the price level OP_1, both the firms are able to sell their entire outputs.
- The firm1 will sell OB and firm2 will sell BB_1 at this price level. The price level OP_1 seems to provide stability to the model.

- But Edgeworth in his model explain that this price level is not stable. There is an inherent instability in the model. The cause for the instability in the model is that, each firm realizes that its rival is selling its entire output and it will therefore not be able to alter its price and each firm thinks that it can raise his price to OP and can make profit.
- This again sets the chain of actions and reactions. If the firm 1 raises its price to OP. Firm 2 will assume that firm 1 will retain its price level at OP and finds that if it raises its price to a level slightly below OP it can sell its entire output at a higher price and make profit.
- As a reaction to the move of firm 2, the firm 1 will reconsider his situation and react. Firm 1 observes that its price is higher than the price of firm 2 and its sale has reduced.
- Again, assuming firm 2 to retain its price, firm 1 will reduce its price slightly below the price of firm 2.
- The price war between both the firms resumes. This price war continues and as a result the price remains unstable and keeps on fluctuating i.e., moving up and down between OP and OP_1 where OP is the monopoly price and price OP_1 is the competitive price.
- There is no unique equilibrium in Edgeworth's duopoly model.We can thus conclude that in Edgeworth's duopoly model the equilibrium is indeterminate. The price in Edgeworth's duopoly model constantly oscillates between the monopoly price and competitive price. The assumptions of the Edgeworth's duopoly model have been criticized by the critics.

Stackelberg Model

Development over Cournot model. One duopolist is sufficiently sophisticated to recognise that his competitor acts on Cournot assumption. This recognition allows the duopolist to determine reaction curve of his rival and incorporate it in his own profit function.

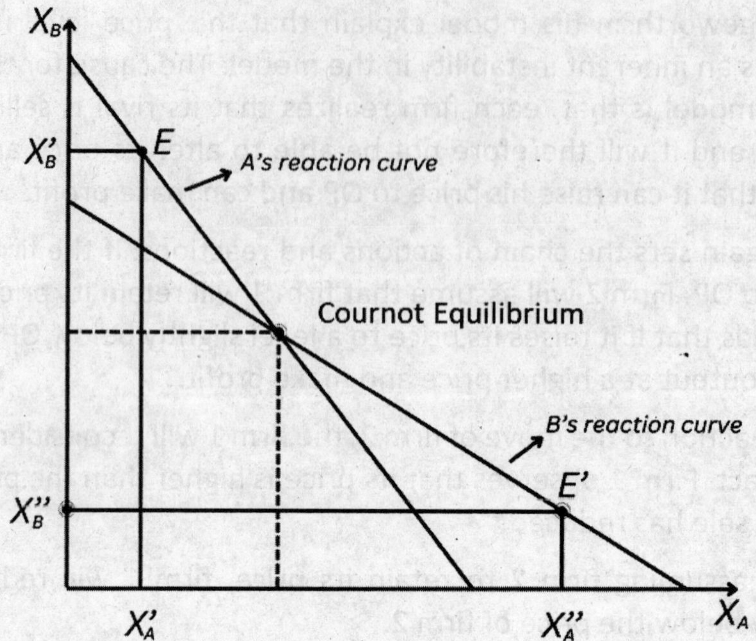

- E' is **Stackelberg equilibrium** with A the leader. It represents maximum profit A can achieve given B's reaction function. B is worse off at OX''_B as compared to Cournot equilibrium
- E is **Stackelberg equilibrium** with B the leader

Cournot Equilibrium (Middle intersection point)

Both firms choose their output simultaneously.

Each assumes the other firm will not change output.

Reaction curves intersect at this point = mutual best responses.

Stable Nash Equilibrium.

Stackelberg Equilibria (Leadership model) Unlike Cournot, here one firm moves first (leader), and the other responds optimally (follower).

<u>Situation 1</u> A: Leader B: Follower

<u>Situation 2</u> A: Follower B: Leader

<u>Situation 3</u> Both A and B want to be leaders. Disequilibrium arises. Outcome is economic warfare.

Situation 4 Both A and B want to be followers. Situation 4 is indeterminate solution

Kinked Demand Curve (Sweezy 1939)

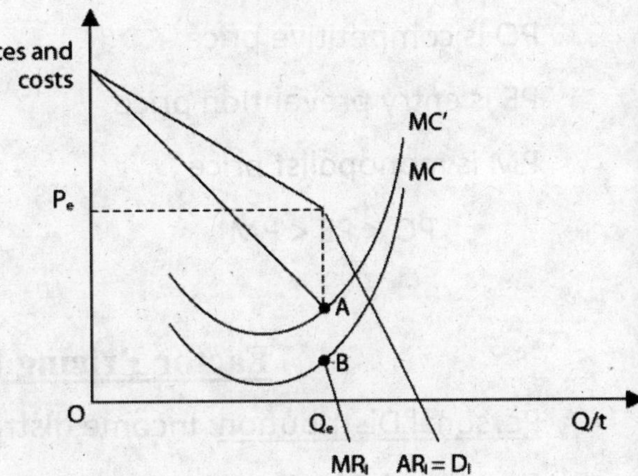

- Prices and quantities are rigid at Kink. If a firm raises price, then others will not raise their prices. If a firm reduces price, others will also reduce it.
- Decline in costs; keep the prices stable but the gap in elasticities increase. As a result, the break in MR curve increases.
- Decline in demand keep the prices stable.
- Due to kink in demand curve, MR is discontinuous.
- Discontinuity of MR implies the range within costs may change without affecting equilibrium price and quantity.
- Upper portion of demand curve (D_1) is elastic portion of demand curve (large fall in sales if producer increases price)
- Lower portion of demand curve is less elastic portion (very little increase in sales can be obtained by reducing price)

Chamberlin Model (small group model)

- Two firms, homogeneous goods
- Chamberlin assumes that monopoly solution can be achieved without collusion.
- One firm recognize the interdependence and will predict the action of other firm and set its output.

At the end, each firm to acts as monopoly and 1/2 of the output is produced and maximized joint profits without collusion.

Limit Price (Bains)

It is price set which does not allow firm to enter the market. It is between competitive price and monopolist price.

PO is competitive price

PE is entry prevention price

PM is monopolist price

- PO < PE < PM

Factor Pricing [Theory of Distribution]

<u>Personal Distribution</u>: Income distribution among individuals.

<u>Functional Distribution</u>: How income is distributed between various factors of production.

<u>Marginal Productivity</u>: Additional product due to employment of an additional unit of a factor.

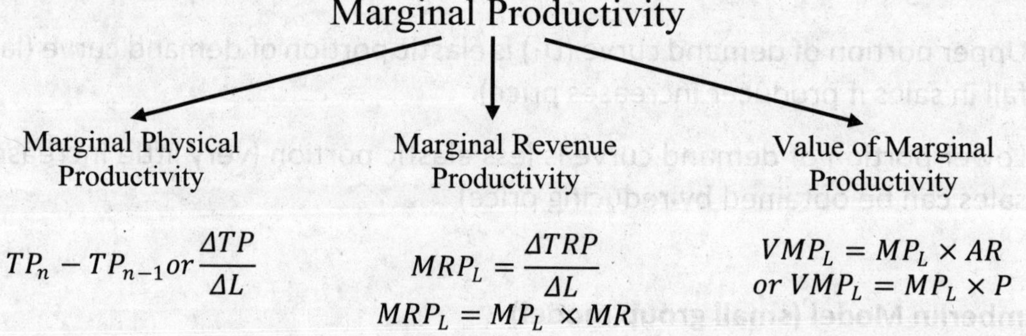

Under Perfect Competition VMP = MRP

Other than it, VMP > MRP

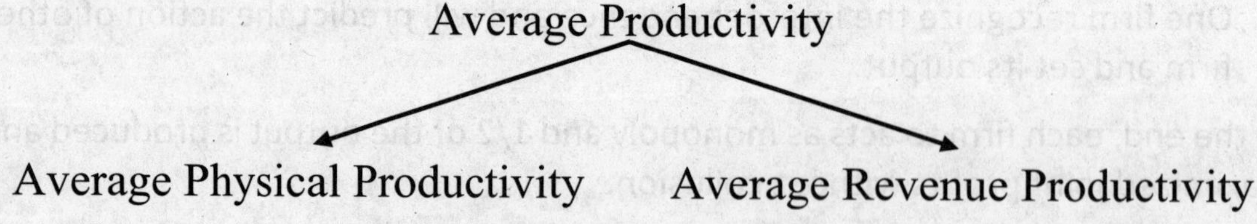

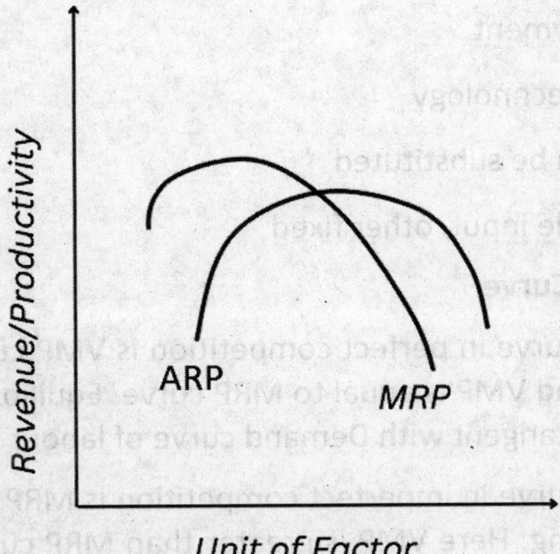

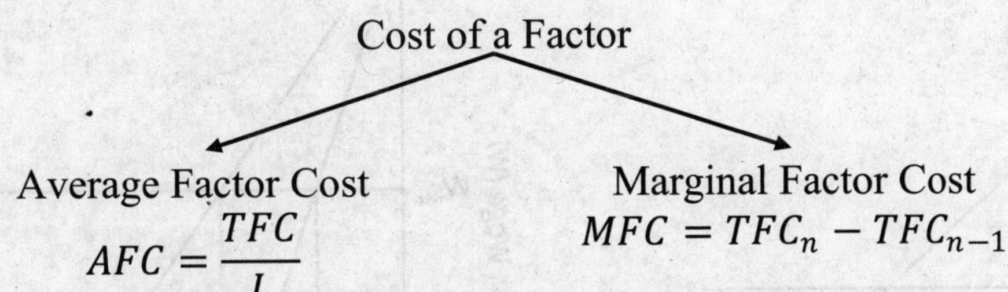

Marginal Productivity Theory (Von Thunen 1826)

Equilibrium MRP = w

If MRP > w, hire more labor

If MRP < w, lay off labor.

Assumptions:

(1) Perfect competition in product market.

(2) Perfect competition in factor market.

(3) Variable proportion type production function [Output can be increased by changing the factor ratio].

(4) Divisible Factor

(5) Full Employment

(6) Constant Technology

(7) Factors can be substituted

(8) One variable input, other fixed

Demand for Labour Curve

Demand for labour curve in perfect competition is VMP curve of labour that is downward sloping and VMP is equal to MRP curve. Equilibrium is where supply curve of labour(W*) tangent with Demand curve of labour (VMP).

Demand for labour curve in imperfect competition is MRP curve of labour. It is also downward sloping. Here VMP is greater than MRP curve. (Here imperfect competition in product market but perfect competition in factor market). Equilibrium is where MRP curve (D_L) equals MFC Curve (S_L).

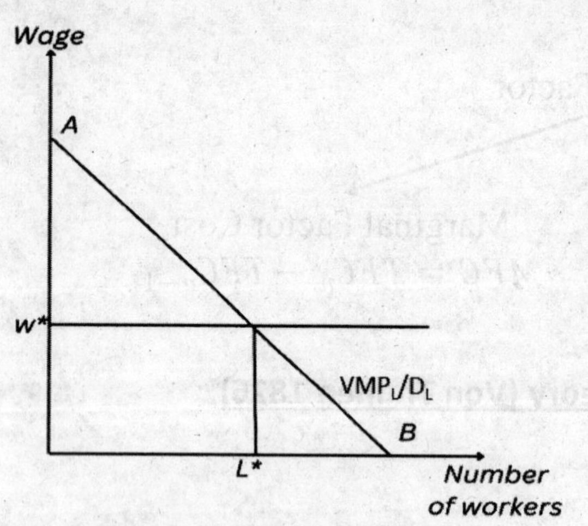

Demand for Labour Curve in Perfect Competition

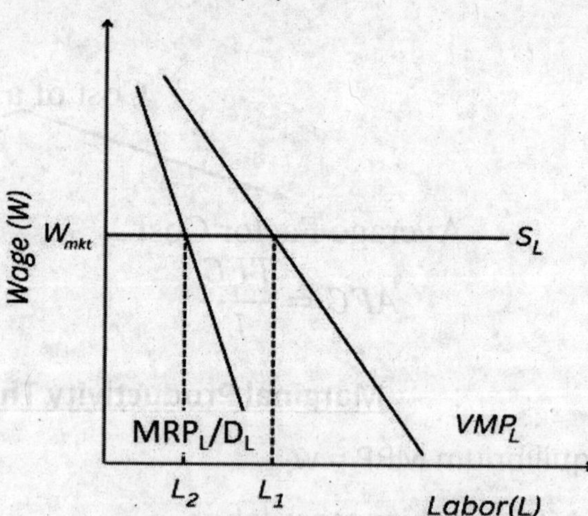

Demand for Labour Curve in Imperfect Competition

Supply Curve of Labor

Supply curve of labor is back ward bending as at higher wages; workers prefer desire to work. Till the point supply of labor curve is upward sloping Substitution effect is more than income effect, that means Increase in wage Induce workers to work more. Workers Substitute leisure hours for work hours. When the supply of labour curve bends backward income effect is stronger than substitution effect, that means increase in wage induce workers to prefer leisure

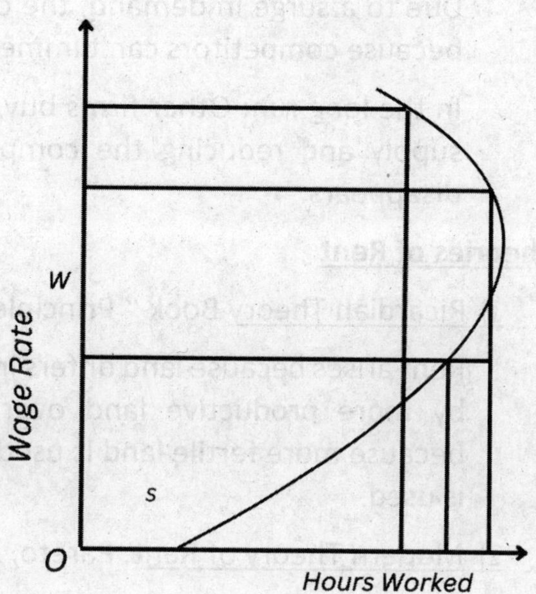

Monopolistic Exploitation

It is difference between VMP (Value of marginal product) and MRP (marginal revenue product.

Economic Rent

Amount that firms are willing to pay for an input less the minimum amount necessary to buy it.

Quasi-Rent Given by Alfred Marshall

Quasi-rent refers to the temporary earnings or surplus **income** that a factor of production (like machinery, buildings, or specialized equipment) earns over and above its opportunity cost in the short run. Unlike economic rent, which can persist in both the short and long run, quasi-rent exists only in the short run because it arises due to temporary supply constraints.

Imagine a company owns a specialized machine that produces high-demand microchips.

- In the short run: The machine cannot be easily replaced or reproduced. Due to a surge in demand, the company earns extra profits (quasi-rent) because competitors can't immediately supply the same chips.
- In the long run: Other firms buy or develop similar machines, increasing supply and reducing the company's surplus earnings. The quasi-rent disappears.

Theories of Rent

1) Ricardian Theory Book " Principle of Political economy and Taxation"

   Rent arises because land differs in fertility & location. It is a surplus earned by more productive land over least productive land. Rent emerges because more fertile land is used first. As demand grows, less fertile land is used.

2) Modern Theory of Rent: Pareto, Joan Robinson, Boulding.

   According to Modern Theory, rent is a Difference between actual earning of a factor over its transfer earnings.

Transfer earnings of factor: Minimum amount necessary to buy the factor of production

- Perfectly elastic supply of factor of production: No economic rent.
- Perfectly inelastic supply of factor of production: Entire income is economic rent, no transfer earnings.
- Less than perfectly elastic supply: Economic rent occurs, transfer earnings also occur.

Some theories and introducers

Subsistence theory of wages/ Iron law of wages [given by Adam Smith]

Minimum level of wages sufficient enough to meet the basic necessities of life.

Wage Fund Theory [Introduced by Adam Smith, developed by JS MILL].

Residual Claimant Theory [given by Walker]

The monopoly theory of distribution (given by Michal Kalecki)

Theories of Interest

1) Productivity theory of interest (Turgot)

2) Loanable fund theory of interest: Given by Wicksell (Neo-Classical) and further developed by Ohlin and Robertson

3) Liquidity preference theory (Keynes)

Theories of Profit

- Hawley's Risk bearing theory of profit
- Uncertainty theory of profit (Knight)
- Rent theory of profit (Walker)

Welfare Economics

Partial Equilibrium: It does not consider interdependence between the market.

General equilibrium: Interdependence is considered.

Pareto Optimality: According to this criterion any change that makes at least one individual better-off and no one worse-off is an improvement in social welfare. i.e., the change is desirable. In that case, we say that the initial state was Pareto-non optimal. Conversely, a change that makes no one better-off and at least one worse-off is a decrease in social welfare. The criterion can be stated in a somewhat different way: a situation in which it is impossible to make anyone better-off without making someone worse-off is said to be Pareto-optimal or Pareto-efficient.

Assumptions:

a. Factor prices are known.

b. Technology is given.

c. Prices are given.

d. Consumers and producers are rational.

e. ordinal measure of utility.

f. It is free from value judgement.

Scan here to watch full video lecture on Pareto Optimality

Conditions:

For the attainment of a Pareto-efficient situation in an economy three marginal conditions must be satisfied:

(a) Efficiency of distribution of commodities among consumers (efficiency in exchange);

(b) Efficiency of the allocation of factors among firms (efficiency of production);

(c) Efficiency in the allocation of factors among commodities (efficiency in the product-mix, or composition of output)

Efficiency of distribution of commodities among consumers: Distribution of the given commodities X and Y between the two consumers is efficient if it is impossible by a redistribution of these goods to increase the utility of one individual without reducing the utility of the other. There is Edgeworth box for the given commodities X and Y. Only points on the Edgeworth contract curve satisfy the Pareto-optimality condition. Thus, the contract curve shows the locus of Pareto-optimal or –efficient distribution of goods between consumers. Consumption contract curve is the locus of points of tangencies of in difference curves of two consumers consume X and Y commodity. For example, point z is inefficient, since a redistribution of the commodities such as to reach any point between a and b increases the utility of both consumers. A movement to 'a' increases the utility of 'B' without reducing the utility of 'A'. Similarly, the distribution implied by 'b' increases the utility of 'A' without reducing the utility of 'B'.

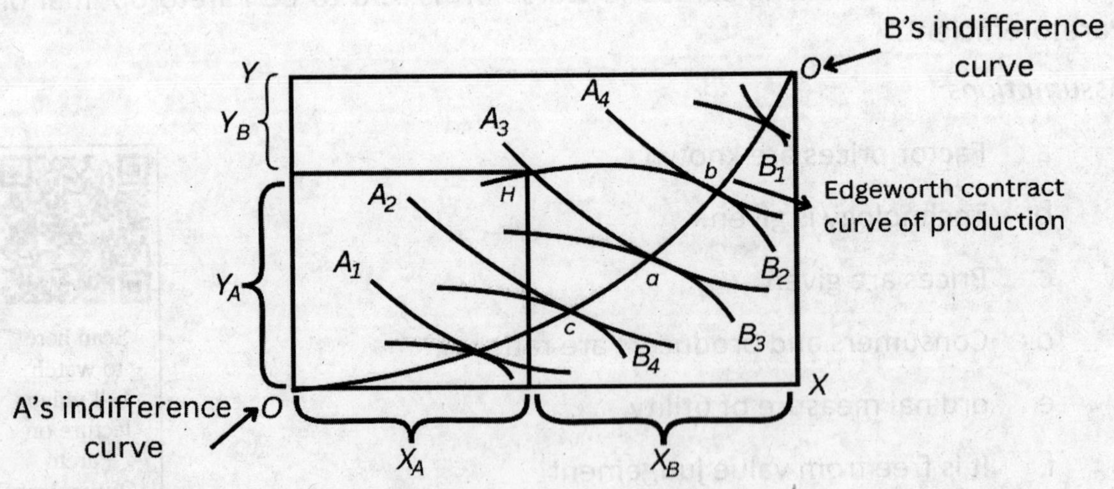

Pareto Optimality will always lie on the contract curve, which implies that there are no leftovers. However, there is no unique solution on the contract curve.

$$Efficiency\ in\ consumption:-\ \boxed{MRS^A_{XY} = MRS^B_{XY} = P_X/P_Y}$$

Therefore, the marginal condition for a Pareto-optimal or -efficient distribution of commodities among consumers requires that the MRS between two goods be equal for all consumers.

Efficiency Of Allocation of Factors Among Producers

Production contract curve is the locus of points of tangencies of isoquants curves of two producers produce X and Y commodity.

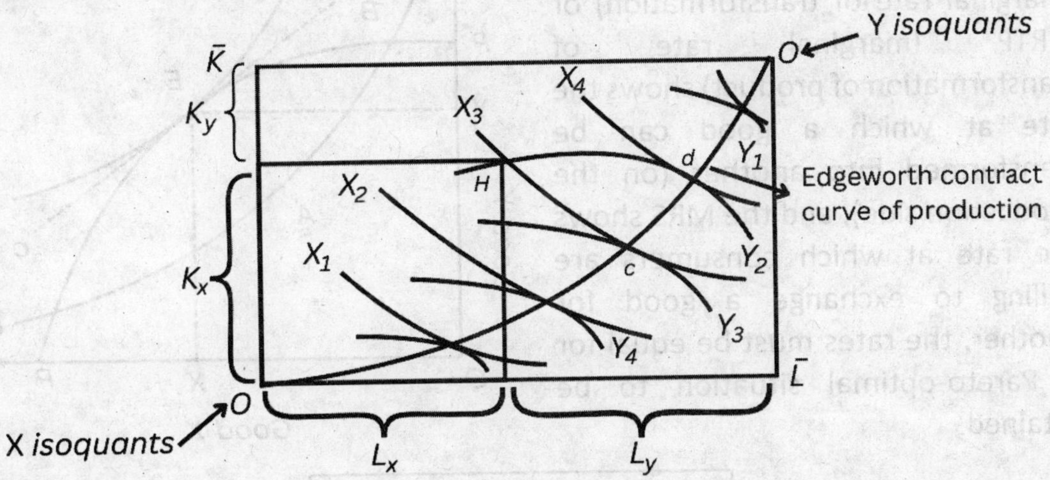

Only points on the contract curve of production are Pareto-efficient. Point H is inefficient, since a reallocation of the given K and L between the producers of X and Y such as to reach any point from c to d inclusive results in the increase of at least one commodity without a reduction in the other.

Efficiency in Production:

$$\boxed{MRTS^A_{LK} = MRTS^B_{LK} = P_L/P_K}$$

The marginal condition for a Pareto-optimal allocation of factors (inputs) requires that the MRTS between labour and capital be equal for all commodities produced by different firms.

Efficiency in Exchange and Production:

- The third possible way of increasing social welfare is a change in the product-mix. The slope of the PPC is called the 'marginal rate of product transformation ($MRPT_{xy}$), and it shows the amount of Y that must be sacrificed in order to obtain an additional unit of X. In other words, the MRPT is the rate at which a good can be transformed into another.
- The marginal condition for a Pareto-optimal or -efficient composition of output requires that the MRPT between any two commodities be equal to the MRS between the same two goods:

Since the MRPT (marginal rate of product transformation) or MRT (marginal rate of transformation) or MRTP (marginal rate of transformation of product) shows the rate at which a good can be transformed into another (on the production side), and the MRS shows the rate at which consumers are willing to exchange a good for another, the rates must be equal for a Pareto-optimal situation to be attained.

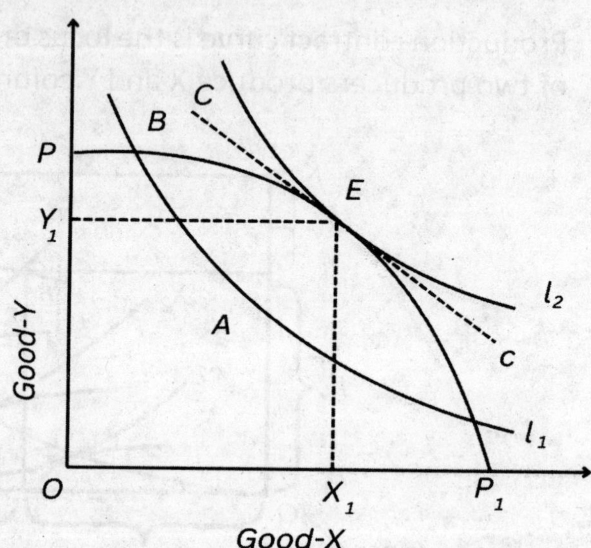

$$MRT_{XY} = MRS^{A}_{XY} = MRS^{B}_{XY}$$

Second Order Conditions:

These are related to the slope.

a. Indifference curve is downward sloping and convex to the origin.

b. Product possibility curve is concave to the origin

First Fundamental Theorem

Under the assumptions of perfect competition and no market power, pareto efficient allocation emerge.

In other words, General competitive equilibrium is Pareto optimal. It ensures Pareto efficiency but not Social Justice.

Second Fundamental Theorem

Any efficient equilibrium is achievable through operation of competitive market with redistribution of wealth.

New Welfare Economics: Kaldor Hicks Compensation Criteria

Someone is made better off and someone is made worse off by a social change. Such change will increase the social welfare if those who gain from the change could compensate the losers and still be better off than before.

Scitovsky - Double Criteria

To rule out the possibility of contradictory results in K-H test, Scitovsky formulated a double criterion which requires the fulfilment of K-H test and also non fulfilment of reversal test.

Social Welfare Function - Bergson Samuelson (BS)

BS social welfare function is an ordinal index of society's welfare and is function of utility level of all individuals constituting the society.

$$W = W(U_1, U_2, U_3, \ldots, U_n)$$

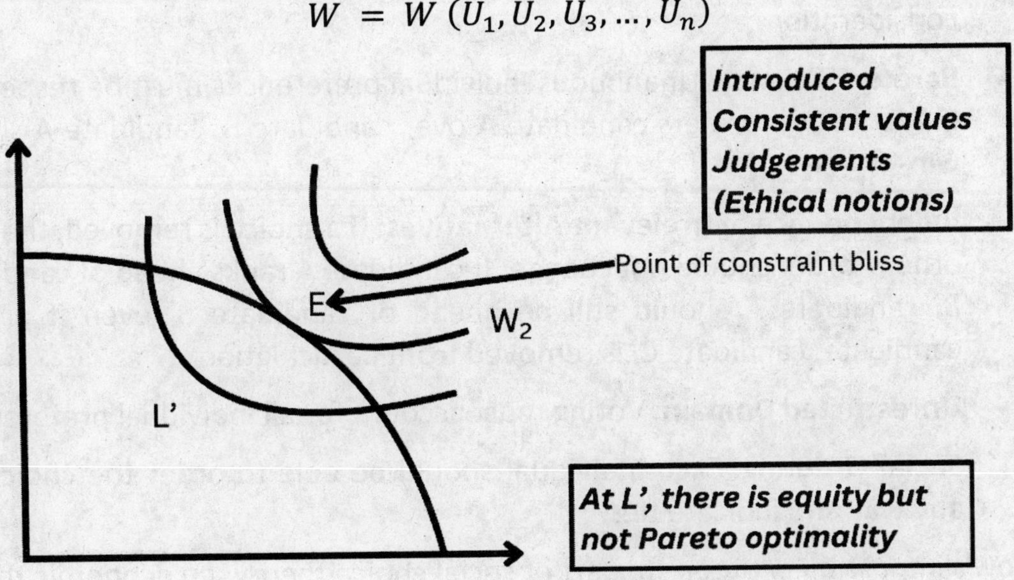

Grand Utility Possibility Frontier

➢ It is the locus of Pareto optimal points.

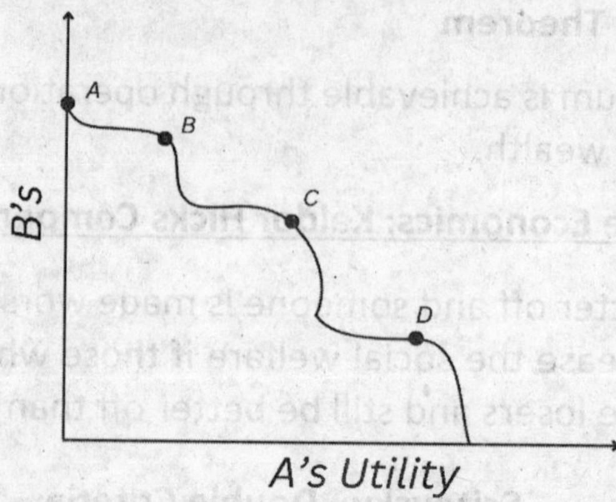

Arrow's Theory of Social Choice (Arrow Impossibility Theorem)

Prof. Arrow pointed out that the Social Welfare Function which reflects the preferences of all individuals constitute a society is an impossible task. Individual have different social choices. Therefore, there is inconsistent social choices. According to it, in all cases where preferences are ranked, it is impossible to formulate a social ordering without violating one of the following conditions:

- **Non-dictatorship**: The wishes of multiple voters should be taken into consideration.
- **Pareto Efficiency**: Unanimous individual preferences must be respected: If every voter prefers candidate A over candidate B, candidate A should win.
- **Independence of Irrelevant Alternatives**: If a choice is removed, then the others' order should not change: If candidate A ranks ahead of candidate B, candidate A should still be ahead of candidate B, even if a third candidate, candidate C, is removed from participation.
- **Unrestricted Domain**: Voting must account for all individual preferences.
- **Social Ordering:** Each individual should be able to order the choices in any way and indicate ties.

Arrow's impossibility theorem, part of social choice theory, an economic theory that considers whether a society can be ordered in a way that reflects individual preferences, was lauded as a major breakthrough.

Example of Arrow's Impossibility Theorem

Let's look at an example illustrating the type of problems highlighted by Arrow's impossibility theorem. Consider the following example, where voters are asked to rank their preference of three projects that could be used for: A; B; and C. This country has 99 voters who are each asked to rank the order, from best to worst, for which of the three projects should receive the annual funding.

- 33 votes A > B > C (1/3 prefer A over B and prefer B over C)
- 33 votes B > C > A (1/3 prefer B over C and prefer C over A)
- 33 votes C > A > B (1/3 prefer C over A and prefer A over B)

Therefore,

- 66 voters prefer A over B
- 66 voters prefer B over C
- 66 voters prefer C over A

So a two-thirds majority of voters prefer A over B and B over C and C over A---a paradoxical result based on the requirement to rank order the preferences of the three alternatives.

Arrow's theorem indicates that if the conditions cited above i.e., Non-dictatorship, Pareto efficiency, independence of irrelevant alternatives, unrestricted domain, and social ordering are to be part of the decision-making criteria then it is impossible to formulate a social ordering on a problem such as indicated above without violating one of the following conditions.

Baumol's Sales Maximization Model

Main aim of the model is to maximize the sales or revenue from sales subject to some minimum level of profits.

Marris Model of Maximizing Growth Rate

- ➢ Managers do not aim to maximize profit; they aim to maximize the balanced growth rate of the firm.

Marris talked about constraints

1) Managerial constraint related to skills of manager

2) Financial constraint

$$Debt\ Ratio\ or\ Leverage\ Ratio \rightarrow \frac{Debt}{Gross\ Value\ of\ Assets}$$

$$Liquidity\ Ratio \rightarrow \frac{Liquid\ Assets}{Total\ Assets}$$

$$Retention\ Ratio \rightarrow \frac{Retained\ Profits}{Total\ Assets}$$

$$Maximize\ G = \underbrace{Gd}_{\substack{Growth\ Rate \\ of\ Demand}} = \underbrace{Gs}_{\substack{Growth\ Rate \\ of\ supply}}$$

Williamson's Managerial Theory

Managers are motivated towards their own self-interest and they try to maximize their own utility function.

Utility of Managers = f (Monetary expenses, no. of staff, Management slack, discretionary investment)

Cobweb Phenomenon

Cobweb phenomenon is economic theory stipulating that price fluctuations lead to fluctuations in supply, causing a cycle of rising and falling prices. For example, seeing higher prices, farmers sow the seeds for the crops to benefit from higher prices. This results in surplus production, more than the demand, resulting in a price crash, often referred to as the 'problem of plenty'. Seeing the low prices, farmers switch to different crops or produce less of the same crop, leading to lower than usual production for that particular crop. This increases the prices of crops, completing the cyclical variations in price and production.

$$Y_t = \alpha + \beta P_{t-1} + U_t$$

Adaptive expectations and cobweb model

Farmers look back on most recent prices in order to forecast prices. When they expect high prices to continue, they produce too much and end up with low prices and vice versa.

Cobweb Model: - Convergent case: Stable equilibrium

In stable case, prediction error becomes smaller every period. After several periods, price and quantity comes close to the point where supply and demand cross.

$E_d > E_s$. In other words, slope of demand is less than that of supply

Divergent Case: - Unstable Equilibrium

In unstable case, prediction errors get larger every period.

$E_d < E_s$. In other words, slope of demand is more than that of supply.

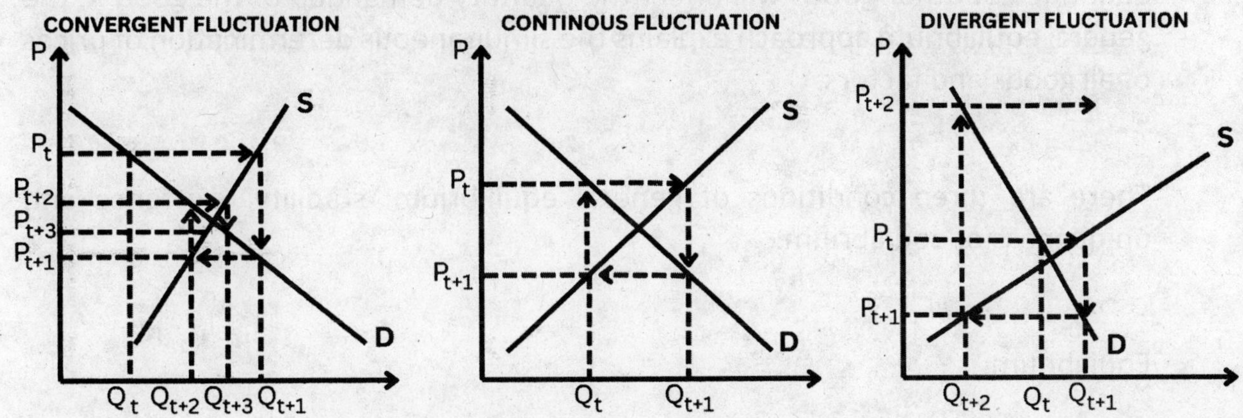

Inada Conditions

Assumptions about the shape of production function that guarantee the stability of an economic growth path in a Neo-classical growth model. A production function satisfies these conditions are referred to as well behaved production function.

I. No output can be produced without any capital i.e. f (0) =0

II. Marginal product of capital is positive for all levels of capital - labour ratio f'(K) >0 for all k

III. Marginal product of capital diminishes as capital for laborer increases f''(K) < 0 for all k

Marshall's Partial Equilibrium Analysis

We seek to explain the price determination of commodity, keeping the prices of other commodities constant.

Walras General Equilibrium Analysis

The price of a good is not explained to be determined independently of the prices of other goods. Since the changes in price of good X affect the prices and quantities demanded of other goods and in turn the changes in prices and quantities of other goods will affect the quantity demanded of the good X, the general equilibrium approach explains the simultaneous determination of prices of all goods and factors.

There are three conditions of general equilibrium: stability, existence and uniqueness of equilibrium.

Equilibrium:

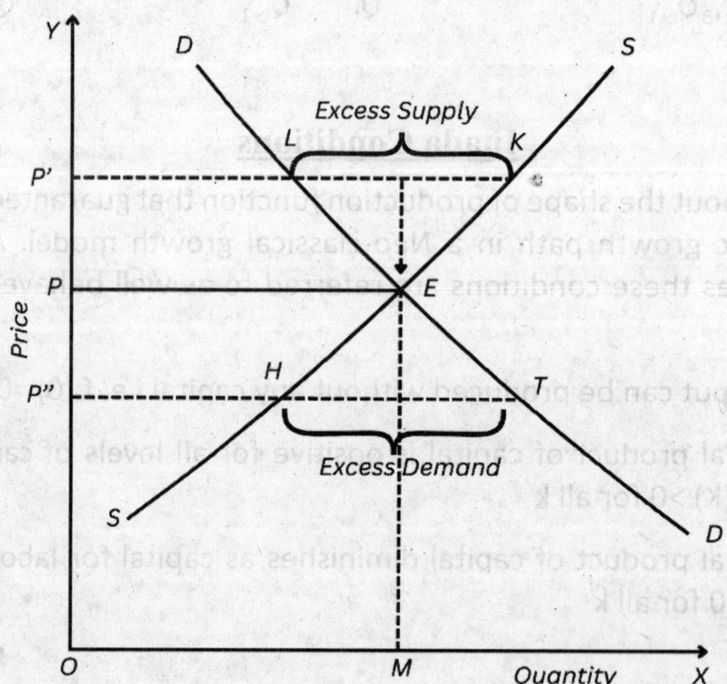

Non-existence of Equilibrium

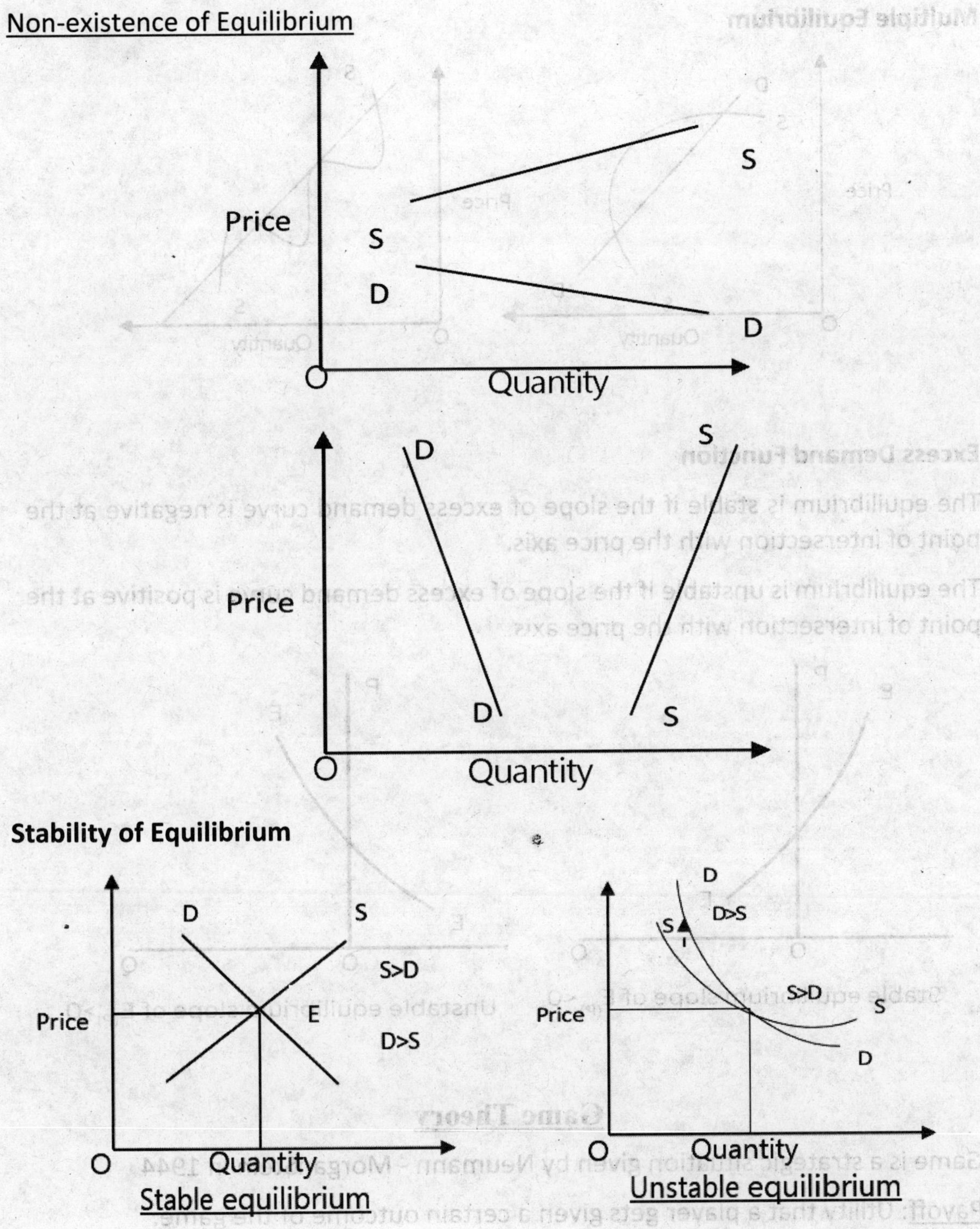

Stability of Equilibrium

Stable equilibrium

Unstable equilibrium

Multiple Equilibrium

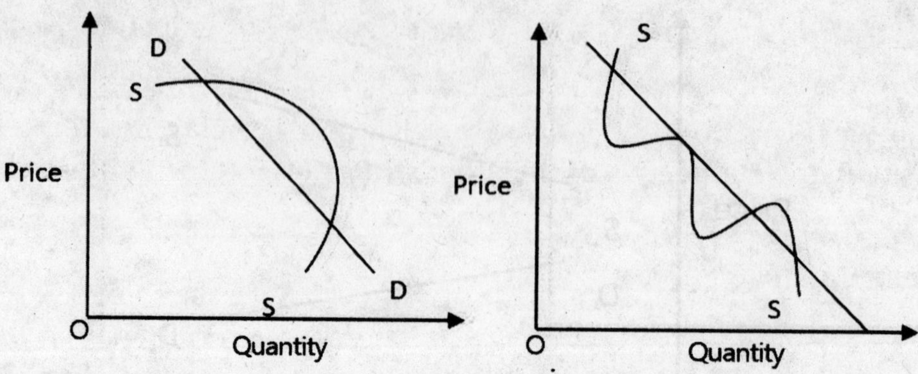

Excess Demand Function

The equilibrium is stable if the slope of excess demand curve is negative at the point of intersection with the price axis.

The equilibrium is unstable if the slope of excess demand curve is positive at the point of intersection with the price axis.

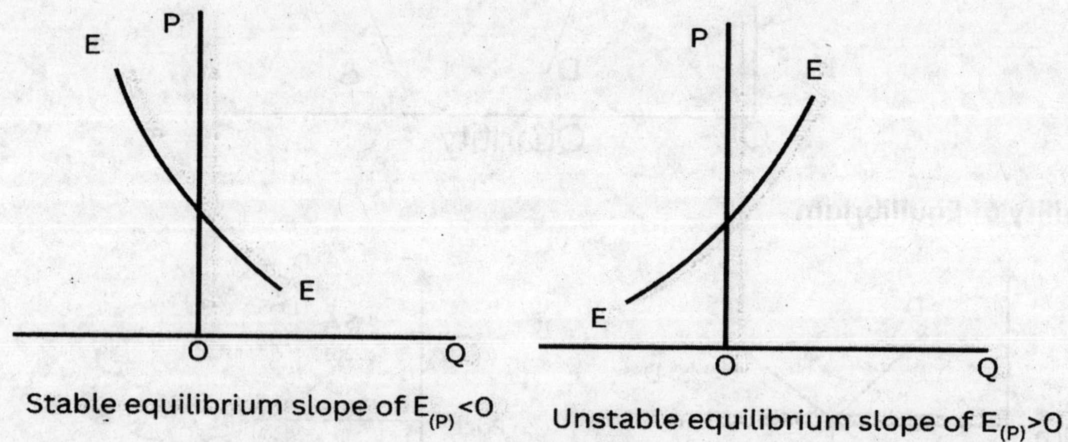

Stable equilibrium slope of $E_{(P)} < 0$ Unstable equilibrium slope of $E_{(P)} > 0$

Game Theory

Game is a strategic situation given by Neumann - MorganStein in 1944

Payoff: Utility that a player gets given a certain outcome of the game.

Pay off Matrix: Shows players, their actions and their pay offs in a game.

Pure strategy: The player will surely follow a particular action.

Mixed strategy: The player will be indifferent between several pure strategies, and he will select the strategy according to the probability distribution.

Optimal strategy: It is the course of plan which puts the player into the most favorable situation, irrespective of the other strategies.

Zero Sum Game: When the gain of one competitor is the loss of the other, then it is a zero-sum game.

Minimax: Minimum loss out of maximum losses.

Maximin: Maximum out of Minimum profits.

Fair Game: It is the point where minmax and maximin are equal to zero.

How To Find Saddle Point

Minimum element of first row is 7 and 7 is maximum in third column.

	1	2	3
(I)	10	9	7
(II)	8	8	6
(III)	9	9	6

	1	2	3
(I)	10	9	7
(II)	~~8~~	~~8~~	~~6~~
(III)	9	9	6

	1	2	3
(I)	10	9	7

(7) is Saddle Point

Cooperative Games

Games in which negotiations of binding contracts are possible, i.e. Bargain b/w buyers and sellers.

Tit for Tat Strategy: Players respond in kind to an opponent's previous play, Cooperative to Cooperative opponents and retaliating against un- cooperative ones.

Non-Cooperative Games

Video Lecture on Nash Equilibrium & Dominant Strategy

Nash equilibrium

Firm A will adopt best strategy, given other's strategy.

Dominant Strategy

Firm A will adopt best strategy regardless of firm B will do

Numerical Problem

		Firm B	
	Adv.	Adv.	Not Adv.
Firm A		10,5	15,0
	Not Adv.	6,8	10,2

Firm A will choose 10 from 10 and 6 and will choose 15 from 15 and 10.

Firm A will advertise, no matter firm B will do or not.

Firm B will choose 5 from 5 and 0 and choose 8 from 8 and 2. Firm B will advertise, no matter firm A will do or not.

Both choices are consistent.

Both 'A' and 'B' has dominant strategies. Nash equilibrium is (10,5).

Asymmetric Information

Asymmetric information is an economic theory that describes a situation where one party in a transaction has more information than the other. This imbalance can lead to inefficient outcomes and market failures.

Moral Hazard

It occurs when there is change in behaviour of one party occurs after agreement. It is also called Hidden Action problem as one side of the market can't observe the action of other. Insured consumers are likely to take greater risk, knowing that a claim will be paid by their cover. For example, an individual with car insurance may drive more recklessly, knowing that any accident costs will be covered by the insurer.

Adverse selection [Market of Lemons]

Given by Akerlof. Adverse Selection arises when there is asymmetric information before a contract is made, where one party has more or better information than the other.

The Lemon Problem (used car market example)

Buyers of used cars can't tell whether a car is good (peach) or bad (lemon). Only sellers know the quality of their cars. Thus, buyers offers only an average price as they cannot tell the difference. Consequently, sellers of good cars exit the market because they are not getting a fair price and only lemons remain in the market, causing a market failure.

Macroeconomics

Classical Model of Output and Employment

The classical economists believed in the existence of full employment in the economy. To them, full employment was a normal situation and any deviation from this regarded as something abnormal.

Assumptions:

1. Full employment →Resources are fully employed. Any deviation from full employment leads to bring economy back to original situation by the act of market forces. There can be frictional and voluntary unemployment in the state of full employment.

Full employment is a situation in which everyone who is willing to work and able to do work gets work.

2. Say's law of market → Supply creates its own demand i.e., AD = AS and S = I

   No overproduction, No underproduction.
3. Laissez - faire system → No government control. Market forces of demand and supply operate.
4. Money is neutral → Money only acts as a medium of exchange.
5. Perfect competition
6. Closed economy
7. No money illusion [workers easily determine price levels in economy and hence demand real wages]
8. Existence of two sectors- Real and Monetary
9. Rate of interest = f [savings (+), Inv. (-)]
10. Prices, wages are flexible in both upward and downward direction
11. S_L = f (W/P), where W= Nominal wages & P = price level, and W/P is real wage

12. $D_L = f((W/P), MRP_L)$, where MRP is marginal revenue productivity
13. Long run analysis

Classical Dichotomy

By the term classical dichotomy, we mean that there exist two independent sectors in the economy- real sector and monetary sector. There is a complete independence of real variables from nominal variables. This implies that the money is neutral in nature. It acts as a medium of exchange only. Money impacts prices and hence only affects the nominal variables, keeping the real variables unchanged. Real factors are determined by variables totally different from nominal variables

Determination of Output and Employment

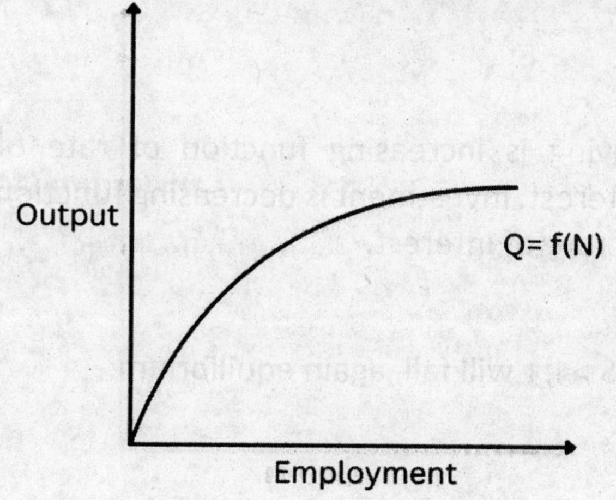

Output is increasing function of the number of workers. But after a point diminishing returns to labour start.

Labour market equilibrium

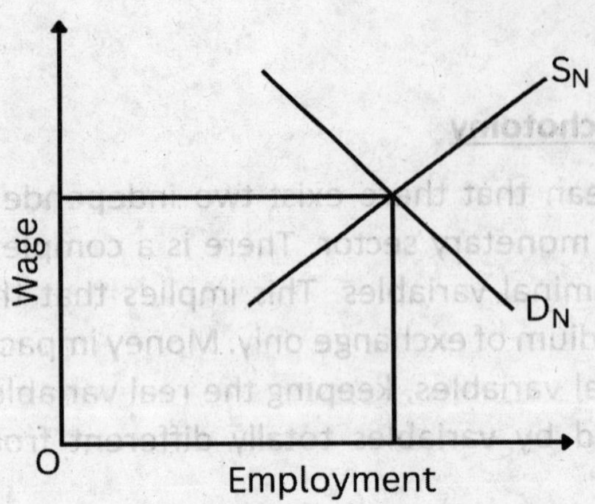

D_N is decreasing function of real wage rate. S_N is increasing function of real wage rate.

Goods Market Equilibrium

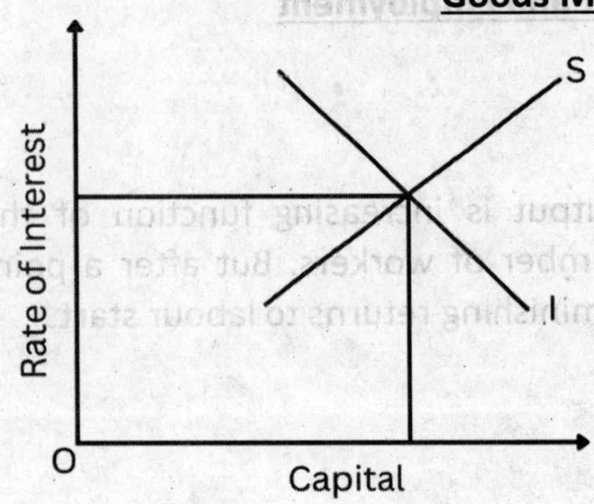

Saving is increasing function of rate of interest. Investment is decreasing function of rate of interest.

If S > I, r will fall, again equilibrium.

Money Market Equilibrium

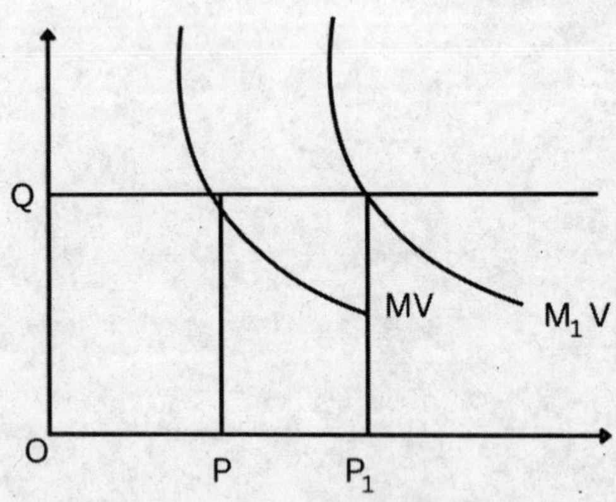

Based on quantity theory of money (MV=PT) that is price level is a function of money supply.

MV= money supply curve

If MV shifts forward (money supply increases) then price level increase given the same level of output.

Criticisms by Keynes

1) Underemployment equilibrium.
2) Refutation of say's law.
3) Self-adjustment not possible
4) Equality of S and I through income changes
5) Money is not neutral
6) State intervention essential
7) Rejection of quantity theory of money
8) Long run analysis is unrealistic

Keynesian Macroeconomic Theory

Keynes in his book 'General theory of Employment, Interest and Money' challenged the validity of classical theory of employment.

Assumptions:

1) Full employment not possible [under employment equilibrium].
2) Workers suffer from money illusions.
3) D_L =f (w/p). D_L is function of real wages

   S_L = f(w). S_L is function of nominal wages because workers cannot estimate the effect of price levels on their income.
4) Money also acts as a store of value
5) Short-run analysis.

Classicals focused on supply side
Keynesian's focused on demand side

Keynes's Money-Wage Rigidity Model

Workers resist to change in money wages but don't resist change in real wages. So, unemployment can be reduced through change in price level but not by money wages.

1. Money Illusion. One key reason why firms often hesitate to cut wages, even when there is an excess supply of labour, is due to money illusion among workers.

   Money illusion refers to the tendency of workers to think in terms of nominal wages rather than real wages. In other words, they focus on the amount of money they receive rather than its purchasing power.

   They fail to recognize that when prices rise, the value of money (its purchasing power) declines. As a result, even if workers' wages remain the same in money terms, rising prices may reduce their real income — but they do not react as strongly to this as they would to a direct cut in the amount of money they receive.

2. Wage fixation through contracts

3. Minimum Wage Laws

4. Efficiency Wages: Efficiency of workers depends positive on real wage they are paid.

Effective Demand Principle

In Keynes theory, the level of 'effective aggregate demand' determines equilibrium national income. The level of effective demand will be where the aggregate demand curve equals aggregate supply.

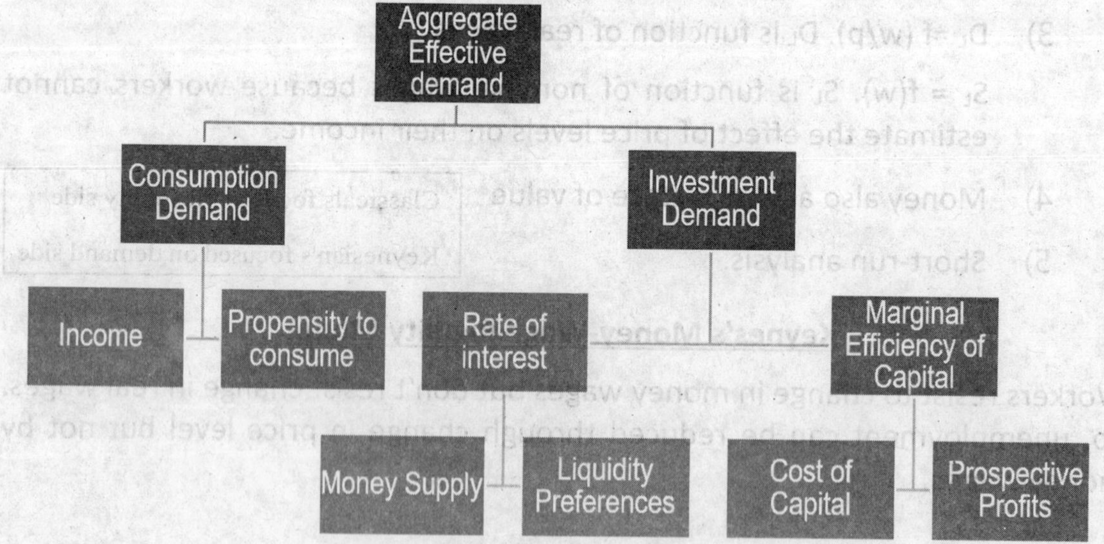

Equilibrium income or output AD = AS

C + I = C+ S

Aggregate supply remains constant in short run. Savings = f(income) while investment =f (MEC, r)

Underemployment equilibrium (problem of demand deficiency)

N_2N_F is called involuntary unemployment—a situation at which people are willing to work but do not find jobs.

This unemployment, according to Keynes, is due to the deficiency of aggregate demand. This unemployment can be removed by stimulating aggregate demand.

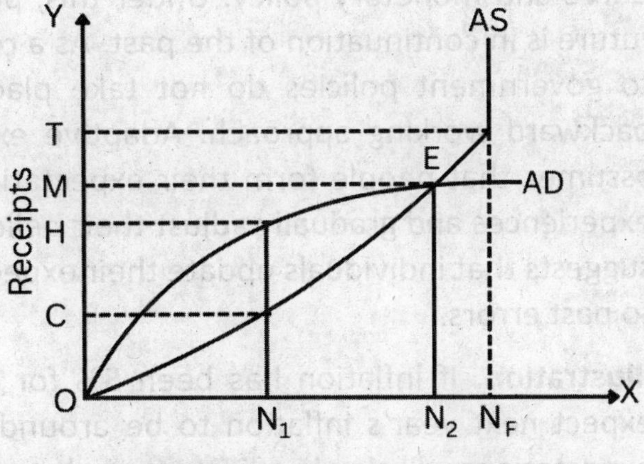

Inflationary Gap

The amount by which income is more than the full employment level.

Deflationary Gap

Amount by which income is less than full employment level.

Adaptive Expectations

Watch full video on Adaptive & Rational Expectations

The Adaptive Expectations hypothesis was introduced by Irving Fisher and later formalized by Philip Cagan in his 1956 study on hyperinflation.

In 1958, Nerlove applied the adaptive expectations framework to agricultural supply models. It was further developed by Milton Friedman in his work on the Phillips Curve and monetary policy. Under this, people believe that future is in continuation of the past. As a result, changes due to government policies do not take place rapidly. It is a backward working approach. Adaptive expectations theory assumes that people form their expectations about the future based on past experiences and gradually adjust their beliefs as new data becomes available. It suggests that individuals update their expectations slowly over time in response to past errors.

Illustration. If inflation has been 5% for the past three years, people might expect next year's inflation to be around 5%. If inflation then jumps to 7%, expectations will slowly adjust upward over time.

Rational Expectations

The theory was given by John Muth in 1961 and later popularized by Robert Lucas in the 1970s. It is a forward-looking approach and people are considered to be rational. Rational expectations suggest that individuals and firms use all available information, including past data, current policies, and economic theories, to form expectations as accurately as possible. Unlike adaptive expectations, rational expectations assume that people do not make systematic errors when predicting the future. In other words, any errors in forecasting are random in nature.

New Classicals

New classical economics emerged in the early 1970s through the work of Robert Lucas. Some of the names of the new classical economists are: Thomas Sargent. Neil Wallace. The new classical macroeconomics is based on the rational expectations hypothesis. This means that people have rational expectations about economic variables. The implication is that people make intelligent use of available information in forecasting variables that affect their economic decisions.

According to this hypothesis, forecasts are unbiased and based on all available information. The hypothesis holds that people make unbiased forecasts. A more controversial assumption is that people use all available information and economic theory in making decisions.

This implies that people understand how the economy works and how the government policies alter macroeconomic variables such as the price level, the level of employment and aggregate output. And because of rational expectations, the government cannot fool the people with systematic economic policies.

One of the most important contentions of rational expectations is the ineffectiveness of systematic fiscal and monetary policies in reducing unemployment. The basic idea is that a predictable attempt to stimulate the economy would be known in advance, and would have no effect on the economy. This is known as the policy ineffectiveness theorem. With rational expectations and flexible prices and wages, anticipated government policy cannot affect real output or employment.

According to the theory, any new policy will be ineffective because it would be anticipated before it is being introduced. This was known as policy ineffectiveness/irrelevant impotency theory which was given by Lucas.

- Equilibrium will be established at the point where equality is reached between long run supply, short run supply and demand.

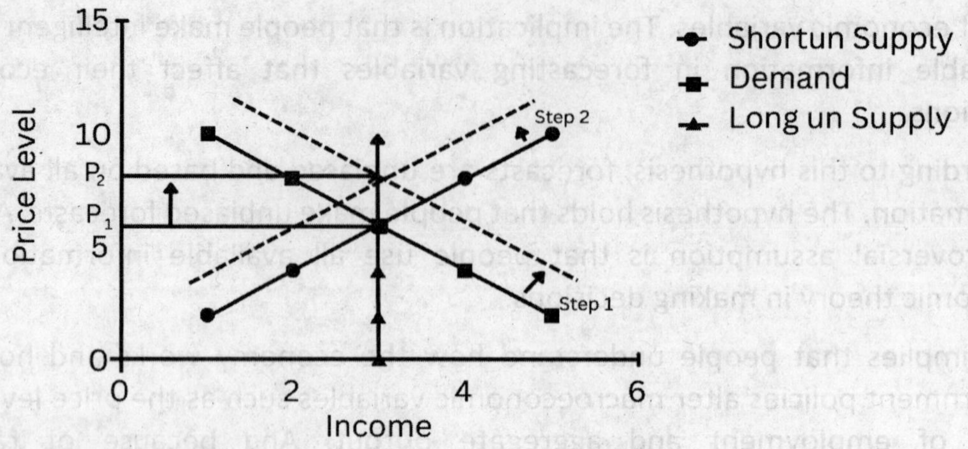

New Keynesians

The term "New Keynesians" was coined by Parkin and Bade in 1982. The main aim of this school of thought was to improve upon the Keynesian theory. Keynes theory did not provide any rationale for the wage-price rigidity.

Therefore, their main aim was:

a. Provide a rationale behind wage-price rigidity.

b. Provide micro-foundations to macro theories.

Assumptions taken by New Keynesians were:

a. Involuntary unemployment is possible.

b. Imperfectly competitive market structures.

c. Considered both supply and demand shocks.

d. Considered asymmetric information and incomplete labour markets.

e. The New Keynesians have talked about nominal and real wage-price rigidity.

According to New Keynesians, relative prices remain constant. Why prices are assumed to be constant?

a. Prevalence of menu costs, that is, costs of making the price adjustment.

c. Price Wars

d. Co-ordination failures: The firms do not co-ordinate with each other and hence they reach a recessionary situation.

Differences

Feature	New Classical Economics	New Keynesian Economics
Founders	Robert Lucas, Edward Prescott, Thomas Sargent	Gregory Mankiw, David Romer, Jordi Galí
Price & Wage Flexibility	Fully flexible (markets clear instantly)	Sticky prices and wages (due to contracts, menu costs, etc.)
Role of Market Failures	Markets are efficient and adjust quickly	Market imperfections (price/wage stickiness cause inefficiencies)
Business Cycle Theory	Real Business Cycle (RBC) Theory – fluctuations are driven by real shocks (e.g., technology, productivity)	Demand shocks and rigidities drive business cycles
Monetary Policy Effectiveness	Ineffective in the long run (monetary neutrality/ policy ineffectiveness)	Effective, especially in the short run, due to price/wage stickiness
Fiscal Policy Effectiveness	Ineffective (Ricardian equivalence – people anticipate taxes and adjust savings)	Can be effective, particularly in liquidity traps or recessions
Unemployment	Voluntary	Involuntary (due to wage rigidity and demand shortages)
Business Cycle Drivers	Supply-side factors (technology, productivity shocks)	Demand-side factors (monetary/fiscal shocks, sticky prices)
Government Intervention	Minimal (markets self-correct)	Necessary to stabilize the economy

Aggregate Supply Curves

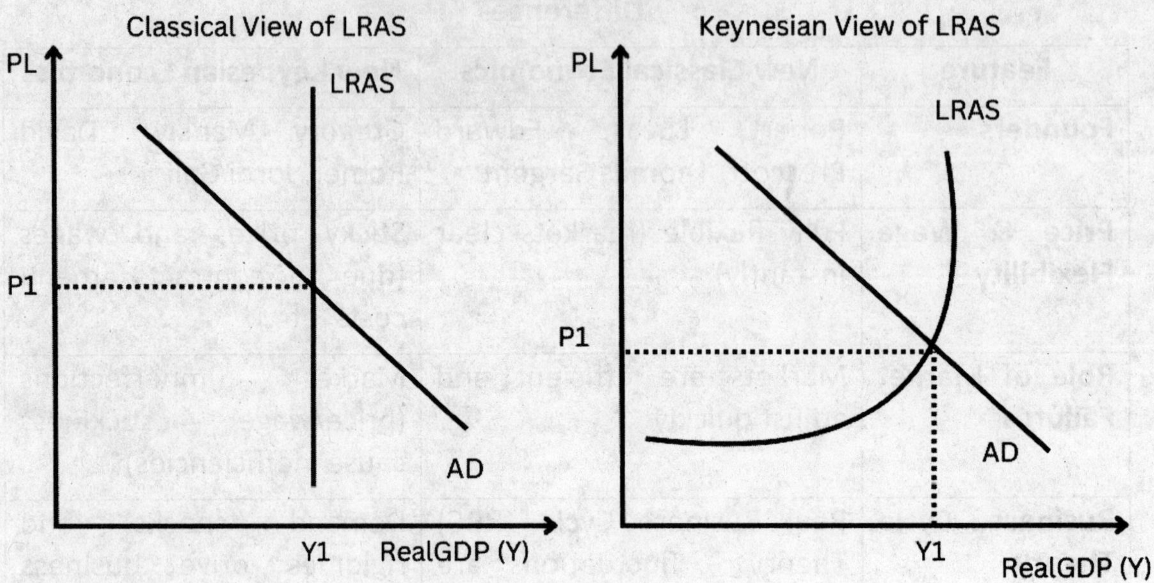

Here, LRAS Curve: Long Run Aggregate Supply Curve

Paradox of Thrift

The paradox of thrift is an economic theory that suggests that when people save more during a recession, it can lead to a decrease in aggregate demand, which can then decrease gross output and total savings. This theory is based on the idea that when people cut spending to save more, aggregate savings will eventually decrease because one person's spending is another person's income.

The paradox of thrift is part of the under-consumption theories of the business cycle, which suggest that economic downturns are caused by high savings and weak consumption. British economist John Maynard Keynes popularized the theory in his 1936 book The General Theory of Employment, Interest, and Money.

Consumption Function

Absolute Income Hypothesis

It was given by Keynes in 1936. He considered a short run consumption function which is linear in nature. It is stated that aggregate consumption is a function of aggregate current disposable income.

$C = a + by$

b is MPC

a is autonomous consumption

$APC = C/Y$

$MPC = dc/dy$

According to Keynes, when income increases, consumption also increases, but not in the same proportion. Thus, the relationship between consumption and income are non-proportional and reversible overtime.

Features:

- Short-run theory
- In short run, APC > MPC
- When income increases, APC decreases.
- APC + APS = 1
- MPC + MPS = 1
- 0 < MPC < 1

The relation between income and consumption is based on psychological law of consumption.

Psychological Law of Consumption

When income increases, consumption increases but not as much as increase in income.

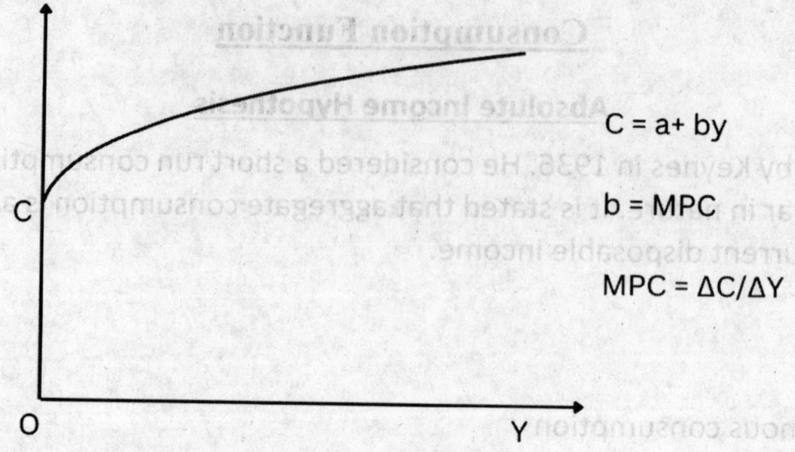

Long run consumption function by Kuznets

On the other hand, Kuznets found that consumption function is of the following form:

C = bY

Here APC=MPC=b

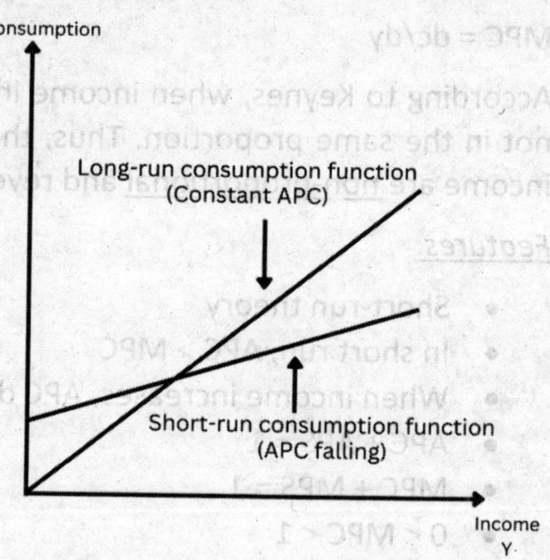

In Kuznets' consumption function there is no intercept term (that is, autonomous consumption). Kuznets' consumption function curve starts from the origin and is very near to 45° line depicting that the propensity to consume (b) is very high. Kuznets concluded that there was no tendency for the average propensity to consume to decline as disposable income rises.

Keynes' consumption function (C = a + bY) and Kuznets' consumption function (C = bY) are different. Whereas in Keynes' consumption function APC falls as income rises, in Kuznets' consumption function it remains constant over a long period. Further, the value of marginal propensity to consume which is less than one is much higher in Kuznets' function as compared to that of Keynes.

Relative Income Hypothesis

It was given by Dusenberry in 1949. The relative income hypothesis (RIH) is a theory that states that a person's attitude towards consumption is more influenced by their income in relation to others.

According to Dusenberry, the tendency of humans not only to keep up with 'Joneses' but also to surpass the 'Joneses'. Joneses are rich neighbors. Thus, consumer preferences are interdependent. It is difference in relative incomes that determines the consumption expenditure in community.

Difference from absolute income hypothesis:

1. Consumption also depends on relative income besides absolute income.
2. The relationship between consumption and income are irreversible.

Demonstration Effect by Duesenberry

The effect is based on imitations, i.e. consumption habits of the people will be influenced by people around them. Households with relatively lower incomes and living in the community of higher incomes, spend more proportion of their income then the households with high incomes. In other words, if income increases, consumption also increases with respect to consumption pattern of others.

Ratchet Effect by Duesenberry (Past Peak of Income Hypothesis)

If income increases, consumption increases.

If income decreases, consumption remains constant because of the demonstration effect and then a consumer gets accustomed to the consumption standards.

Long run constant APC: Rich has lower APC and poor has higher. In long run, lower and higher APC would balance in aggregate.

Permanent Income Hypothesis

It was given by Milton Friedman in 1957in his book "A theory of consumption function". Income has permanent (Y_P) and transitory (Y_t) component. Permanent income is that people expect to persist in future. Transitory income is that people do not expect to persist in future. Consumption also has permanent (C_p) and transitory (C_t) component.

Assumptions:

1) No covariance between permanent income and transitory income.
2) No covariance between transitory income and transitory consumption.
3) No covariance between permanent consumption and transitory consumption
4) Only relation between permanent consumption and permanent income exists.

$C_P = K.Y_P$

K = APC

In long run APC is constant. In short run, APC decreases with increase in income.

$APC_{rich} < APC_{poor}$

Life Cycle Income Hypothesis

Given by Ando - Modigliani in 1957. An individual will base his consumption on the lifetime income. The theory states that individuals seek to smooth consumption over the course of a lifetime – borrowing in times of low-income and saving during periods of high income.

Assumptions:

1) Person knows when he will die and when he will enter the labour market.
2) No changes in prices.
3) Consumption level is constant over the lifetime
4) Little relation between current income and current consumption

In long run APC = MPC

The theory states consumption will be a function of wealth, expected lifetime earnings and the number of years until retirement.

Consumption will depend on

$$C = \frac{W + RY}{T}$$

C = consumption

W = Wealth

R = Years until retirement. Remaining years of work

Y = Income

T= Remaining years of life

Investment Function

Investment is a function of real interest rate.

$$I = a - bi$$

Induced investment- It is profit or income motivated.

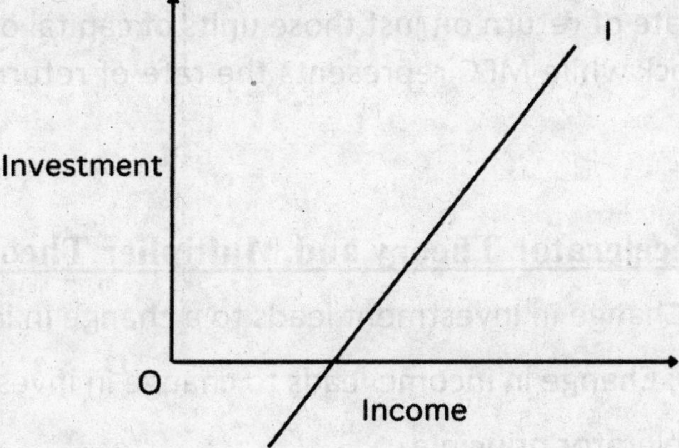

Autonomous investment: It is independent of the level of income and it is income inelastic.

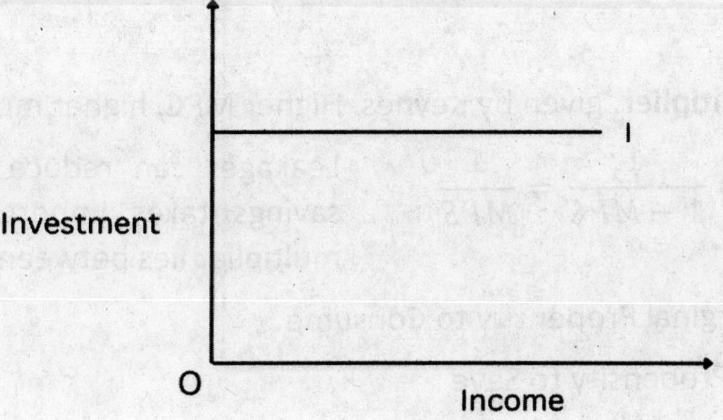

Determinants Of the Level of Investment

MEC [Marginal efficiency of capital]: Rate of return expected from an additional unit of capital asset. It is the ratio between the prospective yield of additional capital goods and their supply price. Prospective yield is the aggregate net return from an asset during its lifetime, while the supply price is the cost of producing this asset.

If MEC > r investors will invest

If MEC < r investors will not invest

Equilibrium MEC = r

Marginal Efficiency of Investment (MEI)

It represents the rate of return on just those units of capital over and above the existing capital stock while MEC represents the rate of return on all successive units of capital

Accelerator Theory and Multiplier Theory

Multiplier: Change in investment leads to a change in income.

Accelerator: Change in income leads to change in investment.

Clark gave the accelerator principle.

The concept of multiplier was first given by 'R. F. Kahn' in 1931, namely Employment Multiplier.

Investment Multiplier: given by Keynes. Higher MPC, higher multiplier.

$$K = \frac{\Delta Y}{\Delta I} = \frac{1}{1 - MPC} = \frac{1}{MPS}$$

Leakages can reduce multiplier i.e. savings, taxes, imports etc. Value of multiplier lies between 1 and infinity

Here, MPC: Marginal Propensity to Consume

MPS: Marginal Propensity to Save

Foreign Trade Multiplier: with increase in exports, by how much does the income increase.

$$K_f = \frac{1}{MPM + MPS}$$

MPM: Marginal Propensity to Import

MPS: Marginal Propensity to Save

Keynes Multiplier > Foreign Trade Multiplier

Super Multiplier: Given by Hicks

Change in autonomous investment → Change in income → Change in induced investment

Combination of Multiplier and Accelerator mathematically, it is called super multiplier.

$$K_S = \frac{1}{MPS - MPI}$$

where MPI: Marginal Propensity to Invest

Government Expenditure Multiplier: It reflects the change in income due to change in government expenditure.

$$K_G = \frac{\Delta Y}{\Delta G} = \frac{1}{1-b}\text{, where } b \text{ is } MPC$$

Tax Multiplier: It reflects the change in income due to change in taxes. Taxes imposed will reduce the consumption partially.

$$K_T = \frac{\Delta Y}{\Delta T} = \frac{-b}{1-b}\text{, where } b \text{ is } MPC$$

Remark: Tax Multiplier < Government Multiplier

Balanced Budget Multiplier

Balanced Budget Multiplier = Govt. Expenditure Multiplier + Tax Multiplier

A measure of the change in aggregate production caused by equal changes in government purchases and taxes. An important point to note here is that balanced budget multiplier is equal to one only in case of lump sum taxes. In case of proportional tax, the balanced budget multiplier is less than 1.

$$Balanced\ Budget\ Multiplier = \frac{1}{1-b} + \frac{-b}{1-b} = 1$$

Foreign Repercussions / Backwash effects

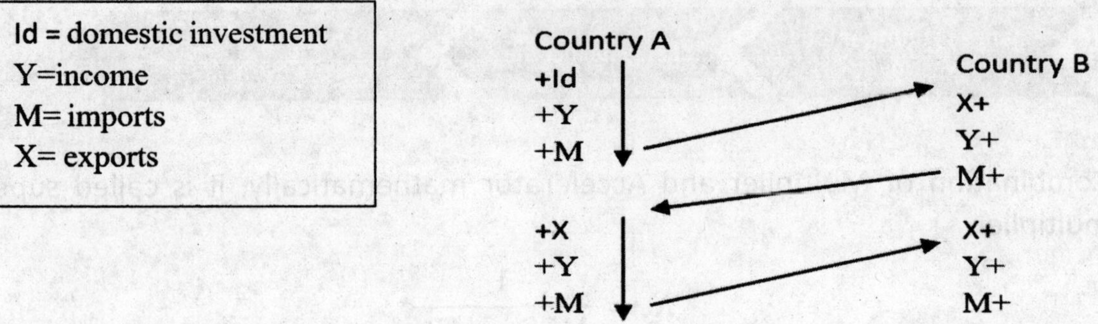

A country's exports and imports affect national income of other country which in turn effect foreign trade and national income of first country. This is called foreign repercussions/ Backwash effects/ feedback effect

Tobin Q theory of investment

James Tobin was the first person to explain the relation between the stock market and investment and that is why it is also referred as "Tobin's Q" theory.

$$Q = \frac{Market\ Value\ Of\ The\ Firm}{Replacement\ Cost\ Of\ Capital}$$

$$Or$$

$$Q = \frac{Value\ The\ Stock\ Market\ Places\ On\ The\ Firm's\ Asset}{Cost\ Of\ Producing\ Those\ Assets}$$

If Q ratio is high → it means the price of share is high. Therefore, Firms will invest more. If Q > 1 → Firm will buy physical capital, that is, add to the capital stock.

In other words, when Q > 1, firms find it profitable to acquire additional capital because value of capital exceeds the cost of acquiring it. Thus, when Q > 1 → Investment will increase.

National Income

Monetary value of all final goods and services produced by the residents of a country. It is a flow concept.

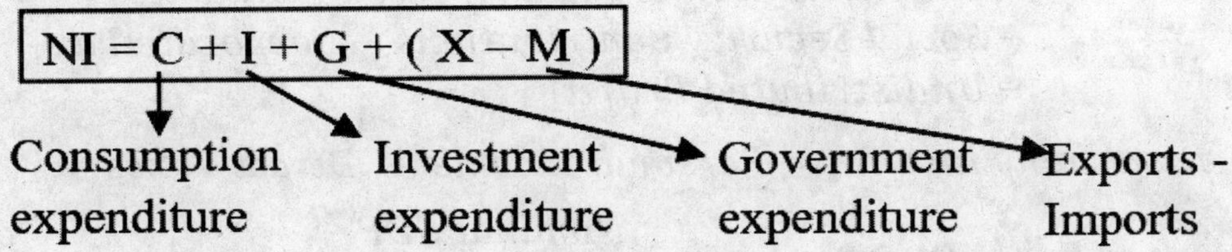

Depreciation is deducted from the gross value to get net value. Net factor income from abroad (NFIA) is added to the domestic product to get national income.

GDP: Gross Domestic Product

Monetary value of all final goods and services produced in a country in a period of one year

$$NDP = GDP - Depreciation$$

here, NDP: Net Domestic Product

$$GNP = GDP + NFIA$$

here, GNP: Gross National Product

NFIA: Net Factor Income from Abroad

$$NNP = GNP - Depreciation$$

NNP_{FC}: *National Income* [*Value of G & S is taken at production point*]

$$NNP_{MP} = NNP_{FC} + Indirect\ taxes - Subsidies$$

here, MP: Market Price

FC: Factor Cost

$$Real\ National\ Income = \frac{NNP\ at\ Current\ Prices}{Price\ Index} \times 100$$

$$Per\ Capita\ Income = \frac{National\ Income}{Population\ In\ A\ Year}$$

$$GDP = GVA + Taxes - Subsidies$$

here, GVA: Gross Value Added

$$\begin{aligned} &Personal\ Income \\ &\quad = National\ Income + Transferred\ Payments \\ &\quad - Social\ Security\ Contributions - Corporate\ Tax \\ &\quad - Undistributed\ Profit. \end{aligned}$$

$$Disposable\ Income = Personal\ Income - Direct\ Taxes$$

$$GDP\ Deflator = \frac{Nominal\ GDP}{Real\ GDP}$$

Nominal GDP: GDP at current prices

Real GDP: GDP at constant prices

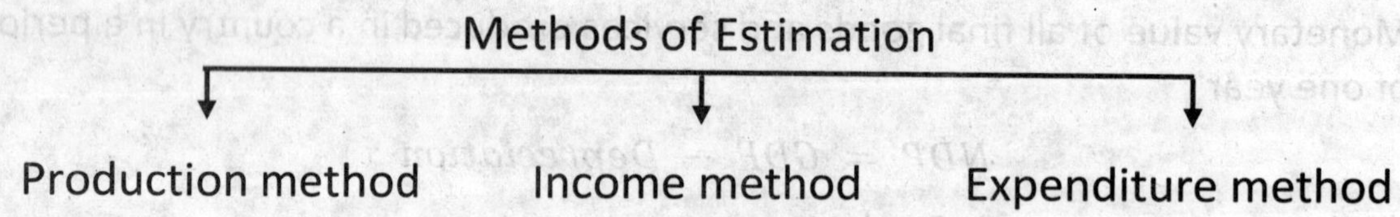

There are three methods to calculate national income:

Income method: Sum total of payments to factors of production (rent, wages, interest, profit)

Product method: Total value of final goods and services produced in a country during the year. Data of all productive activities can be assessed at market prices

Expenditure method: Total expenditure incurred in a year. (Y = C + I +G + X - M)

Items not included in National Income Calculation –

1. Transfer payments, i.e., pension, scholarships, unemployment allowance, old age pension, gifts, donations, etc.

2. Illegal activities, i.e., smuggling, black marketing, etc.
3. Unpaid services like household work
4. Sale of second hand goods like sale of used cars.

Numerical Problems

Question 1. When MPS is 0.25 and initial increase in autonomous spending is Rs. 100, then the expenditure multiplier and resultant increase in GDP respectively are:

(a) 1, Rs.100

(b) 0.75, Rs.75

(c) 4, Rs.400

(d) 1.33, Rs.133

Answer **(c)**

Solution:

$$MPS = 0.25$$

$$Autonomous\ Spending = 100$$

$$Expenditure\ Multiplier: \frac{Change\ in\ income}{Change\ in\ expenditure}$$

$$K = \frac{1}{MPS}$$

$$K = \frac{1}{0.25}$$

$$K = 4$$

Since Change in autonomous spending = 100. Thus, Increase in GDP = K x Change in autonomous spending = 4 x 100 = 400

Question 2. What will be the aggregate Domestic Income NDP (FC) of the economy for 2022-23; if

GDP (Market Price) = 27,654 crores

Depreciation =2847 crores

Indirect taxes less subsides = 2160 crores

(December 2021 and June 2022)

(a) 24,807 (b) 22,647

(c) 26,967 (d) 28,467

Answer – (b)

Solution: NDP_{FC} = GDP_{MP} - Depreciation - NIT = 27654 – 2847 – 2160

NDP_{FC} = 22647

Question 3. Given that LM function is Y=100+ 10i and the IS function is Y 160-20i, find the correct value of equilibrium level of income and rate of interest from the given options.

(a) 120 and 2 (b) 90 and 3

(c) 150 and 2 (d) 120 and 3

Answer: (a)

Solution:

$$100 + 10i = 160 - 20i$$

$$10i + 20i = 160 - 100$$

$$30i = 60$$

$$i = \frac{60}{30} = 2$$

$$Y = 100 + 10i$$

$$Y = 100 + 10 * 2$$

$$Y = 120$$

Demand For Money Theories

Classical Theory

Watch full video on Demand for Money Theories

Also known as Fisher's Quantity Theory of Money.

The transactions version of the quantity theory of money was provided by the American economist Irving Fisher in his book- The Purchasing Power of Money (1911). According to Fisher, "Other things remaining unchanged, as the quantity of money in circulation increases, the price level also increases in direct proportion and the value of money decreases and vice versa".

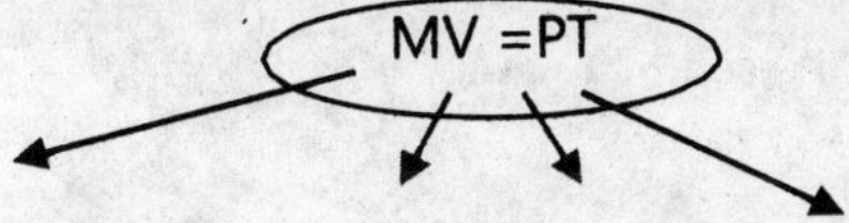

MV represent supply of money, PT represents demand

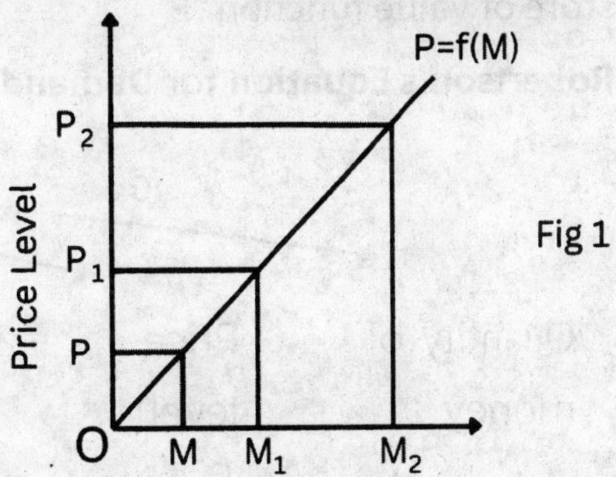

Fig 1

Assumptions:

1. T, V are constant.
2. Money supply is not affected by price level. Full employment of resources.
3. Any↑ in money supply → ↑ in price level

Fig 2

Diagram:

In the diagram, it can be seen that as the quantity of money increases, the price level also increases in direct proportion and the value of money decreases and vice versa.

Cambridge Version / Cash Balance Approach

Initially given by Marshall and modified by Pigou, Robertson, Keynes.

Marshall's Equation

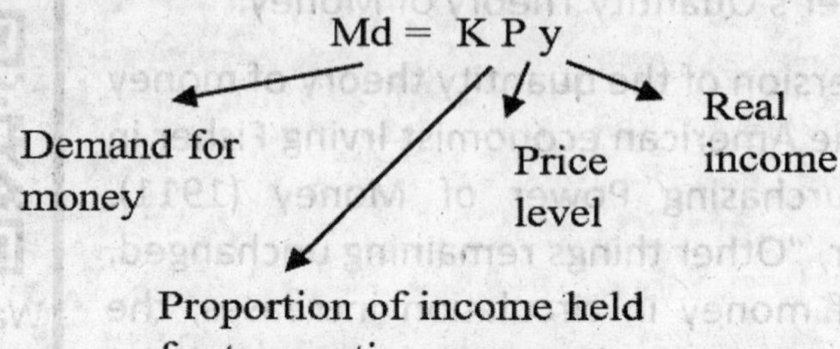

Besides the medium of exchange, the Cambridge approach also considered the store of value function.

Robertson's Equation for Demand for Money

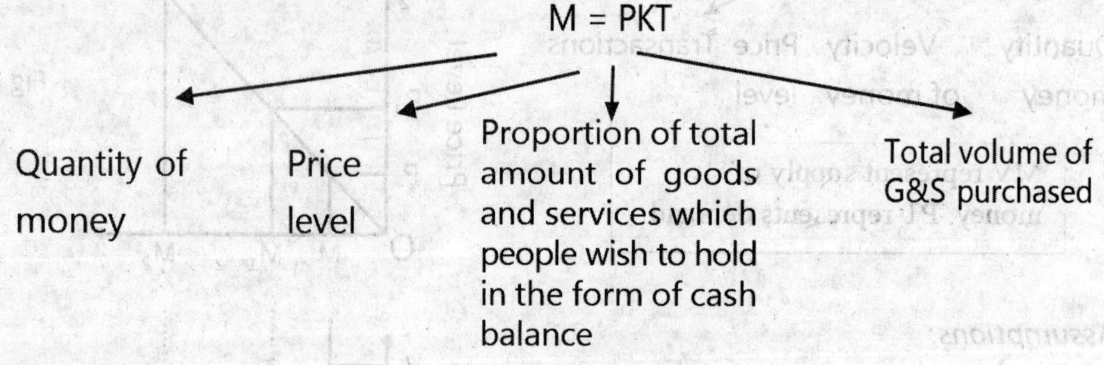

Pigou's Equation

P = K R /M

Here, P: Value of money

K: Proportion of total resources which people wish to hold in the form of titles to legal tender.

M: Number of actual units of legal tender money

Keynesian Theory of Money

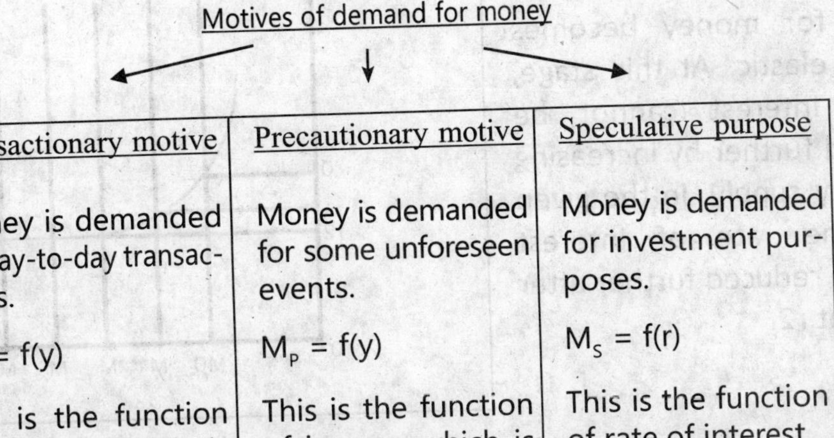

Motives of demand for money

Transactionary motive	Precautionary motive	Speculative purpose
Money is demanded for day-to-day transactions.	Money is demanded for some unforeseen events.	Money is demanded for investment purposes.
$M_T = f(y)$	$M_P = f(y)$	$M_S = f(r)$
This is the function of income which is interest inelastic.	This is the function of income which is interest inelastic.	This is the function of rate of interest.

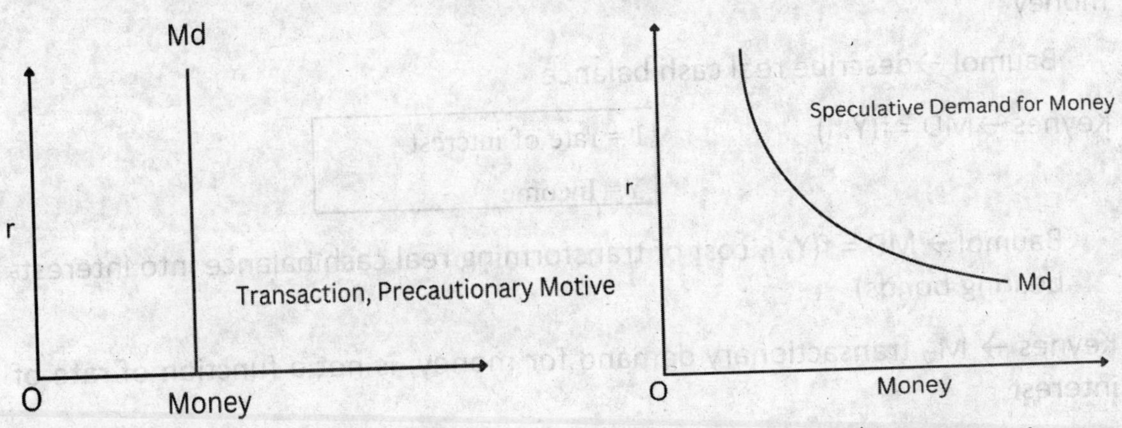

There is a negative relation between speculative demand for money and rate of interest. Rate of interest ↑, Bond price ↓, Demand for money is low Consumer would want to sell bonds, if the bond prices are high. Consumer would want to buy bonds if bond prices are low.

Liquidity Trap

Interest rate is so low that the demand for money becomes infinitely elastic. At this stage, rate of interest cannot be decreased further by increasing the money supply. In the given figure, the rate of interest cannot be reduced further after reaching at r2.

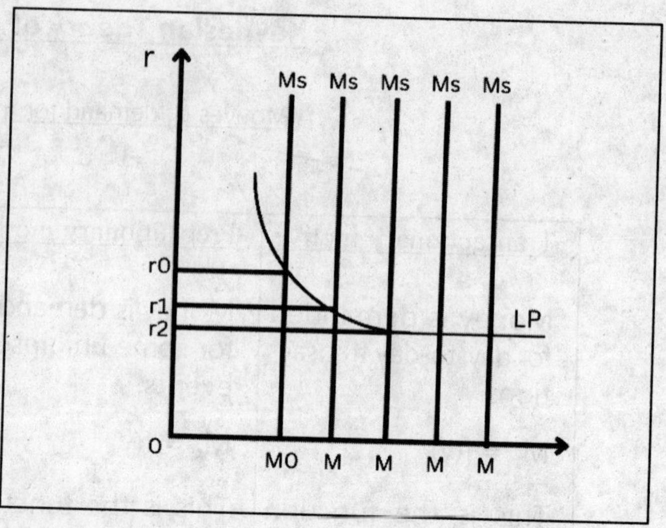

Baumol's Inventory Approach to Transaction Demand for Money

1) Keynes → described Transaction, Precautionary and Speculative demand for money

   Baumol →describe real cash balance

2) Keynes →MD = f(Y, I)

I = rate of interest
Y= Income

   Baumol→ MD = f(Y, I, cost of transforming real cash balance into interest-bearing bonds)

3) Keynes → M_t, transactionary demand for money, is not a function of rate of interest

   Baumol → M_t is a function of rate of interest

Baumol explains the transaction demand for money from the viewpoint of inventory control. Baumol asserts that as businessmen keep inventories of goods and materials to facilitate transactions, and individuals also hold inventory of money to buy goods and services. Individuals incur costs on these inventories as they have to forgo interest which they could earn if they had kept their wealth in saving account or FD or invested in bonds. This interest income forgone is the cost of holding money for transaction purpose.

In this way Baumol and Tobin highlighted that transaction demand for money is not independent of rate on interest. They both argue that transaction demand depends on rate of interest. People hold money for transaction purpose "to bridge gap between the receipts of income and its spending"

Baumol has shown that average amount of cash withdrawal which minimizes cost is given by square root formula:

$$M_D = \sqrt{\frac{2by}{r}}$$

where b: brokers fee, r: rate of interest, y: income

Remarks:

- Higher r will lead to lesser MD (demand for money) as it will encourage individuals to keep more funds in saving deposits to earn higher interest.
- Higher b will lead to higher MD as it will discourage individuals to make more trips to bank.
- Higher Y leads to higher MD

In other words, if b is high, then individual demands more money. If r is high, then individual demand for less money. Therefore, according to Baumol and Tobin, transaction demand for money slopes downward as it is negatively related with rate of interest.

Tobin's Portfolio Approach to Demand for Money

According to Tobin, individuals diversify their portfolio by holding balanced combination of safe and risky assets. In Keynes analysis, all individual holds wealth in either all money or all bonds depending upon his estimate of future rate of interest. But according to Tobin, individual can hold both cash & bond simultaneously. According to Tobin, individual's behaviour shows risk aversion. They prefer less risk to more risk at a given rate of return.

At higher rate of interest demand for holding money (liquidity) will be less and people will hold more bonds in their portfolio.

Tobin's portfolio demand function for money as an asset slopes downward like Keynes' speculative demand for money.

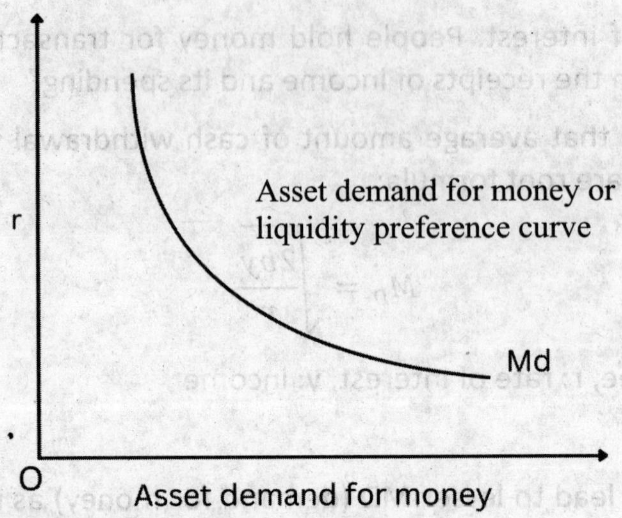

Friedman's Restatement of Quantity Theory of Money

According to Friedman, demand for money is stable function whereas Keynes said that it is unstable.

$M_d = K\ P\ Y$

where M_d: money demand,

P: Price,

Y: real income,

K: constant

Friedman's money demand function can be written as

$M_d = f\ (P, Y, R_d, R_b, R_e)$

R_b = Rate of interest on bonds.

R_e = Rate of interest on equities

R_d= Return on durable goods

R_d is negatively related with demand for money.

R_b is negatively related with demand for money.

R_e is also negatively related with demand for money.

Nominal income (PY) is positively related with demand for money.

Friedman found that income elasticity of Demand for money is greater than one while interest elasticity is negligible.

Differences

Keynes	Friedman
Demand for money is unstable	Demand for money is stable
He segmented money demand into transaction, precautionary, speculative motive	He does not segmented money demand into components.

Real Balance Effect given by Patinkin in his work "Money, interest and prices.": As price increase, purchasing power of money decreases and as a result demand will decrease

Wealth effect given by Pigou: As wage-price decreases (wage price deflation), wealth, consumption and employment increases. It depicts the relation between consumption, wealth, employment and output during deflation.

Trade Cycles

They are alternate phases of business activity.

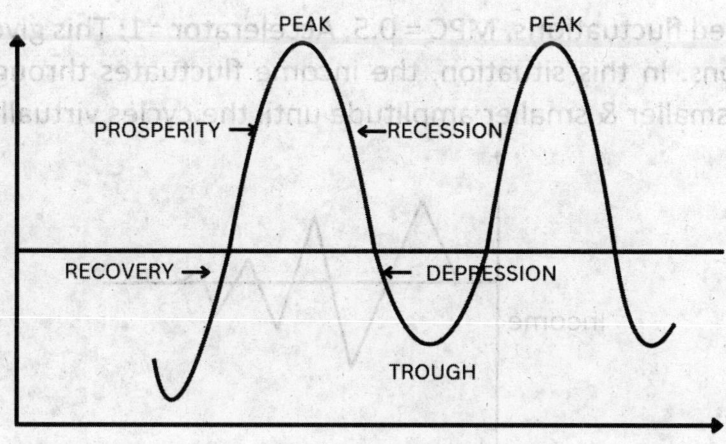

Four Phases of Business Cycle

Samuelson's Theory of Trade Cycle

Samuelson in his article " Interaction between multiplier analysis and principle of accelerator " constructed a multiplier accelerator model which is also known as Dynamic Model of trade cycle. Samuelson's theory of trade cycle used the concepts of both multiplier and accelerator.

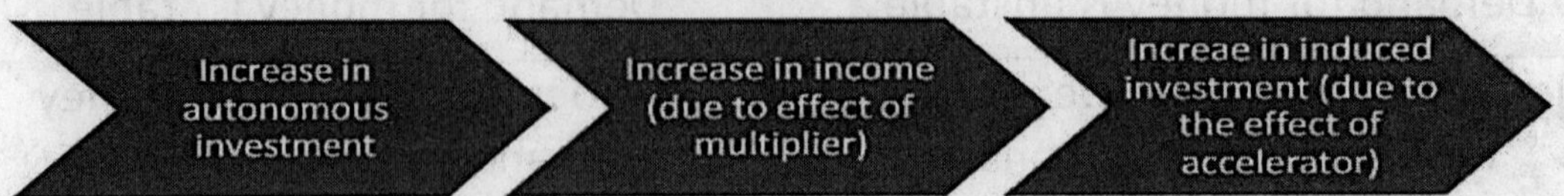

a) Cycle less growth path, MPC= 0.5, Accelerator = 0 : In this type of situation, level of income is influenced by multiplier because value of acceleration is zero (0).

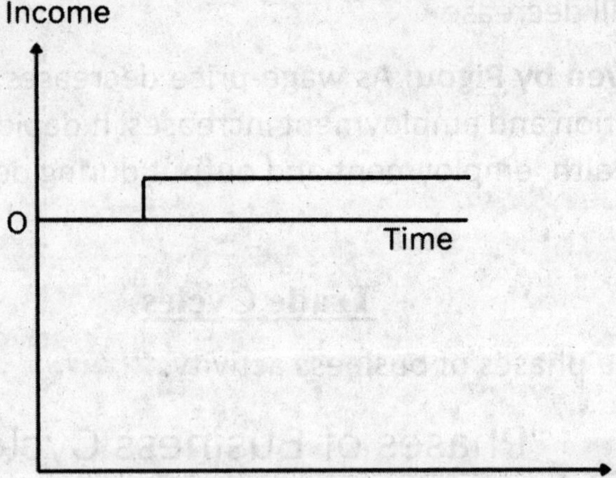

b) Dampened fluctuations, MPC = 0.5, Accelerator =1: This gives us damped oscillations. In this situation, the income fluctuates through a series of cycle of smaller & smaller amplitude until the cycles virtually disappear.

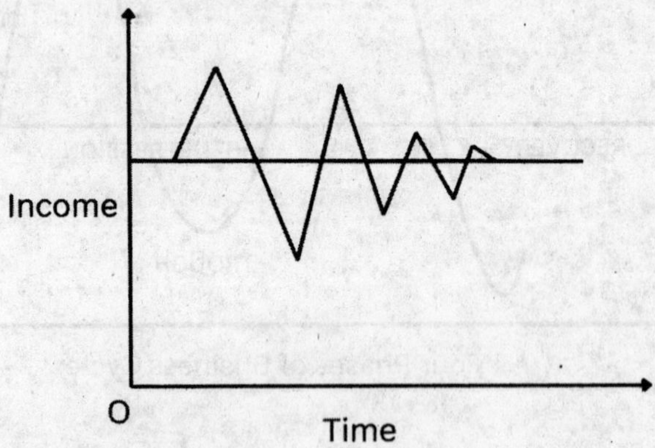

c) Constant Amplitude, MPC=0.5, Accelerator = 2 : This gives us regular & continuous cycle where more are less same values repeat themselves.

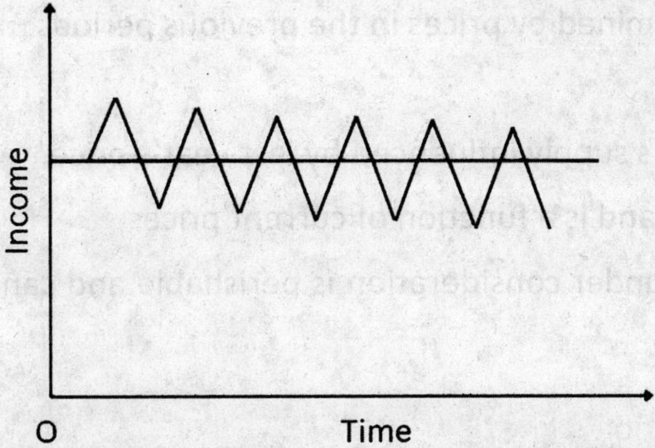

d) Anti-damped Cycles / Explosive Cycles, Accelerator = 3, MPC = 0.5: In this situation the income fluctuates through series of cycle of wider & wider amplitude.

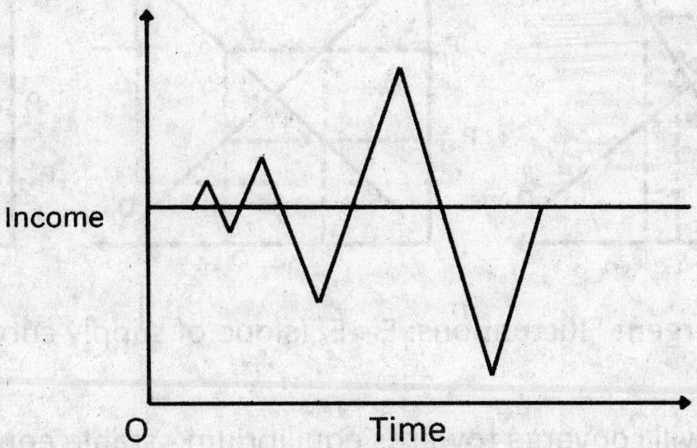

e) Explosive path, MPC= 0.5, Accelerator = 4: This gives us ever increasing income gradually. In other words, income increases at an increasing rate.

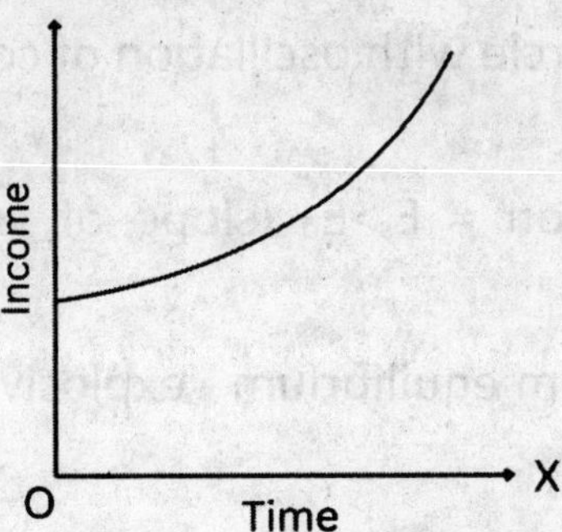

Cobweb Theory of Trade Cycle

The Cobweb theory analyses the movements of prices and outputs when supply is wholly determined by prices in the previous periods.

Assumptions:

- Current year's supply influenced by last year's price.
- Current Demand is a function of current prices
- Commodity under consideration is perishable and can be stored only for one year.

Three types of cobwebs: convergent, divergent and continuous.

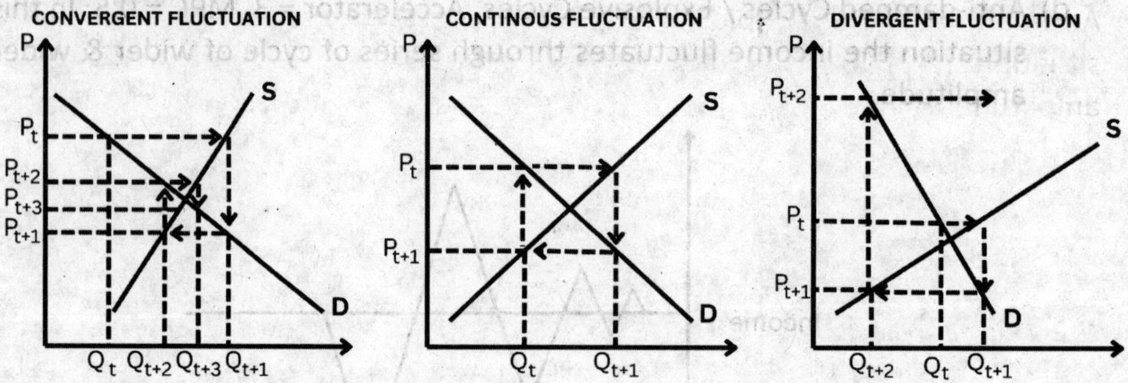

1. Convergent Fluctuations: $E_d > E_s$ (slope of supply curve > slope of demand curve)

   Price will converge towards equilibrium - stable equilibrium

2. Continuous Fluctuation: $E_d = E_s$ (slope of supply curve = slope of demand curve)

   P and Q move in a circle with oscillation of constant amplitude around an equilibrium point

3. Divergent Fluctuation = $E_s > E_d$ (slope of supply curve < slope of the demand curve)

   Price will diverge from equilibrium - explosive situation - unstable

Hicksian Theory of Trade Cycle

Hicksian theory of trade cycle was given in his work "A Contribution to The Theory of Trade Cycles". He also stated that both the multiplier and accelerator will lead to the generation of cycles.

Assumptions:

1. Constant value of multiplier and accelerator
2. The relation between multiplier and accelerator is lagged
3. Gross investment does not fall below zero. The average capital output ratio is greater than unity. (Reverse action of multiplier takes place but reverse action of accelerator does not take place.)

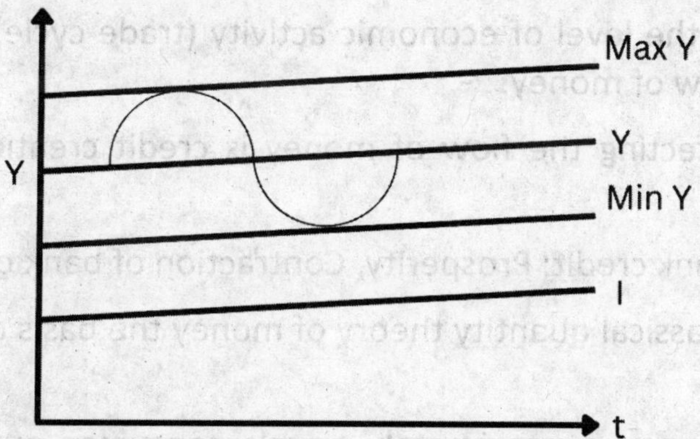

Max Y: Ceiling to output expansion

Min Y: floor to downward movement of output

I: Autonomous investment

Y: Equilibrium growth

Greater the investment lag, more economy moves along ceiling.

Reverse action of multiplier takes place but not of accelerator because investment cannot fall below the zero.

Ingredients of theory:

1. **Warranted rate of growth**: It is a rate which will sustain itself. According to Hicks, it is multiplier accelerator interaction which weaves the path of economic fluctuation around the warranted rate of growth.

2. **Consumption function**: It takes the function $C_t = aY_{t-1}$, i.e., consumption is a function of previous period income. Consumption lags behind income and multiplier is treated as lagged relation.

3. **Autonomous and induced investment**: Accelerator based on induced investment and multiplier based on autonomous Investment.

Pure Monetary Theory of Trade Cycles (By Hawtrey)

→Book: The monetary theory of trade cycle (1929)

→Trade cycle is a purely monetary phenomenon.

→ All changes in the level of economic activity (trade cycle) are reflections of changes in the flow of money.

→Main factor affecting the flow of money is credit creation by the banking system.

→Expansion of bank credit: Prosperity, Contraction of bank credit: Depression.

→He made the classical quantity theory of money the basis of his theory of the trade cycle.

→The flow of money approximately equals consumer outlay which can be written as MV=PT. Increase in quantity of money leads to rise in output, cost and prices. A reduction in quantity of money causes reduction in demand, output, and price.

Hayek Theory of Trade Cycle

→Hayek based his theory of trade cycle on Wicksell's theory of income determination.

→Wicksell's had analysed the equilibrium of the economic system with the help of a distinction between the natural rate and money rate of interest natural rate of interest.

→Natural rate of interest is that at which the demand for loanable funds equals the supply of loanable funds. Money rate of interest is that which actually prevails in the market at a particular time. When the money rate diverges from real rate of interest, there is disequilibrium in the economic system.

→If the money rate is above the natural rate of interest, there is contraction. If the money rate happens to be less than natural rate, there is expansion

→Hayek theory is called monetary overinvestment theory because it considers 'overinvestment' of the economy's resources in the capital good sector. The sole cause of business cycle and the over investment takes place when there is too much expansion of money

Phillips Curve (1958)

It is stated that there is a negative relationship between wages and unemployment.

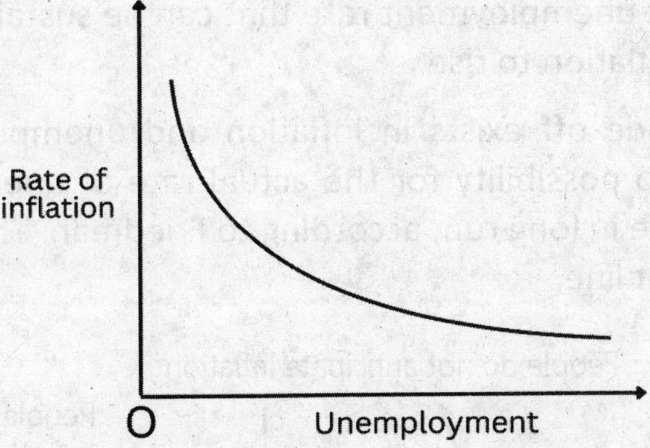

Later on, Phillips curve was established showing a negative relationship between rate of inflation and rate of unemployment.

Assumptions:

1) PC is a short run curve and static in nature.
2) Downward-sloping and take the shape of a rectangular hyperbola.
3) Non - linear relationship.
4) Price expectations are static.

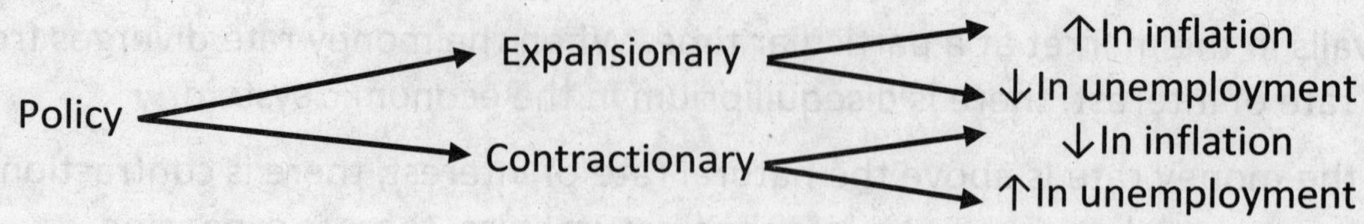

Long-run PC

Given by Milton Friedman. (Augmented Phillips curve/Adaptive Expectations Philip curve)

Natural Rate of Unemployment (NRU): Given by Friedman.

NRU is a combination of frictional and structural unemployment.

Tobin has given it a new name "non-accelerating inflation rate of unemployment"

NAIRU is the lowest unemployment rate that can be sustained without causing wage growth and inflation to rise.

In long run, no trade off exists in inflation and unemployment. People are rational. There is no possibility for the actual rate of unemployment to differ from the natural rate in long run, according to Friedman. Therefore, in long run, PC is vertical straight line.

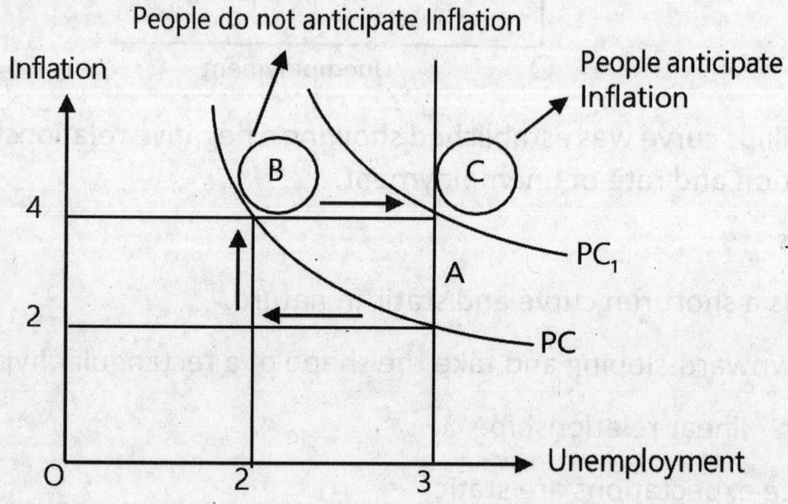

The economy is at point A. if the government makes an expansionary policy to increase inflation and reduce unemployment. The economy moves to point B. But in long run people anticipate that inflation reduces purchasing power.

Workers demand higher wages. So, process hiring of new workers will stop. Unemployment do not reduce, and economy is a point C. So, in long run, inflation has little effect on unemployment. So monetary policy leads to inflation but not permanent effect on unemployment.

Friedman view on Phillips curve is adaptive expectation hypothesis which is based on the prediction of the individuals from the past behaviour.

Monetarism embraced the adaptive expectations theory to mean that people would stumble once or twice on the same stone, but not a third.

In summary, monetarists sustained that the Phillips curve will hold up in the short term, but not in the long term. In the long term, the Phillips curve is completely vertical and determines the natural rate of unemployment, as Friedman puts it in his article "The role of Monetary Policy", 1968.

Acc. to rational expectation hypothesis, Phillips curve is vertical straight line. Trade off can't exist as rate of inflation fully and correctly anticipated by workers.

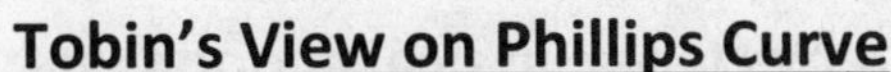

Tobin's View on Phillips Curve

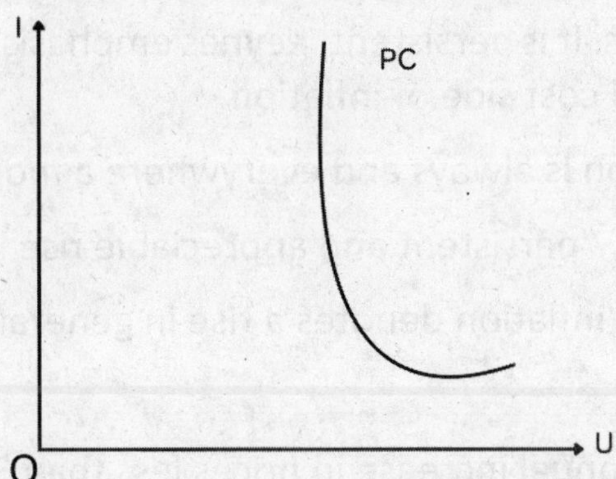

Kinked shape, apart like a normal Phillips Curve and the rest is vertical.

Solow's View on Phillips Curve

PC is vertical at positive rate of inflation and is horizontal at negative rates of inflation.

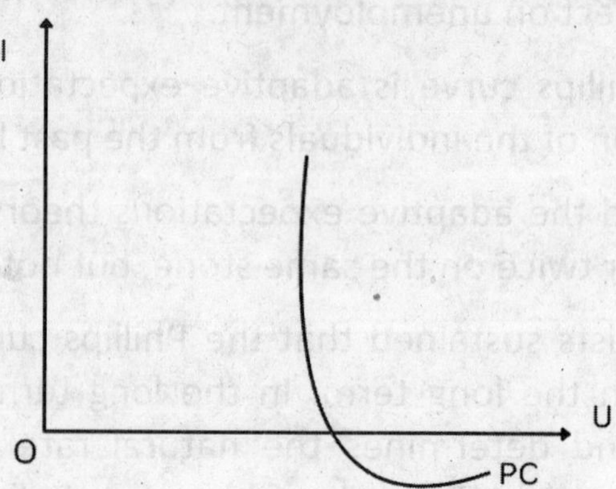

Inflation

Inflation was first defined by Neo- classical economists.

It is a long-term process. It is persistent. Keynes emphasis that demand is a cause of inflation. He ignored cost side of inflation.

Friedman said, "Inflation is always and everywhere a monetary phenomenon."

Shapiro described it as, "persistent and appreciable rise in general price level"

Samuelson remarked, "inflation denotes a rise in general price level"

Types of inflation

Creeping inflation → Annual increase in prices less than 3%

Walking inflation → Rate is 3% to 7%

Running inflation → 10% to 20%

Hyperinflation → 20%to 100%

Demand pull inflation: Inflation due to rise in aggregate demand of goods and services.

Cost push inflation: inflation due to decrease in aggregate supply of goods and services because of an increase in cost of production. Its further classification:

- o Wage push
- o Profit push inflation

Open inflation: Inflation that is visible & uncontrolled by government i.e., free market prices increasing during a boom

Suppressed inflation: Inflation that exists but is hidden due to price control or restrictions

Stagflation: High unemployment + High inflation + stagnant economic growth

Inflation tax: decline in purchasing power of money due to inflation.

Real Business Cycle Theory

The theory belongs to neo-classicals. According to it, business cycles accounted for real (in contrast to nominal) shocks. The real business cycle (RBC) theory was introduced by Finn E. Kydland and Edward C. Prescott in the 1982

1. **Technological shock**: Because of technological shocks, productivity will increase.

2. **Labour market:** Favorable technology leads to increase in marginal productivity of labour. As a result, wages and employment will increase and vice-versa.

3. **Interest rate**: Favorable technology leads to increase in marginal productivity of capital. As a result, interest rates reduce which leads to boom and vice versa.
4. **Flexibilities of wages and prices**: wages and prices adjust quickly to the market (AD=AS), invisible hand exists in the economy.

5.**Classical dichotomy** (Neutrality of money): Money is neutral which means it does not affect real variables, it only effects price level. Money supply is endogenous in real business cycle theory. With favorable technology, output increases – money demand, money supply and price will also increase.

6. **Government role is limited**.: Invisible hand operates. Fiscal policy has limited role.

Monetary Policy

INSTRUMENTS OF MONETARY POLICY

- QUANTITATIVE
  - BANK RATE
  - OPEN MARKET OPERATION
  - CASH RESERVE RATIO
  - SLR
  - REPO RATE & RESERVE REPO RATE
- QUALITATIVE
  - RATIONING OF CREDIT
  - MARGINAL REQUIREMENT
  - MORAL SUASION
  - REGULATION OF CONSUMER CREDIT
  - DIRECT ACTION

Credit control measures adopted by Central Bank of a country.

Quantitative Measures of Credit Control

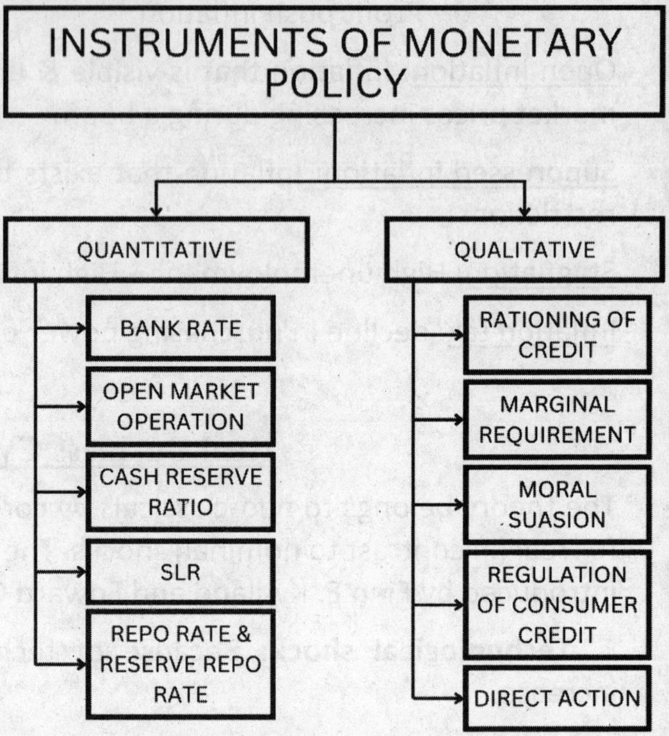

Bank Rate: To reduce money supply, bank rate is increased. RBI charges bank rate to commercial banks for long term loans.

Open market operations: sale and purchase of securities in the money market by the central bank.

Liquidity adjustment facility (LAF) is a monetary policy tool which allows banks to borrow money through repurchase agreements. LAF is used to aid banks in adjusting the day-to-day mismatches in liquidity. LAF consists of repo and reverse repo operations.

Repo Rate: RBI charges to commercial banks for short term loans. ↑ in repo rate, ↓ in money supply. Repo rate is technically a repurchase agreement in which the commercial banks offer securities such as Treasury Bills to the RBI in return for short term funds.

Scan for a video lecture on this topic

Reverse repo: RBI borrows from banks short term loans at reverse repo rate.

BR > Repo Rate > Reverse Repo

Cash reserve Ratio: It is percentage of money, which a bank has to keep with RBI in the form of cash.

SLR > CRR

Statutory liquidity Ratio :It is the percentage of money, which a bank has to reserve with itself. It cannot give loan out of it.

Note: Read figure of all these current policy rates from RBI website.

Marginal standing facility (MSF)

- Marginal standing facility (MSF) is a window for banks to borrow from the Reserve Bank of India in an emergency when inter-bank liquidity dries up completely. The Marginal standing facility is a scheme launched by RBI while reforming the monetary policy in 2011-12.
- It is a penal rate at which banks can borrow money from RBI when they are completely exhausted of all borrowing assistance. The Marginal Standing facility allows banks to borrow money with an interest rate above the repo rate and can be termed as the Marginal standing facility rate.

Standing Deposit Facility

Standing Deposit Facility allows the RBI to absorb liquidity (deposit) from commercial banks without giving government securities in return to the banks.

MCLR (Marginal cost of funds-based lending rates)

Banks have been mandated to provide the loans on MCLR replacing base rate which was used earlier. Banks cannot lend below the MCLR as defined by the bank

Qualitative Measures of Credit Control

1. Rationing of credit -priority sector should be given preference in lending loans from others.
2. Margin requirements It is difference between market value of security and maximum loan value. Increase in margin requirements decrease the amount of loans and thus reduce money supply.
3. Moral suasion RBI has been sending letters periodically to the commercial banks requesting them too corporate with it.

4. <u>Direct action</u> It refers to the directions issued by the central bank to the commercial banks regarding their lending policies

<u>Dear money policy(contractionary) is used during inflation</u>

1) Increase in bank rate, CRR and SLR can reduce the money supply
2) To reduce money supply, open market operations i.e., Treasury bills, bonds etc. are sold in open market.

<u>Cheap money policy (expansionary) is used during deflation</u>.

In this case, rates are decreased, open market operations are bought by government of a country or by Central Bank.

Fiscal Policy

It is the revenue and expenditure policy of the government. Its instruments are government expenditure & taxes.

<u>During inflation/ Boom</u> : expenditure ↓ and taxes ↑

Surplus Budget: Government Revenue > Government Expenditure

Borrow more from the public also reduce money supply

<u>During deflation/ depression</u> : expenditure↑ and taxes ↓

Deficit budget: Government revenue < Government expenditure

<u>Crowding out effect</u> :Reduction in private expenditure caused by an increase in government expenditure through deficit budget.

Government expenditure ↑, Aggregate Demand ↑, rate of interest ↑, private investment ↓

<u>Three forms of discretionary fiscal policy</u> :

1) Change tax, constant government expenditure.
2) Change government expenditure, constant taxes.
3) Variations in both.

IS - LM Model

Given by Hicks and Hansen

Product Market :IS curve shows equilibrium in the product market. It relates different equilibrium levels of national income with various rate of interest.

↓in rate of interest→ ↑in investment→ ↑in AD→ ↑in income.

Equation: Y = a - bi

where Y is income and i is rate of interest.

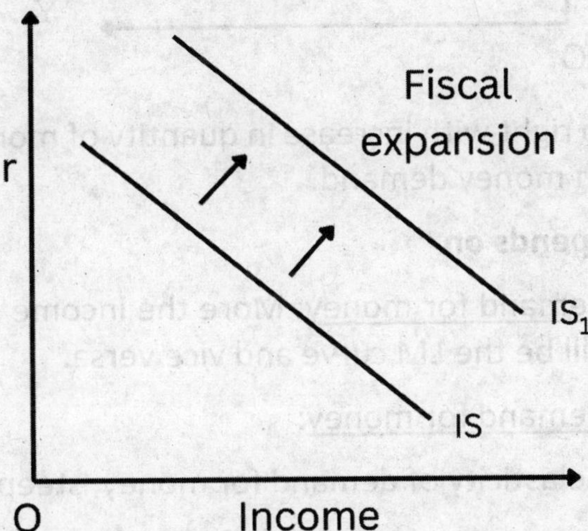

IS shifts to left when taxes increase and shifts to right when Govt. Expenditure and Autonomous investment increases.

Slope of IS curve depends on

1) Interest elasticity of investment Demand Higher the elasticity of demand, flatter will be the IS curve and vice versa.
2) Size of the Multiplier More the size of the multiplier, flatter will be the IS curve and vice versa.

Money market: Money market equilibrium is represented by LM curve. LM curve gives combinations of values of income and rate of interest that produce money market equilibrium.

↑increase in income → demand for money ↑ →rate of interest ↑

Equation: $Y = a + bi$

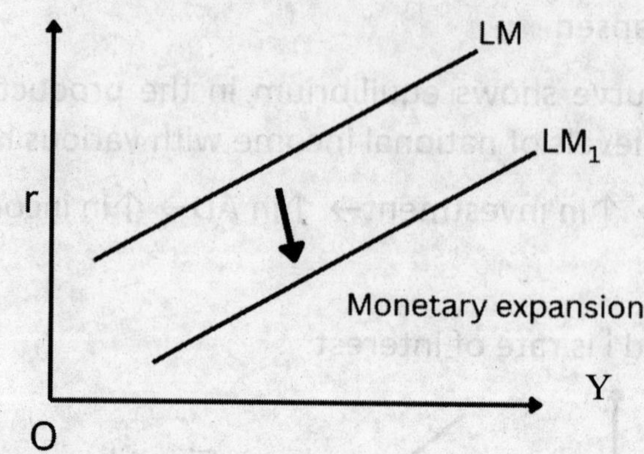

LM shift downward to right with increase in quantity of money and shift upward to left with increase in money demand.

Slope of LM curve depends on

Income elasticity of demand for money: More the income elasticity of demand for money, steeper will be the LM curve and vice versa.

Interest elasticity of demand for money:

→ Lesser the interest elasticity of demand for money, steeper the LM curve and vice versa.

Effectiveness of Monetary Policy

Shape of LM	Shape of IS	Effectiveness
Steeper	Flatter	More
Flatter	Steeper	Less
Vertical	Horizontal	Highly Effective
Horizontal	Vertical	Totally Ineffective

Effectiveness of Fiscal Policy

Shape of IS	Shape of LM	Effectiveness
Steeper	Flatter	More
Flatter	Steeper	Less
Vertical	Horizontal	Highly Effective
Horizontal	Vertical	Totally Ineffective

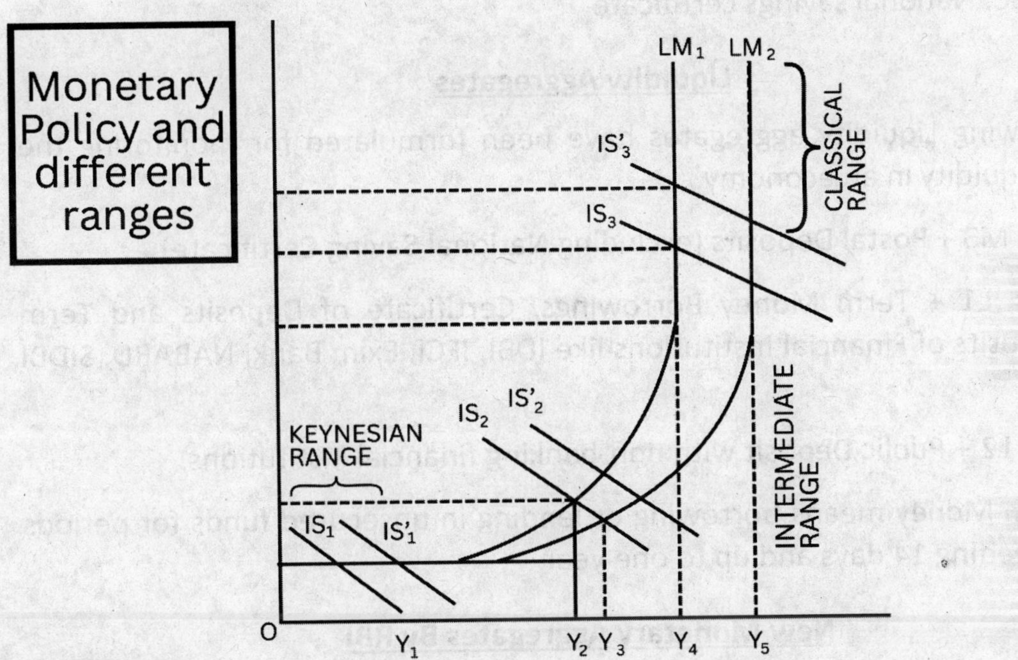

Keynesian Range: LM curve perfectly elastic. Monetary policy ineffective. fiscal policy effective (no ↑ in income)

Classical Range: LM curve perfectly inelastic. monetary policy highly effective Fiscal policy not effective.

Money Supply

Money supply refers to the total stock of money circulating in an economy at a given point of time

Measures Of Money Supply

M1 = C + DD + other deposits [Narrow def.]

where DD: Demand Deposits

C: Currency

M2 = M1 + Demand Deposits with the post office

M3 = M1 + Time deposits [Broader def.]

M4 = M3 + All deposits with post office [Excluding NSC]

where NSC: National savings certificate

M1 - Most liquid
M4 - least liquid

Liquidity Aggregates

The following Liquidity aggregates have been formulated for monitoring the state of liquidity in an economy.

- L1 = M3 + Postal Deposits (excluding National Saving Certificate)
- L2 = L1 + Term Money Borrowings, Certificate of Deposits and Term Deposits of Financial Institutions like IDBI, IFCI, Exim Bank, NABARD, SIDBI etc.
- L3 = L2 + Public Deposit with non-banking financial institutions.
- Term Money means borrowing or lending in unsecured funds for periods exceeding 14 days and up to one year

New Monetary Aggregates By RBI

- **Weekly Compilation**

M0 (High Powered Money) = Currency in Circulation + Bankers' Deposits with RBI + 'Other' Deposits with RBI*

- **Fortnightly**

M1 = Currency with the Public + Demand Deposits with the Banking System + 'Other' Deposits with RBI *= Currency with the Public + Current Deposits with the Banking System + Demand Liabilities Portion of Savings Deposits with the Banking System + 'Other' Deposits with RBI*

M2 = M1 + Time Liabilities Portion of Savings Deposits with the Banking System + Certificates of Deposit issued by Banks + Term Deposits of residents with a contractual maturity of up to and including one year with the Banking System = Currency with the Public + Current Deposits with the Banking System + Savings Deposits with the Banking System + Certificates of Deposits issued by Banks + Term Deposits of residents with a contractual maturity up to an including one year with the Banking System + 'Other' Deposits with RBI *.

M3 = M2 + Term Deposits of residents with a contractual maturity of over one year with the Banking System + Call/Term borrowings from 'non-depository' financial corporations by the Banking System.

Note: * 'Other' deposits with RBI comprise mainly: (i) deposits of quasi-government and other financial institutions including primary dealers, (ii) balances in the accounts of foreign Central banks and Governments, (iii) accounts of international agencies such as the International Monetary Fund, etc.

[coins and currency notes consist of money]

Money v/s Near Money

Near money assets serve the store of value function of money temporarily and are convertible in the medium of exchange in a short run i.e., Time deposits, bonds, debentures.

Money Multiplier

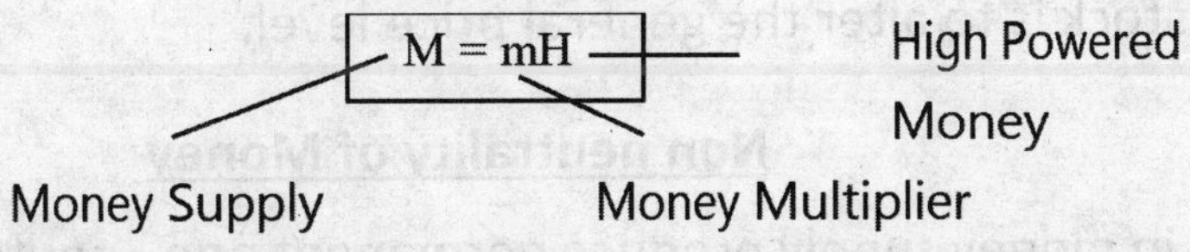

Money multiplier 'm' tells us that with change in H, how much will the money supply in the economy change.

$$M = \frac{cd + 1}{cd + rr + ed} H$$

cd: currency /deposit ratio

ed: excess reserve/ deposit ratio

Watch full video on Money Supply Curve

rr: required reserve/ deposit ratio

H=C+R

where

R=RR+ER(required reserves + excess reserves).

Determinants of money supply:

High Powered Money

Reserve Ratio

Money Multiplier

Inside And Outside Money

Gurley & Shaw have divided total quantity of money in two parts - inside and outside money. Inside money is money created within the private sector. outside money comes from outside private sector.

Neutrality Of Money

It means money is neutral in its effect on the economy. A change in money stock can have no long- run influences on the level of real output, employment, rate of interest or the composition of final output. The only lasting impact of a change in Money stock is to alter the general price level.

Non neutrality of Money

If changes in money supply produce permanent non - neutral effects on the rate of interest, the level of employment, income and output.

Endogenous and Exogenous Money Supply

Money supply curve: It shows the amount of money suppliers are willing and able to supply at various interest rates in the economy.

Exogenous money supply: When money supply is determined by monetary authority and it is not function of rate of interest, then MS curve is vertical.

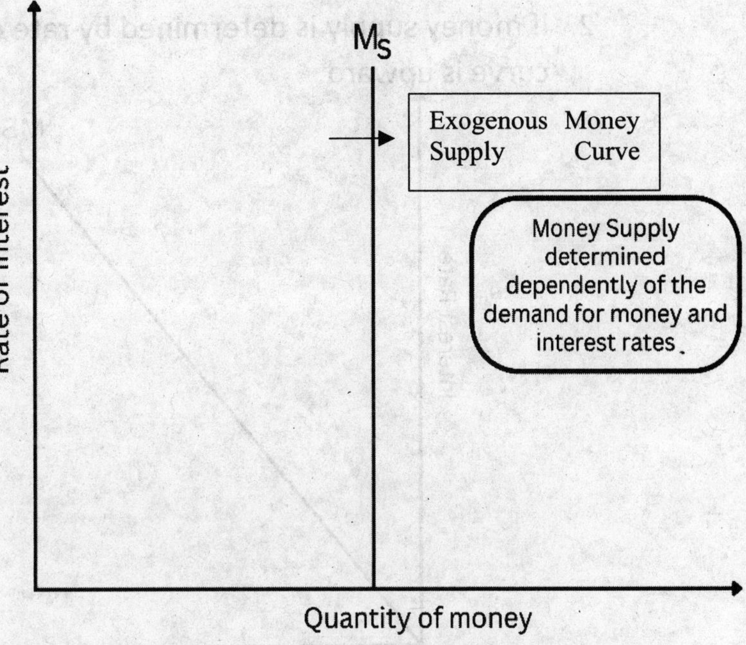

Endogenous money supply: when money supply is not determined by monetary authority, can be presented in the following cases:

1. Income increases, Demand for money increases, supply for money increases. (here rate of interest is exogenous/ constant). In this case MS curve is horizontal.

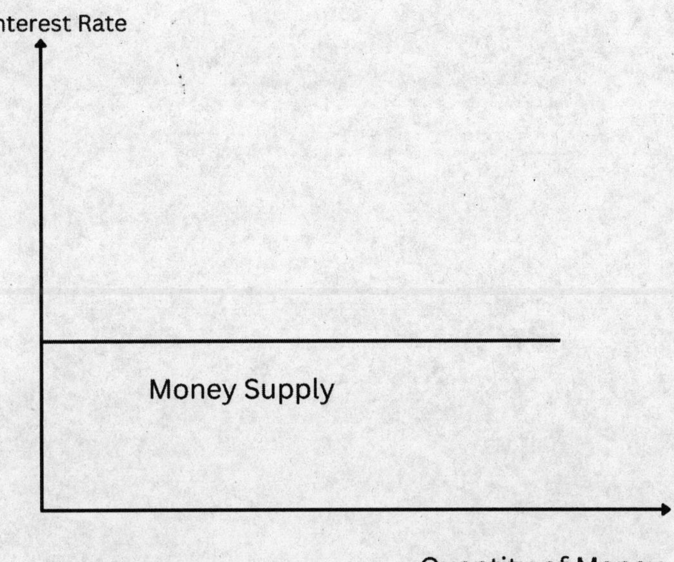

2. If money supply is determined by rate of interest, then money supply curve is upward.

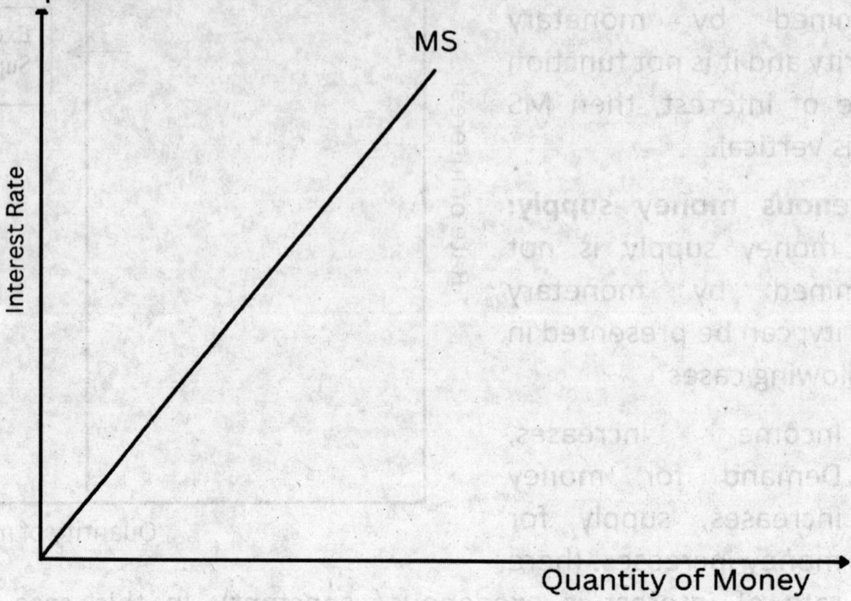

Statistics and Econometrics

Probability Theory

Probability is a device to express the degree of certainty or uncertainty in the numerical form.

$$Probability = \frac{No.of\ Favourable\ outcomes}{No.of\ Total\ outcomes} = \frac{m}{n}$$

Deterministic Experiments (Non-random): Non-stochastic outcome can be predicted with certainty before the experiments is conducted [The stone is dropped from a window]

Non-Deterministic Experiments (stochastic): (Random) Outcome cannot be predicted with certainty, because it depends upon chance. For e.g. tossing of a coin

Mutually Exclusive events (Disjoint):

$$P(A \cup B) = P(A) + P(B)$$

Not mutually exclusive:

$$P(A \cup B) = P(A) + P(B) - P(A \cap B)$$

Independent Events: Happening of one event does not affect happening of another event

$$P(A \cap B) = P(A).P(B)$$

$$P(A|B) = P(A)$$

$$P(B|A) = P(B)$$

Dependent Events: Happening of one event effect happening of other event

$$P(A \cap B) = P(A).P(B|A)$$

Types of Cards in a Deck

Suits (Clubs, Hearts, Spades, Diamonds)

The simplest way to break down the types of cards in a deck is by suit. There are four suits in a standard deck of cards:

- Clubs
- Hearts
- Spades
- Diamonds

Because there are four suits in a deck, there are four of each individual card value in a deck.

For example, there are four Kings, four Jacks, four Queens, etc. in every standard deck of cards... One of each suit.

Accounting for all 52 cards and four suits, there are 13 cards of each suit in a deck.

Probability Numerical Problems

Question 1: A bag contains 5 red, 7 white and 3 green balls. One is randomly drawn from the bag. What is the probability that it is green?

$$Probability = \frac{m}{n} = \frac{3}{15} = \frac{1}{5}$$

Question 2: There are 26 red cards and 26 black cards in a deck — Hearts and Diamonds are red; Clubs and Spades are black. A card is thrown from a well shuffled pack of playing cards. Find the probability that it is either a diamond or a king.

A: Diamond card

B: a King card

$$P(A) = \frac{13}{52}$$

$$P(B) = \frac{4}{52} \qquad P(A \cap B) = \frac{1}{52}$$

$$P(AUB) = P(A) + P(B) - P(A \cap B)$$

$$P(AUB) = \frac{13}{52} + \frac{4}{52} - \frac{1}{52} = \frac{16}{52} = \frac{4}{13}$$

Question 3: Three light bulbs are selected at random from 20 bulbs of which 5are defective. What is the probability that

I. None are defective

$$\frac{5c_0 15c_3}{20c_3} = \frac{15 \times 14 \times 13}{20 \times 19 \times 18}$$

II. Exactly one defective

$$\frac{5c_1 15c_2}{20c_3}$$

III. At least one defective

1 - P (none are defective)

Question 4: In a simultaneous toss of 2 coins, what are the possible outcomes. Find the probability of '2 head'.

Sample space = [HH, TT, HT, TH]

$$P(2\ heads) = \frac{1}{4}$$

Question 5: A box contains 10 bulbs, 4 of which are defective. If 3 of the bulbs are drawn randomly without replacement what is the probability that all 3 bulbs are defective. (December 2018)

(a) 8/10 (b) 8/4

(c) 4/10 (d) 1/30

Answer – (d)

$$Prob = \frac{No.of\ favourable\ cases}{No.of\ total\ cases}$$

$$= \frac{4c_3}{10c_3}$$

$$= \frac{\frac{4 \times 3 \times 2}{3 \times 2 \times 1}}{\frac{10 \times 9 \times 8}{3 \times 2 \times 1}}$$

$$= \frac{24}{720} = \frac{1}{30}$$

Moments

1. Central moments or moments about Actual Mean (u)

$$u_r = \frac{\sum(x - \bar{x})^r}{N}$$

$$u_1 = \frac{\sum(x - \bar{x})^1}{N} = 0$$

$$u_2 = \frac{\sum(x - \bar{x})^2}{N} = Variance$$

2. Moments about assumed mean

$$u'_r = \frac{\sum(x - A)^r}{N}$$

3. Moments about origin

$$v_1 = \frac{\sum(x - 0)^r}{N}$$

$$v_1 = \frac{\sum(x)^1}{N} = Mean$$

u_2 and u_3 measures skewness. u_2 and u_4 measures Kurtosis.

Kurtosis

It determines the shape of the curve, i.e. degree of flatness or peakedness of the curve. It refers to how the items in a distribution are concentrated in the center.

Measure of Kurtosis

$\beta_2 = u_4/u^2$ $\beta_2 = 3$ Mesokurtic

$\gamma_2 = \beta_2 - 3$ $\beta_2 > 3$ Leptokurtic

$\beta_2 < 3$ Platykurtic

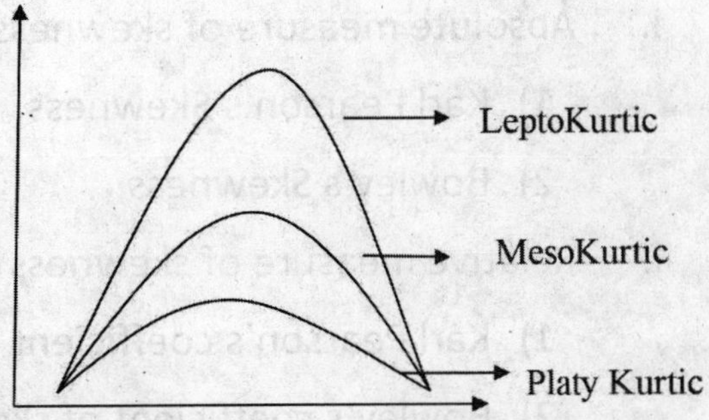

Skewness

Measure the direction in which the values are dispersed. It measures degree of symmetry or asymmetry of the series.

$\beta_1 = u_3^2/u_2^3$

$\gamma_1 = \sqrt{\beta_1}$

$\gamma_1 = 0$ => Symmetric Distribution

$\gamma_1 > 0$ => Positively Skewed Distribution

$\gamma_1 < 0$ => Negatively Skewed Distribution

For a series to be symmetrical, the sum of positive deviation from median should be equal to the sum of negative deviation from the median.

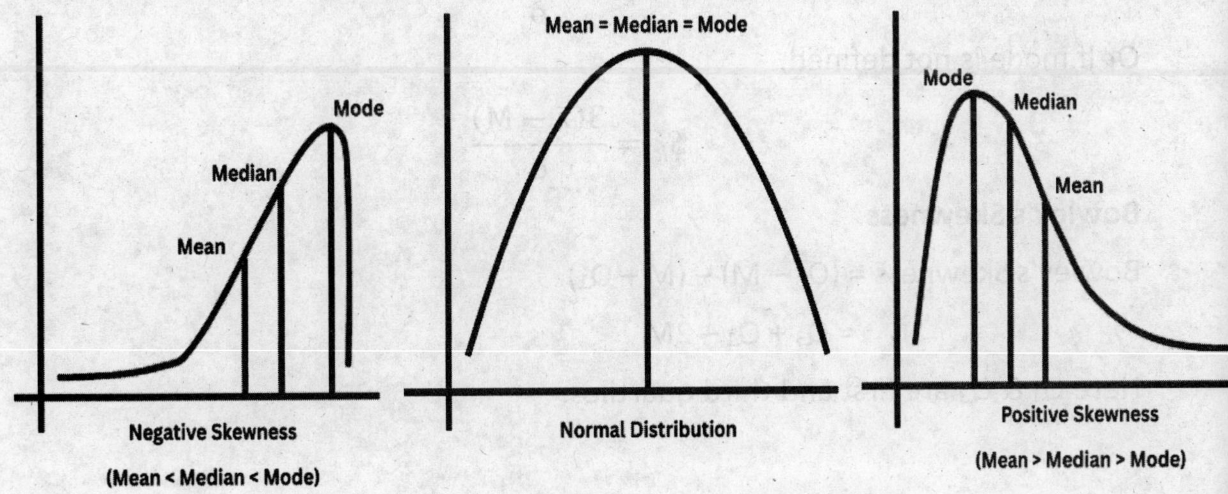

Measure Of Types of Skewness

i. Absolute measure of skewness
   1) Karl Pearson's Skewness
   2) Bowley's Skewness

ii. Relative measure of skewness
   1) Karl Pearson's coefficient of skewness.
   2) Bowley's coefficient of skewness

Karl Pearson's Skewness:

KPS = $\bar{x} - z$

Or

If mode is not defined, then we use median,

KPS = $3(\bar{x} - M)$,

Here $\bar{x}$: Mean

Z: Mode

M: Median

Karl Pearson's Coefficient of Skewness:

$$S_k = \frac{\bar{x} - z}{\sigma}$$

Or If mode is not defined,

$$S_k = \frac{3(\bar{x} - M)}{\sigma}$$

Bowley's Skewness:

Bowley's Skewness = $(Q_3 - M) - (M - Q_1)$

$= Q_3 + Q_1 - 2M$

Here Q_1 & Q_3 are first and third quartiles.

Bowley's Coefficient of Skewness:

$$S_k(Bowley) = \frac{(Q_3 - M) - (M - Q_1)}{(Q_3 - M) + (M - Q_1)}$$

$$S_k(Bowley) = \frac{Q3 + Q1 - 2M}{Q3 - Q1}$$

Central Tendency

Arithmetic Mean (AM) is the mean or average of the set of numbers which is computed by adding all the terms in the set of numbers and dividing the sum by a total number of terms.

Geometric Mean (GM) of a geometric sequence with 'n' terms is computed as the nth root of the product of all the terms in sequence taken together. GM is most suitable for index numbers, ratios and proportions

Harmonic mean (HM) is one of the types of determining the average. The harmonic mean is computed by dividing the number of values in the sequence by the sum of reciprocals of the terms in the sequence.

Formulae:

1. $GM = \sqrt{AM \times HM}$
2. $Mode: 3M - 2\bar{X}$
3. $AM > GM > HM$
4. If and b are positive numbers, then

$$AM = \frac{a + b}{2}$$

$$GM = \sqrt{ab}$$

$$HM = \frac{2ab}{a + b} = \frac{(GM)^2}{AM}$$

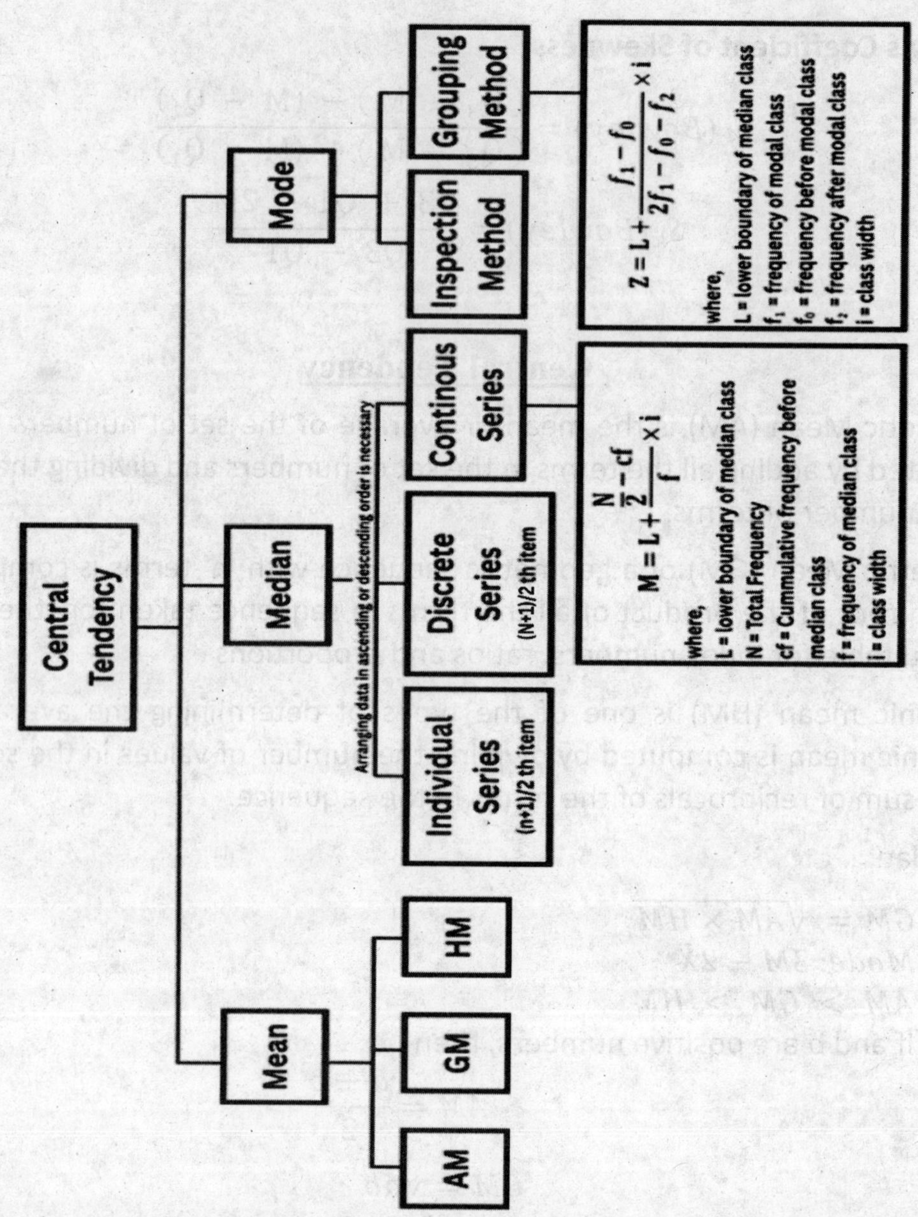

In individual series → n = number of observations

In discrete & continuous series → N = total frequency (Σf)

Properties of Mean

1. Most common form of average and is used only in case of Quantitative data
2. Can be calculated for both grouped as well as ungrouped data.
3. Sum of Deviations of all items from Mean is Zero that is

   $\sum (X - \bar{x}) = 0$
4. Sum of Squared Deviations from the Mean is Minimum.
5. It is capable of further mathematical treatment

$$Combined\ mean = \frac{\bar{x}_1 N_1 + \bar{x}_2 N_2}{N_1 + N_2}$$

6. It can be depicted graphically. The intersection of regression lines (Y on X and X on Y) shows arithmetic means of X and Y.
7. Based on all items of the series.

Properties of Median

1. The sum of deviations from the median will be minimum if we ignore the signs.

   $\sum |X-M| =$ Minimum
2. It can be used in case of qualitative data.
3. It can be graphically depicted.
4. It is not based on all items.

Deciles => Divides series into ten equal parts.

Percentiles => Divides series into hundred equal parts.

Quartiles => Divides series into four equal parts

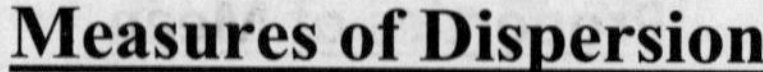

Measures of Dispersion

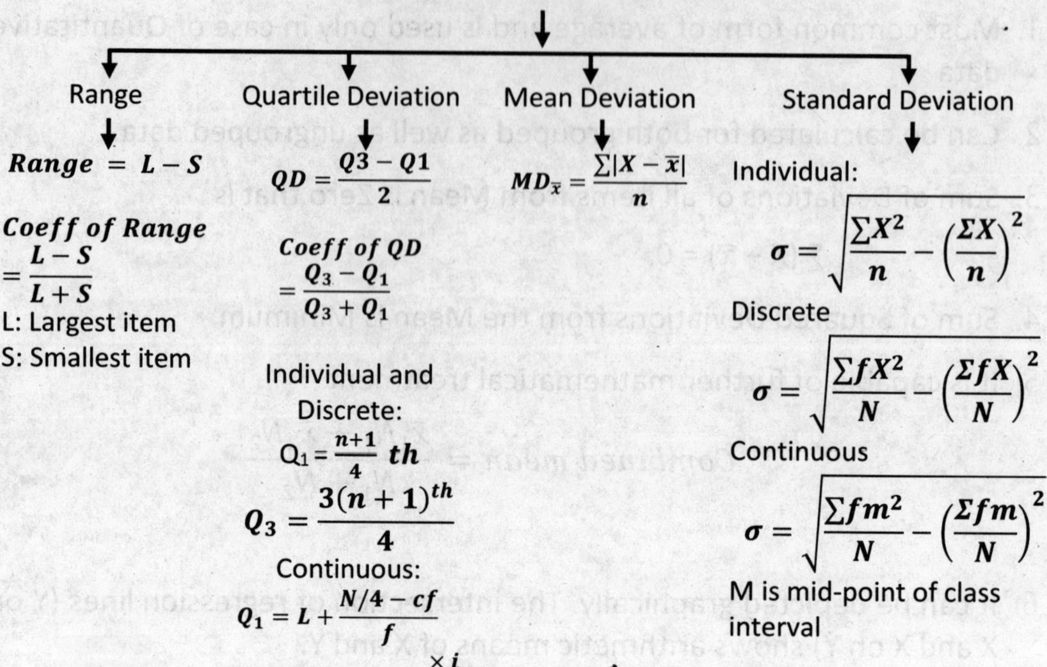

Standard deviation (SD or σ): Standard deviation is a measure which shows how much variation such as spread or dispersion exists from the mean of a data set. SD is independent of origin but not of scale. The square of SD is variance.

$$Variance = \sigma^2$$

$$CV(\%) = \left(\frac{Standard\ deviation}{Mean}\right) \times 100$$

Mean deviation (MD): Mean deviation is the average amount of scatteredness of the items in a distribution from either the mean or median or mode ignoring the sign of deviations. It can be calculated from mean, median and mode.

$$Coefficient\ of\ MD\ about\ Mean: MD_{\bar{X}} = \left(\frac{MD_{\bar{X}}}{\bar{X}}\right) \times 100$$

Quartile deviation (QD): Quartile deviation is a measure of dispersion that is half of the difference between the upper and lower quartile of a data set.

Relation between MD, SD, QD

$$4SD = 5MD = 6QD$$

This is a rule of thumb that holds only under the assumption of a perfectly normal distribution.

Correlation

It determines the relationship between two or more variables. It determines the degree and direction of relationship between two or more than two variables.

- Simple correlation: correlation between two variables
- Partial correlation: relation between two variables keeping other variables constant.
- Multiple correlation: correlation between more than two variables.

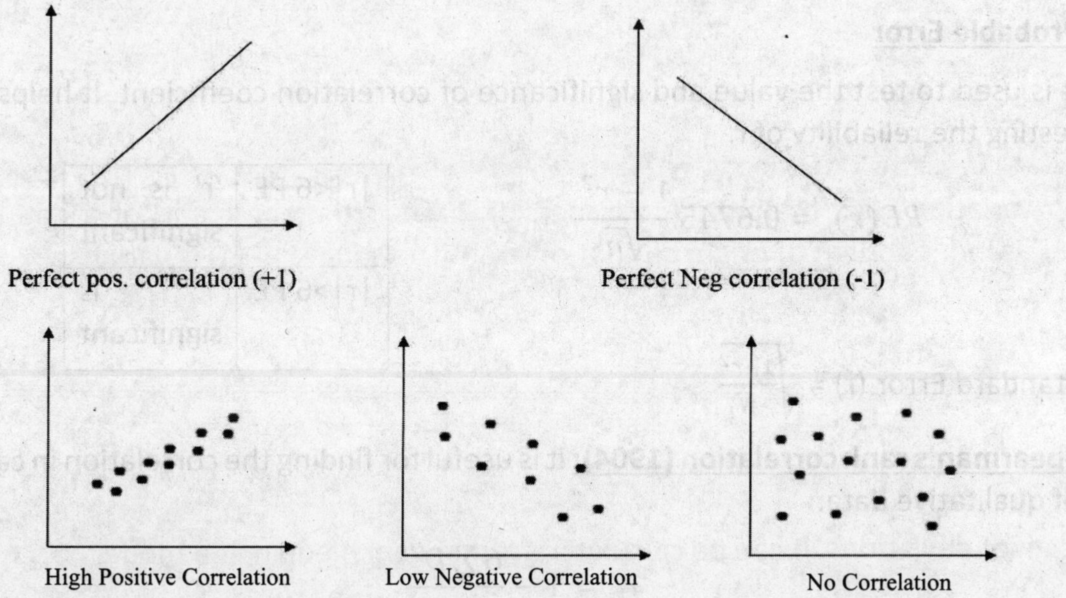

More scattered points, less correlation.

Karl Pearson Coeff. of Correlation

$$r = \frac{\sum(X-\overline{X})(Y-\overline{Y})}{\sqrt{\sum(X-\overline{X})^2}\sqrt{\sum(Y-\overline{Y})^2}}$$

Where, $\overline{X}$ = mean of X variable

$\overline{Y}$ = mean of Y variable

- $-1 \leq r \leq 1$
- "r" is independent of change in origin and scale.
- "r" is under root of the product of two regression coefficient.
- Coefficient of correlation are symmetric $r_{xy} = r_{yx}$

Probable Error

It is used to test the value and significance of correlation coefficient. It helps in testing the reliability of r.

$$PE(r) = 0.6745\frac{1-r^2}{\sqrt{n}}$$

|r|<6 PE	'r' is not significant
|r|>6 PE	'r' is significant

Standard Error (r) = $\sqrt{\frac{1-r^2}{N}}$

Spearman's rank correlation (1904): It is useful for finding the correlation in case of qualitative data.

$$r_k = 1 - \frac{6\sum D^2}{n^3 - n}$$

$$SE = \frac{\sigma}{\sqrt{n}}$$

SE: standard error of the sample

σ: Sample standard deviation

n: number of samples

D: difference between ranks of each pair

Regression

Given by Galton in 1885. It is different from correlation as value of dependent variable is calculated on the basis of given values of explanatory variables.

Properties:

Coefficient of regression is independent of change in origin but not of scale.

Coefficient of regression b_{xy} and b_{yx} are not symmetric.

If r = $\pm$ 1 Regression lines coincide

If r = 0 Regression lines are right angled

$$\text{Regression equation } Y \text{ on } X: \quad \begin{aligned} Y &= a + bX \\ \sum Y &= na + b\sum X \\ \sum XY &= a\sum X + b\sum X^2 \end{aligned}$$

$$Y \text{ on } X = b_{yx} = r\frac{\sigma y}{\sigma x} \qquad b_{yx} = \frac{\sum xy}{\sum x^2}$$

$$b_{yx} = \frac{Cov(x,y)}{Var\ x} \qquad b_{yx} = \frac{Cov(x,y)}{\sigma^2\ x}$$

$$X \text{ on } Y = b_{xy} \rightarrow b_{xy} = r\frac{\sigma x}{\sigma y} \qquad b_{xy} = \frac{\sum xy}{\sum y^2} \text{ or } \frac{Cov(x,y)}{Var\ y} \text{ or } \frac{Cov(x,y)}{\sigma^2\ y}$$

$$b_{yx} = \frac{n\sum XY - \sum X \sum Y}{n\sum X^2 - (\sum X)^2} \qquad b_{xy} = \frac{n\sum XY - \sum X \sum Y}{n\sum Y^2 - (\sum Y)^2}$$

$$r = \sqrt{b_{yx} . b_{xy}}$$

Sampling

Census: census takes each item of the population and is considered to be very authentic and reliable but it is time consuming and costly.

Sampling is collection of samples out of the population. Larger the sample size, more authentic is the sample.

Sampling method:

Probability / Random sampling

All units of population have the same chance of being selected in the sample.

Simple unrestricted method: Techniques used are lottery method, card technique, tippet table.

Systematic sampling: First unit is chosen at random and then every n^{th} unit is chosen for sample. For e.g. I choose any first individual and then every 7th individual to be a part of my sample.

Multi stage sampling: The sample is divided in stages.

Stratified sampling: Population is divided into different strata. Strata are defined in such a way that the population inside one stratum is homogeneous in nature and outside it is heterogeneous.

Cluster sampling: Same as stratified sampling but under cluster sampling, clusters are heterogeneous inside and homogeneous outside.

Clusters/ Strata:	Clustering	Stratification
A		
B		
C		
D		
E		
F		

Stratified	Cluster
• Population divided into few subgroups • Homogeneity within subgroups • Heterogeneity between subgroups • Choice of elements from within each subgroup	• Population divided into many subgroups • Heterogeneity within subgroups • Homogeneity between subgroups • Random choice of subgroups

Non-Probability Sampling

All items of population don't have same chance of being selected

Judgment sampling

Quota sampling

Convenience sampling

Snowball sampling

Sampling Errors

Error is the difference between sample statistic and population parameters.

Probability Distribution

Binomial Distribution

It was discovered in 1700 and first published in 1713 and given by James Bernoulli.

Properties

1. Number of trials is finite and fixed.
2. It is a kind of discrete probability distribution where we have only two cases either a success (occurrence of event) or a failure (non-occurrence).
3. All trials are independent.

4. Probability of success and failure in any trial is constant.

$$\text{Prob}(x=r) = {}^{n}C_{r}\, p^{r}\, q^{n-r}$$

n = no. of trials

p = probability of success

q = probability of failure

r = no. of success

Binomial distribution is also called a limiting case of normal distribution.

$Mean = np$

$SD = \sqrt{npq}$

$Variance = npq$

Poisson Distributions

It was given by Denies Poisson in 1837. It is used when the no. of trails is infinite but probability of success is very small. It is used in case of finding no. of defects, no. of accidents etc. It is discrete prob. distribution.

$$P(X = x) = \frac{e^{-m}.m^{x}}{x!}$$

where, P(X = x): Probability of occurring x events
x = number of occurrences
e = 2.7183 (the base of natural logarithms)
m: the mean of Poisson distribution i.e. the average number of occurrences of an event.
m (mean) = np
SD = √np
Variance = np
Remark: Mean = Variance

Poisson Distribution may be obtained as a limiting case of Binomial Distribution under following conditions:

1. $n \to \infty$ (number of trials indefinitely large)
2. p (the probability of success for each trial) is indefinitely small.

Numerical Problems

Question 1. Find the variance of random variables which constitute the number of heads in a toss of two coins simultaneously.

Solution. Probability of success (head)= 1/2

Probability of failure (toss)=1/2

N = 2

Variance = npq =1/2

OR

Can also be solved by formula of variance of random variable given in next unit

Normal Distribution

Given by AD Moivre, Karl gauss in 1733. Poisson Distribution is limiting case of Normal Distribution.

Properties:

- The distribution is symmetrical., hence it resembles a bell- shaped curve.
- The two tails do not touch the axis.
- Total area under normal curve is 1.
- Belong to mesokurtic distribution
- MEAN = MEDIAN = MODE
- Characteristic function of normal distribution:

  $$\varphi(t) = e^{i\mu t - \frac{1}{2}\sigma^2 t^2}$$

  It has two parts: $i\mu t$ → related to the mean $1/2\sigma^2 t^2$ → related to the variance

- By virtue of symmetry, quartiles are equidistant from median

  i.e. $Q_3 - M = M - Q_1$

  $Q_1 + Q_3 = 2M$

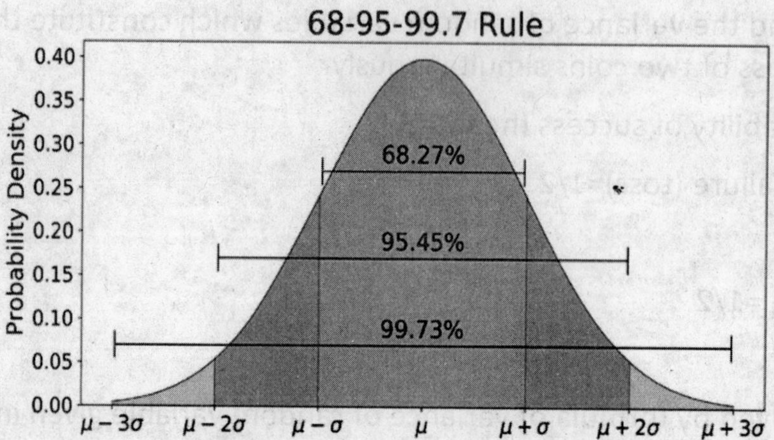

Collectively, these points are known as the empirical rule or the 68-95-99.7 rule. Clearly, given a normal distribution, most outcomes will be within 3 standard deviations of the mean.

- Mean = 0
- SD = 1
- Variance = 1
- Skewness measure = 0
- Measure of Kurtosis = 3
- Moments about Mean (u): $u_1=0$, $u_2=\sigma^2$, $u_3=0$ (as skewness is zero), $u_4=3\sigma^4$

Index Number

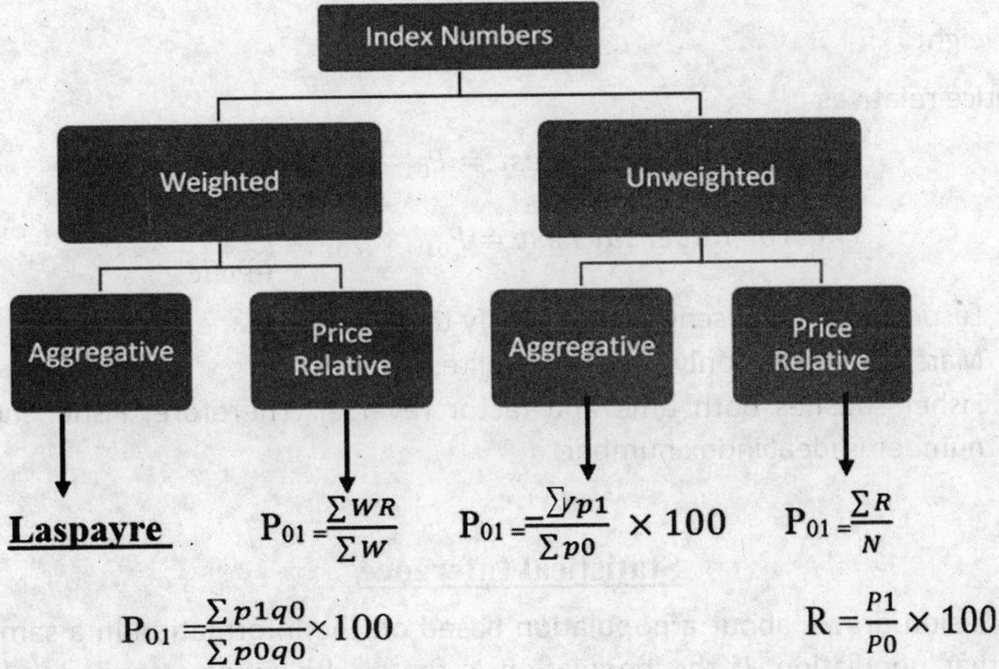

Laspayre $P_{01} = \frac{\sum WR}{\sum W}$ $P_{01} = \frac{\sum yp1}{\sum p0} \times 100$ $P_{01} = \frac{\sum R}{N}$

$$P_{01} = \frac{\sum p1q0}{\sum p0q0} \times 100$$

$$R = \frac{P1}{P0} \times 100$$

Paasche

$$P_{01} = \frac{\sum p1q1}{\sum p0q1} \times 100$$

Fisher

$$\sqrt{L \times P} \rightarrow P_{01} = \sqrt{\frac{\sum p1q0}{\sum p0q0}} \times \sqrt{\frac{\sum p1q1}{\sum p0q1}} \times 100$$

Bowley

$$\frac{L+P}{2} \rightarrow P_{01} = \frac{\frac{\sum p1q0}{\sum p0q0} + \frac{\sum p1q1}{\sum p0q1}}{2}$$

Marshall

$$p_{01} = \frac{\sum p_1q_0 + \sum p_1q_1}{\sum p_0q_0 + \sum p_0q_1} \times 100$$

where p_1 & p_0 are prices of current and base year

q_1 & q_2 are quantities of current and base year

W is weight

R is price relatives

$$Time\ Reversal\ Test = P_{01} \times P_{10} = 1$$

$$Factor\ Reversal\ Test = P_{01} \times Q_{01} = \frac{\Sigma p_1 q_1}{\Sigma p_0 q_0}$$

- Laspeyres and Paasche do not satisfy these tests.
- Marshall satisfies only time reversal test.
- Fisher satisfies both time and factor reversal. Therefore, Fisher index number is ideal index number.

Statistical Inference

A conclusion drawn about a population based on the information in a sample from that population. If the population is finite with mean μ and standard deviation σ or the sampling is without replacement, use the following:

Mean	Variance	Standard Deviation*
$\mu_{\bar{x}} = \mu$	$\sigma_{\bar{x}}^2 = \frac{\sigma^2}{n}\left(\frac{N-n}{N-1}\right)$	$\sigma_{\bar{x}} = \frac{\sigma}{\sqrt{n}} \cdot \sqrt{\frac{N-n}{N-1}}$

σx: sample standard deviation
σ: population standard deviation
n: number of sample observation
N: number of population observation
With replacement formula is

$$\sigma_{\bar{x}} = \frac{\sigma}{\sqrt{n}}$$

Simple Linear Regression Model

SLR is a basic technique for measuring the relationship among the economic variables. It is a model in which one variable 'y' is expressed as function of another variable 'x' and disturbance terms 'u'.

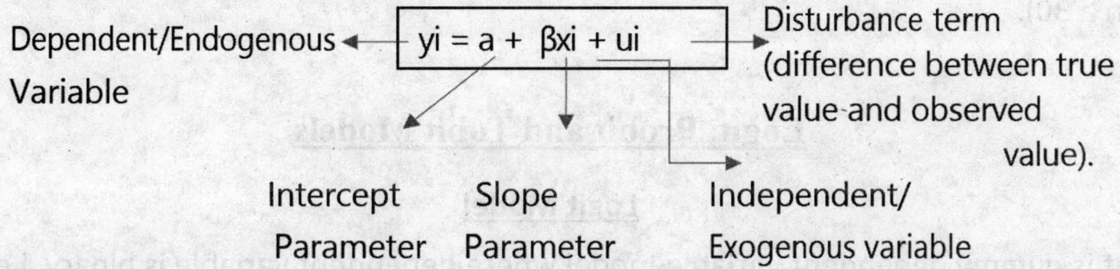

Assumptions:

1. The regression model is linear in parameters though it may or may not be linear in the variables.
2. Zero Mean value of disturbance i.e. E(ui) = 0.
3. Variance is constant. In other words, disturbance term is homoscedastic. i.e. $E(u_i^2) = \sigma_u^2$.
4. Error terms are random.
5. X's are non - random i.e., 1,2, 3, ...
6. u_i has normal distribution.
7. Errors are non - auto correlated i.e., $Cov(u_i u_j) = 0$
8. X's are uncorrelated in multiple linear regression model.
9. Fixed X values such as values taken by regressor X may be considered fixed in repeated samples. i.e. Y records quantity sold each day at same price.
10. X values are independent of error term i.e., $Cov(X_i U_i)=0$.
11. The number of observation (n) must be greater than the number of parameters (k) to be estimated.

Central Limit Theorem

If you take sufficiently large random samples from any population with a finite mean μ and variance σ^2, the sampling distribution of sample mean $\bar{x}$ will tend to be approximately normal. In other words, sampling distribution of mean will always be normally distributed as long as sample size is large enough (usually $n \geq 30$).

Logit, Probit and Tobit Models

Logit Model

It is dummy dependent variable model where dependent variable is binary, i.e., it has two possible outcomes such as 0 or 1. The logit model is based on following cumulative distribution function of Logistic distribution:

$$P_i = Prob(Y_i = 1) = \frac{1}{1 + e^{-(\beta_0 + \beta_1 X_i)}} = \frac{1}{1 + e^{-(Z_i)}}$$

$$where\ Z_i = \beta_0 + \beta_1 X_i$$

$$(1 - P_i) = \frac{1}{1 + e^{(Z_i)}}$$

Thus,

$$\frac{P_i}{1 - P_i} = \frac{1 + e^{(Z_i)}}{1 + e^{-(Z_i)}}$$

$$logit_i = \ln\left(\frac{P_i}{1 - P_i}\right) = Z_i = \beta_0 + \beta_1 X_i$$

- ➔ $\frac{P_i}{1-P_i}$ is the odds of success.
- ➔ Taking the natural log of the odds gives the logit.
- ➔ The logit is modelled as linear function of the independent variable X_i

It is visible from the function that Z_i ranges from -∞ to ∞, P_i ranges between 0 and 1.

Logit is log of odd ratio i.e., ratio of probability of happening an event to the probability of not happening an event. Pi is probability of happening an event i.e., adoption of technology. (1-pi) is probability of not happening an event.

Probit Model

It is also a dummy dependent variable model means dependent variable can only have two possible outcomes like 0 or 1. Probit model follows normal distribution. It is also called normit model. Dependent variable can take only two values i.e. married or not married.

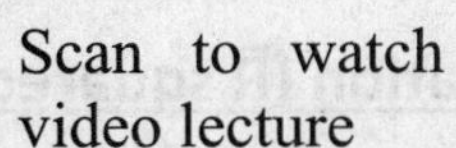

Tobit Model

Tobit model is used when a sample in which information on the regressand is available only for some observations. Such samples are called censored samples. Therefore, Tobit model is also called censored model or limited dependent variable regression model, i.e., suppose we have a set of consumers and we are interested in finding amount of money a person spends on a house in relation to other socio-economic variables. If consumer do not purchase house, we have no data for housing expenditure for such consumer.

Coefficient of Determination (R2)

It measures the proportion of variance in dependent variable that is explained by independent variables in the regression model. It is measure of goodness of fit. It lies between 0 to 1.

$$\underbrace{\Sigma y_i^2}_{\substack{Total\\Variation}} = \underbrace{\hat{\beta}\Sigma x_i y_i}_{\substack{Explained\\Variation}} + \underbrace{\Sigma e_i^2}_{\substack{Unexplained\\Variation}}$$

$$r^2 = \frac{explained\ variation}{Total\ variation}$$

$$r^2 = \frac{\hat{\beta}\sum x_i y_i}{\sum y_i^2}$$

$$= \frac{\sum y_i^2 - \sum e_i^2}{\sum y_i^2}$$

$$= 1 - \frac{\sum e_i^2}{\sum y_i^2}$$

Illustration. If coefficient of correlation, R= 0.7, how much variation in dependent variable is explained in independent variable?

R^2 = 0.49. That means 49% variation in dependent variable is explained by independent variable and remaining 51% variation is unexplained.

Adjusted Coefficient of Determination ($\bar{R}$ squared)

When R^2 is adjusted by degrees of freedom, it is $\bar{R}$ squared.

$$\bar{R}^2 = 1 - \frac{\sum e_i^2}{\sum y_i^2} \div \frac{n-(K+1)}{n-1}$$

$$\bar{R}^2 = 1 - (1 - R^2).\frac{n-1}{n-(K+1)}$$

K: no. of variables

n: no. of observations

OLS (Ordinary Least Square)

It is a type of least square method for finding unknown parameter in linear regression model by principle of least square i.e. minimizing the sum of square of residuals.

$$Min \sum e_i^2 (RSS) = \sum \left(y_i - \hat{\alpha} - \hat{\beta} x_i\right)^2$$

$$Parameter\ \hat{\beta} = \frac{\sum x_i y_i}{\sum x_i^2}$$

$$\hat{\alpha} = \bar{y} - \hat{\beta}\bar{x}$$

RSS: Residual Sum of Square

Gauss Markov Theorem

The BLUE properties of OLS estimates are termed as Gauss Markov Theorem. BLUE : Best Linear Unbiased Estimate. An OLS estimator is said to be a best linear unbiased estimator if it holds following properties:

Scan QR Code for video lecture

1. Linearity: The OLS estimator must be a linear function of the dependent variable Y.
2. Unbiasedness:

$$E[\hat{\beta}_0] = \beta_0$$

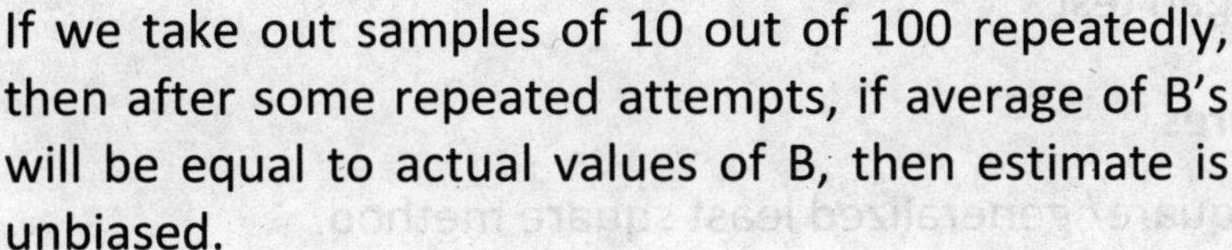
If we take out samples of 10 out of 100 repeatedly, then after some repeated attempts, if average of B's will be equal to actual values of B, then estimate is unbiased.

3. Minimum Variance: An Estimator is best when it has small variance as compared with any other estimators.
4. Efficiency: An estimator is efficient when it possesses both the properties of unbiasedness and of minimum variance is efficient estimator.

Heteroscedasticity

A regression model in which disturbance variance change from observation to observation is known as heteroscedasticity.

Consider the following regression models:

$Y_i = \hat{\beta}_1 + \hat{\beta}_2 X_i + e_i$

i.e., Var (u_i) = σ_u^2 (Homoscedasticity)

Var (u_i) = $\sigma_{u_i}^2$ (Heteroscedasticity)

Consequences: OLS estimates have large variance, so become inefficient but remain unbiased and linear.

Formula for ordinary least square variance (homoscedastic disturbances): $Var(\hat{\beta}_2) = \frac{\sigma^2}{\Sigma x_i^2}$

Formula for ordinary least square variance (heteroskedastic disturbances): $Var(\hat{\beta}_2) = \frac{\sum x_i^2 \sigma^2}{(\sum x_i^2)^2}$

Tests

- Spearman Rank Correlation Test
- Gold Fed Quandt Test
- Glejser Test
- Park Test
- White general test
- Breush pagan test

Remedial measures

Weighted least square/ generalized least square method.

Multicollinearity

It occurs when there is perfect or exact linear relationship among explanatory variables of a regression model, i.e., correlation among x_1, x_2, x_3, ...x_n in following model is termed as multicollinearity (MC). The term multicollinearity was given by Ragnar Frisch.

$Yi = \beta_0 + \beta_1 X_1 + \beta_2 X_2 + \ldots + \beta_n X_n + ui$

Perfect multicollinearity $r_{12} = 1$

Imperfect multicollinearity $r_{12} < 1$

Tests

1. Farrar Glauber Test

2. Frisch's confluence or Bunch Map Analysis

3. Tolerance and VIF (Variance Inflation Factor): $VIF=1/(1-R^2)$

    $(1-R^2)$=Tolerance

    If VIF=1, no MC

    If it is between 1 to 5, moderate MC

    If it is greater than 5, highly MC

Generally, a VIF above 4 or tolerance below 0.25 indicates that multicollinearity might exist. When VIF is higher than 10 or tolerance is lower than 0.1, there is significant multicollinearity that needs to be corrected.

4. Eigen values and Condition Index

A condition index shows the degree of multicollinearity. It is an alternative to other methods like variance inflation factors.

The indices are calculated as "—the square roots of the ratios of the largest eigenvalue to each successive eigenvalue"

Kennedy gives the following rule of thumb for interpreting a condition index; Any index greater than 30 —indicates strong collinearity

Consequences: If there is perfect multicollinearity, OLS estimates are indeterminate, Variance and covariance infinitely large, test of significance become invalid.

If MC is less than perfect, although determinate regression coefficients but large variance (or standard error) exist. So, coefficients can't be estimated with greater precision or accuracy. Because of large variance and covariance, the confidence intervals tend to be much wider, leasing to acceptance of H_0. T ratio tends to be statistically insignificant of one or more coefficients. R^2, the overall measure of goodness of fit can be very high. The OLS estimator and their standard errors can be sensitive to small changes in data.

Solutions

1. Increasing size of sample
2. Use extraneous/external information i.e., priori information criteria
3. Dropping collinear variable
4. Principal component method
5. Combining time series and cross-sectional data, known as pooling data
6. Transformation of variables

Autocorrelation

Correlation between successive values of same variable. In other words, correlation between different values of disturbance term.

If the assumption of $E(u_i u_j) = 0$ is violated, then there is Autocorrelation.

Consequences: Variance of OLS estimates become large (inefficient) but remain unbiased. Prediction inefficient, Invalid test of significance, misleading and unnecessarily widen confidence internals.

Tests

1. Durbin - Watson Test (for small samples)
   D-W statistic is given by
   $$d = 2[1 - \hat{e}]$$
   ê: coefficient of autocorrelation
   d lies between 0 to 4
   if ê = 0, d = 2 (No AC)
   if ê = -1, d = 4 (perfect negative correlation)
   if ê = 1, d = 0 (perfect positive correlation)
2. Non - Neuman Ratio Test (for large samples i.e., greater than 30)
3. L-Jung Box Q (LBQ) statistic

Remedial measures

Generalized least square method

Cochrane- Orcutt iterative method

Dummy Variables

They are qualitative variables/ categorial variables that takes only two values 0 and 1. There are always one less dummy variable than number of categories in a model. If two categories i.e. male and female, we introduce one dummy variable in model.

The dummy variable trap occurs when there is perfect multicollinearity in a regression model due to the inclusion of too many dummy variables. This happens when dummy variables represent all possible categories of a qualitative variable without excluding one as a reference category.

Incorrect Approach (Dummy Variable Trap)

If we include **both** dummy variables for Male and Female:

$$Salary = \beta_0 + \beta_1 Male + \beta_2 Female + u$$

Since a person can only be either male or female, the two dummies are perfectly correlated:

$$Male + Female = 1$$

This results in perfect multicollinearity, making the regression model unsolvable.

Correct Approach (Avoiding Dummy Variable Trap)

To avoid the dummy variable trap, we drop one category (e.g., Female) and set it as the reference group:

$$Salary = \beta_0 + \beta_1 Male + u$$

If Male = 1, then the person is male, If Male = 0, then the person is female. This ensures the model is identifiable and statistically valid.

Test For Structural Stability: Chow Test

Chow test in econometrics refers to the statistical method that checks whether variables of two different regression models are equal. The primary purpose of this test is to determine if any structural change occurs between these variables.

The Chow test is typically used in the field of econometrics with time series data to determine if there is a structural break in the data at some point.

If the test determines that the coefficients are not equal between the regression lines, this means there is significant evidence that a structural break exists in the data. In other words, the pattern in the data is significantly different before and after that structural break point.

Scan for video on Chow Test

Sometimes your data will have a break point or structural point (a period of significant or violent change), splitting a data set into two parts. For example:

- Donations given to an organization before and after a natural disaster.
- Stock market prices before and after Black Friday.
- House prices before and after a significant interest change.
- Asset prices before and after civil war.

Let's say your linear regression analysis of two parts of a data set resulted in the following two linear regression equations:

First part of the data: $y_t = X_1 * b_1 + \mu_1$

Second part of the data: $y_t = X_2 * b_2 + \mu_2$

The Chow test would tell you if the coefficients $b_1 = b_2$ and $\mu 1 = \mu_2$. If they *are* equal, the data set can be represented with a single regression line.

The null hypothesis for the test is that there is no break point (i.e. that the data set can be represented with a single regression line).

Steps

Run a regression for the entire data set (the "pooled regression"). Collect the Error Sum of Squares.

Run separate regressions on each half of the data set. Collect the Error Sum of Squares for the two regressions.

Calculate the Chow F statistic from each subsample. The formula is:

$$CHOW = \frac{RSS_p - (RSS_1 + RSS_2))/k}{(RSS_1 + RSS_2)/(N_1 + N_2 - 2k)}$$

- RSS_P = Residual sum of square from pooled data
- RSS_1, RSS_2 = Residual sum of square from two regressions
- Find the F-critical value from the F-table.
- Reject the null hypothesis if your calculated F-value falls into the rejection region (i.e. if the calculated F-value is greater than the F-critical value).

Bai-Perron Test is also used for detecting Structural Breaks in Time Series

Causality

Causality means that there is a clear cause-effect relationship between two variables. Therefore, there is causation, when action A causes outcome B. Granger causality is an econometric test used to verify the usefulness of one variable to forecast another. A variable is said to Granger-cause another variable if it is helpful for forecasting the other variable. Fail to Granger-cause if it is not helpful for forecasting the other variable.

Scan for video on Causality and Cointegration

Steps to Implement the Granger Causality Test

1. Calculate the Restricted Residual Sum of Squares (RSS_R)
   - Regress current GDP (GDP_t) on lagged GDP terms and other variables, excluding the lagged values of the other variable (M).
   - The restricted model equation:

     $$GDP_t = \sum \beta_j GDP_{t-j} + u_{1t}$$

   - Compute RSS_R (Residual Sum of Squares for the restricted model).
2. Calculate the Unrestricted Residual Sum of Squares (RSS_U)
   - Regress current GDP (GDP_t) on lagged GDP and lagged values of M.
   - The unrestricted model equation:

     $$GDP_t = \sum \alpha_i M_{t-i} + \sum \beta_j GDP_{t-j} + u_{1t}$$

   - Compute RSS_U (Residual Sum of Squares for the unrestricted model).
3. Define the Hypotheses
   - Null Hypothesis (H_0: $\alpha_i = 0$)

     This means the lagged values of M are statistically insignificant, implying that M does not Granger-cause GDP.
   - Alternative Hypothesis (H_1: α_i not equal to 0)

     This means the lagged values of M are statistically significant, implying that M Granger-causes GDP.
4. Compute the F-Statistic
   The F-static formula is

   $$F = \frac{(RSS_R - RSS_U)/m}{RSS_U/(n-k)}$$

   where,

   RSS_R: Residual Sum of Squares from the Restricted Model
   RSS_U: Residual Sum of Squares from the Unrestricted Model
   m: Number of lagged terms
   n: Number of observations
   k: Number of parameters estimated in the unrestricted model

5. Compare the Computed F-Statistic
   - If the computed F-statistic exceeds the critical F-value at the chosen significance level (e.g., 0.05), we reject H_0.
   - Result: M Granger-causes GDP.
   - If the computed F-statistic is below the critical value, we fail to reject H_0.
   - Result: No evidence that M Granger-causes GDP.

The Sims Test is an alternative to the Granger Causality Test used to examine the causality relationship between two or more time series variables.

Cointegration

Cointegration is a statistical property of a group of **non-stationary** time series variables that move together in the long run. Even if individual variables are non-stationary (having trends over time), their linear combination may be stationary, indicating a long-term equilibrium relationship.

Identification Problem

It must be solved before estimation. Model is identified if it is in unique statistical form. Order condition is necessary and rank condition is sufficient for identification.

Paradox Of Identification

Identification of a function depends on the variables absent from it while at the same time being operative in the other function of model. We will able to identify a function by what variables it does not include.

Structural Equation Model

It expresses the endogenous variables as a function of other endogenous variables, predetermined variable and disturbance term. i.e.,

$$C_t = a_0 + a_1 Y_t + u_1$$

$$I_t = b_0 + b_1 Y_t + b_2 Y_{t-1} + u_2$$

$$Y_t = C_t + I_t + G_t$$

Here G_t and Y_{t-1} are predetermined variables,

and u_1, u_2 are disturbance terms.

C_t, I_t, & Y_t are endogenous variables. In other words, they are endogenous regressors as in one equation they appeared as independent/explanatory variable (regressors) and in other equation they appeared as dependent variable.

Reduced Form Model

Endogenous variables are function of only predetermined variables and error term.

Order Conditions

It states that for an equation to be identified the total number of variables excluded from it, must equal to or greater than the number of endogenous variables (number of equations) in the model less than one. If

$K - M < G - 1$: Under identified equation

$K - M = G - 1$: just identified or exactly identified equation

$K - M > G - 1$: Over identified equation

K: Total no. of variables

M: No. of endogenous and exogenous variables in a particular equation.

G: Total no. of equations/endogenous variables in a model.

Illustration

$Y_1 = \alpha_0 + \alpha_1 y_2 + \alpha_3 y_3 + \alpha_4 x_1 + \alpha_5 x_2 + u_1$

$Y_2 = \beta_0 + \beta_1 y_3 + \beta_2 y_1 + \beta_2 x_2 + u_2$

$Y_3 = \gamma_0 + \gamma_1 x_1 + \gamma_2 x_2 + \gamma_3 x_3 + u_3$

According to order condition, the first eq. is

a)Unidentified b) Exact identified c) Over identified

Solution:

K = (y_1, y_2, y_3, x_1, x_2, x_3) = 6

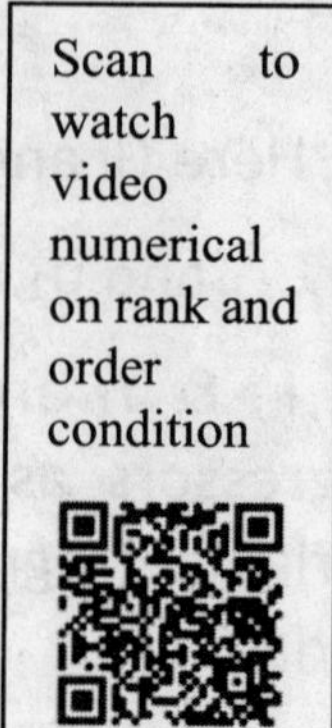

$M = (y_1, y_2, y_3, x_1, x_2) = 5$

$G = 3$

K – M	G - 1	
6 - 5	3 – 1	
1 <	2	⇨ Unidentified

Rank Condition: In Case of Structural Model

In a system of G equation, any particular equation is identified if and only if it is possible to construct at least one non zero determinant of order G-1 from coefficient of variables excluded from that particular equation but contained in other equation of model.

Scan for a video lecture on endogenous & exogenous variable

In case of Reduced Form Equation

In a system of G endogenous variables, any particular equation is identified if and only if it is possible to construct at least one non zero determinant of order G-1 from reduced form coefficients of exogenous variables excluded from particular equation but contained in other equation of model.

Simultaneous Equations

The simultaneity problem arises because some of the regressors are endogenous and are therefore likely to be correlated with disturbance term. Joint dependence of variables is called SEM (simultaneous equation model). In other words, dependent variable is function of other dependent variables rather than just independent variables. We can't apply OLS in SEM as it led to simultaneous bias. Estimates will be biased and will not efficient estimator. Three commonly used single equation methods are OLS, ILS and 2SLS. OLS is inappropriate in the context of simultaneous equation models, as it led to simultaneous equation bias. Estimates obtained from ILS and 2SLS are consistent but they may not satisfy small sample properties of unbiasedness and minimum variance.

Simultaneous Equation Bias:
OLS estimates are biased, inefficient and inconsistent. $E(u_i x_i)$ not equal to 0. That means correlation between error term and explanatory variable exist. There is a test of simultaneity to test whether explanatory variable (endogenous regressors) is correlated with error term in the model. It is called Hausman specification test.
Note: Regressors are called endogenous when they are not statistically independent of error term.

1. **Indirect least square (ILS) or Reduced form method.**

It is method of obtaining the estimation of structural coefficient from OLS estimation of reduced form coefficients. This method is appropriate for exactly identified equations.

Steps 1. Obtain reduced form equation from structural model

2.Apply OLS and find reduced form coefficients

3.Solve for structural parameters from reduced form coefficient.

2. **Instrumental variable method:** In this method, a proxy has to be found which is strongly correlated with endogenous variable and uncorrelated with error term. Appropriate for over identified equations

3. **Two Stage least square:** Appropriate for just identified and over identified equations.

4. **Three Stage Least Square:** It is simultaneous equation method as it is applied to all equations of model simultaneously. Appropriate for over identified equations.

Recursive Model

$y_1 = f(x_1, x_2, \ldots, x_k, u1)$

$y_2 = f(x_1, x_2, \ldots, x_k, y_1, u_2)$

$y_3 = f(x_1, x_2, \ldots, x_k, y_1, y_2, u_3)$

- First equation includes only predetermined variables (Independent) at the right.
- Second equation includes predetermined and endogenous variables at the right.
- System is recursive and triangular.
- OLS can be applied directly on each equation of recursive model.
- OLS are unbiased and consistent.
- Endogenous variable in one equation may appear as explanatory variable in another.
- Causal Direction: y1 influences y2, but y2 does not affect y1. Similarly, y1 and y2 influence y3, but y3 does not influence them. In other words, each equation shows unilateral causal dependence. Hence the name causal models. There is no interdependence among endogenous variables in the same equation.

Time Series Data

Values that a variable takes at different times. Collected at a regular interval such as daily, weekly, monthly. Components of time series:

1. Secular variation (long term). It is also called trend value (T)
2. Seasonal variation (Short term) (S)
3. Cyclical variation (C)
4. Irregular or random variation i.e., variation due to wars, floods or natural calamities (I).

<u>Additive model</u>: T + S + C + I (Components are independent)

Multiplicative model: T x S x C x I (Components may not be necessarily independent).

Methods of measuring trend: graphical method, semi-averages, moving averages and least square method.

Stationary Time Series

Time series is assumed to be stationary which means that its means and variance does not vary with time. Stationary also means series without trend or seasonal component.

Scan QR Code for video lecture

Random Walk (R-W) model represents non-stationary time series as its variance varies in time periods. A process x_t is called random walk if $y_t = y_{t-1} + u_t$

R-W without drift (there is no drift parameter): $y_t = y_{t-1} + u_t$

R-W with drift: $y_t = a+y_{t-1} + u_t$

There is a drift parameter 'a'. Y_t drifts upward or downward depending on 'a' being positive /negative.

Tests of Stationarity

1. Dicky fuller Test - used for first order Autoregressive model.
2. Augmented Dicky Fuller Test (ADF) – used for higher order Auto –Regressive Model and when error term is correlated (autocorrelation).

   Hypothesis is set as follows:
   H_0: Series is non stationary or series has unit root
   H_1: series is stationary or it has not unit root.
3. KPSS (Kwiatkowski Phillips Schimdt Shin) test:
   Hypothesis is set as follows:
   H_0: Series is trend stationary or series has not unit root
   H_1: series is non stationary or it has unit root.

If in case, ADF concludes non stationary and KPSS concludes stationary, then series is trend stationary. To make it strictly stationary, trend is to be removed.

If ADF concludes stationary and KPSS concludes non stationary, then series is difference stationary. Differencing used to make series stationary.

Approaches For Time Series Forecasting

Forecasting methods i.e. ARMA (Auto-Regressive Moving Average), ARIMA (Auto-Regressive Integrated Moving Average) and Exponential smoothing are approaches for time series forecasting. First step to use these models is to make time series stationary as model cannot forecast non stationary time series.

Types of Errors

Type I Error – Hypothesis is true, but our test rejects it.

Type II Error – Hypothesis is false, but our test accepts it.

Possible Hypothesis Test Outcomes		
	Actual Situation	
Decision	H0 True	H0 False
Accept H0	No error	Type II error
	Probability = 1 - α	Probability = β
Reject H0	Type I error	No error
	Probability = α	Probability = 1 - β

Level of Significance: The maximum size of Type I error, which we are ready to risk is called as level of significance. It can be 5% or 1 %. If we fix 5% level, it means we are 95% confident that our decision to reject null hypothesis is true.

Power of Test: The probability of committing Type II error is denoted by β. Power of test is defined as the value '1-β'. It is the probability of rejecting H0 when it is false. Our aim is to fix level of significance at 'α' and then maximize '1-β'.

Confidence intervals (CI): Range of values you expect your estimate to fall between. In other words, probability that a parameter will fall between a set of values.

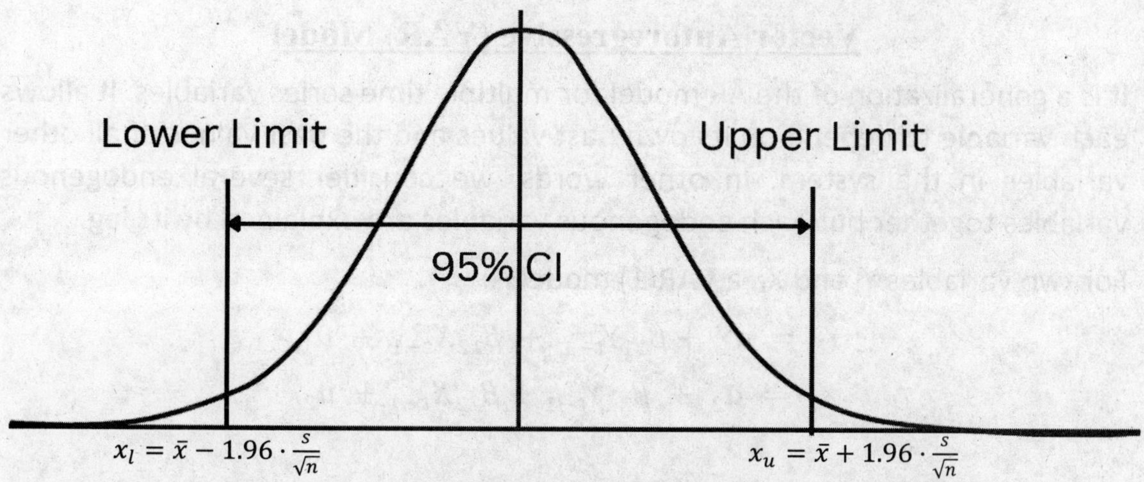

Here, x_l: lower limit, x_u: upper limit, $\bar{x}$: mean, s: standard deviation

Distributed Log Models

When in regression equation, current value of dependent variable (y) depends upon the current value of independent variable (X_t) and its lagged values (X_{t-1}, X_{t-2}) etc., then such a model is known as Distributed log model.

$$Y_t = \beta_0 + \beta_1 X_t + \beta_2 X_{t-1} + u_t$$

Auto Regressive (AR) Model

An Auto Regressive model is a time series model in which the current value of the dependent variable (Y_t) is explained using its own past (lagged) value.

It is AR(2) model:

$$Y_t = \beta_0 + \beta_1 Y_{t-1} + \beta_2 Y_{t-2} + u_t$$

Vector Autoregressive (VAR) Model

It is a generalization of the AR model for multiple time series variables. It allows each variable to depend on its own past values and the past values of all other variables in the system. In other words, we consider several endogenous variables together but each endogenous variables are explained by its lag.

For two variables Y_t and X_t, a VAR(1) model is:

$$Y_t = a_1 + \beta_{11}Y_{t-1} + \beta_{12}X_{t-1} + u_{1t}$$
$$X_t = a_2 + \beta_{21}Y_{t-1} + \beta_{22}X_{t-1} + u_{2t}$$

Generalized Least Square Model

The procedure of transforming the original variable in such a way that the transformed variables satisfy the assumption of the classical model and then applying OLS to it is known as the method of Generalized Least Square Model.

GLS is OLS on the transformed variables that satisfy the least square assumption. It provides solution of heteroscedastic and autocorrelated disturbance and capable of providing estimators that are BLUE.

GLS	OLS
Minimize weighted residual sum of square (RSS).	Minimize unweighted or equally weighted residual sum of square.
Weights are given to observation according to variability. Weights assigned to each observation is inversely proportional to variance. Each observation coming from population with large variance will get smaller weight.	Equal weights are assigned to each observation.

Hypothesis Testing

Null Hypothesis: It assumes that there is no difference between population parameter and sample statistics.

Alternative Hypothesis: Alternative Hypothesis is accepted when null hypothesis is rejected. It can be two tailed, right tailed or left tailed.

Small Sample Tests

1. T-test: developed by William Gosset.
2. Applicable where sample is less than 30.
3. Degree of Freedom = n-1
4. T-test is used for test of significance of regression coefficient in regression model. Formula is:

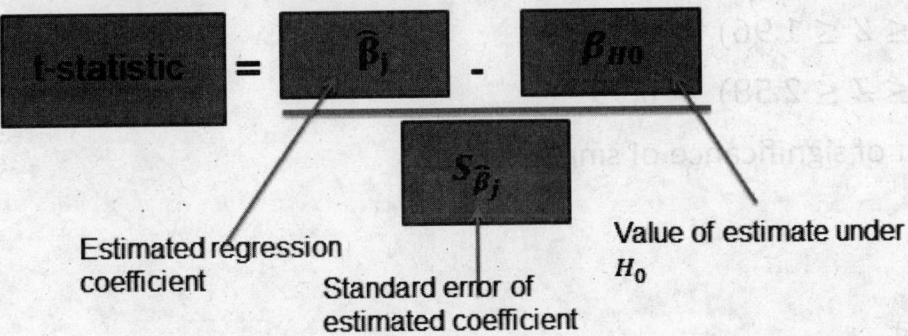

5. It is used to test significance of an observed sample correlation coefficient. Formula is:

$$t = r\sqrt{\frac{N-2}{1-r^2}}$$

6. Used where population variance is unknown.
7. Used to test of significance of single mean and difference of means (in paired and unpaired samples).

Large Sample Test

1. Z-test: Given by Fisher.
2. Used when sample size is more than 30.
3. Used where population variance is known.

4. Used to test of significance for single proportion, difference in proportions, test of significance of single mean and difference of means.

5. It is based on standard normal distribution.

6. For each significance level, the z test has single critical value

At 5% significance level for two tailed test, z value is 1.96

At 1% significance level for two tailed tests , it is 2.58

At 5% significance level, for one tailed test, it is 1.645

At 1% significance level for one tailed test, it is 2.33

7. Area under normal probability curve:

$$P(-3 \leq Z \leq 3) = 0.9973$$

$$P(-1.96 \leq Z \leq 1.96) = 0.95$$

$$P(-2.58 \leq Z \leq 2.58) = 0.99$$

8. Formula to test of significance of single mean:

$$Z_c = \frac{\bar{x} - \mu)}{\sigma/\sqrt{n}}$$

9. Z score formula

$$z = \frac{x - \mu}{\sigma}$$

σ: Standard deviation

μ: Mean

Numerical Problems

Question 1. Hari's score in the statistics in the first year is 76, whereas the class average is 68 with standard deviation of 5. What is Hari's Z-score?

(a) 1.5 (b) 1.6 (c) 1.2 (d) 1.4 (December 2021 and June 2022)

Answer - (b)

Solution: To calculate Hari's Z-score, we can use the formula: Z = (X - μ) / σ

Where: X is Hari's score

μ is the mean (class average)

σ is the standard deviation

Given: Hari's score (X) = 76 Class average (μ) = 68 Standard deviation (σ) = 5

Plugging in the values into the formula, we have: Z = (76 - 68) / 5

Z = 8 / 5

Z = 1.6 Therefore, Hari's Z-score is 1.6.

Question 2. A principal at a school claim that the students in his school are above average intelligence level. A random sample of 30 students IQ score have mean score of 112.5. The mean population IQ is 100 with standard deviation of 15. Whether principal claim is right or wrong.

Solution: H_0: u = 100 At 5% level of significance

H_1: u > 100 Critical value =1.645

$$Z = \frac{\bar{x} - u}{\frac{\sigma}{\sqrt{n}}} = \frac{112.5 - 100}{\frac{15}{\sqrt{30}}} = 4.56$$

4.56 > 1.645, Null Hypothesis is rejected, thus principal claim is right.

Question 3. The OLS regression output of wages on education (years of schooling S) and cognitive ability scores(CA) comes out to be:

$$\text{wages} = \underset{(1.98)}{-3.36} + \underset{(0.12)}{0.64S} + \underset{(0.05)}{0.15\,CA}$$

With figures in parenthesis giving standard error.

The explained sum of square is 4745.75 with degree of freedom 2 and residual sum of square is 33651.28 with degree of freedom 567, which of the following statements are true?

A. For one year increase in schooling, wage per hour increases by 640 Rs, on the average, when CA is kept constant.

B. The value of t-statistic of CA is 3.

C. The F statistic is given by $F = \frac{4735.75/2}{33651.28/567}$

D. The F statistic is given by $F = \frac{33651.28/567}{4735.75/2}$

Choose the correct answer:

1. A, C
2. A, B, D
3. A, B, C
4. A, D

Answer: 3

Solution: Wages =- 3.36+0.64s+0.15CA

Wages depend on schooling and cognitive ability scores.

0.64 means - for 1 year increase in schooling, wages increase by Rs. 640. When CA is held constant. (there is positive sign, so wages and S has positive relation)

Test statistic for CA,

$$CA = \frac{(\hat{\beta} - \beta)}{SE(\hat{\beta})} = \frac{0.15}{0.05} = 3$$

$$F\ static \ = \frac{ESS/df}{RSS/df} = \frac{4735.75/2}{33651.28/567}$$

ESS: explained sum of square

RSS: residual sum of square

Variance Ratio Test

1. F test: given by Fisher
2. F test is used to test two independent estimations of variance.

$$Variance\ Ratio \ = \frac{S_1{}^2}{S_2{}^2}$$

3. Testing of overall significance of regression by F-test.
4. Value of F-test lies between 0 to ∞.

Chi-Square Test

Given by Karl Pearson. It is non- parametric test. Value lies between 0 to 1. Sample size must be greater than 50.

The square of a standard normal variable is called a chi-square variate with 1 degree of freedom. If x is a random variable following normal distribution with mean μ and standard deviation σ, then (x- μ)/ σ is standard normal variate (Z).

$$Z^2 = \left(\frac{x-\mu}{\sigma}\right)^2$$

is a chi-square (χ^2) variate with 1 degree of freedom.

Application:

1. Used to test goodness of fit (R^2). It is used to test if the deviation between observation (observed values) and theory (expected values). Formula is:

   $$x^2 = \sum \frac{(O_i - E_i)^2}{E_i}$$

   where O_i = observed value(actual value)

   E_i= expected value

2. Used to test independence of attributes. A contingency table is a frequency distribution table that organizes data for a chi-square test of independence. It's also known as a cross-tabulation or two-way table. They are constructed by listing all the levels of one variable as rows in a table and the levels of the other variables as columns, then finding the joint or cell frequency for each cell. The cell frequencies are then summed across both rows and columns. For the contingency table having r rows and c columns, the test statistic follows chi-square distribution with (r-1) (c-1) degree of freedom provided.

Parameteric Test v/s Non-parametric Test

	Parametric test	Non-parametric test
1.	Used for ratio or interval data	For ordinal or nominal data
2.	Used for normal distribution	Any distribution
3.	Mean is usual central measure	Median is usual central measure
4.	Information about population is completely known	No information available
5.	Specific assumptions made regarding population	Assumption free test
6.	Z test, F test, Paired t test, unpaired t test, one way ANOVA, Pearson correlation are parametric test.	Chy square test, Wilcoxon rank sum test, Mann Whitney U test, Kruskal Wallis test, Spearman correlation are non-parametric test.

ANOVA (Analysis of Variance)

Given by Fisher.

ANOVA break down the total variation of a variable into additive components which may be attributed to various separate factors. E.g. variation in yield may be attributed to X1 (type of seed), X2 (type of fertilizer), X3 (type of irrigation). So, we may break down the total variation in yield in to three separate components.

ANOVA Table

Source of variation	Degrees of freedom	Sum of Square	Mean Sum of Square	F-statistic
X	$V_1 = k - 1$	SSR (Sum of Square Regression)	MSR (Mean Square due to regression)	$F = \frac{MSR}{MSE}$ OR $F = \frac{\left(\frac{SSR}{k}\right)}{\left(\frac{RSS}{n-k-1}\right)}$
Error	$v_2 = n - k$	RSS (Sum of Square Residuals or Residual Sum of Square)	MSE (Mean Square due to Errors)	

If calculated value of F is greater than critical value (tabulated value), then H0 is rejected. (overall regression is significant).

Other Formulae

$$F = \frac{explained\ variation\ /(k-1)}{unexplained\ variation/(n-k)}$$

$$F = \frac{R^2/(k-1)}{(1-R^2)\ /(n-k)}$$

Specification Error

It arises due to

a. inclusion of irrelevant variables in model.
b. exclusion of relevant variables in model
c. incorrect functional form.

RESET (Ramsey Regression Equation Specification Error test) is a statistical test for specification error in a linear regression model.

Mathematical Economics

Sequence and Series

Collection of objects in order form is termed as **sequence**.

For e.g. Population of human beings at different times form a sequence.

The amount of money deposited in a bank over a number of years forms a sequence.

Sequences following specific patterns are called progressions, for e.g., arithmetic progression and geometric progressions.

Series

Let a_1, a_2, a_3, - - - - - - a_n be a given sequence. Then the expression $a_1 + a_2 + a_3 + - - - a_n$ is called the series associated with the given sequence. Series is represented as sigma notation $\sum_{K=1}^{n} a_K$

Arithmetic progression

Let as consider an A.P with first term a and common difference d, i.e. a, a+d, a+2d, ------------n^{th} Term of the A.P. is $a_n = a + (n - 1)d$

a = first term   l = last term   d = common difference

n = number of terms S_n = sum to n terms of A.P

$$S_n = \frac{n}{2}[2a + (n - 1)d] \text{ or } S_n = \frac{n}{2}[a + l]$$

Geometric Progression

A, ar, ar^2, ar^3 is a geometric progression

Where a is the first term and r is common ratio.

$$a_n = ar^{n-1}$$

$$s_n = \frac{a(1 - r^n)}{1 - r}$$

Geometric mean of two positive numbers a and b is the number $\sqrt{ab}$

Arithmetic mean of two positive numbers a and b is $A = \frac{a+b}{2}$

Sum to n terms of special series

i) $1 + 2 + 3 + \cdots \ldots\ldots\ldots\ldots\ldots\ldots.. n$ $(sum\ of\ first\ n\ natural\ numbers)$

$$S_n = \frac{n(n+1)}{2}$$

ii) $1^2 + 2^2 + 3^2 + \cdots \ldots\ldots\ldots\ldots\ldots n^2$ $(sum\ of\ squares\ of\ the\ first\ n\ natural\ numbers)$

$$S_n = \frac{n(n+1)(2n+1)}{6}$$

iii) $1^3 + 2^3 + 3^3 + \cdots \ldots\ldots\ldots\ldots\ldots n^3$ $(sum\ of\ cubes\ of\ the\ first\ n\ natural\ numbers)$

$$S_n = \frac{[n(n+1)]^2}{4}$$

Theory of Sets

Set is a well-defined collection of objects. [This collection must be mathematical valid] i.e. A is a set of natural numbers. Collection of beautiful girls does not form a set.

Two ways of expressing a set

i) **Roster form** or Tabular form for e.g. A is a set of natural numbers from 1 to 10. It is written as A= {1,2,3,4,5,6,7,8,9,10}

ii) **Set builder form**

A is a set of natural numbers can be written as **A** = {x ∈ N,1≤ *x* ≤10} or **A** = {x*:* *x* is a natural number and 1≤ *x* ≤10}

Important types of sets

Open set: It does not include boundary point i.e. x>5

Closed set: It includes all the boundary points i.e. x>=5

Finite set: Set having finite number of elements

Infinite set: Set having infinite number of elements.

Properties: The union of finite number of a closed set is closed set.

Intersection of finite number of open sets is an open set.

Empty set is both open and closed. (If a set has no elements, then it is called an empty set. As there are no points in an empty set, it does not contain any of the boundary points, so it is an open set. Since there are no points on the boundary, it includes all its boundary points so it is closed).

Disjoint set: If two sides have no element in common, then they are disjoint sets.

i.e., A = {All odd numbers}

B = {All Even Numbers}

Then A and B are disjoint set.

Subset: If every element of set A is an element of B, then A is called subset of B written as

A ⊆ B

i.e. A = {2,4,6}

B = {2,4,6,7,8} then A ⊆ B

Equal sets: Two sets of A and B are said to be equal if every member of B is a member of A and conversely every member of A is a member of B

i.e., A = {2, 4, 6, 8}

B = {2, 4, 6, 8} then A = B

Equivalent sets: They have same number of elements

i.e., A = {1, 2, 3}

B = {x, y, z}

Then A and B are equivalent sets.

Null Set: It contains no element

i.e. [A = {x : x is a married bachelor}] = Φ

Power set: Power set is the set of all subsets of a set A and is denoted by

P (A). If A = {a, b, c}

Then subsets of A are Φ, {a}, {b}, {c}, {a, b}, {b,c}, {c,a}, {a,b,c}

P (A) = [Φ, {a}, {b}, {c}, {a, b}, {b, c}, {c, a}, {a, b, c}]

Union of two sets: The set of all elements which are either in set A or in set B or in both is called union of two sets A and B and is denoted by A ∪ B.

i.e., A = {1,2 3, 4,5} & B = {4,6,8,10 }. Find A ∪ B.

A ∪ B = {1, 2 3, 4, 5, 6, 8, 10}

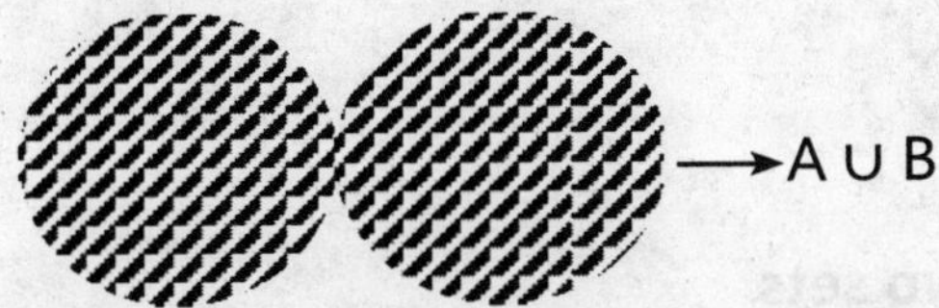

Intersection of Two Sets: The intersection of two set A and B is the set A ∩ B composed of those elements which belong to both A and B.

i.e., A = {a, b, c, d} and B = {c, d, e}. Find A ∩ B

A ∩ B = {c, d}

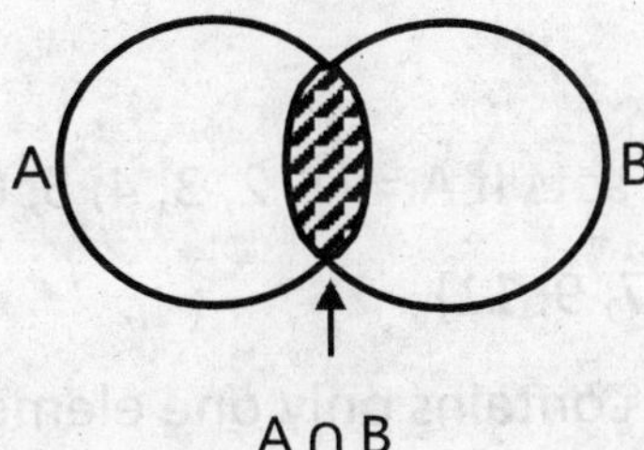

Commutative laws for union and Intersection of two sets.

A ∪ B = B ∪ A

A ∩ B = B ∩ A

Associative laws for union and intersection for two sets.

A ∪ (B ∪ C) = (A ∪ B) ∪ C

A ∩ (B ∩ C) = (A ∩ B) ∩ C

Distributive law

A ∩ (B ∪ C) = (A ∩ B) ∪ (A ∩ C)

A ∪ (B ∩ C) = (A ∪ B) ∩ (A ∪ C)

Complement of A Set

Let U be the universal set and A be its sub - set, the set of all those elements of U which do not belong to A, is called complements of A and is written as A^C

i.e. $U = \{x: x \text{ is a natural number } < 12\}$

$A = \{1, 2, 5, 6, 10, 11\}$

$A^C = \{3, 4, 7, 8, 9\}$

De Morgan's Law

$(A \cup B)^C = A^C \cap B^C$

$(A \cap B)^C = A^C \cup B^C$

Cartesian product of two sets

$If\ A = \{1, 2, 3\}, B = \{2, 4\}\ find\ A \times B$

$A \times B = \{(1,2), (1,4), (2,2), (2,4), (3,2)\ (3,4)\}$

Difference of sets

If A = {5, 6, 9, 10, x, y} & B = {9, x, 15, 12}

A – B = {5, 6, 10, y}

Symmetric difference of two sets If A = {1, 2, 3, 4, 5, 6} & B = {3, 5, 7, 9, 11}

(A – B) ∪ (B – A) = {1, 2, 4, 6, 7, 9, 11}

Unit set or singleton set → It contains only one element: -

A = {0} is a unit set.

Universal set → it is the total of elements under consideration.

i.e. U = {1, 2, 3, 4, 5, 6} is a universal set obtained by throwing a dice.

Idempotent Property:

a) A ∪ A = A b) A ∩ A = A

Identity Property

A ∪ Φ = A A ∩ U = A

Complement Law

A∪A^C=U A ∩ A^C = Φ

Functions

Function shows the relationship between variables. For e.g., if Y is dependent variable and X is an independent variable then Y = $2X^2$ is a function.

Explicit function → It is that function in which a dependent variable Y is a function of an independent variable X.

For e.g. Y =5 x + 3

Implicit function is that function which shows the mutual relationship between variable Y and X.

For e.g. $x^2 + y^2 + 2xy = 0$

Linear function: Highest power unity.

$$Y = 5x + 3$$

Quadratic function: Highest power of X is 2.

$$Y = 2x^2 + 7x + 6$$

Exponential function: It is in the form

$$f(x) = a^x$$

Polynomial function: It is in the form

$$f(x) = a_0x^n + a_1x^{n-1} + a_2x^{n-2} + \cdots \cdot a_n$$

$$Y = 5x^4 + 3x^3 + 6x^2 - 7x + 8$$

Constant function: degree zero.

$$i.e. y = a$$

Rational Function: It is in the form.

$$Y = \frac{f(x)}{g(x)}$$

$$Y = \frac{5x^2 + 6}{6x - 1}$$

Composite function: Function of a function

$$Y = f\ (u)\ and\ U = g(x)$$

$$Y = f\ [\ g(x)\ ]\ is\ composite\ function\ of\ x.$$

Reciprocal function: It is in the form

$$y = \frac{1}{x}, where\ x \neq 0$$

Quadratic function: A quadratic function is a polynomial function that has a highest exponent of 2.

The curve of quadratic function is parabolic. It can be U-shaped or inverted U-shaped.

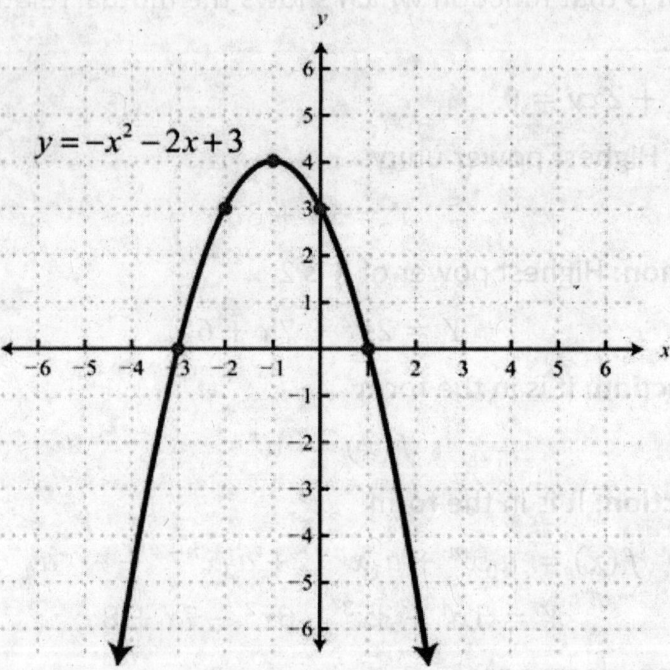

Exponential function: An exponential function is a Mathematical function in the form f (x) = a^x, where "x" is a variable and "a" is a constant which is called the base of the function and it should be greater than 0. The most commonly used exponential function base is the transcendental number e, which is approximately equal to 2.71828.

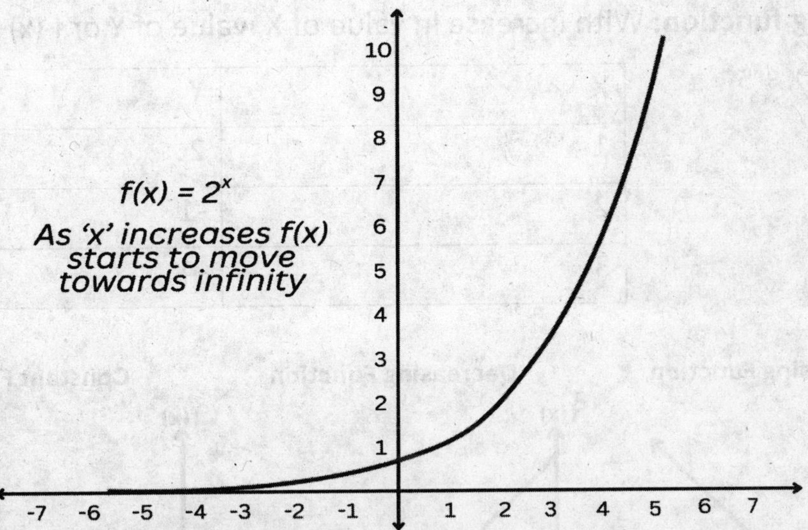

Cubic function: A cubic function is a polynomial function of degree 3 and is of the form f (x) = $ax^3 + bx^2 + cx + d$.

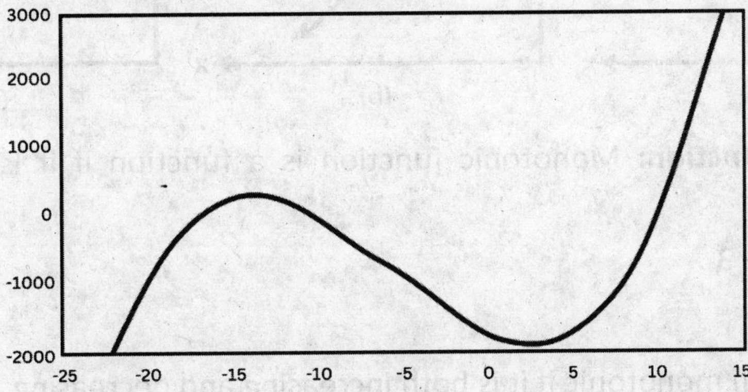

Linear function: A linear function is a function which forms a straight line in a graph. It is generally a polynomial function whose degree is utmost 1 or 0.

Increasing function: With increase in values of X, values of Y or f(x) also increasing.

i.e., Y = 2X + 3.

X	Y
1	5
2	7
3	9

Decreasing function: With increase in value of X, value of Y or f (x) decreasing.

i.e., Y = - 3X + 5

X	Y
1	2
2	-1
3	-4

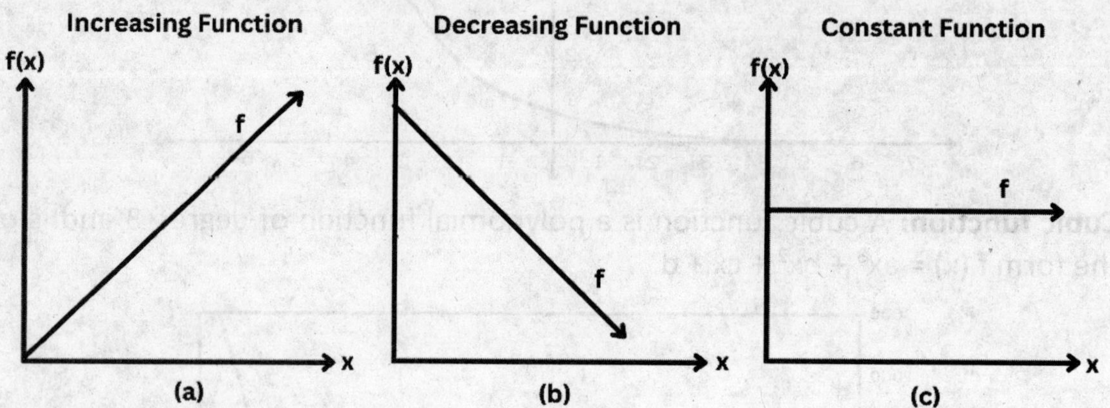

Monotonic function: Monotonic function is a function if it is increasing or decreasing.

i.e., Y = 2x + 3

$Y = -x^5$

Function is non monotonic if it is both increasing and decreasing. i.e., $Y = X^2$

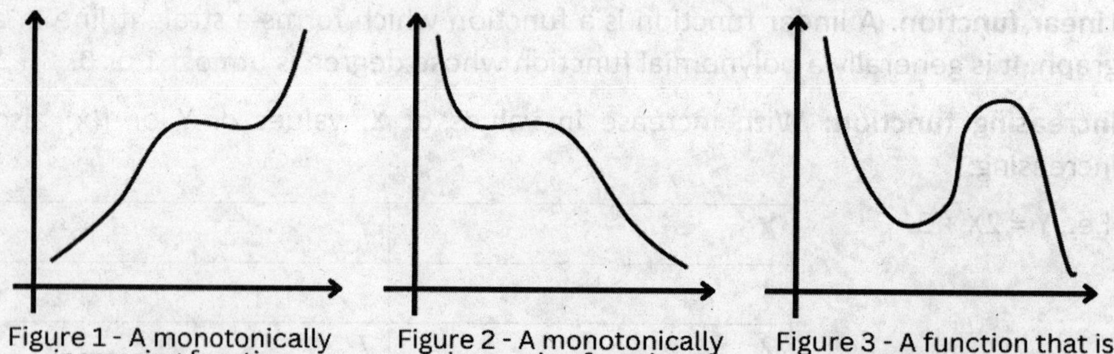

Figure 1 - A monotonically increasing function

Figure 2 - A monotonically decreasing function

Figure 3 - A function that is not monotonic

Limits

If 'x' be a real variable and 'a' be a fixed constant, then by limit x approach to a, we mean that X attains value very near to 'a '.

For e.g., find the limit of function f(x) = 2x + 3 as x → 2

$$\lim_{x\to 2} 2x + 3 = 2(2) + 3 = 7$$

Continuity

A function f (x) is said to be continuous at a given point when its left-hand limit and right-hand limit is equal to the value of function at that point

$$\underbrace{\lim_{X\to a^-}}_{\substack{\text{Left handed limit} \\ \text{Here } a^- \text{ denotes the} \\ \text{Value of } x \text{ which is} \\ \text{Very close to a but} \\ \text{Slightly less than a.}}} f(x) = \underbrace{\lim_{X\to a^+}}_{\substack{\text{Right handed limit} \\ \text{Here } a^+ \text{ denotes the} \\ \text{Value of } x \text{ which is} \\ \text{Very near to a but} \\ \text{Slightly more than a.}}} f(x) = f(a)$$

Matrix

Let us consider the equations,

3x + 4y - 5z = 0 6x - 7y + 2z = 0

The Coefficient of these two equations can be written as:

$$A = \begin{bmatrix} 3 & 4 & -5 \\ 6 & -7 & 2 \end{bmatrix}$$

This rectangular array is called a matrix.

$$\boldsymbol{Diagonal\ Matrix} = \begin{bmatrix} d_1 & 0 & 0 \\ 0 & d_2 & 0 \\ 0 & 0 & d_3 \end{bmatrix}$$

Scaler Matrix

$$= \begin{bmatrix} 1 & 0 & 0 \\ 0 & 1 & 0 \\ 0 & 0 & 1 \end{bmatrix} [\textit{Diagonal matrix whose diagonal elements are equal}]$$

Symmetric Matrix

A matrix A is called symmetric if it is equal to its transpose, i.e., $A = A^T$ ($a_{ij} = a_{ji}$).

$$A = \begin{bmatrix} a & h & g \\ h & b & f \\ g & f & c \end{bmatrix} \qquad B = \begin{bmatrix} 1 & 2 & 4 \\ 2 & 7 & 3 \\ 4 & 3 & 8 \end{bmatrix}$$

Here $A = A^T$ and $B = B^T$

Skew Symmetric Matrix

A matrix A is called skew symmetric matrix if its transpose is equal to its negative, i.e., $A^T = -A$ ($a_{ij} = -a_{ij}$)

$$A = \begin{bmatrix} 0 & h & g \\ -h & 0 & f \\ -g & -f & 0 \end{bmatrix}$$

Orthogonal Matrix: A square matrix is said to be orthogonal if A'A = AA' = 1

Singular Matrix when $|A| = 0$

Non-Singular Matrix when $|A| \neq 0$

Properties Of Matrix Addition

Commutative law: A+B = B+A

Associative law: (A + B) + C = A + (B + C)

Properties of multiplication of matrices: Associative law: (AB)C=A(BC)

Distributive law: A (B + C) = AB + AC

(A + B) C = AC + BC

Properties of transpose of matrix:
(i) (A')'=A
(ii) (kA)'=kA'
(iii) (A+B)'=A' + B'
(iv) (AB)' = B'A'

Inverse of A Matrix

It is defined usually for square matrices. For any m*n square matrix, there exists an inverse matrix. If A is the square matrix, then A^{-1} is the inverse of matrix A and satisfy the property:

$AA^{-1} = A^{-1}A = I$, where I is identity matrix.

Also, determinant of the square matrix should not be equal to zero.

Steps to find inverse of matrix:

1. Find determinant
2. Then find cofactors and adjoint of matrix: The transpose of a cofactor matrix of the square matrix is called the adjoint of the matrix. The transpose of a matrix is a new matrix created by switching the rows and columns of the original matrix.
3. Then apply formula for inverse

$$A^{-1} = \frac{1}{|A|} Adj\ A$$

For a system of equation, unique solution of equation AX+B is $X=A^{-1}B$ where determinant of A is not equal to zero.

Illustration. Find inverse of a matrix

$$A = \begin{bmatrix} 1 & 3 & 3 \\ 1 & 4 & 3 \\ 1 & 3 & 4 \end{bmatrix}$$

$$|A| = 1\begin{vmatrix} 4 & 3 \\ 3 & 4 \end{vmatrix} - 3\begin{vmatrix} 1 & 3 \\ 1 & 4 \end{vmatrix} + 3\begin{vmatrix} 1 & 4 \\ 1 & 3 \end{vmatrix}$$

$$= 1|16-9| - 3|4-3| + 3|3-4|$$

$$= 1(7) - 3(1) + 3(-1)$$

$$= 7 - 3 - 3 = 1$$

$$A_{11} = \begin{vmatrix} 4 & 3 \\ 3 & 4 \end{vmatrix} = 16 - 9 = 7 \qquad (+1)$$

$$A_{12} = \begin{vmatrix} 1 & 3 \\ 1 & 4 \end{vmatrix} = 4 - 3 = 1 \qquad (-1)$$

$$A_{13} = \begin{vmatrix} 1 & 4 \\ 1 & 3 \end{vmatrix} = 3 - 4 = -1 \qquad (+1)$$

$$A_{21} = \begin{vmatrix} 3 & 3 \\ 3 & 4 \end{vmatrix} = 12 - 9 = 3 \qquad (-1)$$

$$A_{22} = \begin{vmatrix} 1 & 3 \\ 1 & 4 \end{vmatrix} = 4 - 3 = 1 \qquad (+1)$$

$$A_{23} = \begin{vmatrix} 1 & 3 \\ 1 & 3 \end{vmatrix} = 3 - 3 = 0 \qquad (-1)$$

$$A_{31} = \begin{vmatrix} 3 & 3 \\ 4 & 3 \end{vmatrix} = 9 - 12 = -3 \qquad (+1)$$

$$A_{32} = \begin{vmatrix} 1 & 3 \\ 1 & 3 \end{vmatrix} = 3 - 3 = 0 \qquad (-1)$$

$$A_{33} = \begin{vmatrix} 1 & 3 \\ 1 & 4 \end{vmatrix} = 4 - 3 = 1 \qquad (+1)$$

$$Adj\ A = \begin{bmatrix} 7 & -1 & -1 \\ -3 & 1 & 0 \\ -3 & 0 & 1 \end{bmatrix}$$

$$= \begin{bmatrix} 7 & -3 & -3 \\ -1 & 1 & 0 \\ -1 & 0 & 1 \end{bmatrix}$$

$$A^{-1} = \frac{1}{|A|} Adj\ A$$

$$= \frac{1}{1}\begin{bmatrix} 7 & -3 & -3 \\ -1 & 1 & 0 \\ -1 & 0 & 1 \end{bmatrix} = \begin{bmatrix} 7 & -3 & -3 \\ -1 & 1 & 0 \\ -1 & 0 & 1 \end{bmatrix}$$

For equation Formula is

$X = A^{-1}B$

To find cofactors sign takes place $= \begin{bmatrix} + & - & + \\ - & + & - \\ + & - & + \end{bmatrix} \begin{bmatrix} + & - \\ - & + \end{bmatrix}$

For minors, there are no signs.

Rank of Matrix

It is the order of the largest square submatrix where determinant is not zero. i.e.,

$$A = \begin{bmatrix} 3 & 6 & 6 \\ 0 & 4 & 5 \\ 3 & 2 & 1 \end{bmatrix}$$

Determinant of A is zero. We can find a 2*2 submatrix whose determinant is not zero. So rank is 2.

Rule for Matrix Multiplications

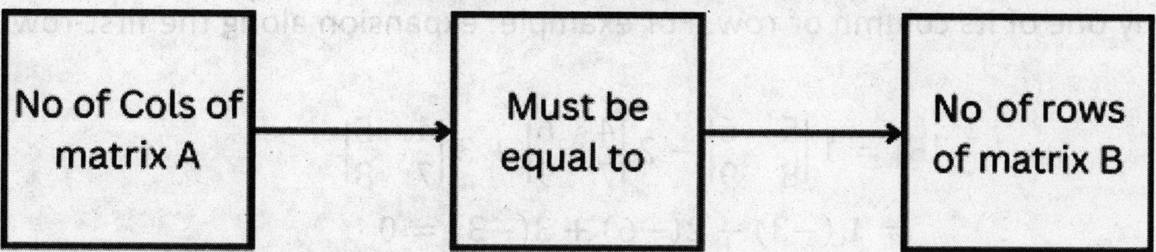

1st Row is multiplied with 1st column.

$$A = \begin{bmatrix} 1 & 2 \\ 4 & 6 \end{bmatrix} \qquad B = \begin{bmatrix} 3 & 1 \\ 2 & 5 \end{bmatrix}$$

$$A = \begin{bmatrix} 1 \times 3 + 2 \times 2 & 1 + 5 \times 2 \\ 4 \times 3 + 6 \times 2 & 4 \times 1 + 6 \times 5 \end{bmatrix}$$

Important Properties of Determinants

1. The determinant remains unaltered if its rows are changed into columns and the columns into rows. This is known as the property of reflection.

2. If all the elements of a row (or column) are zero, then the determinant is zero.

3. If all elements of a row (or column) are proportional (identical) to the elements of some other row (or column), then the determinant is zero.

4. The interchange of any two rows (or columns) of the determinant changes its sign.

5. If all the elements of a row (or column) of a determinant are multiplied by a non-zero constant, then the determinant gets multiplied by the same constant.

6. The "triangle property" of a determinant state that if all elements of a matrix below and above the main diagonal are zero (meaning the matrix is triangular), then the determinant of that matrix is simply the product of the elements on the main diagonal.

$$\begin{vmatrix} a & b & c \\ 0 & e & f \\ 0 & 0 & i \end{vmatrix} = \begin{vmatrix} a & 0 & 0 \\ d & e & 0 \\ g & h & i \end{vmatrix} = a \times e \times i$$

7. The determinant of the matrix can be computed by using Laplace expansion along any one of its column or row. For example: expansion along the first-row yields:

$$|B| = 1\begin{vmatrix}5 & 6\\8 & 9\end{vmatrix} - 2\begin{vmatrix}4 & 6\\7 & 9\end{vmatrix} + 3\begin{vmatrix}4 & 5\\7 & 8\end{vmatrix}$$

$$= 1\,(-3) - 2(-6) + 3(-3) = 0$$

Laplace expansion along the second column yields the same result.

$$|B| = -\,2\begin{vmatrix}4 & 6\\7 & 9\end{vmatrix} + 5\begin{vmatrix}1 & 3\\7 & 9\end{vmatrix} - 8\begin{vmatrix}1 & 3\\4 & 6\end{vmatrix}$$

$$= -2(-6) + 5(-12) - 8(-6) = 0$$

Input Output Technique

Given by Leontief in 1951. It is used to analyze inter industry relationship in order to understand the interdependencies of the economy. As the inputs of one industry is the output of the other industry and vice versa. Wassily Leontief, who was a Soviet-American economist, developed the input-output analysis method, earning him the Nobel Prize in Economics in 1973.

Illustration

Suppose we have an equation X = AX + D and we need to find Leontief inverse.

A: Matrix of inter industry coefficient

D: Final demand matrix

X – AX = D

B = (I - A) X

X = $(I - A)^{-1}$ D

$(I - A)^{-1}$ is an input output inverse or Leontief inverse.

For three sectors:

$$A = \begin{bmatrix}0.3 & 0.4 & 0.2\\0.2 & 0.0 & 0.5\\0.1 & 0.3 & 0.1\end{bmatrix},\ D = \begin{bmatrix}100\\40\\50\end{bmatrix},\ X = \begin{bmatrix}X_1\\X_2\\X_3\end{bmatrix}$$

$X = (I - A)^{-1}D$

$$I - A = \begin{bmatrix} 0.7 & -0.4 & -0.2 \\ -0.2 & 1.0 & -0.5 \\ 0.1 & -0.3 & 0.9 \end{bmatrix}$$

After finding cofactors

$$Adj(I - A) = \begin{bmatrix} 0.75 & 0.23 & 0.16 \\ 0.42 & 0.61 & 0.25 \\ 0.40 & 0.39 & 0.62 \end{bmatrix}$$

$$= \begin{bmatrix} 0.75 & 0.42 & 0.40 \\ 0.23 & 0.61 & 0.39 \\ 0.16 & 0.25 & 0.62 \end{bmatrix}$$

$(I - A) = 0.75 \times 0.7 + 0.23(-0.4) + (0.16)(-0.2)$

= 0.401

$$(I - A)^{-1} = \frac{1}{(I - A)} Adj(I - A)$$

$$\frac{1}{0.401}\begin{bmatrix} 0.75 & 0.42 & 0.40 \\ 0.23 & 0.61 & 0.39 \\ 0.16 & 0.25 & 0.62 \end{bmatrix}$$

$x = (I - A)^{-1}D$

$$\begin{bmatrix} x_1 \\ x_2 \\ x_3 \end{bmatrix} = \frac{1}{0.401}\begin{bmatrix} 0.75 & 0.42 & 0.40 \\ 0.23 & 0.61 & 0.39 \\ 0.16 & 0.25 & 0.62 \end{bmatrix}\begin{bmatrix} 100 \\ 40 \\ 50 \end{bmatrix}$$

$$= \frac{1}{0.401}\begin{bmatrix} 0.75 \times 100 + 0.42 \times 40 + 0.40 \times 50 \\ 0.23 \times 100 + 0.61 \times 40 + 0.39 \times 50 \\ 0.16 \times 100 + 0.25 \times 40 + 0.62 \times 50 \end{bmatrix}$$

In this way you can solve it further.

Hawkins Simon Conditions

a) Determinant of the Matrix (I - A) should always positive.

b) The diagonal elements should be positive.

Let us take apply these conditions on the following matrix and analyze what does this condition imply

$$|I - A| = \begin{vmatrix} 1 - a_{11} & -a_{12} \\ -a_{21} & 1 - a_{22} \end{vmatrix}$$

a) $1 - a_{11} > 0$ or $a_{11} < 1$

b) $(1 - a_{11})(1 - a_{22}) - a_{12}a_{21} > 0$

Open Input Output Model

When the model beside the 'n' industries contain an open sector (household) which computes the final demand for the product of each industry and which supplies a primary input by 'n' Industries themselves, then model is an open model (I-A) X = D

Close Input Output Model

When final demand and primary input do not appear, i.e., (I – A) X = 0

Disappearance of final demand means that we will have a homogenous equation system.

Linear Programming Problem

Linear programming given by Dantzig

Linear programming may be defined as a method of optimizing a linear function, of a number of constraints stated in the form of linear inequalities.

Objective function: In LPP, the objective is to maximize the profit etc. or to minimize the cost etc. Max. = 3X+4Y.

Structural constraint: In LPP, the constraints limit the stage to which we can pursue our objective.

Non - negativity constraints: the non- negativity constraints are that which assume that there cannot be negative values of the variables involved in the problem, i.e., $x \geq 0$, $y \geq 0$

Feasible solution: All possible solutions that satisfy the constraints.

Infeasible solution: It is the situation when the feasible region is empty.

Feasible region: It is a set of all possible, feasible solutions.

Optimal solution: In linear programming (LPP), an optimal solution is the feasible solution that gives the maximum or minimum value of the objective function.

Unbounded region: It is the region where the feasible region is continuing endlessly.

Slack variable: In an optimization problem, a slack variable is a variable that is added to an inequality constraint to transform it into an equality. We add slack variable in equation to make it equal. It is used in less than ($\leq$) inequality that represents unused resources.

Surplus variable: it is used in more than ($\geq$) inequality that represent use of excess resources. We subtract surplus variable from equation to make it equal.

Illustration 1. Suppose we want to solve the following LP:

Maximize: $Z = 3x_1 + 2x_2$

Subject to: $x_1 + x_2 \leq 10$ (Constraint 1)

$x_1 + 2x_2 \geq 6$ (Constraint 2)

$x_1, x_2 \geq 0$

We can transform the constraints into equalities:

1. For Constraint 1 (using a slack variable s_1):

$$x_1 + x_2 + s_1 = 10, \quad s_1 \geq 0$$

2. For Constraint 2 (using a surplus variable s_2):

$$x_1 + 2x_2 - s_2 = 6, \quad s_2 \geq 0$$

Now the LPP is ready for the simplex method.

Graphical method to solve LPP

Illustration 2. Minimize $0.6X_1 + X_2$ objective function

$10X_1 + 4X_2 \geq 20$................(1)

$5X_1 + 5X_2 \geq 20$..................(2)

$2X_1 + 6X_2 \geq 12$..................(3)

$Put\ X_1 = O\ in(1), X_2 = 5$

$Put\ X_2 = O\ in(1), X_1 = 2$

$Put\ X_1 = O\ in(2), X_2 = 4$

$Put\ X_2 = O\ in(2), X_1 = 4$

$Put\ X_1 = O\ in(3), X_2 = 2$

$Put\ X_2 = O\ in(3), X_1 = 6$

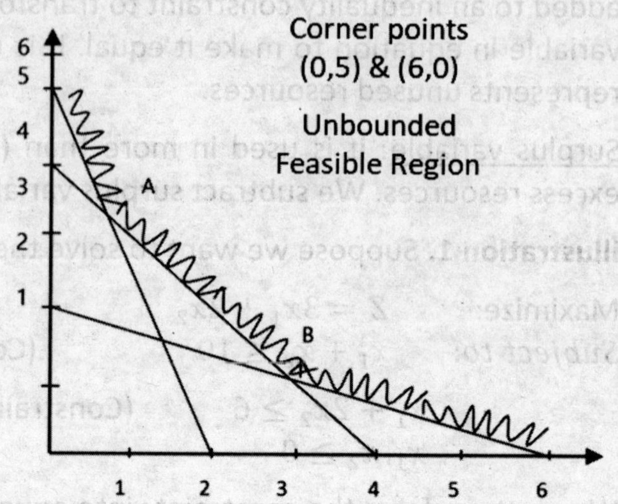

For point A,

Solve

$10X_1 + 4X_2 = 20$

$5X_1 + 5X_2 = 20$

$X_2 = 3.3$

$X_1 = 0.6$

For point B,

Solve

$5X_1 + 5X_2 = 20$

$2X_1 + 6X_2 = 12$

$X_2 = 1$

$X_1 = 3$

Now (0,5), (6, 0), (3, 1), (0.6, 3.3), put these points in objective function

$Z = 0.6X_1 + X_2 \rightarrow (0,5) = 5$

$Z = 0.6(6) + 0 \rightarrow (3,6) = 5$

$0.6(3) + 1 \rightarrow 2.8$

$0.6(0.6) + 3.3 \rightarrow 3.66$

Function is minimized where objective function gives minimum value. So, function is minimized at (3,1)

[Optimal solution]

$\boxed{X_1 = 3, X_2 = 1}$

Illustration 3. Solve the following linear programming problem graphically:

Maximize Z = 4x + y

subject to the constraints:

x + y ≤ 50

3x + y ≤ 90

x ≥ 0, y ≥ 0

Solve by above mentioned method.

Graph with bounded feasible region will be as follows

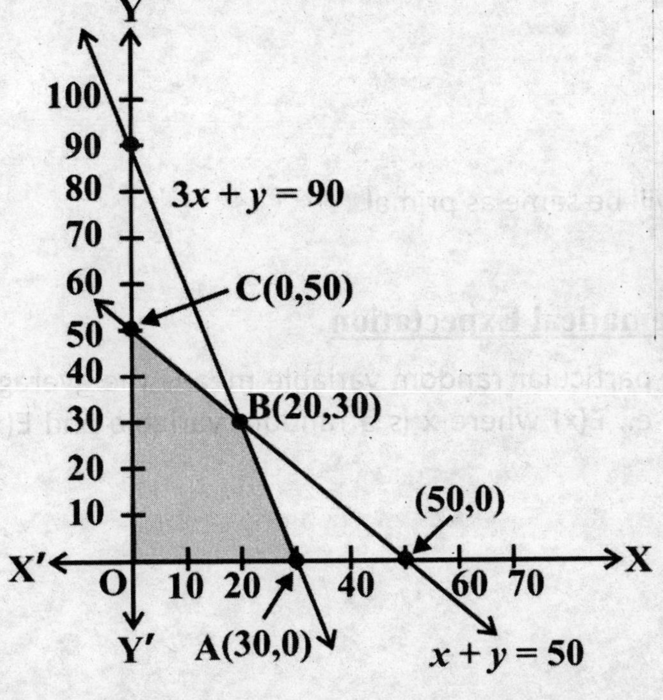

Corner Point	Corresponding value of Z	
(0, 0)	0	
(30, 0)	**120** ←	Maximum
(20, 30)	110	
(0, 50)	50	

Hence, maximum value of Z is 120 at the point (30, 0).

Some Key Points:

- It is known that the optimal solution of an LPP either exists uniquely, does not exist or exists infinitely.
- So, if a LPP admits two optimal solutions, it has an infinite number of optimal solutions.
- Dual of dual is primal.

Primal:

Maximize $6X_1 + X_2 + 4X_3$ subject to

$3X_1 + 7X_2 + X_3 \leq 15$

$X_1 - 2X_1 + 3X_3 \leq 20$

$X_1, X_2, X_3 \geq 0$

Dual:

Minimize $15Y_1 + 20Y_2$

$3Y_1 + Y_2 \geq 6$

$7Y_1 - 2Y_2 \geq 1$

$Y_1 + 3Y_2 \geq 4$

$Y_1, Y_2 \geq 0$

If we do its dual again, then it will be same as primal.

Mathematical Expectation

Mathematical expectation of a particular random variable means the average value of the random variable i.e., E(x) where x is a random variable and E(x) means mean(avg) of 'x'.

$Var(x) = E(x^2) - [E(x)]^2$

Random variable is a variable whose value is unknown. Properties of Mathematical Expectations:

E (a) = a ; where 'a' is constant

E (x + a) = E (x) + a

E (x + y) = E (x) + E (y)

E (x, y) = E (x) . E (y) [x and y are independent r.v's]

V (a x) = a2 V(x)

E (a x) = a E (x)

Var (x + a) = V (x)

Calculus

Derivative Rules

Product Rule: if $y = uv$, then $y' = u'v + uv'$

Quotient Rule: if $y = u/v$, then

$$y' = \left(\frac{u'v - uv'}{v^2}\right)$$

Chain Rule: if $y = y(z)\ and\ z = z(x)$, then

$$\frac{dy}{dx} = \frac{dy}{dz}\frac{dz}{dx}$$

Integration By parts Formula

$$\int uv\,dx = u\int v\,dx - \int \left(u'\int v\,dx\right)dx$$

Extremum (Maxima / Minima)

Optimization problem: A problem which seeks to maximize or minimize a linear function subject to certain constraints as determined by a set of linear inequalities is called an optimization problem.

Watch full video by scanning this QR Code

One variable case:

Necessary condition: Put first derivative of function (if we have to max. profit then first find profit function= Revenue -Cost) equal to zero and find the value of variable. (We can equate MR=MC to maximize profit).

Sufficient condition: if we have to minimize then second derivative should be positive.

If we have to maximize, then second derivative should be negative.

(or slope of MR should be less than slope of MC).

Two variable Case:

Necessary condition: Put first derivative (partial derivative) w.r.t. both variables equal to zero and find values of both variables.

Sufficient condition: For maxima

$$f_{xx} < 0 \; or \; |H_1| < 0$$

$$f_{xx}f_{yy} > f_{xy}f_{yx} or \; |H_2| (hessian \; determinant \; of \; second \; order) > 0$$

Here H is hessian matrix.

$$H = \begin{vmatrix} f_{xx} & f_{xy} \\ f_{yx} & f_{yy} \end{vmatrix}$$

Sufficient condition: For minima

$$f_{xx} > 0$$

$$f_{xx}f_{yy} > f_{xy}f_{yx}$$

Three Variable Case

Necessary Condition: Put first derivative (partial derivative) w.r.t three variables equal to zero and find values of three variables.

Sufficient Condition: For maxima: $|H_1| < 0, |H_2| > 0, |H_3| < 0$

For minima: $|H_1| < 0, |H_2| < 0, |H_3| < 0$

$$H = \begin{vmatrix} f_{xx} & f_{xy} & f_{xz} \\ f_{yx} & f_{yy} & f_{yz} \\ f_{zx} & f_{zy} & f_{zz} \end{vmatrix}$$

Constrained optimization:

To find values of three variables, we will use Lagrangean multiplier.

L = (objective function) - λ (subjective function)

OR

$$\mathcal{L}(x_1, x_2, x_3, \dots \dots x_n, \lambda) = f(x_1, x_2, \dots x_n) + \lambda[g(x_1, x_2, \dots x_n)]$$

[Note: Sign in between the objective function & the constraint can be either positive or negative.]

Sufficient (second order) conditions: For constrained extremum case, we shall encounter bordered hessian in place of hessian matrix.

The bordered Hessian is built as follows:

$$\begin{bmatrix} 0 & g_{x_1} & g_{x_1} & \cdots & g_{x_1} \\ g_{x_1} & \mathcal{L}_{x_1x_1} & \mathcal{L}_{x_1x_2} & \cdots & \mathcal{L}_{x_1x_n} \\ g_{x_2} & \mathcal{L}_{x_2x_1} & \mathcal{L}_{x_2x_2} & \cdots & \mathcal{L}_{x_2x_n} \\ \vdots & \vdots & \vdots & \ddots & \vdots \\ g_{x_n} & \mathcal{L}_{x_nx_1} & \mathcal{L}_{x_nx_2} & \cdots & \mathcal{L}_{x_nx_n} \end{bmatrix}$$

For maximum $|\overline{H}_2| > 0, |\overline{H}_3| < 0, \dots \dots \dots \dots$

For minimum $|\overline{H}_2| < 0, |\overline{H}_3| < 0, \dots \dots \dots \dots$

Diagrams for Maxima, Minima

For minima, second derivative is positive

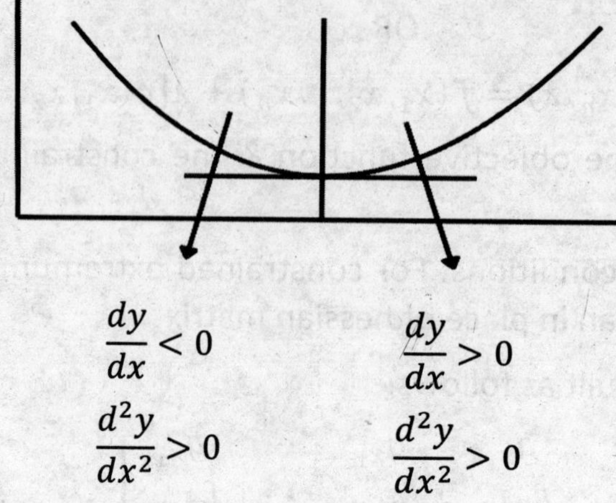

For maxima, second derivative is negative.

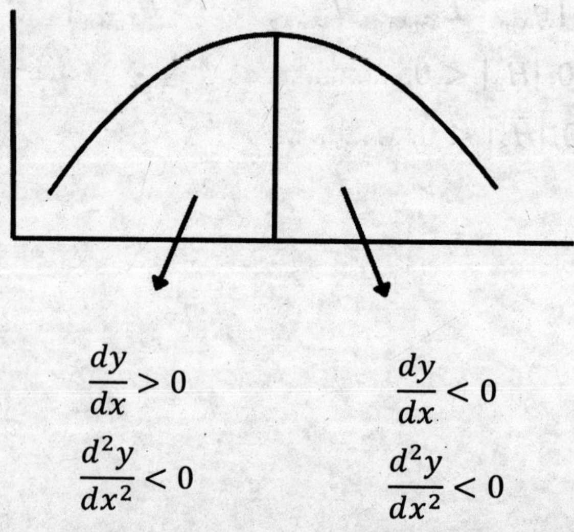

Some formulae

$$MR = dTR/dq$$

$$MR = AR\left[1 - \frac{1}{e}\right]$$

$$MPC = \frac{dC}{dY}$$

$$APC = \frac{C}{Y}$$

$$Multiplier = \frac{1}{1 - MPC}$$

$$APS = \frac{S}{y}$$

$$MPS = \frac{dS}{dY}$$

$$APC + APS = 1$$

$$MPC + MPS = 1$$

$$Profit = Revenue - Cost$$

$$Total\ revenue = price * quantity$$

Numerical Problems

Question 1. For the demand function $p = 10 - 2x - 0.5x^2$, what is price elasticity of demand at $x = 2$

Solution

$$P = 10 - 2x - 0.5x^2$$

$$\frac{dP}{dx} = -2 - x$$

$$\frac{dP}{dx} = -2 - 2 = -4$$

$$P = 10 - 2x - 0.5x^2$$

$$Put\ x = 2$$

$$P = 10 - 4 - 2 = 4$$

$$ed = \frac{-dx}{dP} \times \frac{P}{x}$$

$$= \frac{1}{4} \times \frac{4}{2}$$

$$= \frac{1}{2} = 0.5$$

Question 2. Total cost function of a producer is $C = 10 + 5Q + 2Q^2$. If price is 15, what is Marginal Cost of the producer in equilibrium?

Solution

$$TC = 10 + 5Q + 2Q^2$$

$$MC = \frac{d(TC)}{dQ}$$

$$MC = 5 + 4Q$$

$$TR = pQ$$

$$= 15Q$$

MR=15 or you may directly equate

$MR = MC$

$5 + 4Q = 15.$

$Q = 2.5$

$Put\ Q\ = 2.5\ in\ equation\ (1)$

$MC = 5 + 4(2.5)$

$= 5 + 10 = 15$

Question 3. Demand function is given as $p = 20 - 2x$. Find **consumer surplus** at $p = 4$.

Solution

$$4 = 20 - 2x$$

$$4 - 20 = -2x$$

$$x = 8$$

$$Cs = \int_0^x f(x)\,dx - \rho x = \int_0^8 (20 - 2x)\,dx - 4 \times 8 = \left[20x - \frac{2x^2}{2}\right]_0^8 - 32$$

$$For\ x = 8$$

$$= \left[20 \times 8 - \frac{2(8)^2}{2}\right] - \left[20 \times 0 - \frac{2(0)^2}{2}\right] - 32$$

$$= 160 - 64 - 32$$

$$= 64$$

Question 4. $C = q^3 - 10q^2 + 17q + 66$ and $p = 5$. Find the output at which profits are maximized.

Solution

$$TR = pq = 5q$$

$$MR = 5$$

$$MC = 3q^2 - 20q + 17$$

At equilibrium,

$$MR = MC$$

$$3q^2 - 20q + 17 = 5$$

$$3q^2 - 20q + 12$$

To solve the quadratic equation, $d = b^2 - 4ac = 400 - 4(36) = 400 - 144$

$$d = 256$$

$$q = \frac{-b \pm \sqrt{d}}{2a}$$

$$= \frac{-20 \pm \sqrt{256}}{6}$$

$$\frac{-20 \pm \sqrt{256}}{6} = \frac{36}{6}, \frac{4}{6}$$

$$= 6\ (Slope\ of\ MR < Slope\ of\ MC)$$

Thus, profit maximizing output = 6

Question 5. $I = 50 + 0.2Y$

$S = -150 + 0.4Y$

$G = 50$

I: Investment

S: Savings

G: Govt. Expenditure

Y: National Income

Find equilibrium level of income.

Solution: At equilibrium,

$AD \ = \ AS$

$I + G \ = \ S$

$50 + 0.2Y + 50 = -150 + 0.4Y$

$100 + 150 + 0.2Y - 0.4Y = 0$

$250 - 0.2y = 0$

$0.2Y = 250$

$Y = 1250$

Question 6. GDP Deflator Current Year is 110 GDP & annual growth is 15% . What is the rate of Growth due to real GDP ?

Solution:

$Real\ GDP = Nominal\ GDP - Price$

$= 15 - 10$

$= 5\%$

Question 7. Investment = 200

Govt. Expenditure =75

Net Taxes = 100

$C=25+0.8Y_D$

1) Find tax multiplier.

Solution

$C = 25 + 0.8(Y - 100) = 25 + 0.8Y - 80$

$MPC = 0.8$

$$Tax\ multiplier = -\frac{MPC}{1 - MPC} = -\frac{0.8}{1 - 0.8} = -\frac{0.8}{0.2} = -4$$

2) Find government expenditure multiplier.

Solution

$$Govt.\ expenditure\ multiplier = \frac{-MPC}{1 - MPC}$$

$$= \frac{1}{1 - 0.8} = \frac{1}{0.2} = \frac{10}{2} = 5$$

3) Find equilibrium income.

Solution

$Y = C + I + G$

$Y = 25 + 0.8(Y - 100) + 200 + 75$

$Y = 25 + 0.8Y - 80 + 275$

$Y - 0.8Y = 220$

$0.2Y = 220$

$Y = \frac{220}{2} \times 10$

$Y = 1100$

Question 8. If the demand and supply functions are given P_d = 20 - 5x and P_s = 4x +8; obtain Producer's surplus (December 2022 - shift 1)

(a) 31/9 (b) 32/9 (c) 129/9 (d) 29/9 x 221

Answer: (b)

Solution: At equilibrium,

$P_d = P_s$

$20 - 5x = 4x + 8$

$12 = 9x$

$4/3 = x$

$P = 20 - 5x$

$= 20 - 5(4/3)$

$= 20 - \frac{20}{3}$

$= \frac{60 - 20}{3} = \frac{40}{3}$

$$P_s = P_x - \int_d^x f(x)\,dx$$

$$= \frac{40}{3} \times \frac{4}{3} - \int_d^x f(4x+8)\,dx$$

$$= \frac{160}{9} \frac{-4\left(\frac{16}{9}\right)}{2} - 8\left(\frac{4}{3}\right)$$

$$= \frac{160}{9} - \frac{64}{18} - \frac{32}{3}$$

$$= \frac{320 - 64 - 192}{18}$$

$$= \frac{64}{18} = \boxed{\frac{32}{9}}$$

Question 9. A monopolist faces a linear demand curve p=100-4q, while his cost functions is C= 50+20q. The profit maximising output for this monopolist is (December 2018)

(a) 20 (b) 5

(c) 40 (d) 10

Answer (d)

Solution

For Profit Maximisation

MR = MC

$Now, TR = PQ$

$= (100 - 4Q)Q$

$TR = 100Q - 4Q^2$

$MR = 100 - 8Q$

$MC = 20$

Now,

$$100 - 8Q = 20$$

$$\frac{80}{8} = Q$$

$$\boxed{10 = Q}$$

2nd Condition of profit max is slope of MR should be less than slope of MC. i.e.

$$MR = 100 - 8Q$$
$$= -8$$
$$\boxed{-8 < 0}$$

Question 10. The cost function of a monopolist if C = 40 + 12x and demand function as P = 60 – 3x. What is his profit maximizing output level. (June 2019)

(a) 12 (b) 11

(c) 8 (d) 9

Answer: (c)

Solution:

Profit maximisation

$$MR = MC$$

$$TR = PX$$

$$= (60 - 3x)x$$

$$= 60x - 3x^2$$

$$MR = 6 - 6x$$

$$TC = 40 + 12x$$

$$MC + 12$$

$$60 - 6x = 12$$

$$-6x = 48$$

$$\boxed{x = 8}$$

Question 11. Suppose that for a particular economy for some time period investment = 200. Government expenditure was = 75. Net taxes were fixed at

100 and consumption was given by the consumption function C = 25 + 0.8 Y_d. Where Y_d is disposable income and Y is GDP. What is the value of tax multiplier $(\Delta Y/\Delta T)$

(a) -3

(b) 2

(c) -5

(d) -4

Answer: (d)

Solution:

$$Yd = Y - Taxes$$

$$Tax\ Multiplier = \frac{-MPC}{1 - MPC}$$

$$C = 25 + 0.8\,Yd$$

$$= 25 + 0.8\,(Y - 100)$$

$$= 25 + 0.8Y - 80$$

$$MPC = 0.8$$

$$Tax\ Multiplier = \frac{-0.8}{1 - 0.8}$$

$$= -4$$

Question 12. $Y = X^3 - 12X^2 + 36X + 8$, Identify which one of the following is correct?

A. Y is maximum at X =6 and minimum at X =2

B. Y is minimum at X =6 and maximum at X =2

C. Y has two inflexion point at X =6 and X =2

D. Y is maximum at X =2 and minimum at X =6

Answer: b

Solution:

$Y = X^3 - 12X^2 + 36X + 8$

$Y' = 3X^2 - 24X + 36$

$X^2 - 8X + 12 = 0$

$X^2 - 6X - 2X + 12 = 0$

$X(X-6) - 2(X-6) = 0$

$X = 6,2$

$Y'' = 6X - 24$

$Put\ X = 6$

$Y'' = 8(min)$

$Put\ X = 2$

$Y'' = -12(max)$

$So\ Y\ is\ max\ at\ X = 6\ and\ min\ at\ X = 2.$

Question 13. Integrate $\int x\sqrt{x^2+1}\,dx, x > 0$

1. $\frac{1}{2}(x^2+1)^{\frac{3}{2}} + C$
2. $\frac{1}{3}(x^2+1)^{\frac{3}{2}} + C$
3. $\frac{1}{3}(x^3+1)^{\frac{2}{3}} + C$
4. $\frac{1}{2}(x^3+1)^{\frac{2}{3}} + C$

Answer (b)

$\int \left(x\sqrt{x^2+1}\right) dx$ let x^2+1 = U

Then dU = 2x

But in equation we are having only X, So multiply & divide by 2

$\int \left(\frac{2x\sqrt{x^2+1}}{2}\right) dx$

$\frac{1}{2}\int (U)^{\frac{1}{2}}\, dU$

$\frac{1}{2}\frac{U^{\frac{3}{2}}}{\frac{3}{2}} + C$

$\frac{1}{2} \times U^{\frac{3}{2}} \times \frac{2}{3} + C$

$\frac{1}{3} \times (x^2 + 1)^{\frac{3}{2}} + C$

Question 14. If we have objective function involving a variable:

$U = f(X_1, X_2, X_3, \cdots X_n)\ subject\ to\ \emptyset\{X_1, X_2, X_3, \cdots X_n) = 0.$

The second order condition for extremum to be

A. For maximum $|\bar{H}_2| < 0, |\bar{H}_3| < 0, \dots \dots$

B. For maximum $|\bar{H}_2| > 0, |\bar{H}_3| < 0, \dots \dots$

C. For maximum $|\bar{H}_2| < 0, |\bar{H}_3| > 0, \dots \dots$

D. For minimum $|\bar{H}_2| < 0, |\bar{H}_3| < 0, \dots \dots$

E. For minimum $|\bar{H}_2| > 0, |\bar{H}_3| > 0, \dots \dots$

Choose the correct answer from the options given below:

(a) (A) and (D) only
(b) (B) and (D) only
(c) (C) and (E) only
(d) (B) and (E) only

Answer - (2)

Solution: In constrained extremum case, we shall encounter bordered hessian. These are the conditions for extremum in case of bordered hessian matrix.

For maximum $|\bar{H}_2| > 0, |\bar{H}_3| < 0, \dots \dots$

For minimum $|\bar{H}_2| < 0, |\bar{H}_3| < 0, \dots \dots$

Question 15. Find the extremum of $u = x^2 + y^2 + z^2$ subject to $x + y + z = 1$.

1. $(\bar{x}, \bar{y}, \bar{z}) = \left(\frac{1}{3}, \frac{1}{2}, \frac{1}{2}\right)$
2. $(\bar{x}, \bar{y}, \bar{z}) = \left(\frac{1}{2}, \frac{1}{2}, \frac{1}{3}\right)$
3. $(\bar{x}, \bar{y}, \bar{z}) = \left(\frac{1}{2}, \frac{1}{2}, \frac{1}{2}\right)$
4. $(\bar{x}, \bar{y}, \bar{z}) = \left(\frac{1}{3}, \frac{1}{3}, \frac{1}{3}\right)$

Answer: 4

$$L = (x^2 + y^2 + z^2) - \lambda(x + y + z - 1) \begin{bmatrix} langrange \\ multiplier \end{bmatrix}$$

$$\frac{\partial L}{\partial x} = 2x - \lambda, \frac{\partial L}{\partial y} = 2y - \lambda, \frac{\partial L}{\partial z} = 2z - \lambda$$

$$\frac{\partial L}{\partial \lambda} = -x - y - z + 1$$

$2x - \lambda = 0$	$2y - \lambda = 0$	$2z - \lambda = 0$
$\lambda = 2x$	$\lambda = 2y$	$\lambda = 2z$
$\frac{\lambda}{2} = x$	$\frac{\lambda}{2} = y$	$\frac{\lambda}{2} = z$

$$-x - y - z + 1 = 0$$

$$-\left(\frac{\lambda}{2} + \frac{\lambda}{2} + \frac{\lambda}{2}\right) + 1 = 0$$

$$-\frac{3\lambda}{2} + 2 = 0$$

$$\lambda = \frac{2}{3}$$

$\frac{2}{3} \times \frac{1}{2} = x$	$\frac{2}{3} \times \frac{1}{2} = y$	$\frac{2}{3} \times \frac{1}{2} = z$

So $x = y = z = \frac{1}{3}$

Question 16. Integrate: $\frac{x^2}{x+2}$

(a) $4x\,/\,(x+2)^2\ + c$

(b) $x^2/\,2 + 2x + 4\log(x+2) + c$

(c) $x^2/\,2 - 2x + 4\log(x+2) + c$

(d) $x^2/\,2 - 2x + c$

Answer: (c)

Solution:

```
X+2) X²  (X-2
     X² +2X
     -   -
    ---------
        -2X
        -2X - 4
         +    +
       ---------
              4
```

$$= \int \left(x - 2\frac{4}{x+2}\right) dx$$

$$= \int \left(\frac{(x-2)(x+2)+4}{x+2}\right) dx$$

$$= \int \left(\frac{(x-2+4)}{x+2}\right) dx$$

$$= \frac{x^2}{2} - 2x + 4\log(x+2) + c$$

Question 17. Given the total cost TC = Q3 – 10Q² + 60Q, what will be the minimum average cost? At what level of output will the minimum cost occur? (Q is the level of output)

(a) Minimum average cost is AC min = 35 at Q=5

(b) Minimum average cost is AC min = 175 at Q=5

(c) Minimum average cost is AC min = 170 at Q=1

(d) Minimum average cost is AC min = 45 at Q=1

Answer = (a)

Solution:

AC = TQ/Q

For minima put AC' (first derivative = 0) and AC'' (second derivative should be positive)

$TC = Q^3 - 10Q^2 + 60Q$

$AC = Q^2 - 10Q + 60$

$AC' = 2Q - 10 = 0$

$Q = 5$

For minima AC'' > 0

Now,

$$AC = 5^2 - 10(5) + 60Q$$
$$= 25 - 50 + 60$$
$$= 25 + 10$$
$$= 35$$

Question 18. For the diagram given below which of the following is correct in terms of derivatives?

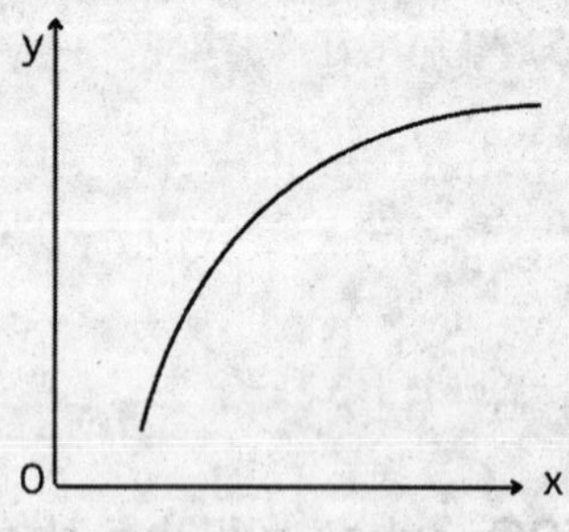

a) $\frac{dy}{dx} > 0, \frac{d^2y}{dx^2} > 0$

b) $\frac{dy}{dx} < 0, \frac{d^2y}{dx^2} < 0$

c) $\frac{dy}{dx} < 0, \frac{d^2y}{dx^2} > 0$

d) $\frac{dy}{dx} > 0, \frac{d^2y}{dx^2} < 0$

Answer: (d)

International Economics

Theories of Trade

Classical Theory of International Trade

According to the classical theory of international trade every country will produce the commodities for the production of which it is most suited in terms of its natural endowment, climate quality of soil, means of transport capital etc. It will produce these commodities in excess of its own requirement and will exchange the surplus with the imports of goods from other countries for the production of which it is not well suited or which it cannot produce at all. Thus, all countries produce and export these commodities in which they have cost advantages and import those commodities in which they have cost disadvantages.

Economists speak about three types of cost difference in production they are:

i) Absolute cost difference.

ii) Equal cost difference

iii) Comparative cost difference.

Absolute Advantage Theory (1776): - "Wealth of Nations"

International trade is beneficial only when the two nations have absolute differences in the cost of production of the commodity in which they specialize.

Assumptions:

(1) Complete specialization.

(2) 2 X 2 X 1 model

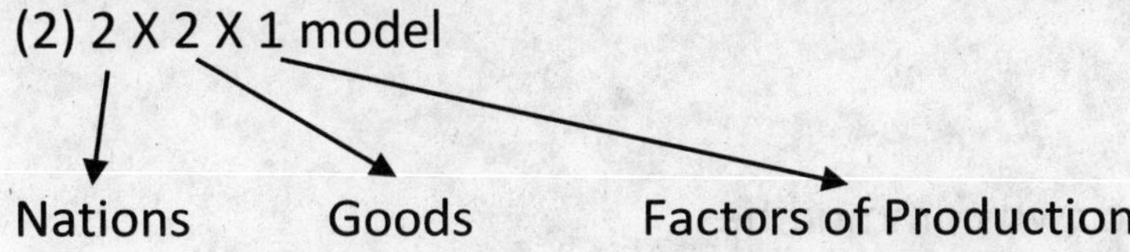

Nations Goods Factors of Production

(3) Perfect Competition.

(4) Full Employment.

(5) Constant returns to scale.

(6) Perfect mobility of factors within the nation but not outside the nation.

<u>*Theory:*</u>

Production of Commodity X and Y in Country A and B

Country	Com -X	Com -Y
A	10	5
B	5	10

Country A has an absolute advantage in the production of X and Country B has an absolute advantage in the production of Y. If A were to specialize in production of Com – X and use both unit of labor on it, its total production will be 20 units of X. If B specialize in production of Y, Its Total Production will 20 units of Y.

Equal Difference in Cost

Smith, in order to strengthen his argument in favour of absolute difference in cost, pointed out that trade is not possible if countries operate under equal difference in cost instead of absolute difference

Ricardo Theory of Comparative Difference in Costs (1817)

According to Ricardo the essence for international trade is not the absolute difference in cost but comparative difference in cost. Even if a country is less efficient in producing all goods (i.e., it has absolute disadvantage) it can still benefit from trade by focusing on its comparative advantage.

Thus, a country will export commodities in which its comparative advantage is the greatest and import commodities in which its comparative disadvantage is the least.

<u>*Assumptions:*</u>

1. There are two countries and two commodities.

2. There is a perfect competition both in commodity and factor market.

3. Cost of production is expressed in terms of labour i.e. value of a commodity is measured in terms of labor hours/days required to produce it.

4. Labor is the only factor of production other than natural resources

5. Labor is homogeneous i.e. identical in efficiency, in a particular country.

6. Labor is perfectly mobile within a country but perfectly immobile between countries.

7. There is free trade i.e. the movement of goods between countries is not hindered by any restrictions.

8. Production is subject to constant returns to scale.

9. There is no technological change.

Theory:

Ricardo shows that trade is possible between countries when one country has an absolute advantage in the production of both commodities, but a comparative advantage in the production of one commodity than in the other.

Labor Required for Producing One Unit

Country	Wine	Cloth
England	120	100
Portugal	80	90

Production of one unit of wine in England requires 120 men for a year, while a unit of cloth requires 100 men for the same period. The production of per unit of wine and cloth in Portugal requires 80 and 90 men. Portugal causes an absolute advantage in both wine and cloth. But Portugal would benefit more by producing wine and exporting it to England as it possesses greater comparative advantage in it. England has a lower opportunity cost for cloth -> comparative advantage in cloth. Portugal will export wine to England in exchange for cloth from him.

Domestic Exchange Ratios

England	Portugal
Wine 120:100 Cloth 1:1.2	Wine 80:90 Cloth 1:0.89
Cloth 100:120 Wine 1:0.83	Cloth 90:80 Wine 1:1.13

England would gain 0.17 (1-0.83) unit of wine by exporting one unit of cloth to Portugal. Similarly, the gain to Portugal by exporting one unit of wine to England will be 0.11(1 -0.89) unit of cloth. Thus, trade is beneficial for both countries.

Opportunity Cost Theory (1936) by Haberler

Difference in opportunity cost leads to comparative advantage. Lower opportunity cost in the production of a commodity has a comparative advantage in that commodity and comparative disadvantage in second commodity.

According to this theory, cost of a commodity is the amount of second commodity that must be given up to release enough resources to produce one additional unit of first commodity. For example:

US Produce 1 unit of A at the cost of 1.5 unit of B and UK produce 1 unit of A at the cost of 2 units of B , then cost of producing A is less in case of US. US has comparative advantage in producing A.

Modern Theory of Trade (Factor Proportion Theory/Factor Endowment Theory) by Heckscher-Ohlin

The approach of two Swedish economists Heckscher and Ohlin to the theory of international trade is called the modern theory of international trade. Heckscher's work in 1919 laid the foundation for the model, and Ohlin's work in 1933 added to it. According to them, "Countries which are rich in labour will export labour intensive goods and countries which are rich in capital will export capital intensive goods. The basis of trade is difference in availability of resources/ factor endowment.

Assumptions:

1) 2×2×2 model (two countries, two commodities, two factors)
2) Perfect competition
3) Full employment
4) Constant returns to scale
5) Perfect mobility with the nation and imperfect in mobility between Nations.
6) Same technology
7) Incomplete specialization in production in both nations. It means even with free trade both nations continue to produce both goods.
8) Good X is labour intensive and good Y is capital intensive in both nations. (no factor intensity reversal).
9) Tastes are equal in both nations.
10) No transportation cost.

Factor intensity: In world of two commodities X and Y and two factors L and K, we say that commodity Y is capital intensive if capital labour ratio (K/L) used in production of Y is greater than capital labour ratio used in production of X.

$(K/L)_Y > (K/L)_X$

where Y is capital intensive and X is labour intensive. Factor intensities for commodities X and Y in nation 1 and 2 has been explained in following figure.

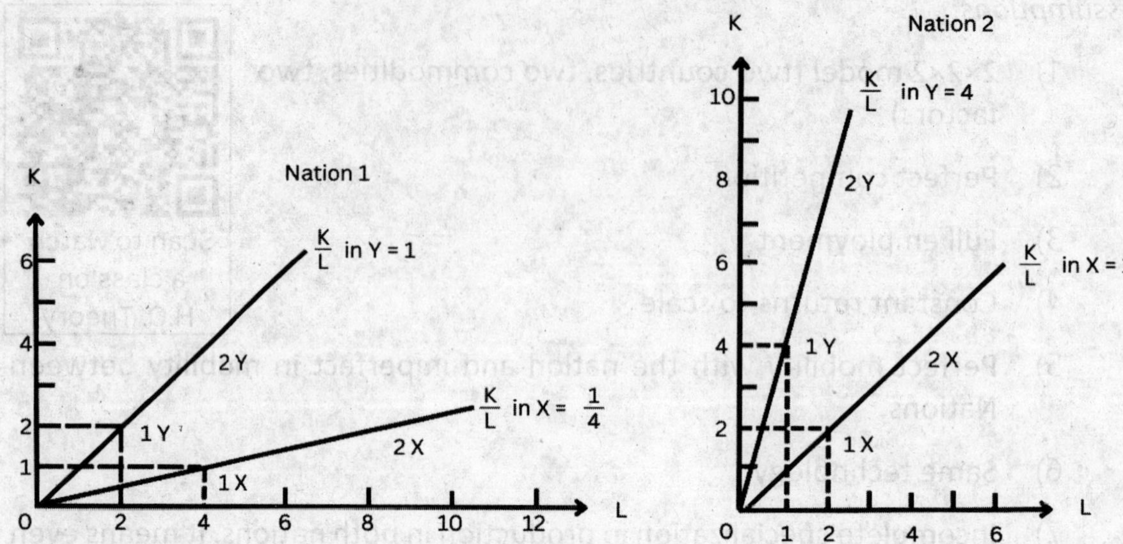

Even commodities Y is Capital intensive in both nations and X is labour intensive in both nations, nation 2 uses higher Capital labour ratio (K/L) than nation 1 for both commodities.

For Y, K/L=4 in nation 2 but K/L = 1 in nation 1

For X, K/L=1 in nation 2 but K/L =1/4 in nation 1.

Factor abundance:

1) **Factor abundance in terms of physical units:** Nation 2 is capital abundant if ratio of total amount of capital to total amount of labour available in nation 2 is greater than in nation 1.

$(K/L)_1<(K/L)_2$

2) Factor abundance in terms of relative factor prices: Nation 2 is capital abundant if ratio of rental price of capital to price of labour (Pk/Pl) is lower in nation 2 than nation 1.

$(P_k/P_l)_1>(P_k/P_l)_2$

Or $(r/w)_1>(r/w)_2$

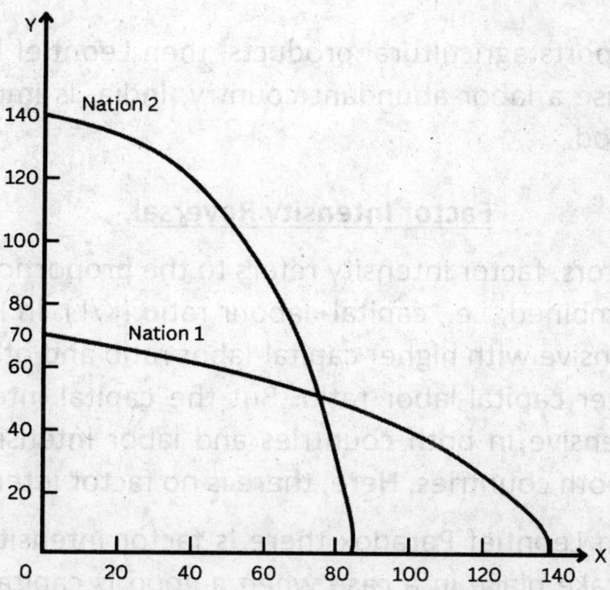

Fig: Shape of Production Frontiers in nation 1 and 2.

Since nation 2 is K abundant and commodity Y is K intensive, nation 2 can produce relatively more of Y than nation 1. Since nation 1 is L abundant and X is L intensive, nation 1 can produce relatively more of X than nation 2. This gives a production frontier for nation 1 that is relatively flatter and wider than that of nation 2.

Brief Overview of Some More Theories of Trade

Leontief Paradox (1953)

Leontief criticised H-O trade theory. He empirically proved it using the example of US economy saying that US being a capital-intensive nation, import capital intensive goods and export labour intensive goods. If a commodity is produced by a labor-intensive process in the labor-rich country and also by the capital-intensive process in the capital-rich country, then factor intensities are reversed in the production of that commodity.

Example: Agriculture is labor-intensive in India but capital-intensive in the US.

- If the US imports agricultural products, then Leontief Paradox_occurs in the US, because a capital-abundant country is importing the capital-intensive product.

- If the US exports agricultural products, then Leontief Paradox occurs in India, because a labor-abundant country, India, is importing the labor-intensive good.

Factor Intensity Reversal

In a model of 2 factors, factor intensity refers to the proportion at which capital and Labour are combined, i.e., capital- labour ratio (K/L). In H-O theorem, one good is capital intensive with higher capital-labor ratio and other good is labour intensive with lower capital-labor ratio. But the capital intensive good must remain capital intensive in both countries and labor intensive good must be labor intensive in both countries. Here, there is no factor intensity reversal.

On the contrary, in Leontief Paradox there is_factor intensity reversal. Factor intensity reversal take place in a case when a good is capital intensive in one country but Labor intensive in other country. In that case H-O theorem will be invalid.

Stolper - Samuelson Theorem (1941)

It depicts the effect of change in commodity prices on real factor rewards. An increase in the relative price of a commodity raises the return or earnings of the factor used intensively in the production of commodity. As a result of International Trade, abundant factor gains and scarce factor lose.

After imposing tariff, abundant factor loses and scarce factor gain. For example, nation is capital intensive and imposition of an import tariff on commodity x (labour intensive commodity) increases P_x/P_y in the nation and increases the earnings of L (nation's scarce factor).

Abundant factor: whose supply is more in country. Countries will tend to export goods that require a factor which is relatively abundant within its own currency.

Scarce factor: whose supply is less in country. A country will import goods that require a factor of production which is relatively scarce within its own economy.

Rybczynski Theorem

Effect of factor endowment changes on output (1955). An increase in a country's endowment of a factor will cause an increase in output of the good which uses that factor intensively and decrease in the output of other good.

Metzler Paradox (1949)

Contradictory of Stolper Samuelson Theorem. There is possibility that imposition of tariff on imports may reduce the relative internal price of that good. Therefore, imposing of tariff became favourable to abundant factor and unfavourable to scarce factor.

Samuelson's Factor Price Equalization Theorem (1948)

Samuelson showed that free commodity trade will, under certain specified conditions, inevitably lead to complete factor price equalization. Prices of factors of production. Such as wage rate or rent of capital will be equalised across countries as a result of International Trade.

Assumes: Two goods, Two factors, same commodity prices, free trade, same technology.

When the prices of the output goods are equalised between countries as they move to free trade, then the prices of the factors will also be equalised between countries.

Before international trade, factor receives lowest price. After international trade, it becomes more expensive. While those with the highest price will tend to become cheaper.

The Kravis Theory of Trade (1956)

It is the domestic availability or non-availability of goods that governs the pattern of trade. Kravis asserted that the nations would export those products which were readily available in the home country. They would tend to import, on the contrary, such products the domestic supply of which had been short of their demand. According to him, the essential basis of international trade has been the 'non-availability of goods at home'.

Linder Hypothesis

Linder Hypothesis is an economic hypothesis that posits countries with similar per capita income will consume similar quality products, and that this should lead to them trading with each other. The theory was proposed by Staffan Linder in 1961. Research has shown that both export prices and demand are strongly correlated with income, specifically for the same quality of goods, though income is used as an approximation for demand.

Gravity Model of Trade

The Gravity Model is a widely used economic theory that predicts the volume of trade between two countries based on their economic sizes (usually measured by GDP) and their geographical distance from each other. According to the Gravity Model:

- Larger economies have more goods and services to trade, leading to higher trade volumes.
- Closer geographical distance reduces transportation costs and trade barriers, leading to higher trade volumes.
- The gravity model of international trade in international economics is a model that, in its traditional form, predicts bilateral trade flows based on the economic sizes and distance between two units. Research shows that there is "overwhelming evidence that trade tends to fall with distance.

Specific Factor Model

The model's name refers to its distinguishing feature—that one factor of production is assumed to be "specific" to a particular industry. A specific factor is one that is stuck in an industry or is immobile between industries in response to changes in market conditions. A factor may be immobile between industries for a number of reasons. Some factors may be specifically designed (in the case of capital) or specifically trained (in the case of labor) for use in a particular production process. In these cases, it may be impossible, or at least difficult or costly, to move these factors across industries.

In specific factor model, trade will have an ambiguous/uncertain(gain or loss) effect on the nation's mobile factors, benefits the immobile factors specific to the nation's export commodities and harm the immobile factor specific to the nation's import competing commodities.

Product Cycle Model

The product cycle model identifies five different stages in the life cycle of a product from the point of view of the innovating and the imitating country.

In stage I, or new-product phase (referring to time OA on the horizontal axis), the product (at this time a specialty) is produced and consumed only in the innovating country.

In stage II, or product-growth phase (time AB), production is perfected in the innovating country and increases rapidly to accommodate rising demand at home and abroad. At this stage, there is not yet any foreign production of the product, so that the innovating country has a monopoly in both the home and export markets.

In stage III, or product-maturity phase (time BC), the product becomes standardized, and the innovating firm may find it profitable to license other domestic and foreign firms to also manufacture the product. Thus, the imitating country starts producing the product for domestic consumption.

In stage IV (time CD), the imitating country, facing lower labor and other costs now that the product has become standardized and no longer requires development and engineering skills, begins to undersell the innovating country in third markets, and production of the product in the innovating country declines. Brand competition now gives way to price competition.

Finally, in stage V (i.e., past point D), the imitating country starts underselling the innovating country in the latter's market as well, and production of the product in the innovating country declines rapidly or collapses. Stages IV and V are often referred to as the product-decline stage. Technological diffusion, standardization, and lower costs abroad thus bring the end of the life cycle for the product. It is now time for the innovating country to concentrate attention on new technological innovations and to introduce new products. Imports Examples of products that seem to have gone through such product cycles are radios, stainless steel, razor blades, television sets, and semiconductors.

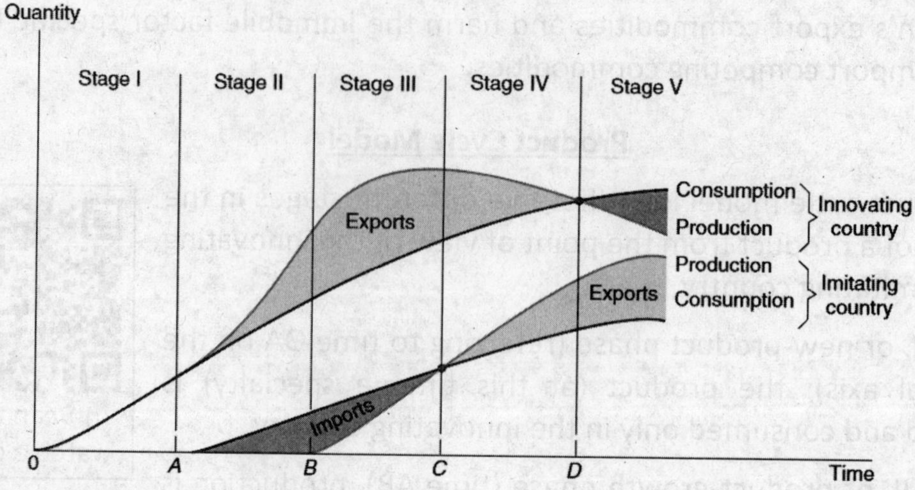

In stage I (time OA), the product is produced and consumed only in the innovating country. In stage II (AB), production is perfected in the innovating country and increases rapidly to accommodate rising demand at home and abroad. In stage III (BC), the product becomes standardized and the imitating country starts producing the product for domestic consumption. In stage IV (CD), the imitating country starts underselling the innovating country in third markets, and in stage V (past point D) in the latter's market as well.

Mill's Theory of Reciprocal Demand

It is used to indicate country's demand for one commodity in terms of quantities of other commodity it is prepared to give up in exchange. Reciprocal demand determined terms of trade of country.

Offer Curve

Also known as Reciprocal demand curve developed by Edgeworth, Marshall, Meade. It shows the various quantities of its exportable commodity, a country is willing to exchange for an importable commodity at various international prices. In other words, an offer curve of a country indicates the quantity of imports and exports, the country is willing to buy or sell in world markets at all possible terms of trade.

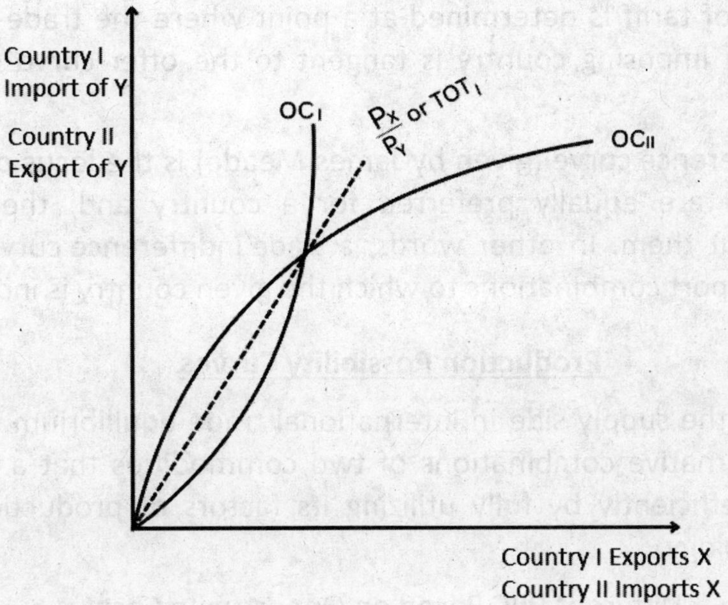

Here, OC I and OC II are offer curves of two countries. X and Y are two commodities. Equilibrium is found at the relative prices for the two goods where each is willing to purchase what the other want to sell. The international terms of trade (P_x/P_y) will be the slope of line passing through the point where the offer curve crosses.

$$Elasticity\ of\ Offer\ Curve = \frac{\%\ change\ in\ imports}{\%\ change\ in\ exports}$$

The less elastic the foreign offer curve, the higher will be the optimum tariff. Where the foreign offer curve has elasticity of one and thus is horizontal, the optimum tariff will be infinity.

Optimum Tariff

An optimum tariff is a tariff that maximizes a country's welfare while balancing trade restrictions with trade improvements. It is the rate at which the net gain will be maximized. It helps the country to reach its maximum rate of satisfaction.

$$Optimum\ tariff - t^* = \frac{1}{e-1}$$

$$e = point\ of\ elasticity\ of\ offer\ curve\ of\ other\ country$$

Optimum level of tariff is determined at a point where the trade indifference curve of a tariff imposing country is tangent to the offer curve of the other country.

The trade indifference curve (given by James Meade) is the locus of such trade positions which are equally preferred for a country and, therefore, it is indifferent about them. In other words, a trade indifference curve represents those export-import combinations to which the given country is indifferent.

Production Possibility Curves

They represent the supply side in international trade equilibrium. They shows the various alternative combinations of two commodities that a country can produce most efficiently by fully utilizing its factors of production with the available technology.

Different PPC Based on Opportunity Cost

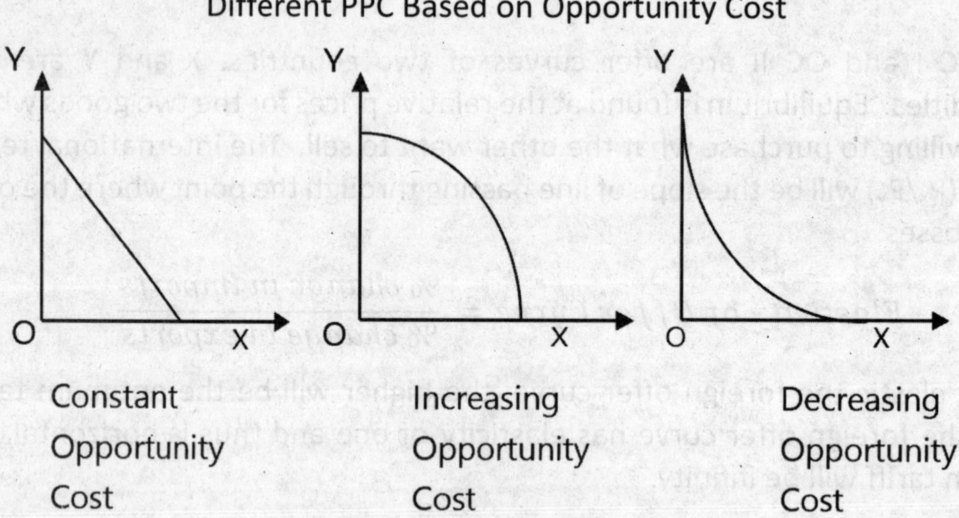

Community Indifference Curve

Represents demand side in international trade equilibrium. It shows the various combinations of two goods which yield same satisfaction to the community.

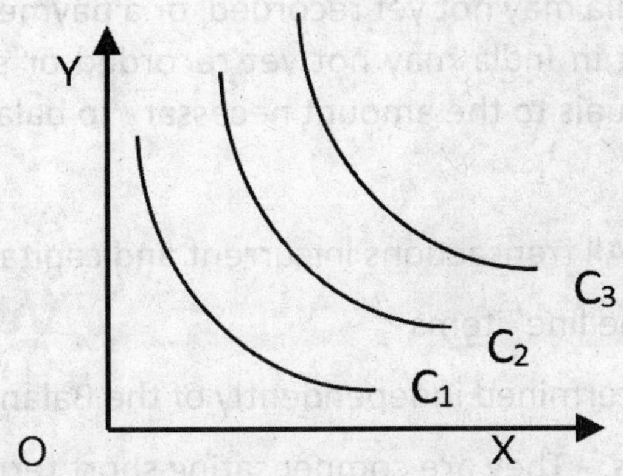

Balance of Payments (BOP)

It is a systematic record of all economic transactions of a country with outside world in a given year.

Trade in goods - Balance of visible trade

Trade in services - Balance of invisible trade

Credit (Receipts)	Debits (Payment)
1) Current account Export – →Goods and services →Unilateral Receipts →Interest, profits, Dividend received	1) Current account Imports – → Goods and services → Unilateral payments → Interest, profits, dividend paid.
2) Capital Account →Borrowing from foreign countries →Investments by foreign countries	2) Capital Account → Lending to foreign countries → Investments in foreign countries

Errors and Omission

The errors may be due to statistical discrepancies & omission may be due to certain transactions may not be recorded. For e.g.: A remittance by an Indian working abroad to India may not yet recorded, or a payment of dividend abroad by an MNC operating in India may not yet recorded or so on. The errors and omissions amount equals to the amount necessary to balance both the sides.

Autonomous items: - All transactions in current and capital account.

→These are 'above the line' items

→Their values are determined independently of the Balance of payments.

Accommodating items: - They are compensating short term capital transactions which are meant to correct a disequilibrium in the autonomous items of balance of payments.

BOP Adjustment Policies of Government

Expenditure changing → Mundell Fleming model [Monetary and fiscal policies]
Expenditure Switching → Devaluation

BOP equilibrium: Receipts =Expenditure.

BOP Disequilibrium: Receipts > Expenditure (surplus)

Receipts < Expenditure (deficit)

Some important points:

- Devaluation: Decline in the value of currency in terms of foreign currency. [Done by government]
- Depreciation: same as devaluation but it occurs as a result of forces of demand and supply(in flexible exchange rate).
- Current account deficit in BOP is financed by capital inflows.
- Foreign exchange reserves are used to meet the deficit in the BOP.
- If there is deficit (M(import)>X(export)) in free floating system, there is net outflow of money. It will increase supply of nation currency in foreign exchange market. External value of currency will fall which leads to depreciation.

Elasticity Approach

Marshall-Lerner Condition

Devaluation of a currency can be successful to correct deficit of balance of payments depending on the elasticities of demand of exports(e_x) and of demand for imports(e_m).

If $e_x + e_m > 1$ Devaluation will be successful

If $e_x + e_m = 1$ Devaluation will have no effect on BOP

If $e_x + e_m < 1$ Devaluation will worsen the BOP

J-Curve

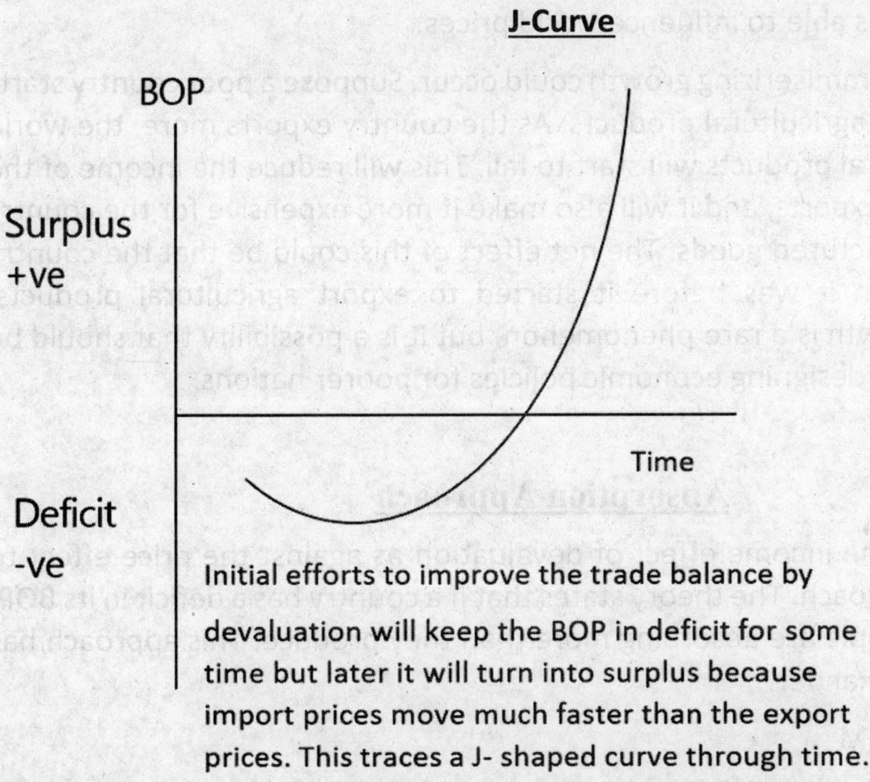

Initial efforts to improve the trade balance by devaluation will keep the BOP in deficit for some time but later it will turn into surplus because import prices move much faster than the export prices. This traces a J- shaped curve through time.

Prebisch - Singer Hypothesis (1958)

It states that there will be a long-term deterioration of TOT in developing countries due to long-term decline in the prices of primary goods which were exported by developing countries in comparison to the prices of manufactured goods imported by the developing countries.

The demand for primary products grows slower over time when income rises but demand for manufactured goods increases as income rises. So income elasticity of demand of manufacture goods is higher.

Immiserizing Growth (1958) by Jagdish Bhagwati

The theory states that a country, if focuses on economic growth could let it to in the fall in Terms of Trade and making the country worse off than before. If growth is heavily export based, it might lead to a fall in the terms of trade of the exporting country. In rare circumstances, this fall in the terms of trade may be so large as to outweigh the gains from growth. If so, this situation would cause a country to be worse off after growth than before. This result is only valid if the growing country is able to influence world prices.

Example of how Immiserizing growth could occur. Suppose a poor country starts to export a lot of agricultural products. As the country exports more, the world price of agricultural products will start to fall. This will reduce the income of the country from its exports, and it will also make it more expensive for the country to import manufactured goods. The net effect of this could be that the country is worse off than it was before it started to export agricultural products. Immiserizing growth is a rare phenomenon, but it is a possibility that should be considered when designing economic policies for poorer nations.

Absorption Approach

It runs through the income effect of devaluation as against the price effect to the elasticity approach. The theory states that if a country has a deficit in its BOP, it means that people are absorbing more than they produce. This approach has developed by Alexander.

$Y = C + I + G + X - M$

$Y = A + B \qquad \text{or } B = Y - A$

Where A is total absorption consists of sum of Consumption, Investment, Government expenditure and B is BOP consists of exports – imports. BOP can improve if either there is increase in income or decrease in absorption. Therefore, trade balance of a country can improves if domestic absorption is reduced.

Expenditure Switching Policy – Devaluation

Devaluation means a reduction in the external value of a currency in terms of other currencies. But there is no change in internal purchasing power of country. Thus, when a country with BOP deficit devalues its currency, domestic price of imports increases, foreign price of exports falls.

Monetary-Fiscal Mix: Internal and External Balance Policies – Mundell Fleming Model

This model was developed by Fleming and Mundell in the early 1960s for the purpose of analysing the role of monetary and fiscal policies in the context of an open economy. This model is called the Keynesian Open Economy Model.

Scan to watch a class

This approach analyses the relationship between two instruments and two targets. The two instruments are monetary policy represented by interest rate and fiscal policy represented by government expenditure. The two objective or targets are full employment (internal balance) and balance of payments equilibrium (external balance).

Main Assumptions:

1) Small open economy.
2) Constant prices and wages
3) An extended version of IS-LM model with balance of payment
4) Impact of monetary and fiscal policy will be analyses in fixed and flexible exchange rates regimes.

The BP Curve in the IS-LM Framework

- The BP curve depicts different combinations of income and interest rate that assure the balance of payment equilibrium.
- The points below the BP curve refer to the balance of payments deficit.
- By analogy, the points above the BP curve refer to the balance of payments surplus.

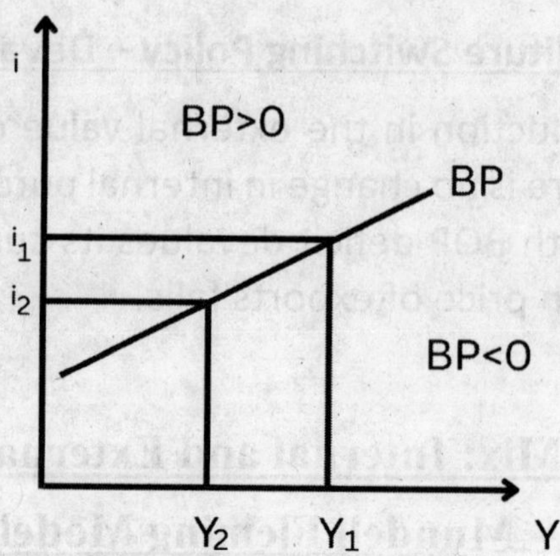

The Slope of BP Curve

The slope of BP curve depends on the international mobility level of capital (parameter K). With perfect capital mobility BP curve is horizontal because:

$K \Rightarrow \infty$ and $i = i *$ (Domestic rate of interest is equal to foreign interest rate)

With no capital mobility K = 0, and BP curve is vertical (interest rate do not influence capital flows). Finally, with imperfect capital mobility BP curve is positively sloped.

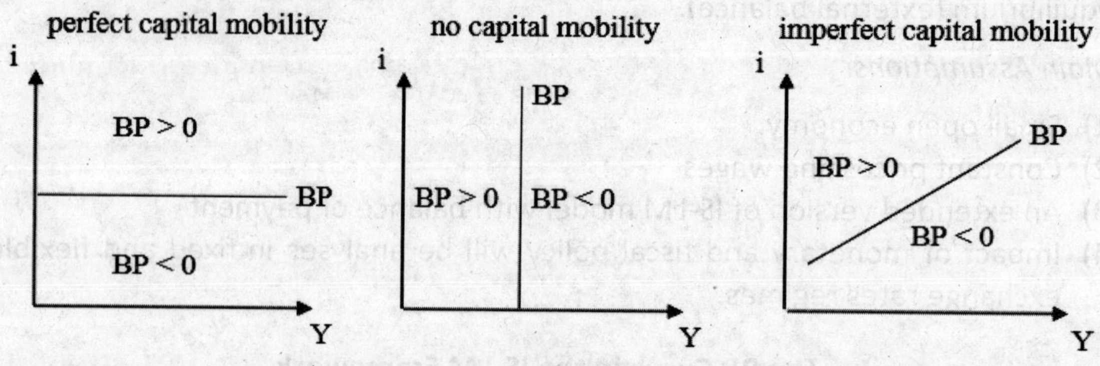

We will analyze the Mundell-Fleming model as follows:

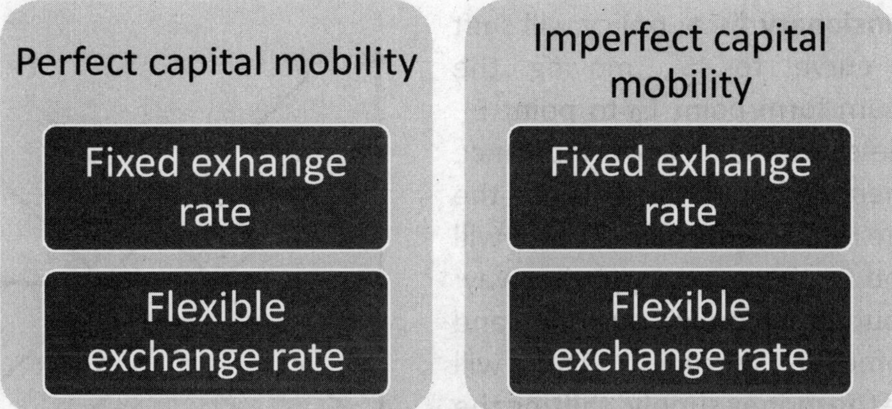

Monetary Policy Under Perfect Capital Mobility and Fixed Exchange Rate

An **expansionary monetary policy** will shift the LM curve to LM', which makes the equilibrium go from point E_0 to E_1. However, since we are below the BP curve, we know the economy has a balance of payments deficit. Since exchange rates are fixed, government intervention is required: the government will purchase domestic currency and sell foreign currency, which will drop the money supply and therefore shift the LM' curve to its original position (which makes the equilibrium go to E_2). Monetary policy has therefore no effect under these circumstances.

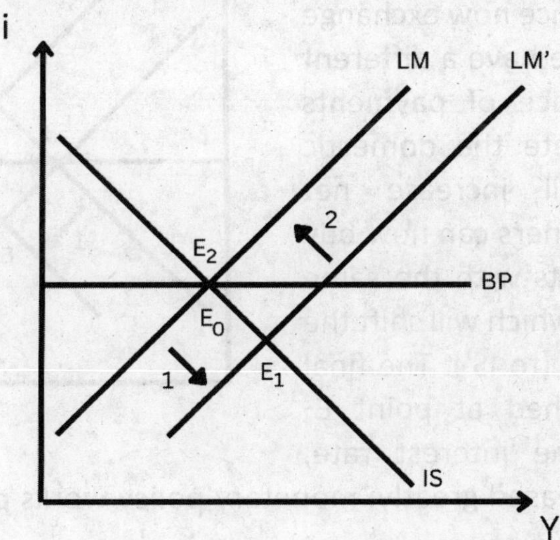

Fiscal Policy Under Perfect Capital Mobility and Fixed Exchange Rate

An **expansionary fiscal policy** will shift the IS curve to IS', moving the equilibrium form point E_0 to point E_1. Since the economy has now a balance of payments surplus, and because the exchange rate is fixed, government will intervene in the exact opposite way: they'll purchase foreign currency and sell domestic currency. This will increase the money supply, shifting the LM curve to the right. The final equilibrium is reached at point E_2 where, at the same interest rate, production has increased greatly: fiscal policy works perfectly under these circumstances.

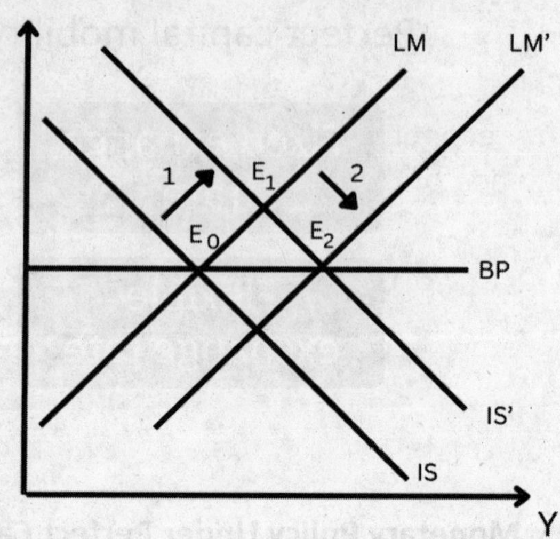

Monetary Policy Under Perfect Capital Mobility and Flexible Exchange Rate

An **expansionary monetary policy** will shift the LM curve to LM', which makes the equilibrium go from point E_0 to E_1. However, since now exchange rates are flexible, we have a different situation: the balance of payments deficit will depreciate the domestic currency. This will increase net exports (since foreigners can now buy more of our products with the same amount of money), which will shift the IS curve to the right (to IS'). The final equilibrium is reached at point E_2 where, at the same interest rate, production has increased greatly: monetary policy works perfectly under these circumstances.

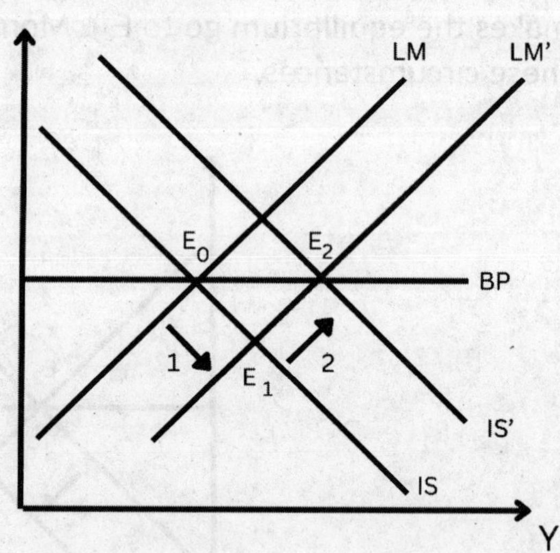

Fiscal Policy Under Perfect Capital Mobility and Flexible Exchange Rate

An **expansionary fiscal policy** will shift the IS curve to IS', moving the equilibrium from point E_0 to point E_1. The economy will therefore have a balance of payments surplus, which in this case of flexible exchange rate will appreciate the domestic currency. This will decrease net exports, since we are able to import more goods and services with less money, while foreigners will import less of our products because of our appreciated domestic currency. This drop in net exports will shift the IS' curve back to its original position. Since now the final equilibrium E_2 corresponds to the initial equilibrium, we know fiscal policy is no good in this case.

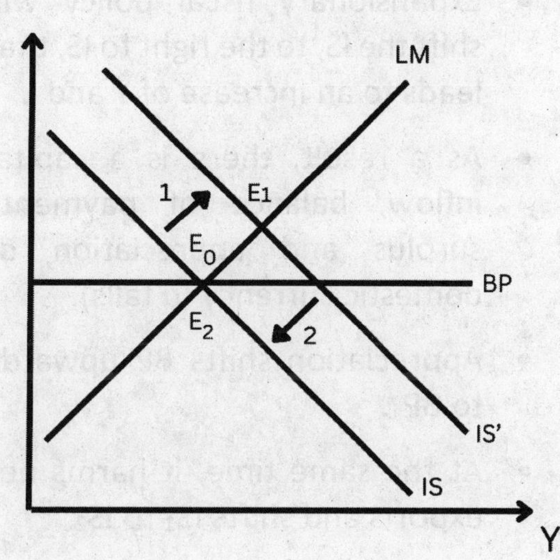

Monetary Policy under Flexible Exchange Rates and Imperfect Capital Mobility

- Expansionary monetary policy will shift LM to the right - there is an increase in Y and a fall in i.
- There is a capital outflow, balance of payments deficit and depreciation of domestic currency.
- Depreciation shifts BP_0 down to BP_1 and leads to an increase in net exports.
- As a result, IS_0 shifts to IS_1.
- Final result: higher Y, lower i (although could be either higher or constant).
- Conclusion - monetary policy is effective.

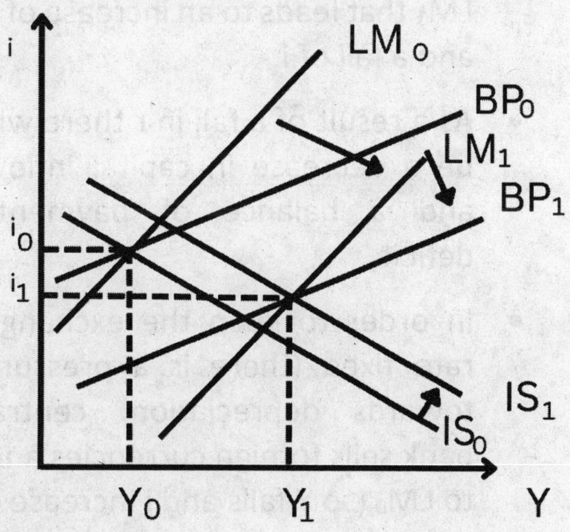

Fiscal Policy Under Flexible Exchange Rates and Imperfect Capital Mobility

- Expansionary fiscal policy will shift the IS, to the right to IS, that leads to an increase of Y and i.
- As a result, there is a capital inflow, balance of payments surplus and appreciation of domestic currency (q falls).
- Appreciation shifts BP upwards to BP_1.
- At the same time, it harms net exports and shifts IS_1 to IS_2.
- Final result: higher Y, higher i.
- Conclusion - fiscal policy is not very effective.

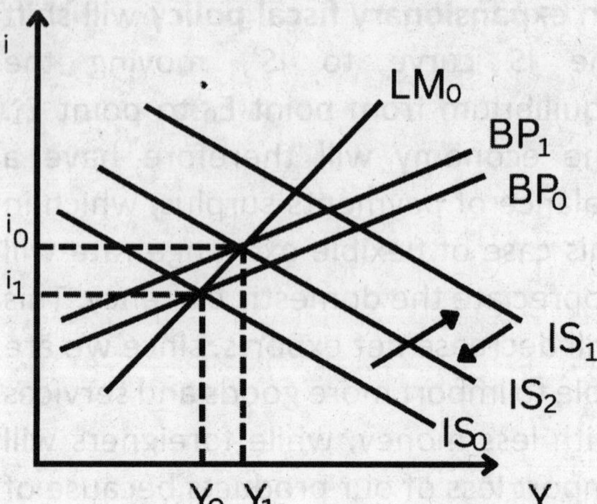

Monetary Policy Under Fixed Exchange Rates and Imperfect Capital Mobility

- Expansionary monetary policy will shift the LM_0, to the right to LM_1 that leads to an increase of Y and a fall of i.
- As a result of a fall in r there will be a decrease in capital inflow and a balance of payments deficit.
- In order to keep the exchange rate fixed (there is a pressure towards depreciation) central bank sells foreign currencies and cuts money supply - this shifts LM_1 back to LM_0 (so Y falls and i increases to the previous level).
- Final result: constant Y, constant i.
- Conclusion - monetary policy is ineffective.

Fiscal Policy Under Fixed Exchange Rates and Imperfect Capital Mobility

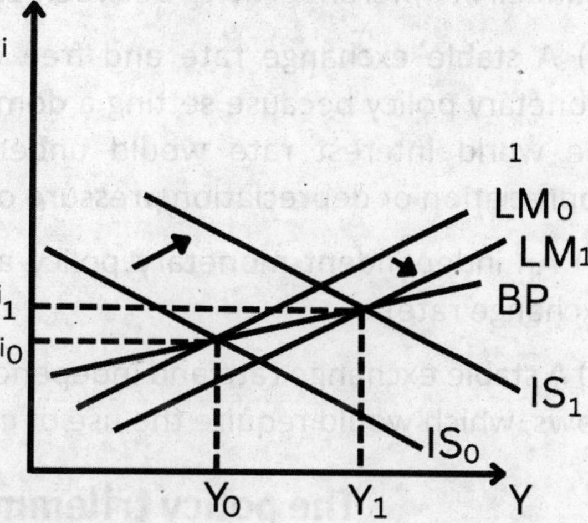

- Expansionary fiscal policy will shift the IS_0, to the right to IS_1 that leads to an increase of Y and i.
- As a result of an increase in i there will be a rise in capital inflow and a balance of payments surplus.
- In order to keep the exchange rate fixed (there is a pressure towards appreciation) central bank increases money supply - this shifts LM_0 to the right to LM_1 (there is a further increase in Y and a fall in i).

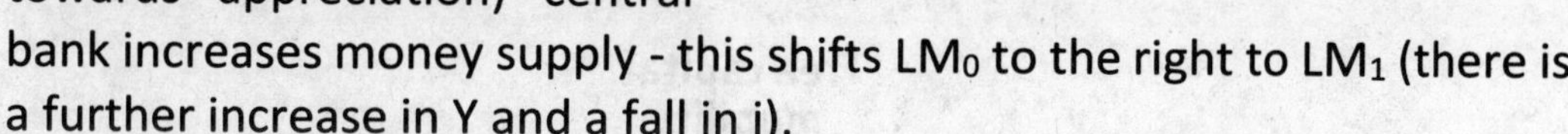

- Final result: higher Y, higher i.

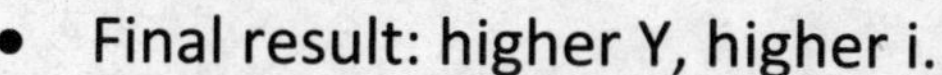

- Conclusion - fiscal policy is effective.

Conclusion Of Mundell Fleming Model (IS-LM-BP Model)

→In case of fixed exchange rate, expansionary fiscal policy more effective.

→In case of fixed exchange rate, monetary policy is not effective.

→In case of flexible exchange rate, fiscal policy ineffective.

→In case of flexible exchange rate, monetary policy is effective.

Impossible Trinity/ Impossible Trilemma/ Policy Trilemma

The impossible trinity is a concept in international economics which states that it is impossible to have all three of the following at the same time:

- a fixed foreign exchange rate
- free capital movement (absence of capital controls)
- an independent monetary policy

It is a finding from empirical studies where governments that have tried to simultaneously pursue all three goals have failed. The concept was developed independently by both John Marcus Fleming in 1962 and Robert Alexander Mundell in different articles between 1960 and 1963. Such as

(a) A stable exchange rate and free capital flows (but not an independent monetary policy because setting a domestic interest rate that is different from the world interest rate would undermine a stable exchange rate due to appreciation or depreciation pressure on the domestic currency).

(b) An independent monetary policy and free capital flows (but not a stable exchange rate).

(c) A stable exchange rate and independent monetary policy (but no free capital flows, which would require the use of capital controls).

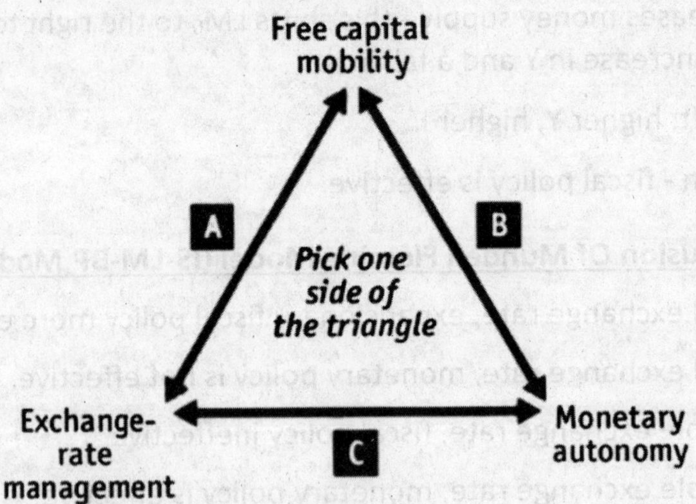

In a few words, no economy can have the following three: perfect capital mobility, fixed exchange rates and an independent and efficient monetary policy. Under the perfect capital mobility assumption, and in order to have an efficient monetary policy, exchange rates must be flexible. Or have fixed exchange rates but assume that monetary policy won't be efficient.

Triffin Dilemma/ Triffin Paradox

The **Triffin dilemma** or **Triffin paradox** is the conflict of economic interests that arises between short-term domestic and long-term international objectives for countries whose currencies serve as global reserve currencies. This dilemma was identified in the 1960s by Belgian-American economist Robert Triffin, who pointed out that the country whose currency, being the global reserve currency, foreign nations wish to hold, must be willing to supply the world with an extra supply of its currency to fulfill world demand for these foreign exchange reserves, leading to a trade deficit. The use of a national currency, such as the U.S. dollar, as global reserve currency leads to tension between its national and global monetary policy. This is reflected in fundamental imbalances in the balance of payments on the current account, as some goals require an outflow of dollars from the United States, while others require an inflow.

Foreign Exchange Rate

1) Nominal exchange rate : Number of units of domestic currency required to purchase one unit of foreign currency.
2) Real exchange rate : Relative prices of two currencies after adjusting for the price levels in those two Nations.
3) Nominal effective exchange rate : The weighted average of nominal exchange rate where weights are the share of trading partners in the foreign trade of a country.
4) Real effective exchange rate : The weighted average of real exchange rate where weights are the shares of a country in foreign trade.

$$Real\ exchange\ rate = \frac{Nominal\ exchange\ rate * Domestic\ price\ index}{Foreign\ price\ index}$$

Illustration

60 Rs are required to purchase USD 1 and 80 Rs required to purchase 1 Pound. These are nominal exchange rates.

Percentage of trade with USA =60%

Percentage of trade with UK = 40%

Nominal effective exchange rate= 60 x 0.6 + 80 x 0.4 = 68

Exchange Rate Determination

Demand for dollars : When dollar price of rupee falls implying that rupee appreciate, then imports increase and demand for dollar will increase.

Supply of dollars : when dollar price of rupee increases, this will discourage the imports and hence supply of dollar increases.

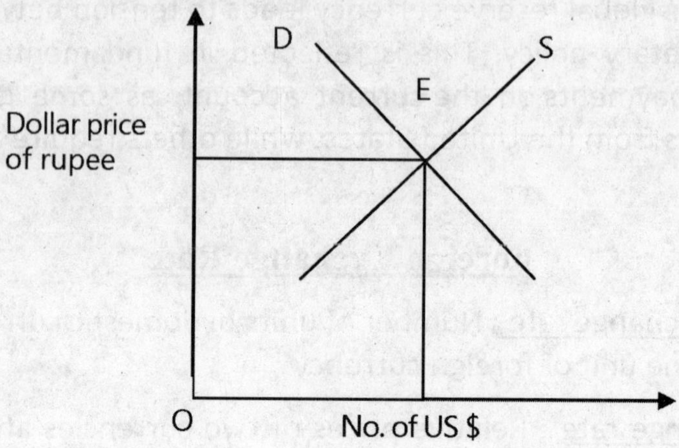

Important point to remember: if domestic interest rate is less than world interest rate, then there will be capital outflow (capital flight) and vice versa.

Exchange Rate

The rate of exchange refers to the rate at which the currencies of two countries are exchanged for each other.

Rate of exchange is the value or price of a country's currency in terms of foreign currency. For e.g., if 1 US dollar is exchanged for ₹40, then the foreign exchange rate is $1 = ₹40.

In foreign exchange market two types of exchange rate operations take place. They are spot exchange rate and forward exchange rate.

Spot Exchange Rate:

Spot rate of exchange refers to the price of foreign currency in terms of domestic currency payable for the immediate delivery of the foreign currency.

Forward Exchange Rate

Forward rate refers to a contract to buy or sell foreign currency at a fixed date in future at a price agreed at present. This pre-determined rate at which the currency is to be bought and sold at a future date is called as the forward rate.

A forward contract is signed between party A and party B face to face (or over the counter), whereas in a futures contract there is an intermediary between the two parties. This intermediary is often called a clearance house, which is a part of a stock exchange.

Fixed Exchange Rates	Flexible Exchange Rate
→Under fixed or pegged ex- change rates, all exchange trans- actions take place at an exchange rate that is determined by the monetary authority. → No fear of currency fluctuations and encourages long-term capital flows. →BOP disequilibrium persists.	→ Under floating or fluctuating exchange rates are determined by market forces. The monetary authority does not intervene for the purpose of influencing the exchange rate. → Uncertainty Therefore, discourages long term capital flows. → BOP disequilibrium automatically corrected.

Theories Of Foreign Exchange Rate

The Mint Parity Theory

The rate at which the standard money of the country was convertible into gold was called the Mint price of gold. If the official British price of gold was £6 per ounce and the US price of gold $36 per ounce, they were the mint prices of gold in the respective countries. The exchange rate between the dollar and the pound would be fixed at $36 / £6. This rate was called the mint parity or mint par of exchange because it was based on the mint price of gold.

The Purchasing Power Parity Theory

Developed by Gustav Cassel in 1920. According to this theory, rates of exchange between two countries are determined by relative price level. For example, if by spending Rs.65. we can buy an amount of goods in India as we can buy with $1/- in America, the rate of exchange between India and America will be Rs.65/- to $1. It has presented in two versions

1) Absolute version of PPP theory.
2) Relative version of PPP theory

Absolute Version:

Exchange rate between two currencies should be equal to the ratio of the price indexes in the two countries. The formula is

$$R_{AB} = \frac{P_A}{P_B}$$

For e.g., Basket of goods cost Rs.1000 in India and $100 in America. That means the exchange rate would be Rs. 10/- = $1.

Relative Version:

Explains changes in the equilibrium exchange rate between two currencies. According to this, equilibrium rate of exchange in the current period (R_1) is determined by equilibrium rate of exchange in base period (R_0) and the ratio of price indices of current and base period in one country to the ratio of price indices of current and base period in other country.

$$R_1 = R_0 . \frac{\frac{P_{B_1}}{P_{B_0}}}{\frac{P_{A_1}}{P_{A_0}}}$$

(P_{B_1} *and* P_{B_0} are the price indices in country B in current and base periods)

Terms of Trade

$$TOT = \frac{Index\ of\ exports\ prices}{Index\ of\ imports\ prices} \times 100$$

Net Barter TOT: The concept was given by Taussig.

$$T_C = \frac{P_{x_1}/P_{x_0}}{P_{m_1}/P_{m_0}}$$

[Index number of export prices/Index number of price of import]

More the ratio, more favourable are the TOT

Gross Barter TOT: The concept was given by Taussig.

$$T_G = \frac{Q_{m_1}}{Q_{m_0}} / \frac{Q_{x_1}}{Q_{x_0}} \left[\frac{Quantity\ Imported}{Quantity\ Exported}\right]$$

Income Terms of Trade: Dorrance

$$T_y = T_c . Q_x \qquad Q_x = quantity\ index\ of\ export$$

$$= \frac{P_x}{P_m} \times Q_x$$

Single Factorial Terms of Trade: (Viner) $T_c . F_x$

$$T_S = \frac{P_x}{P_m} . F_x$$

$$F_x = productivity\ index\ of\ export\ industries$$

Double Factorial Terms of Trade (Viner)

$$T_d = \frac{P_x}{P_m} . \frac{F_x}{F_m}$$

F_m=Productivity index in import sector

Real Factorial Terms of Trade

$$T_r = T_S . R_x$$

R_x =Disutility per unit of factors of production engaged in country's exports.

Utility Terms of Trade

$$T_u = T_r . U$$

U = Relative utility of imports and domestically forgone commodities. Robinson called it Real TOT.

Intra-Industry Trade

It is the trade that occurs between countries but within the same industry. The products that are traded are of a similar type such as oil or cars. It incorporates Economies of scale and monopolistic competition. Value of intra industry index can be measured as

$$T = 1 - \frac{|X - M|}{X + M}$$

Value of T ranges from 0 to 1. If T=0, there is no intra industry trade. If T=1, exports and imports of a good are equal. Intra industry trade is maximum.

Illustration: Index of import prices stands at 102 and that of export prices stand at 106. TOT is:

$$TOT = \frac{P_x}{P_m} \times 100$$

$$= \frac{106}{102} \times 100$$

$$= 104$$

Foreign Exchange Markets

It is a market which deals in foreign currency functions→

1) Transfer function: foreign exchange market transfers the purchasing power of people
2) Credit function :providing credit to exporters and importers
3) Hedging: protection against foreign exchange risk

Kinds of operations

- Spot transactions: payment has to be made within 2 business days.
- Forward or future transactions: signing an agreement for payments on delivering in future.

Activities in FEM		
Hedging	**Speculation**	**Arbitrage**
Protection against losses or covering foreign exchange risk. *Types of risk* Transaction exposure, Accounting / translation exposure, economic exposure.	Opposite of hedging. Speculators are willing to take risk.	Buying the currency from a country where price is lower and reselling it in a country where it is higher in order to earn monetary profits.

Tariffs

Tariffs is a tax levied on export and import of goods. These are the restrictions on free trade.

Types of Tariffs

1) Revenue tariff: Tariff implemented to raise the revenue capacity of the government is known as revenue tariff .

Scan to watch a class on Retaliatory Tariff

2) Protective tariff: Tariff to protect the domestic Industries from foreign competitors.
3) Ad Valorem duty: Charged on the total value of the imported commodity.
4) Specific duty: Charged on the weight of the commodity.
5) Compound duty: Mixture of both ad valorem and specific duty.

Scan to watch a class on Countervailing Tariff

6) Retaliatory tariffs: It is levied by one country on the imports of another country in order to punish them latter for its trade policy.

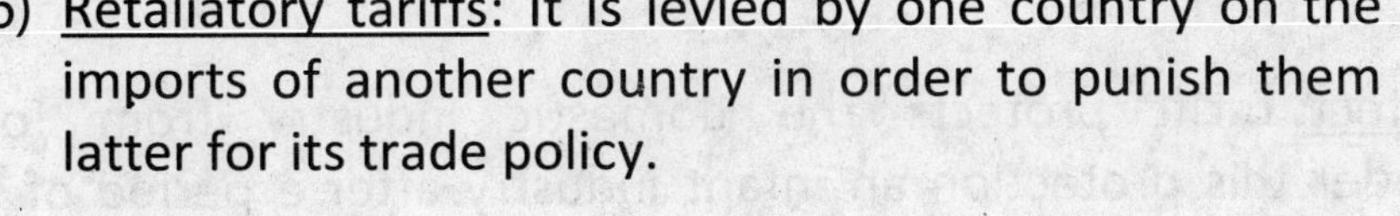

7) Countervailing duty: Imposed on a commodity whose export price is reduced by the other country through an export subsidy.

Non-Tariff Barriers to Trade

Quotas: Ceiling on the quantity to be imported or exported.

Import licensing: Import is dependent on license.

Voluntarily export restraints: Self-imposed limit on exports to a specific country.

Effects of Tariffs

Kindelberger has mentioned eight effects of tariff in a partial equilibrium approach. These include:

1. Protective or Production Effect
2. Consumption Effect
3. Revenue Effect
4. Redistribution Effect
5. Terms of Trade Effect
6. Competitive Effect
7. Income Effect
8. Balance of Payments Effect.

Effects are explained as follows:

Price of the commodity will increase on which tariff is levied.

Domestic production of the commodity increases.

Consumption effect is to reduce the consumption of the commodity on which tariff is imposed.

Revenue effect: Before the imposition of tariff, government revenue is zero. After tariff, government will get revenue.

BOP effect: Favorable BOP effect on tariff imposing country.

Consumer surplus reduces, and producer surplus increases. Loss of consumer's surplus which is neither transferrable to producers nor to the government is called by kindle Berger as the "deadweight loss of the tariff ".

TOT effect: Tariff imposing country improves its TOT.

Income effect: Demand for domestically produced goods increase, as a result income increase.

Competitive Effect: Tariff protects the domestic industry from foreign competition. Under this protection an infant industry after a period of time, grows into an economically strong industry which can fully compete in the world market. But the sluggish and lazy industry may not like to face the competition and remain inefficient even under the protection cover provided through tariffs.

> The infant industry argument was first put forward by Alexander Hamilton in 1791. Friedrich List also contributed to the argument in 1841. The infant industry argument is a theory that new industries need protection from foreign competitors until they can compete on their own. It's often used to justify trade protectionism.

Trade Creation and Trade Diversion

Trade Creation: Occurs when the consumption of higher cost domestic production of the home country is replaced with the lower cost product of the partner country after entering into union.

Trade Diversion: Occurs when after entering into union, the home country imports the product from higher cost partner country instead of from the lower -cost rest of the world country.

Effective Rate of Protection: ERP measures the actual protection given to domestic producers taking into account the tariffs on both final goods and imported goods. In other words, it is degree of protection provided to the domestic good from the imported goods [Important for producers].

Nominal Rate of Protection: It refers to the percentage by which a tariff raises the price of the final good. In other words, it shows by how much price of commodity increase as a result of tariff [Important for consumers].

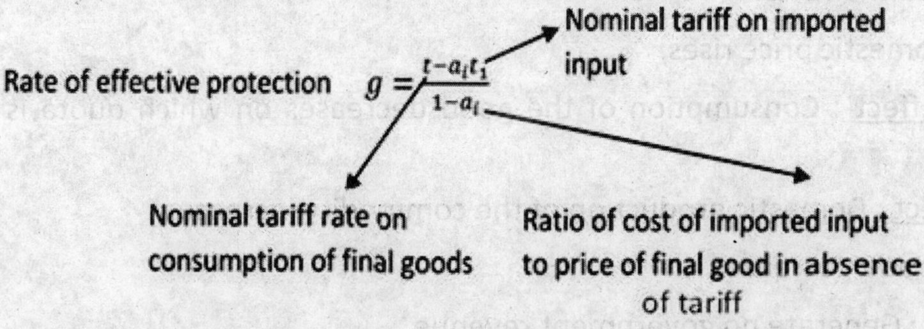

Optimum tariff – $t^* = \frac{1}{e-1}$ e = point of elasticity of offer curve of other country.

PYQ: If the nominal tariff rate (t) on consumers of the final commodity is 10 percent; the ratio of the cost of the imported input to the price of the final commodity in the absence of tariffs a_i = 0.8; and the nominal tariff rate on the imported input t_i = 20%, then find the rate of effective protection. (December 2022 - shift 1)

(a) 10% (b) 8%

(c) 3% (d) -30%

Answer: (d)

$$Rate\ of\ Effective\ tariff = \frac{10/100 - (0 \cdot 8 \times 20/100)}{1 - 0.8}$$

$$= \frac{0.1 - (0.8 * 0.2)}{0.2}$$

$$= -0.3$$

$$= -30\%$$

Quota

A government-imposed limit on the quantity or value of a specific good that can be imported or exported during a given time period.

Effects of Quotas

Partial equilibrium effects:

Price effect : Domestic price rises.

Consumption effect : Consumption of the good decreases on which quota is imposed.

Production effect : Domestic production of the commodity increases.

Trade effect : Trade decreases.

Revenue effect : Generate no government revenue

Consumer surplus decreases but producer surplus increases

BOP effect : favorable to Quota imposing country

Difference Between Quota & Tariff

Quota	Tariff
→ Trade reducing effects are more certain	→ Trade reducing effects are less certain
→ More vulnerable to corruption	→ Less vulnerable to corruption
→ More restrictive	→ Less restrictive
→ Generate no revenue for the economy	→ Generate revenue for the economy

Dumping: The export by a country of a product at a price that is lower in the foreign market than the price charged in the domestic market.

Predatory dumping - Predatory dumping is a type of anti-competitive behavior in which a foreign company prices its products below market value in an attempt to drive out domestic competition.

Sporadic dumping: Manufactures practice sporadic dumping to get rid of excess merchandise. A manufacturer with unsold inventories avoids starting a price war in the home market to preserve his competitive position. Excess supplies are destroyed. Example, Asian farmers dumped small chickens into the sea. Another method is to have the excess supply dumped in a foreign market where the product is normally not sold. Thus, sporadic dumping is aimed at liquidating excess stocks that may arise occasionally.

Persistent dumping (Long period dumping): Persistent dumping as the name itself implies is the most permanent type of dumping. It involves consistent selling at lower prices in one market than in the rest of the market. This practice is based on the fact that markets vary in terms of overhead costs and demand characteristics. It happens when there is a constant demand for the product in the foreign market.

Japan, for example, sold consumer electronics at high prices in its own country. This is because it has no foreign competition. But it lowered prices in the U.S market in order to maintain market share.

Economic Integration

Economic integration refers to the process by which countries reduce trade barriers & coordinate economic policies. It occurs in stages from least to most integrated.

Scan to watch a video on Economic Integration

1) Preferential Trade Agreement: Countries argue to lower tariffs on certain products from members countries only not all product.
2) Free trade area: Group of nations remove all tariffs & quotas on trade among them but maintain independent trade policies towards non-members. Example NAFTA (North American Free Trade Association) .
3) Custom Union: FTA + common tariff policy with non-members.
4) Common Market: It has features of free trade area and custom union, and moreover, there is a free movement of labour and capital.
5) Economic Union: Highest level of integration. Common market + there is monetary and fiscal unification.

EU→ CM → CU → FTA
(Highest Integration) (Lowest Integration)

The Gains from Trade

Gains from trade refers to net benefits that a country obtains by trading with other countries. In other words, gains from trade represent the increase in total output, efficiency, and welfare that results from specialization and exchange compared to self-sufficiency.

Potential Gains from Trade

- Defined as the difference in the domestic cost ratios of producing goods in two countries.
- Formula:

$$G_P = \left[\frac{C_X}{C_Y}\right]_A - \left[\frac{C_X}{C_Y}\right]_B$$

- Where C_X and C_Y are the costs of producing goods X and Y.
- A and B represent two different countries.
- This equation represents the difference in opportunity costs, which determines comparative advantage.

Actual Gains from Trade

- Defined as the difference in the price ratios of two commodities between two trading countries.
- Formula:

$$G_A = \left[\frac{P_X}{P_Y}\right]_A - \left[\frac{P_X}{P_Y}\right]_B$$

- Where P_X and P_Y are the prices of goods X and Y.
- This measures how trade affects actual prices and benefits nations based on market conditions.

International Organisations and Groups

GATT [General Agreement on Tariffs and Trade]

Formed in 1947

Headquarters in Geneva (Switzerland)

Principles of GATT: Non-Discrimination

- Most favoured nation clause: treating other people equally
- National treatment: treating foreigners and locals equally.

Objective -promotes free trade.

Uruguay round replaced GATT with WTO.

GATT important rounds:

Geneva Round 1947

Annecy round 1949

Torquay round 1951

Geneva round 1955-56

Dillon round 1960-62

Kennedy round 1962-67

Tokyo round 1973-79

Uruguay round 1986-94

World Trade Organisation (WTO), 1995

The legal and institutional foundation of multilateral trading system.

Important meetings of WTO:

Date	Place
1996	Singapore
1998	Geneva
1999	Seattle
2001	Doha
2003	Cancun Fiasco
2005	Hongkong
2009	Geneva Switzerland
2013	Bali, Indonesia
2015	Nairobi, Africa
2017	Argentina
2022	Geneva
2024	Abu Dabi (UAE)

Scope of WTO:

TRIPS [Trade related Intellectual Property Rights] Related to patents, copyrights etc.

TRIMS [Trade related investment measures] Abolition of protection to domestic investment and to allow 100% foreign equity participation in certain cases.

GATTS [General Agreement on Trade and Services] service trade is included in WTO

AOA (Agreement on Agricultures)-

- Domestic support: Reduction of agricultural subsidies.
- Export subsidies abolished
- Market access : Reduction in tariff and non-tariff barriers of agriculture products.

Agriculture Subsidies

(1) Green box: No or minimum trade distorting effects. They are non-actionable under WTO.

(2) Red box: All agricultural subsidies which are considered to distort trade and production fall. They are prohibited by WTO.

(3) Blue box: Red Box subsidies with conditions. They are actionable by trading partners if their interests are adversely affected. The effected countries can appeal to dispute settlement body of WTO and go for countervailing measures.

Agreement on Textiles and Clothing: Reduction in tariff on textile and clothing.

Agreement on Anti-dumping: Set rules for allowing countries to take action against dumping in order to defend its domestic industries.

International Monetary Fund [IMF]

IMF established on 1945

(World Economic Forum and Global Financial Stability Reports are published by IMF).

Basic functions:

(1) Short term lending to countries to solve their BOP disequilibria.

(2) Maintains exchange rate stability.

(3) Remove foreign exchange restrictions.

(4) Balanced growth of trade.

Special Drawing Rights (SDR), 1969: It is a unit of account for IMF members and each member is given SDR's in proportion to their quotes.

International Bank for Reconstruction and Development (IBRD), 1945

Main function is to help poor countries and developing countries by providing loans which are long term in nature. Help is also extended to the countries affected or destroyed in Wars.

The world bank group consists of five organizations:

The International Bank for Reconstruction and Development, 1945

The International Bank for reconstruction and Development (IBRD) lends to governments of middle – income and creditworthy low—level income.

The International Development Association 1960

The International Development Association (IDA) provides interest free loans – and grants to governments of the poorest countries.

Together, IBRD and IDA make up the World Bank.

The International Finance Corporation 1956

IFC is the largest global development institution focused exclusively on the private sector. It helps developing countries achieve sustainable growth by financing investment, mobilizing capital in the international financial markets and providing advisory services to businesses and governments

The Multilateral Investment Guarantee Agency 1988

The multilateral investment guarantee agency (MIGA) was created in 1988 to promote foreign direct investment into developing countries to support economic growth, reduce poverty, and improve people's lives.

The International Centre for Settlement of Investment Disputes 1966

The international center for settlement of investment disputes (ICSID) provides international facilities for conciliation and arbitration of investment disputes

Difference Between IMF and WB

WB	IMF
Long terms loans	Short term Loans
Help poor countries	Overseas the monetary system of world
Promote economic development	Balanced Growth (Maintain economic stability)

SAARC (South Asia Association for Regional Cooperation)

- Intergovernmental organization for the development of economic and regional integration.
- Established in December 1985.
- Its objective is to Promote welfare of south Asians and to improve their quality of life.
- Its Headquarter is at Kathmandu, Nepal.
- It has 8 member countries: India, Bangladesh, Nepal, Sri Lanka, Maldives, Bhutan, Afghanistan, Pakistan.
- SAPTA (SAARC Preferential Trading Arrangement).

European Union

- **Established in 1993** (Belgium)
- International organization consists of European Countries.
- No. of members are 27.
- EU awarded noble peace prize in 2012.
- UK made exit from EU on 31st Jan 2020 known as BREXIT

ASEAN (1967) – Association of South East Asian Nations.

- The motto of ASEAN is **"One Vision, One Identity, One Community"**.
- 8th August is observed as ASEAN Day.

- ASEAN Secretariat – Indonesia, Jakarta.
- Ten member countries:

    1. Indonesia
    2. Malaysia
    3. Philippines
    4. Singapore
    5. Thailand
    6. Brunei
    7. Vietnam
    8. Laos
    9. Myanmar
    10. Cambodia

India is not a member.

- Its meeting held in 2023 at Indonesia with the theme 'ASEAN Matters: Epicentrum of growth'.

The Group of Twenty (G20)

The Group of Twenty (G20) is the premier intergovernmental forum for international economic cooperation. The forum plays an important role in shaping and strengthening global architecture and governance on all major international economic issues.

India holds the Presidency of the G20 from 1 December 2022 to 30 November 2023. The theme of India's G20 Presidency is - "**Vasudhaiva Kutumbakam**" or "**One Earth . One Family . One Future**"

G20 MEMBERS:

The Group of Twenty (G20) comprises 19 countries (Argentina, Australia, Brazil, Canada, China, France, Germany, India, Indonesia, Italy, Japan, Republic of Korea, Mexico, Russia, Saudi Arabia, South Africa, Türkiye, United Kingdom and United States) and the European Union. The G20 members represent around 85% of the global GDP, over 75% of the global trade, and about two-thirds of the world population.

Bretton Woods System

Held in 1944. The IMF and World Bank were created on the day the Bretton Woods Agreements were signed.

Reasons:

(1) Impact of Great Depression on world economics.

(2) World WAR II

Collapse of Bretton Woods System:

→Process of collapse started in 1971.

In 1973, the system was completely removed.

Reasons:

(1) Large current account deficit by USA.

(2) Vietnam War

(3) Two different, markets of Gold

→Which led to instability in the supply & demand equilibrium of gold. Two markets were – Private and Official.

Public Economics

Market Failure

Scan for a video lecture on this topic

Market failure is a situation in which allocation of goods and services by a free market is not fair, often leading to a net loss of economic value. The failure for the market to successfully achieve allocative efficiency, because there is an over or under provision of a good. Market failure is one of the reasons of non-attainment of pareto optimality. A simple example of market failure is when a monopolist seller sets high rates to the products leaving no choice for the buyers other than to purchase the overpriced goods.

Causes of Market Failure

1. Externality:

The presence of externality in consumption and production also lead to the divergence of social costs from private costs and of social benefits from private benefits. Externalities occur when the production or consumption of a good or service has an effect upon a third party.

1) **Positive externality of production** of a good or service creates external benefits for third parties (MPC > MSC).

Here, MPC: Marginal private cost

MSC: Marginal social cost

Examples: industrial training in firms, research into new technologies.

2) **Positive externalities of consumption** occur when the consumption of a good or service creates external benefits for third parties (MSB > MPB).

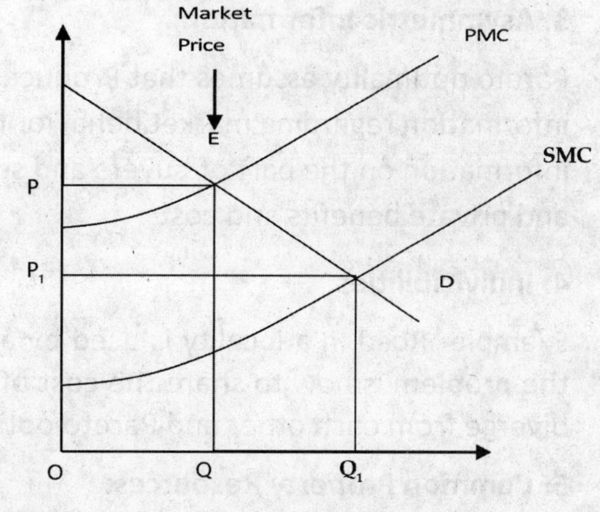

Here, MPB: Marginal private benefit

MSB: Marginal social benefit

Examples: immunisations, education, healthcare.

3) **Negative externalities of production:** occur when the production of a good or service creates external costs that are damaging to third parties (MSC > MPC).

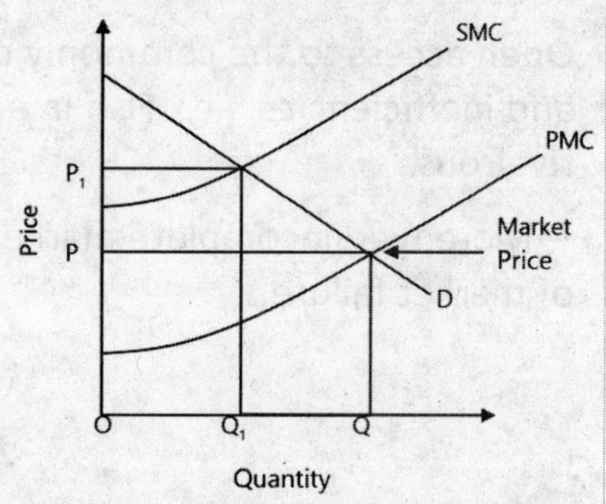

Examples: carbon emissions from factories, factory waste disposal, noise pollution, fossil fuels.

4) **Negative externalities of consumption**: occur when the consumption of a good or service creates the external costs that is damaging to third parties (MSB < MPB)

Examples: smoking, alcohol, cars, loud music, coal fires

2. Public Goods:

A public good is one who has properties of non-excludable and non-rivalrous.

Non-excludable: A good is non-excludable if it is not possible (or very difficult) to prevent anyone from consuming it.

Non-rivalrous: A good is non-rivalrous if one person's consumption does not reduce the availability of the good for others.

3. Asymmetric Information:

Pareto optimality assumes that Producers and Consumers have perfect information regarding market behavior but in real world, due to an asymmetric information on the part of buyers and sellers, they are unable to equate social and private benefits and costs.

4. Indivisibilities:

Example- Road in a locality is used by a number of persons in the locality. But the problem is how to share the cost of maintenance. Thus, MSC and MSB will diverge from each other and Pareto optimality will not be achieved

5. Common Property Resources:

Open access to the commonly owned resources is a crucial ingredient of waste and inefficiencies, i.e., Fish in a lake. CPR has properties of non-excludable and rivalrous.

→Moreover, incomplete markets and imperfect markets are some other causes of market failure.

Types Of Goods

Scan for a video lecture on this topic

Public goods: A public good is one whose consumption or use by one individual does not reduce the amount available for others. An example of a public good is water which is available to one person and is also available to others without any additional cost. Its consumption is always joint and equal. It is **non-excludable** if it can be consumed by anyone. It is **non-rivalrous** if no one has an exclusive right over its consumption. Its benefits can be provided to an additional consumer at zero marginal cost. Thus, public goods are both non-excludable and non- rivalrous. Public goods once produced, are available to all in identical amounts, demand for them is vertical sum of each individual's demand.

Moreover, environmental quality is generally considered as a public good and when it is valued at market price, it leads to market failure. The Paretian condition for a public good is that its marginal social benefit (MSB) should equal its marginal social cost (MSC). But the characteristics of a public good are such that the economy will not reach a point of Pareto optimality in a perfectly competitive market. Public goods create externalities. The externality starts when the marginal cost of consuming or producing an additional unit of a public good is zero but a price above zero is being charged. This violates the Paretian welfare maximization criterion of equating marginal social cost and marginal social benefit. This is because the benefits of a public good must be provided at a zero marginal social cost. There exists Free Rider problem. Free Rider are the Individuals who receive benefit of public good without paying for it.

Private goods: they are excludable and rival. They don't lead to market failure. Market demand curve for private goods is horizontal summation of each individual demand curve because every individual demand different quantity.

Common property resources: They are non-excludable and rivalrous. i.e. Fish in a lake They lead to market failure.

Club goods: They are excludable and non-rivalry. Such as movie tickets.

Congestible goods: They can be non-excludable and non-rivalry i.e. public road.

They can be excludable and non-rivalry such as toll road.

They can be rivalry and non-excludable i.e., traffic on road.

They can be rivalry and excludable if there is traffic road with toll.

Public Revenue

Income received by the government through its sources. It includes taxation policies, fee, fines etc.

Sources of Public Revenue

Taxes : These are compulsory payment to the government without expecting any direct benefit.

Direct Taxes: Progressive in nature, burden cannot be imposed on another person

i.e. income tax.

Indirect Tax: Can be shifted to another person. Regressive in nature i.e., sales tax, excise, custom etc. [Administrative cost is more in case of direct taxes] .

Corporation Tax: Imposed on profits of company.

Custom Duty: Imposed on imports and exports of commodity.

Excise Duty: Tax on production and sales.

Capital-gains tax: It is a tax imposed on the profit earned from the sale of a capital asset.

Specific tax: A specific tax is a fixed amount of tax placed on a particular good. It is also referred to as a per-unit tax, and the tax will depend on the quantity sold i.e., Rs 10 specific tax per unit of ice-cream.

Ad valorem tax: Taxes that are levied as a percentage of the assessed value of a piece of property. i.e. 10% tax on cell phone.

Lump sum tax: A lump-sum tax is a special way of taxation, based on a fixed amount, rather than on the real circumstance of the taxed entity. In this, the entity cannot do anything to change their liability. In contrast with a per unit tax, lump-sum tax does not increase in size as the output increases. A monopolist can't shift the lump sum tax to the consumer. It is added in fixed cost so marginal cost of monopolist remain unchanged. It reduces monopolist profit but does not affect output.

GST: It is a comprehensive destination based indirect tax introduced in India on 1st July, 2017. It unified various indirect taxes levied by the Central & State Governments into a single tax, making it a "One Nation, One Tax" system.

Old Slabs: 0, 5%, 12%, 18%, 28%

In September 2025, The GST rates in India have been simplified to three main slabs: 5%, 18%, and 40%

Items or transactions that are not covered by GST, such as petroleum products (which are subject to separate state taxes), alcohol for human consumption, and some specified goods like stamps and currency, are considered non-GST supplies.

Canons of Taxation

Given by Adam Smith

Canon of Equality: Burden of tax is equally shared.

Canon of Economy: Cost of collecting tax should be the minimum

Canon of Certainty: The contributor should be clear of all the information regarding the time of payment, amount to be paid etc.

Canon of Convenience: People should not face inconvenience while paying taxes.

Non-Tax Revenue

1) Interest receipt on loans.
2) Revenues from government activities like Railways
3) Receipts of currency notes, mint, etc.

Theories of Distribution of Tax - Burden

1) Benefit Principal : Given by Lindahl

   Taxes should be charged in proportion of the benefits received.ie toll tax

2) Ability to Pay Theory : Seligman

   Taxes charged should be according to the 'ability to pay' of the tax payer.

   Impact of tax : immediate burden of tax

   Shifting of tax : implies transferring the burden of tax from one person to another.

   Incidence of tax : Ultimate burden of Tax

Propounders	**Concept**
Mrs. Ursula Hicks	Formal incidence: It is on the person who is legally liable to pay the tax. Effective incidence: It is on the person who ultimately bears the burden of the tax.
Dalton	Money burden: If a consumer has to spend Rs. 50 more on sugar monthly because of tax, then it is money burden that he has to bear. Real burden: If consumer has to decrease the consumption of sugar, it means loss of economic welfare, it is real burden.

Theories Of Shifting of Tax

Modern theory :Given by Marshall

Case 1: $E_d = E_S$

Tax burden equally distributed amongst consumers and producers.

Scan for a video lecture on this topic

Case 2: $E_d < E_S$

Tax burdens is more on the buyer as compared to seller

Case 3 : $E_d > E_S$

Tax burdens are more on the seller as compared to buyer.

Case 4: $E_d = \infty$ (perfectly elastic)

Burden of tax falls wholly on producer.

Case 5: $E_d = 0$ (perfectly inelastic)

Burden of tax falls wholly on buyer.

Case 6: $E_S = \infty$ (perfectly elastic)

Burden of tax wholly on buyer.

Case 7: When $E_S = 0$ (perfectly inelastic)

Burden of tax falls wholly on seller.

Concepts Related to Incidence of Taxation

Tax incidence : change in tax policy (keeping public expenditure to be constant) which further leads to change in distribution of income.

Expenditure incidence: Change in expenditure policy (keeping tax constant), further leads to change in distribution of income.

Balanced Budget incidence: Study of change in distribution of income due to changes in both taxation and expenditure policy.

Differential tax incidence: Implies substituting one tax for another, as summing money income to be the same.

Tax buoyancy: Change in tax revenue to a change in national income (include additional efforts of government in form of expanding tax base, increasing tax rate and imposing new taxes). If the revenue collection from tax increase by 1% with 1% increase in GDP, then tax is considered buoyant.

Tax buoyancy can be expressed as follows:

$E_Y^b = (\Delta T^b / \Delta Y) \times (Y / T^b)$

$E_Y^b = \text{ buoyancy of tax revenue to national income}$

$T^b = \text{total tax revenue}$

$\Delta T^b = \text{(annual) change in total tax revenue}$

$Y = \text{Aggregate national income}$

$\Delta Y = \text{(annual) change in national income}$

Tax Elasticity: Automatic changes in yield of total revenue to a change in national income.(without any change in tax base, tax rate or new tax).

For tax elasticity, Tax revenue and change in tax revenue is net, not gross. Only the part of tax revenue change that occurs without policy changes is considered for tax elasticity (i.e., net of discretionary changes)

$$E_Y^T = \left(\frac{\Delta T}{\Delta Y}\right) \times \frac{Y}{T}$$

Here T is net tax revenue (excluding effects of discretionary changes)

Laffer Curve

- It depicts inverted U-shaped relationship between tax rates and tax revenues. The curve shows that tax revenue increases as tax rates increase up to a certain point, then decreases.
- The ideal tax rate is at the peak of the curve, where revenue is maximized.
- Tax rates that are too high can discourage investment and consumption, while tax rates that are too low can lead to insufficient revenue.

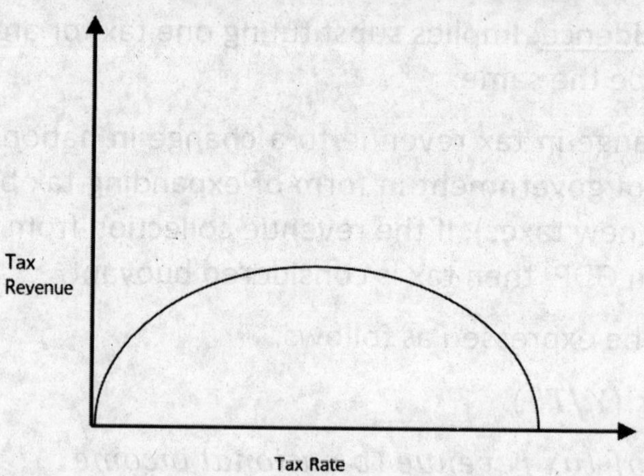

<u>Taxable capacity</u>: Amount of money that can be raised through taxation without causing burden.

Effects Of Taxation

Given by Dalton

<u>On Production</u>: Taxation reduces the ability to work, save and invest

<u>On Distribution</u>: Regressive tax increase inequalities while progressive tax decrease inequalities

<u>On Employment</u>: Tax reduce Income → Fall in demand → Employment↓

<u>On Inflation</u>: Tax reduce purchasing power → Low demand → Low prices.

Horizontal And Vertical Equity of Taxation

Horizontal equity is the economic principle that people with similar incomes should pay the same amount of taxes, while vertical equity is the principle that people with higher incomes should pay more taxes.

Tax Reform Committees

Taxation Enquiry Commission →1925

Kaldor's Tax Reforms/ Indian Tax Reform Committee→ 1956

Wanchoo Committee on Direct Taxes/ Direct Taxation Enquiry Committee→ 1970

Lk Jha Committee/ Indirect Taxation Enquiry Committee→ 1977

Chelliah Committee→ 1991

Rekhi Committee→ 1993

Vijay Kelkar Committee Report/Simplification and Rationalization of Direct Indirect Taxes →2002

Rastogi Committee→2005

Parthasarathi Shome Committee→2012

Arbind Modi Committee / Task Force on Direct Tax Code→2017

Akhilesh Ranjan Committee→2019

Chronological Ordering of Taxes:

- Land Revenue Tax
- Income Tax
- Excise Duty
- Stamp Duty
- Motor Vehicle Tax
- Entertainment Tax
- Sales Tax
- Estate Duty
- Expenditure tax, Gift tax, Wealth tax, Capital Gains Tax
- SUR Tax
- Corporation Tax
- MODVAT

- Death Duty
- Service Tax
- CENVAT
- VAT
- Fringe Benefit Tax
- GST

FRBM Act

Fiscal Responsibility and Budget Management Act, 2003

Objective:
To institutionalize fiscal discipline, reduce fiscal deficit, improve macroeconomic management, and ensure long-term stability in the Indian economy.

Key Targets (Original):

Reduction in fiscal deficit to 3.3% at the end of each financial year.

Reduction in revenue deficit to 0.5% in each financial year. It should be zero within 5 years which would end on March 31, 2009.

Note: Add current target from latest Union budget.

Public Expenditure

Expenditure incurred by public authorities for welfare of citizens.

Theories of Public Expenditure

1) Wagner's Law of Increasing State Activities

The theory holds that for any country, public expenditure rises constantly as income growth expands. According to his study, as public expenditure increases, role of the public sector also increases.

Government plays its role in following ways:

a. Protect people from internal and external aggression

b. Provides social services in respect of culture, education, health, etc.

c. Participation in material production.

Due to these governmental activities, its role becomes more important as compared to the private sector. Thus, Income elasticity of government services is greater than 1, implying that the level of government services changes more than the level of output in the economy. In short, during the process of economic development, the government expenditure increases more than proportionally as compared to the per-capita community output. Moreover, Government's role, both intensively and extensively, increases over a period of time.

Concept of X inefficiency: Lebenstein introduced it in 1966. It refers to inefficient use of productive resources. In Govt. sector, because of overstaffing, beau acratic delays, rigid rules and regulations, portion of public expenditure goes waste.

2) **Peacock - Wiseman Hypothesis**

Public Expenditure does not increase in a smooth manner but in a jerky, step like fashion. they talked about three effects -

a) Displacement effect : Movement from previous level of expenditure to a new and higher level.
b) Inspection effect : Along with the rise in Public Expenditure, government will also make some improvements in public revenue by adjusting tax. This will lead to new equilibrium in public finance.
c) Concentration effect : Tendency of Central Government activities increases at a faster rate than the state government.

3) **Colin- Clark Hypothesis**

It tells the optimum level of public expenditure. According to this theory, if government expenditure is more than 25% of the total economic activity, then it leads to inflation.

Canons of Public Expenditure

Given by Findlay Shirras

Canons of Benefit: It should benefit maximum number of people

Canon of Economy: should not be overspending

<u>Canon of Sanction</u>: Spending can be done only up to a certain limit without sanction from higher authorities.

<u>Canon of Surplus</u>: Budget should be in balance or surplus but not deficit budget.

<u>Classification of Expenditure</u>

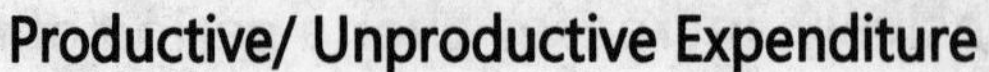

Productive/ Unproductive Expenditure

↓	↘
Effect on production such as building goods.	No effect on production such as defense.

Transfer and Non-transfer Expenditure

↓	↘
Unilateral payments that do not involve receipt of G & S in return. i.e. old ages pensions.	Bilateral payment and involves exchange of G & S.

Revenue and Capital Expenditure

↓	↘
Does not lead to creation of assets and are recurring in nature.	Leads to creation of assets

<u>Effects of Public Expenditure</u>

<u>On Production</u>: Positive impact.

<u>On Distribution</u>: Reduces inequalities

<u>Growth effects:</u> Public Expenditure ↑ → Demand ↑ → Economic activities↑

Dalton's Principle of Maximum Social Advantage

The Principle of Maximum Social Advantage states that public finance leads to economic welfare when public expenditure & taxation are carried out up to that point where the benefits derived from the MU (Marginal Utility) of expenditure is equal to the Marginal Disutility or the sacrifice imposed by taxation.

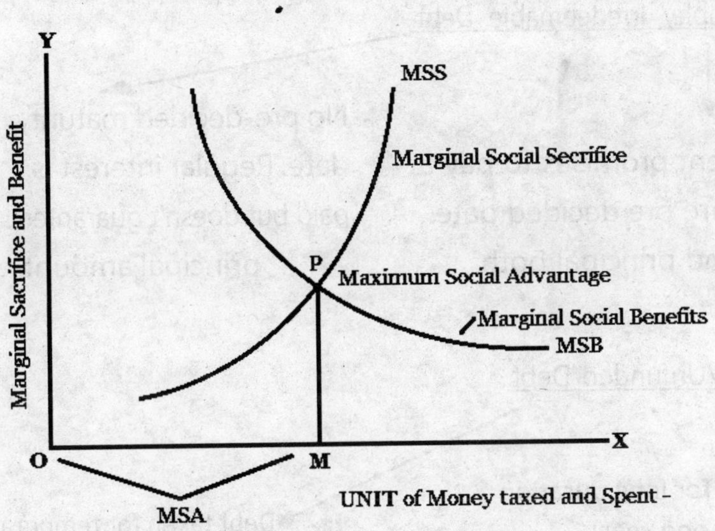

Public Debt

Public Debt is used to finance public expenditure when revenue is not enough.

Classification

1) Internal /External Debt

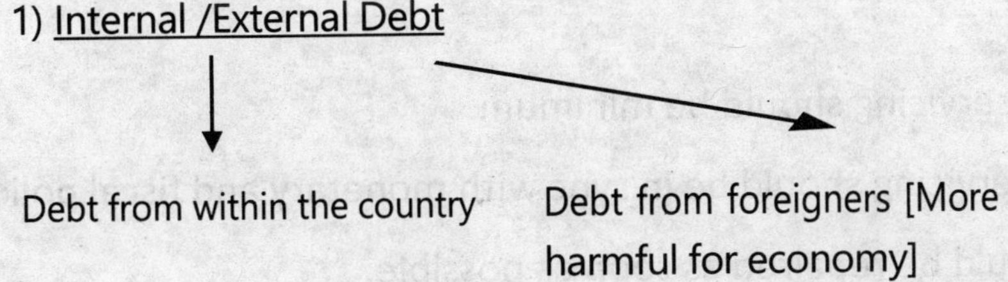

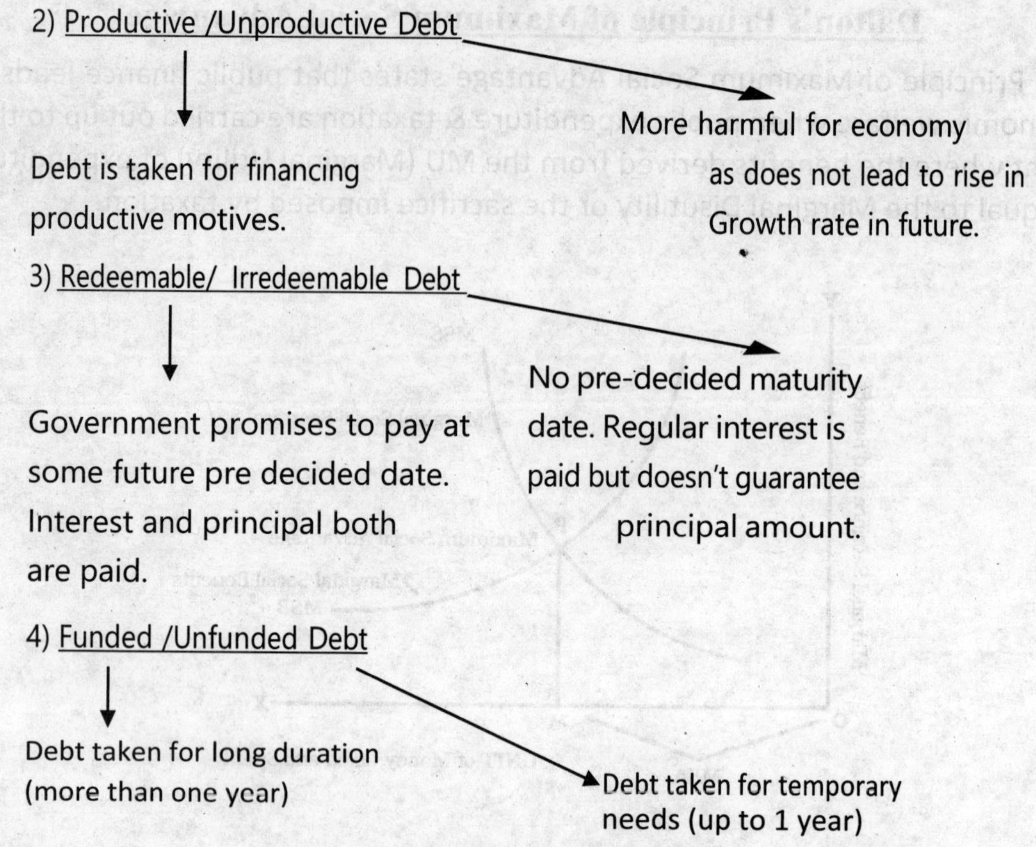

Public Debt Management

Public debt management means managing the debt and repayment of loans in such a way that such debt should not affect the economic situation of the country in an adverse manner.

Principles:

1) Cost of debt servicing should be minimum.
2) Public debt servicing should be in sync with monetary and fiscal policy.
3) The debt should be repaired as soon as possible.
4) Period of maturity should be wisely chosen.

Debt Servicing:

→Cost of meeting interest payments and regular contractual repayments of principal on a loan.

Public Budget

It is a statement of revenue and expenditure incurred by government. Balanced Budget: Estimated receipts are equal to estimated expenditure. Surplus Budget: Estimated receipts are more than estimated expenditure. It has contractionary effect on economy. Deficit budget: Estimated receipts are less than estimated expenditure. More money pumped into the economy. Thus, rise in income levels.

A budget gives **three estimates**:

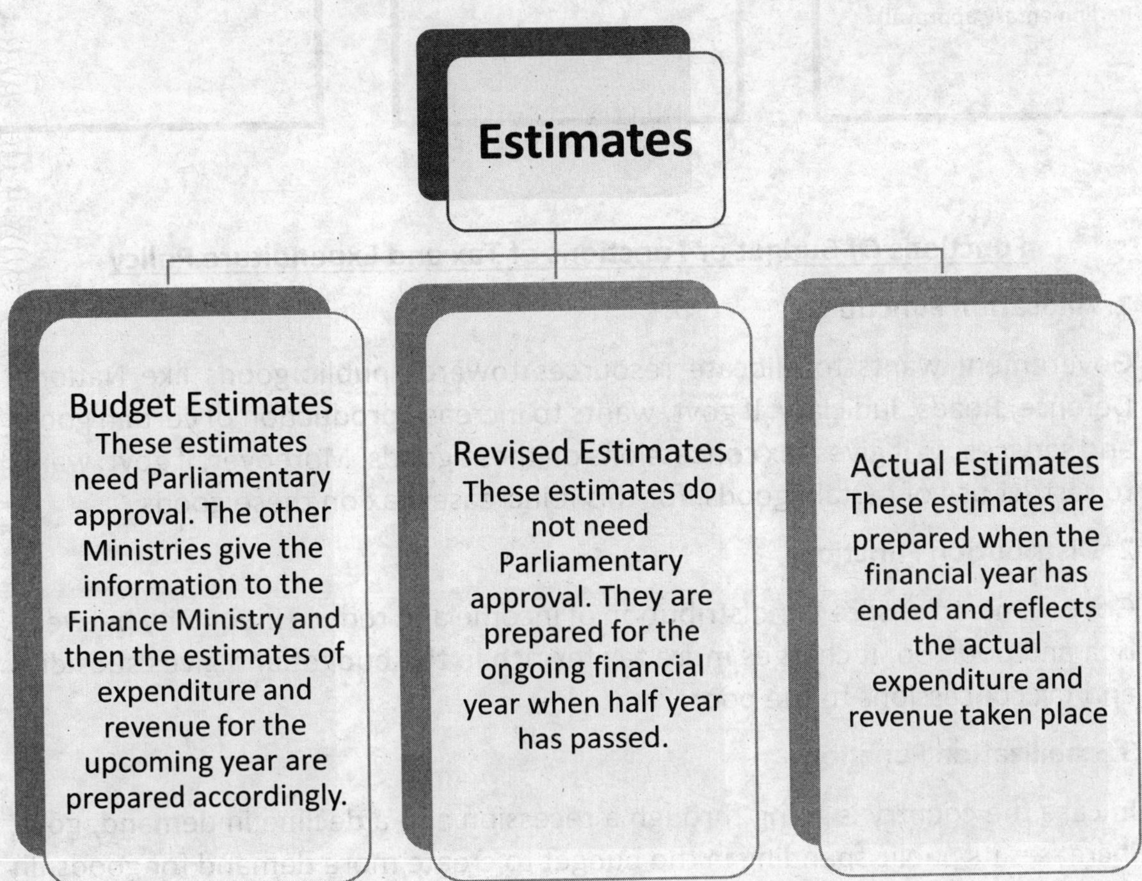

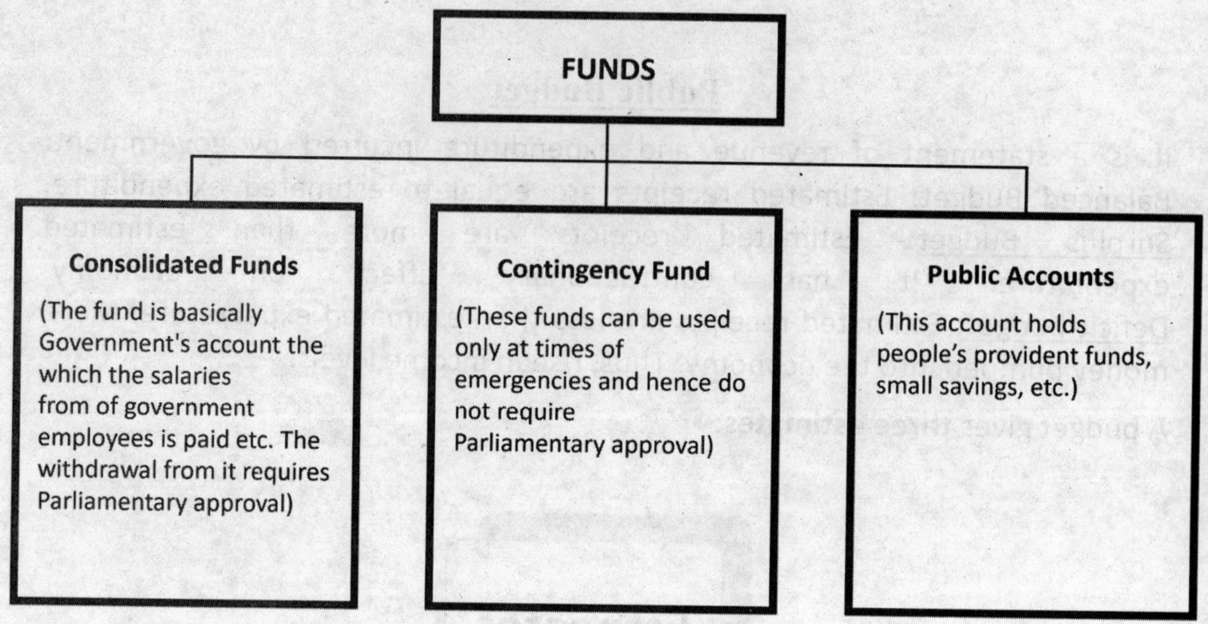

Functions Of Budget or Functions of Tax and Expenditure Policy

1. Allocation Function

Government wants to allocate resources towards public goods like National Defence, Roads, Judiciary. If govt. wants to increase production of certain goods and services, so it gives tax concessions on these goods. Moreover, if govt. wants to restrict use of certain goods, for this it increases tax on these goods.

2. Distribution Function

Govt. wants to ensure fair distribution of income and reduce inequality between rich and poor. So, it charges more tax for rich in the budget and gives subsidies and tax concessions to the poor.

3 Stabilization Function

In case the country is going through a recession and a decline in demand, govt. increases its public spending in the budget to create more demand for goods. In case the country is going through inflation, govt. decreases its spending in the budget to reduce demand for goods.

Kinds of Budget

1) i) Multiple Budget: Budget prepared in two parts

ii) Unified Budget: Entire budget is assessed together

2) i) Revenue Budget: It is short term project consists of revenue receipts and revenue expenditure.

ii) Capital Budget: It is based on long term project consists of capital receipts and capital expenditure.

Revenue Receipts: tax and non-tax revenue

Capital Receipts: borrowing, disinvestment

Techniques of Budgeting

1. Incremental Budgeting:

It is also known as Line-Item Budgeting/ Incrementalism. Under this, the budget is presented in financial terms. It doesn't highlight the purpose of expenditure which is a major drawback of this type of budget. Also, under line-item budgeting, last year's budget is revised to a little extent, that is, it is just an extension to the previous budget. The purposes of this budget are:

a. Accountability

b. Regularity

c. Legality of resources

The advantage is that it reduces the cost of decision making while the disadvantage is that there is no revaluation of programme takes place under Incremental budgeting

2. Zero Based Budgeting

Budget starting from the scratch [from zero] [Developed by Peter Phyrr in 1970]. Under Zero-Based budgeting, each department is required to justify its expenditures and budget requests from the scratch. The programmes are evaluated at various levels of resource allocation and its performance is measured. No balance to be carried forward.

3. Performance Budgeting

This budget was used prior to 1968. Under this kind of budgeting, the resources were allocated on the basis of performance depending on:

a. Final outcome of the budget.

b. Strategy adopted while implementing the budget.

c. Activities undertaken as a part of the budget.

3. Programme Budgeting

It is also known as Programme Planning. It means that out of the available strategies, the authorities choose the best and the most economical in terms of use resources, cost, etc.

The major difference between performance budgeting and programme budgeting is that the latter is more comprehensive as compared to the former. Moreover, programme budgeting is forward looking while performance budgeting is backward looking, that is, it analyses the event which have already occurred.

Some Notes:

Deficit Financing: Filling the gap between public revenue and expenditure [Printing more notes to financial deficit].

Pump Priming: One Shot hike in public expenditure, done when economic activity in private sector is low.

Concept of Deficits

Revenue Deficit = Revenue Expenditure - Revenue Receipts.

Capital Deficit = Capital Expenditure - Capital Receipts.

Budget Deficit = Capital Deficit + Revenue Deficit.

Primary Deficit = Fiscal Deficit - Net Interest Payment.

Effective Revenue Deficit = Revenue Deficit - Grants for Creation of Capital Asset.

Monetized Deficit = Increase in Net RBI Credit to The Government.

Fiscal Deficit = Total Expenditure - Total Revenue [Excluding Borrowings]

It is an indication of total borrowings needed by the government.

Illustration: If the revenue deficit of an economy is 3% of GDP, the primary deficit is 2% of GDP and the fiscal deficit is 7% of GDP, the capital expenditure to GDP ratio of that economy would be:

1. 5% of GDP

2. 1% of GDP

3. 4% of GDP

4. 2% of GDP

Answer: 3

Solution: Fiscal Deficit = total expenditure -total receipts(excluding borrowings, because borrowings are the capital receipts)

FD = (capital expenditure + revenue expenditure) – Revenue receipt

FD =Capital expenditure+ revenue deficit

7 = CE +3

7-3 =CE

4%=CE

Collusion

Collusion occurs when rival firms agree to work together. E.g., setting higher prices in order to make greater profits. It is a way for firms to make higher profits at the expense of consumers and reduces the competitiveness of market.

Collusion between firms is harmful to consumer. This is because firms can collude to raise prices.

Money and Banking

Note: Money supply and monetary policy already covered in macroeconomics.

Reserve Bank of India (RBI)

Central banking institution which controls the monetary policy of India. Established on April 1, 1935 on the recommendations of Hilton Young Commission. RBI was nationalized in 1949.

Functions-General	Development
Issue of currency	Extending Banking
Banker to Govt.	Development of Agriculture Credit
Banker's Bank	Credit Institution
Exchange Management	
Credit Control	
Publication of Data	

Commercial Banks

Scheduled: Banks which are included in the 2nd schedule of RBI Act 1934 and whose paid of capital is Rs. 5 Lac or more.

Functions:

Primary	Secondary
Accepting deposits	Sale/Purchase of shares
Making Advancing	Provides letter of credit.
Credit Creation	Work as trusty

Banking Institutions

NABARD

National bank for Agriculture and Rural Development is an apex development finance institution fully owned by Government of India.

Founded in 1982 Headquarter → Mumbai

Established on the recommendations of Shivaraman committee.

Regional Rural Banks

Regional Rural Banks (RRBs) are commercial banks in India that provide credit and other services to rural areas. They were established in 1975 to support the rural economy. Established on the recommendations of Narasimham working group 1975. They Provide credit to small and marginal farmers, agricultural labourers, artisans, and small entrepreneurs. They support the development of agriculture, trade, commerce, and industry in rural areas.

Cooperative Banks

Established on the cooperative principles of cooperation, self-help and mutual help and is engaged in the normal banking activities.

Their interest rate is high on Savings and low on credit.

The three tiers of cooperative banks in India are:

Primary Agricultural Credit Societies (PACS)

The base-level institutions that serve local people in rural and urban areas

Central Cooperative Banks (CCBs)

The district-level institutions that provide money to primary cooperative banks

State Cooperative Banks (StCBs)

The state-level institutions that connect cooperative banks with the Reserve Bank of India

Credit Rating Agencies

It is a company that assigns credit ratings, that is rating of a debtor's ability to pay back the debt by making timely interest payments and of the likelihood of default.

→ CRISIL (credit rating information services of India Limited) →1988

→ ICRA (Investment information and credit rating Agencies) → 1991

→ CARE (credit analysis and Research Limited) → 1993

Non-Banking Financial Institutions

Institutions which provide banking services without meeting the legal definition of bank, that is, one that does not hold a banking license. NBFI's hinder the operation of effective monetary policy. If central bank tries to control lending by commercial banks, it will not be successful if the lending of NBFI's are not under its control.

Money Market and its Instruments

Money Market deals with short term funds. Its instruments are:

Treasury Bills

Issued by the central bank on behalf of the government, to curb temporary liquidity shortfalls. They not yield interest but issued at redemption price. A Treasury bill doesn't pay interest, so calculating its return is a bit different than with most other investments. It is a short-term government debt security with a maturity of less than one year. Unlike many other debt securities that make regular interest payments to investors, Treasury bills yield no interest. Rather, the bills are sold at a discount to their redemption price. For example, a Treasury bill with a face value of $1,000 might sell for $985.

The first calculation involves subtracting the T-bill's price from 100 and dividing this amount by the price. This figure tells you the T-bill's yield during the maturity period. Multiply this number by 100 to convert to a percentage.

$$Yield = \frac{100-price}{price} \times 100$$

Next, multiply the yield you just calculated by 365 and then divide by the number of days in the maturity period that you determined earlier. This will give you the T-bill's annualized investment return.

$$Annualized\ return\ yield = \frac{365}{days\ to\ maturity}$$

Repo

Commercial banks take loans from RBI at repo rate.

Reverse Repo

Commercial banks lend to RBI at reverse repo rate.

Commercial Papers

They are short-term unsecured, promissory notes issued by the corporations and Financial Institutions are some discounted values.

Bills of Exchange

A bill of exchange is a written order that instructs someone to pay a specific amount of money to another person. It's a legal instrument used to guarantee payment, especially in international trade to help exporters and importers to fulfill transactions.

Certificate of Deposits

It is type of federally insured savings account that has a fixed interest rate and fixed date of withdrawal known as maturity date.

Call Money Market

Market for extremely short period loans i.e. one to fourteen days

<u>Money Market Classification</u>

Organised

- RBI
- Commercial banks
- Development banks
- Investment institutions
- RRB's
- Foreign banks

Unorganised

- Indigenous bankers
- NBFI's (Chit funds and Nidhis)
- Money lenders

Capital Market

Deals with lending and borrowing of medium and long-term credit.

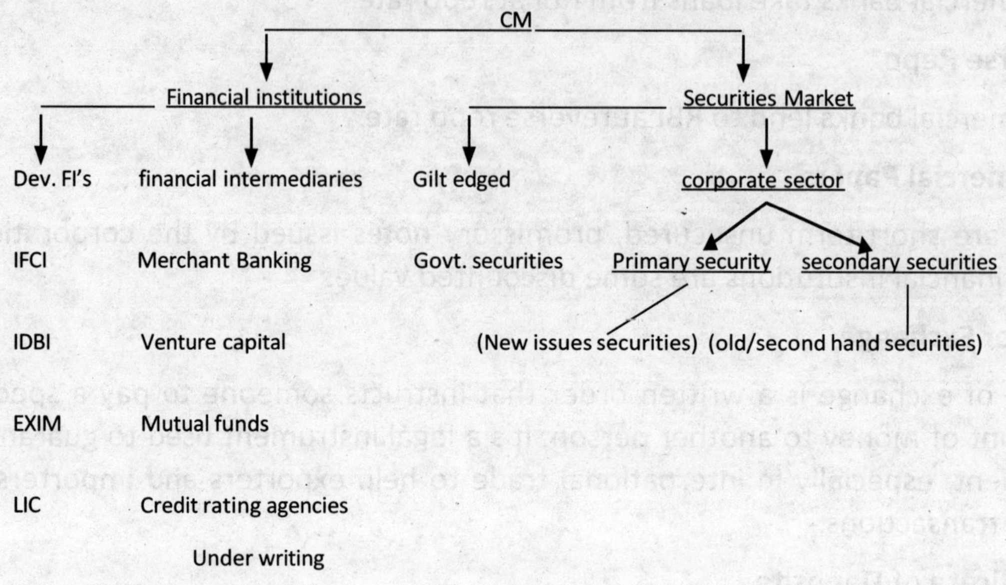

IDBI → 1964 (Provide credit to protect industrial state of economy

↓

Industrial Development Bank of India

SIDBI → 1990 (helps to grow MSME to grow with easy availability of finance)

↓

Small Industrial Development Bank of India

UTI Act in 1963 (encourage poor and middle-income groups to pool their savings)

In 1964, the Unit Trust of India (UTI) launched its first investment scheme, Unit Scheme 1964

IFCI → 1948 (Medium and long-term financial assistance to large industries)
↓
Industrial Finance Corporation of India

IIBI → 1977 (Provide term loan assistance for project finance, assets, credit, etc.)
↓
Industrial Investment bank of India

ICICI → 1955 (finance small and medium enterprises)
↓
Industrial credit and Investment Corporation of India

IRBI- 1971 (provide financial assistance to industrial enterprises)
↓
Industrial Reconstruction Bank of India

Capital Market Reforms

Secondary Market deals with stock exchange.

Biggest → National stock exchange

Oldest → Bombay stock exchange

1. National Stock Exchange (biggest stock exchange) (Index – Nifty) set up in1992. It recognized as stock exchange by SEBI in 1993 and commenced its operations in 1994 with launch of wholesale debt market on June 30, 1994. Equity market segment of NSE commenced operations on Nov 3, 1994.
2. Bombay Stock Exchange – 1875, Index SENSEX (oldest stock exchange).
3. BADLA trading banned by SEBI in 1993, effective from march 1994.
4. SEBI - Securities and Exchange Board of India formed in 1988. Statutory status was given in 1992. It was established to regulate and develop the securities market

   Functions -

   i) Promote interest of investors

ii) Promote development and to regulate securities market

iii) To prevent insider trading and of unfair practices

iv) Investor's education and training

5. Introduction of Electronic Trading (1996): The National Stock Exchange (NSE) introduced electronic trading, replacing the traditional open outcry system.
6. Deregulation of Interest Rates (1994): Allowed market-determined interest rates, enhancing the efficiency of capital allocation.
7. Introduction of Dematerialization (1996): Transition from physical to electronic shares, which increased transparency and reduced the risk of fraud.
8. Foreign Institutional Investors (FII) Participation (1992): Allowed FIIs to invest in Indian capital markets, increasing capital inflow and market liquidity.
9. Implementation of the Depositories Act (1996): Established depositories to ensure the safe and efficient transfer of securities.

Derivatives

Derivatives are financial contracts that derive their value from an underlying asset, for e.g., futures, options & forwards.

Forward And Future Contracts

These are agreements to buy or sell an asset at a set price on a specific date in the future. The main difference between the two is that forwards are customized agreements, while futures are standardized contracts

Basis	Forward Contract	Future Contract
Trading	Private agreement between two parties	Traded on an exchange through an intermediary
Terms	Flexible terms and conditions	Standardized terms
Risk	Higher counterparty risk	Lower default risk

Settlement	Settles at the end of the contract	Prices settled daily until the end of the contract

Banking Sector Reforms

Narsimha Committee

→ Narsimha committee had brought banking sector reforms

→ Two phases - 1991 and 1998

→ Main aim was to improve the banking sector.

Main provisions:

1) Reduces statutory liquidity ratio and cash reserve ratio
2) liberal view for allowing foreign banks to the country
3) Should have 4 - tier banking system

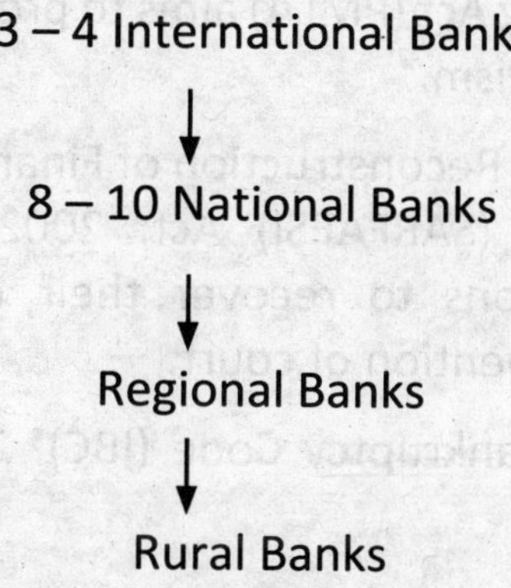

4) More autonomy to the banks
5) Computerization of banking system
6) Asset reconstruction fund was formed to take care of NPA'S

Nationalization of Banks

On 19 July, 1969, 14 banks were nationalized. In 1980, second phase of nationalization begins.

Important Banking Acts

- Reserve Bank of India Act, 1934: This act establishes the Reserve Bank of India (RBI) as the central banking institution in India.
- Banking Regulation Act, 1949: The Banking Regulation Act is a crucial legislation that regulates and supervises the banking sector in India.
- Negotiable Instruments Act, 1881: The Negotiable Instruments Act (NIA) provides a legal framework for negotiable instruments such as promissory notes, bills of exchange, and cheques.

  NIA Section 138: Section 138 of the Negotiable Instruments Act, 1881, states that issuing a cheque which bounces due to insufficient funds is a punishable offense. The punishment includes: Imprisonment for up to two years, A fine of up to twice the amount of the cheque or Both imprisonment and a fine
- Prevention of Money Laundering Act, 2002: Money laundering poses a serious threat to the financial system and economy. The Prevention of Money Laundering Act (PMLA) aims to prevent money laundering and the financing of terrorism.
- Securitization and Reconstruction of Financial Assets and Enforcement of Security Interest (SARFAESI) Act, 2002: This act empowers banks/ financial institutions to recover their Nonperforming assets (NPA's) without the intervention of court.
- Insolvency and Bankruptcy Code (IBC), 2016: it addresses the issue of NPA's in India.

Growth and Development Economics

Economics Growth and Development

Economic Growth: It is related to a quantitative sustained increase in the country's per capita income.

Economic Development: It is a wider concept than economic growth. It means "GROWTH PLUS CHANGE". An economy can grow but it may not develop because poverty, unemployment and inequalities may continue to persist.

Development = Growth + Standard of living

↓

Broader concept than growth

Generally speaking, economic development refers to the problems of UDC's and economic growth to those of the DC's.

Characteristics Of an Underdeveloped Economy

1. General poverty
2. Agriculture- main occupation
3. Dualistic economy
4. Underdeveloped or underutilized natural resources
5. Unemployment / under employment
6. Orthodox social attitude
7. Persistence of customs and traditions
8. Lack of enterprise and initiative
9. Lack of capital formation
10. Technological backwardness

Indices of Economic Development

GNP - Gross National Product

Initially the change in GNP was considered to be an indicator of development. But it has its flaws. It was an index of production only. It did not talk about the quality of life of people.

PQLI - Physical Quality of Life Index

Given by Morris D. Morris in 1979. Three indicators-

a) Life expectancy at age 1

b) Infant mortality (number of deaths per 1000 live births) [IM]

c) Literacy- General ability to read and write [L]

Value of index ranges from 0 to 100 with 0 to be the worst and 100 to be the best.

$$PQLI = \frac{Life\ \ Exp.at\ Age\ 1 + IM\ + L}{3}$$

HDR - Human Development Report

The United Nations Development Programme (UNDP) annually releases the HDR with 5 composite indices, which are:

1. Human Development Index
2. Inequality-adjusted Human Development Index (considers 'Inequality' as the fourth pillar)
3. Gender Development Index
4. Gender Inequality Index
5. Multidimensional Poverty Index

HDI - Human Development Index

Given by Amartya Sen and Mehboob -Ul - Haq in 1990 and published by UNDP

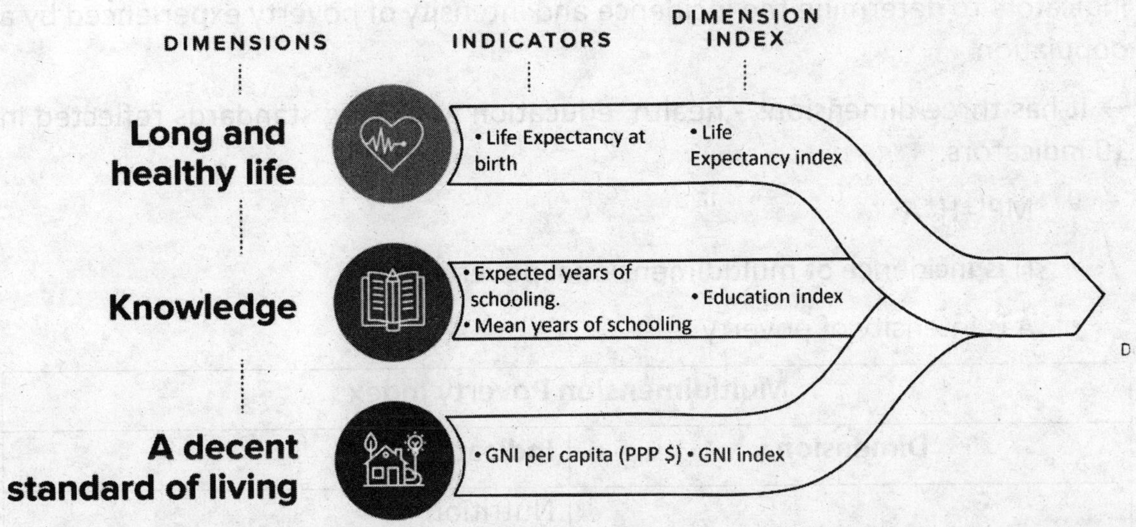

GM of three indicators

$$\sqrt[3]{Longenity \quad . \quad Education \quad . \quad Income}$$

HDI value ranges b/w 0 and 1, where 0 is considered to be worst while 1 is best.

HDI Value	Level of DEV.
0 to 0.499	Low level of HD
0.5 to 0.799	Medium level of HD
0.8 to 1.0	High level of HD

Inequality adjusted HDI

Accounts for inequalities in life expectancy, schooling and income. It will be equal to HDI if there is no inequality across people.

Multi-Dimensional Poverty Index

The Global Multidimensional Poverty Index (MPI) was developed in 2010 by the Oxford Poverty & Human Development Initiative (OPHI) and the United Nations Development Programme and uses health, education and standard of living indicators to determine the incidence and intensity of poverty experienced by a population.

→ It has three dimensions - health, education and living standards reflected in 10 indicators.

- MPI=H*A
- H is incidence of multidimensional poverty
- A is intensity of poverty

Multidimension Poverty Index	
Dimension	**Indicator**
Health	Nutrition
	Child Mortality
Education	Years of Schooling
	School attendance
Living Standard	Cooking fuel
	Improved sanitation
	Safe drinking water
	Electricity
	flooring
	Asset ownership

Gender Inequality Index

Human Development Report (HDR) 2010 introduced it. It has three critical dimensions for women- Reproductive health, empowerment and labor market participation.

Gender Development Index

HDR 1995 launched it. It attempted to capture achievements through the same set of basic capabilities as included in HDI i.e., life expectancy, educational attainment and income but adjust the HDI for gender inequality.

Gender Empowerment Measure

HDR 1995 introduced it. It indicated whether women are able to actively participate in economic and political life. Focused on political participation [measured by women's shares of parliamentary seats], economic participation [shares of high level and professional positions] and power over economic resources (income gap).

Global Hunger Index

GHI scores are based on the values of 4 component indicators.

1) Undernourishment: share of the population whose caloric intake is insufficient.
2) Child stunting: share of children under the age of 5 who have low height for their age.
3) Child wasting: share of children under age 5 who have low weight for their height.
4) Mortality rate of children under age 5.

Composition of GHI Scores and Severity Designations

Note: All indicator values are standardized.

GHI Severity of Hunger Scale				
≤ 9.9 Low	10.0 – 19.9 Moderate	20.0 – 34.9 Serious	35.0 – 49.9 Alarming	≥ 50.0 Extremely Alarming

100-point scale

The Human Poverty Index

The Human Poverty Index is an indicator of the standard of living in a country, developed by United Nations (UN) to complement the Human Development Index (HDI) and was first reported as part of Human Development report in 1997. It was considered to better reflect the extent of deprivation in developed countries compared to HDI. In 2010, it was replaced by the UN's Multidimensional Poverty Index.

The HPI concentrates on the deprivation in the three essential elements of human life already reflect in the HDI: Longevity, Knowledge and a decent Standard of Living

The Human Poverty Index for developing countries (HPI-1)

While the HDI measures average achievement, the HPI-1 measures deprivations in three basic dimensions of human development captured in the HDI:

1. A long and healthy life - vulnerability to death at a relatively early age, as measured by the probability at birth of not surviving to age 40.
2. Knowledge - exclusion from the world of reading and communications, as measured by the adult literacy rate.
3. A decent standard of living: Lack of access to overall economic provisioning, as measured by the unweighted average of two indicators, the percentage of the population not using an improved water source and the percentage of children under weight-for-average

Calculating the HPI-1 is more straightforward than calculating the HDI. The indicators used to measure the deprivation already normalized between 0 and 100 (because they are expressed in percentages), so there is no need to create dimension indices as for the HDI.

The Human Poverty Index for OECD countries (HPI-2)

The HPI-2 measures deprivations in the same dimensions as the HPI-1 and also captures social exclusion. Thus, it reflects deprivation in four dimensions:

1. A long and healthy life: Vulnerability to death at a relatively early age, as measured by the probability at birth of not surviving to age 60.

2. Knowledge-exclusion from the word of reading and communications, as measured by the percentage of adults (ages 16-65) lacking functional literacy skills.
3. A decent standard of living as measured by the percentage of people living below the income poverty line (50% of median adjusted household disposable income)
4. Social exclusion-as measured by the rate of long-term unemployment (12 months or more)

Theories of Development

Classical Theory of Development

Adam Smith

Adam Smith is father of Political economy and is the founder of classical school of economics. Smith's work is "An enquiry into the nature and causes of the wealth of nations"(1776). One of the smith most important contribution was to introduce the notion of increasing returns based on division of labour. He saw the division of labour as the very basis of a social economy. The division of labour determines the level of labour productivity but it is limited by the extent of market. Specialization provides greater scope for capital accumulation. Smith recognized that increasing returns based on the division of labour were much more a feature of industry than agriculture.

Scan for video on Classical and Marxian Theory

His views on development-

1) Capital accumulation should be encouraged.
2) Promoted the concept of division of labor and specialization.
3) Favored laissez-faire policy.
4) Promoted concept of invisible hand. Here invisible hand means market forces of demand and supply.
5) According to him, development is not sudden; rather it is cumulative and slow process.

Assumptions -

1. Laissez-faire
2. Two sectors Agriculture and Industry
3. Agriculture is subject to law of diminishing returns
4. Two inputs - labor, capital
5. Subsistence law of wages
6. Say's laws of market
7. Perfect competition

Ricardian Theory of Development

Ricardo gave the theory of development in his book "Principles of political economy and taxation" (1817). He gave the main role to the capitalists who accumulate capital from the profits which is primary source of capital accumulation. Ricardo predicted that capitalist economies would end up in a stationary state with no growth, also owing to diminishing returns in agriculture. Like smith, according to Ricardo also, growth and development is a function of capital accumulation and capital accumulation depends on reinvested profits.

Two stages -

1) Progressive state: Rate of profits rules high.
2) Stationary state: Rate of profit is zero.

To begin with at OL level of employment, when the population is small and land is fertile, higher rate of profit prevails. But as population increases, inferior grades of cultivation are brought under cultivation, law of diminishing returns operates. At OL_1, output reaches its highest point at Q. The rate of profit becomes zero Point Q indicates stationary State.

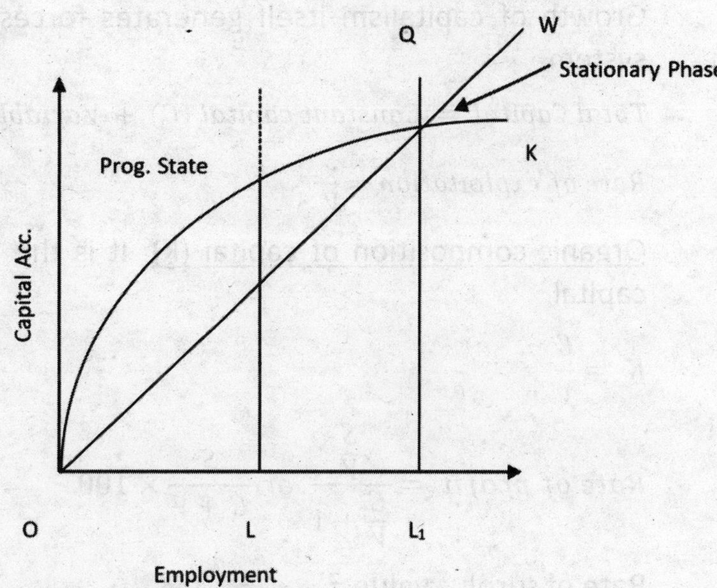

Marxian Theory of Development

Given in Marx's book "Das capital" in 1867. Main ideas of development are: -

a) Materialistic interpretation of history
b) Theory of class struggle
c) Theory of surplus value
d) Concept of Reserve Army
e) Economic development under capitalism

Historical materialism: Movements in society will be in the following stages.

a) Primitive society
b) Slavery system
c) Feudalism
d) Capitalist society
e) Socialistic society

Theory of class struggle: Clash of interest of two groups - capitalist and working class.

According to this theory, birth of capitalist is the cause of their destruction. Growth of capitalism itself generates forces that bring about destruction of system.

$$Total\ Capital\ = Constant\ capital\ (C)\ +\ Variable\ capital\ (V)\ +\ Surplus\ value(S)$$

$$Rate\ of\ exploitation = \frac{S}{V}$$

<u>Organic composition of capital (K)</u>: It is the amount of labour equipped with capital.

$$K = \frac{C}{v}$$

$$Rate\ of\ profit = \frac{\frac{S}{V}}{\frac{C}{V}+1}\ or\ \frac{S}{C+V}\times 100$$

Rate of surplus value = $S' = \frac{s}{v} \times 100$

↓

Indicate degree of exploitation of labour

<u>Reserve Army of Labour</u>: Technically displaced persons

Two ways to increase surplus value:

1) By keeping wages at the subsistence level.
2) By increasing productivity. Increasing productivity implies technological progress. TP is capital absorbing but labour saving. The result is technological unemployment

<u>Destruction of capitalism</u>: Rate of profit of capitalistic reduce because of the following reasons:

1) <u>Organic composition of capital</u>: There is inverse relation between rate of profit and organic composition of capital over a long period.
2) <u>Under consumption</u>: Excess of supply in relation to demand. Prices are reduced. Thus, rate of profits decline.

Main Assumptions:

1) Two classes :
   - Bourgeoise
   - Proletariat
2) Wages of workers are determined at subsistence level
3) Labour theory of value. labour is Principal source of value generation
4) Factors of production are owned by capitalists
5) Capitalist exploits workers
6) Two types of capital: constant and variable
7) Labour is homogeneous and perfectly mobile
8) Perfect competition

Necessary time/ labour → 2 hrs. a day for Rs. 20

But Labour work → 8 hours a day for Rs.20

Surplus Labour = Total labour - Necessary labour = 8 hours - 2 hours = 6 hours

Surplus value = Total value - wages = 80 - 20 = Rs. 60

Schumpeter Theory of Development

Schumpeter ideas about economic development first appeared in his book "The theory of economic development" in 1911. According to him, Development is a spontaneous and discontinuous change in the flow channels which cause a disturbance in equilibrium and hence to alters and displaces the equilibrium state forever. According to Schumpeter, "development will happen only when circular flow is disturbed. The circular flow can only be disturbed through innovation.

Five kinds of innovations:

a) New product
b) New method of production
c) New source of raw material

d) New industrial organization

e) New market

Qualities of innovator:

1) He should have a technical know how

2) Must able to manage funds

→Through the process of development, old things are replaced by new things. This process is termed "Creative Destruction" essential for progress but disruptive to existing equilibrium. Primary wave of expansion will be followed by secondary waves.

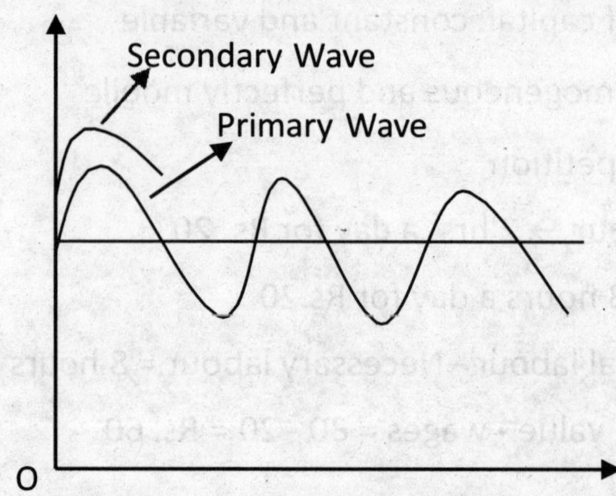

Why downturn of economic starts: When innovation becomes popular, other entrepreneurs follows it. In other words, When the original innovation proves profitable, other competitors follow it in "swarm-like clusters." Innovation in one field induces innovation in other fields. New products replacing old, speculation takes place, old firms vanished. Innovators start repaying loans out of profit.

Structural Transformation Models

These theories and models emphasize structural constraints in developing economies, such as dualism, dependency, and underdeveloped institutions.

Lewis Theory of Development

Given by Arthur Lewis in 1954. Also known as "Model of unlimited supply of labour." It states that with the movement of labour from rural to urban sector, the traditional society transforms into modern society.

Assumptions

1) Dual economy means coexistence of agriculture/ subsistence/ traditional sector and industrial /manufacturing modern sector.

2) Development in an economy takes place due to transfer of labour from agriculture to industrial sector. As a result of movement of labour from traditional to modern sector, the capital in the latter accumulates and output expands, thus leading this economy towards development.

3) No capital accumulation in the agriculture sector.
4) The number of workers in rural sector are more as compared to that in the industrial sector. (Disguised unemployment in agriculture sector).
5) There are diminishing returns to labour.
6) Wage rate is higher in capitalistic sector.

Growth process: If some workers are withdrawn from the primary sector and prepared to work in the capitalist sector at the prevailing wage rate, the Marginal productivity of these workers should be higher than their paid-out wages, so that profits are expected to rise. Capitalist are expected to reinvest their surplus which would stimulate the process of capital formation. It would cease at a point when the workers are prepared to work only at capitalistic wage rate equal to their productivity. Capitalist can stimulate their capital through bank credit.

Fei Ranis Model

Given in 1964 in the work of fie-Ranis. "Development of the labour surplus economy." It is an improvement over Lewis model. This model also assumes coexistence of a dual economy that is agricultural and industrial economies. Development consists of reallocation of surplus agricultural works, whose contribution to output is zero, to the industrial sector where they become productive at a wage equal to the institutional wage in agriculture.

Assumptions:

1. Dual economy
2. Land is fixed
3. Output of agriculture is function of land and labour
4. Output of industry is function of capital and labour

Fie - Ranis analyze the development of a labour surplus economy into three phases.

First phase: The disguised unemployed, who are not adding to agricultural output (whose MPP=0) , are transferred to the industrial sector at the constant institutional wage.

Second phase: Agricultural workers add to agricultural output but produce less than the institutional wage (whose MPP< institutional wage), they get transferred. Then the point will eventually reach when farm workers produce output equal to the institutional wage.

This begins the 3rd phase which marks the end of the takeoff and beginning of the self-sustained growth when farm workers produce more than the institutional wage they get. In this phase, the surplus labour is exhausted. In this stage agricultural sector becomes commercialized. Here MPP= institutional wage or MPP > institutional wage.

1st Phase MPP = 0

2nd phase MPP < institutional wage

3rd phase MPP = Institutional wage

MPP: Marginal physical productivity

Balanced Growth Theory

Promoted by Ragnar Nurkse, Lewis, Young, Rodan. According to it, all sectors should grow together.

Crux: The investments should be made simultaneously in all the sectors.

Following are the theories of balanced growth

1) Big Push Theory : By Rosenstein Rodan. He gives three types of indivisibilities and example of shoe making factory to explain the balanced growth.

2) Vicious circle of poverty (Nurkse) : To break vicious circle of poverty, application of capital to wide range of industries is needed. Just as balanced diet is needed for the growth of body, similarly, balanced growth is needed for economic development.

3) Lewis theory of development : Balance between agriculture and industries, material and human capital, export and import etc. is necessary.

Merits

1) Creates economies of scale

2) Leads to specialization and division of labour

3) Wide extent of market

Demerits

1) Not suitable for underdeveloped economy.

2) Ignores the effect of inflation on the economy.

Unbalanced Growth

Propounded by 'Hirschman' in his work 'The strategy of economic development' (1958). Other proponents were Singer, Rostow, Kindleberger, Streeten. The theory focused upon creating imbalance between the factors of an economy. Investment should be made in leading sectors which will further create economies for other sectors. According to this concept, investment should be made in selected sectors rather than simultaneously in all sectors of the economy.

Unbalancing The Economy With SOC

Social overhead capital (SOC) has been defined as "comprising those basic services without which primary, secondary and tertiary productive activities cannot function." A large investment in SOC will encourage private investment later in DPA (Directly Productive Activities). Growth of raw materials owing to growth of a set of industries. For example, cheaper supply of electric power may encourage the establishment of small industries. Expansion of steel industry will encourage growth of industries making machines, tools etc. using Steel as their basic Input. It will create forward linkage.

Unbalancing The Economy With DPA

An imbalance can also be created via DPA. A government might directly or indirectly invest in DPA instead of investing in SOC. Growth of a set of industries stimulates the growth of those which supply raw materials. If DPA investment is undertaken first, the shortage of SOC facilities is likely to raise production costs substantially. In course of time, it might stimulate investment in SOC also. It will create backward linkage.

Theory of Big Push

Given by Rosenstein Rodan in 1943.

The idea behind this theory is this that a big push or a big and comprehensive investment package can be helpful to bring economic development. In other words, a certain minimum amount of resources must be devoted for developmental programs, if the success of programs is required. This theory is of the view that through 'Bit by Bit' allocation no economy can move on the path of economic development, rather a specific amount of investment is considered necessary for economic development.

The theory talks about indivisibilities that generate through external economies which will result from wide scale production and hence cheap raw materials and wide extent of markets. Indivisibilities leads to increasing returns. If so many mutually supporting industries which depend on each other are started, the economies of scale will be reaped. Such external economies which are attained through specific amount of investment will become helpful for economic development.

Indivisibilities :

1) Production Indivisibilities : The theory states that initial capital requirements (i.e., transport, infrastructure etc.) should be high. Greater level of output would result in decreased cost and thus capital output ratio decreases.
2) Demand Indivisibilities : Investment in a number of ventures at the same time would be profitable. Rodan gave example of shoe making industry. If

capital of the country is invested in shoe making industry. All the people will not spend all their income on shoes, but will spend on buying other goods. If no increase in production of other sectors, then income of other people has not gone up. They will not be able to buy shoes. Thus, shoe making industry will come to a halt.

So, investment in a single industry can be risky as demand is limited in UDCs. According to Rodan, investment should be made in interdependent industries

3) Supply Indivisibilities/ Indivisibilities in Supply of Savings : A specific amount of investment can be made in the presence of specific savings. But in case of UDCs, because of lower incomes, the savings remain low. Therefore, when incomes increase due to increase in investment, savings must increase. The way out of 'vicious circle', " is to have first an increase in income and to provide mechanism which assure that in every second stage marginal rate of saving will be very much higher than the average rate of saving."

Critical Minimum Effort Thesis

In his book "Economic Backwardness and Economic Growth", Prof Lebenstein has propounded well known "Critical minimum effort theory". According to this, underdeveloped countries (UDC's) need certain critical level of investment in order to be out of their vicious circle of poverty.

The theory talks about shocks [Income depressing factors] and stimulants [Income increasing factors]. In case of UDC's shocks are greater than stimulants. In case of developed countries (DC's) shocks are less than stimulants.

Incentives

Zero Sum	Positive Sum
Zero effect on economic growth. [Distribution effect]	They promote and induce eco- nomic growth [Production effect]

Stimulants are

- Attitude of people and motivation aspect
- Activities of growth agents (innovators)

- Creation of positive sum incentive and discourage zero sum incentives.

Income depressing factors (shocks) are

- Reluctance to accept new ideas and innovations.
- High capital output ratio
- Expenditure influenced by conspicuous consumption and demonstration effect.

Low Level Equilibrium Trap

Given by Nelson in his work "Theory of low-level equilibrium trap". It is based on Malthusian theory of population. Population and per capita income are positively related only till some point, beyond which rise in per capita income would not have much effect on Population levels.

Vicious Circle of Poverty

Given by Nurkse & Gunar Myrdal

Crux: *"A country is poor because it is poor"*

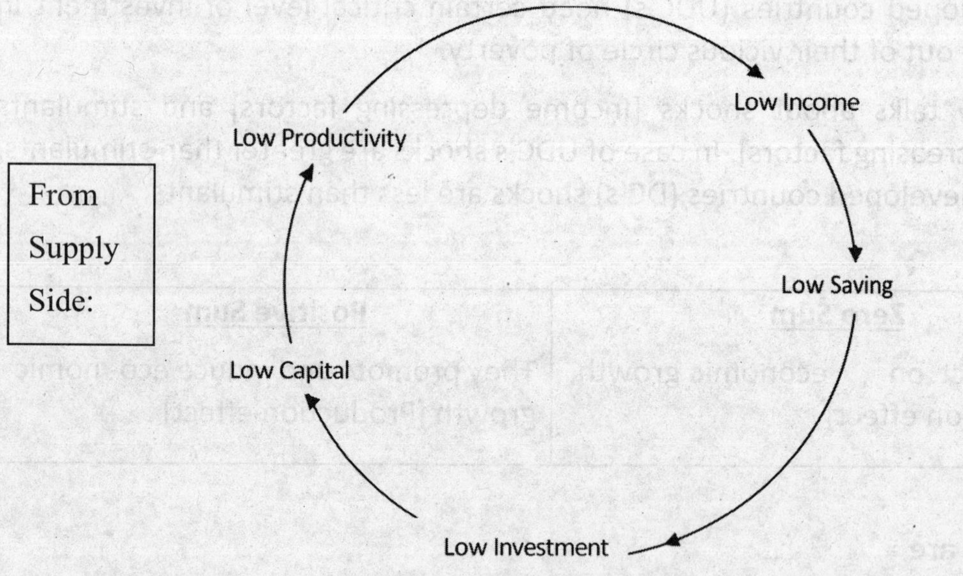

From Demand Side:

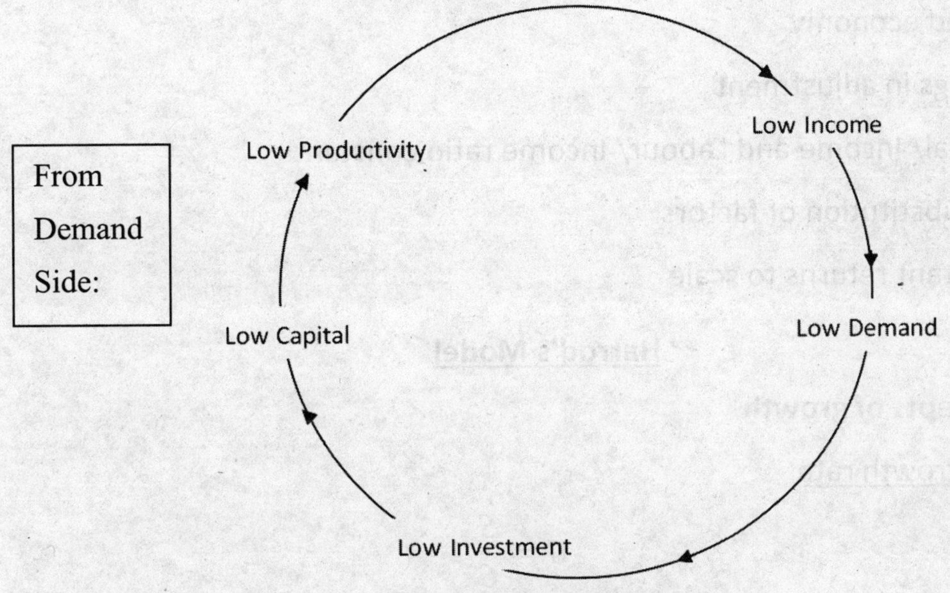

Harrod-Domar Model

Scan for video on Harrod-Domar and Solow Model

Harrod - Domar model: The model was developed independently by Harrod in 1939 and Domar in 1946.

Harrod and Domar extended the Keynesian analysis of income and employment to long-run problem of economic growth and therefore considered both the income and capacity effects of investment.

The Harrod and Domar models seek to determine that unique rate at which investment and income must grow so that full employment level is maintained over a long period of time, i.e., equilibrium growth is achieved. Both of them assigned to capital accumulation a crucial role in the development process. But they emphasized the double role of the investment process, namely generating income (increasing demand) and adding to the productive capacity of the economy. The classical economists confined their attention to the capacity side only, whereas the earlier Keynesian economists studied the problem of demand only whereas Harrod and Domar considers both sides.

Assumptions:

1) Full employment
2) No government interference

3) Closed economy

4) No lags in adjustment

5) Capital/ Income and Labour/ Income ratio constant

6) No substitution of factors

7) Constant returns to scale

Harrod's Model

Three concepts of growth

1) Actual growth rate

$$G = \frac{S}{C}$$

G: growth rate of output

S: saving rate

C: capital output ratio

2) Warranted growth rate: full capacity or potential growth rate which tells us the entrepreneurial equilibrium.

$$G_w = \frac{S}{C_r}$$

C_r → Required capital to maintain warranted growth rate.

3) Natural growth rate: It is the maximum growth rate or full employment that can be achieved. It is ceiling growth. It is not necessary that the warranted rate of growth is the maximum attainable rate of growth. G_n depends on availability of labour and natural resources.

Knife-edge equilibrium: If $G = G_W = G_n$

There can be deviations from the steady path.

Case 1

$$G < G_W - Depression \ - Depression$$
$$C > C_r - Depression$$

Case 2

$$G > G_W - Inflation \quad - Inflation/boom$$
$$C < C_r - Inflation$$

Domar's Model

Domar equations

i) Demand Side → $Y_d = \frac{1}{\alpha} I$

α → MPS I = Net Investment

ii) Supply Side → $Y_S = OK$

O = Productivity of Capital

K = Real capital

→ Condition for achieving steady growth

$$\Delta Y_d = \Delta Y_s$$

$$\frac{1}{\alpha}\Delta I = \sigma \Delta K \qquad \Delta K = I$$

$$\frac{1}{\alpha}\Delta I = \sigma I$$

$$\frac{\Delta I}{I} = \sigma.\alpha$$

Razor – edge equilibrium and the condition to maintain steady growth.

$$\frac{\Delta I}{I} > \sigma.\alpha \rightarrow Inflation$$

$$\frac{\Delta I}{I} < \sigma.\alpha \rightarrow Depression$$

Similarities

1) Similar assumptions
2) Saving, Investment, a condition for steady growth
3) Assume fixed K/O and L/O
4) Knife edge equilibrium is necessary in both.

Dissimilarities

Domar's model is based on the principle of multiplier while Harrod's model is based on the principle of acceleration.

Neo Classical Growth Theory - Solow Model

The basic neo classical growth model was first developed by Solow and Swan in 1956. Meade also in his book 'A neo classical theory of economic growth' constructed model to study the process of equilibrium growth i.e., steady state growth.

Robert M. Solow's 'A Contribution to the Theory of Economic Growth' was published in 1956 that introduced the Solow model. Also known as exogenous growth model or Neoclassical Growth Model, it focuses on long run economic growth. Technical progress and population growth rate are treated to be exogenous in nature.

Difference from H-D Model

1) In HD model, substitution of labour capital is not possible, but in Solow model it is possible.
2) Under HD model, there is tendency of divergence from equilibrium, while in case of Solow; there is tendency of convergence towards equilibrium.

Assumptions

a) Substitution of capital for labour is possible
b) Constant Returns to scale.
c) Full employment
d) Perfect competition
e) Prices and wages are flexible.
f) Diminishing returns to factor
g) Two factors of production that are paid according to their marginal productivity.

h) Output is regarded as net output after making allowances for the depreciation of capital.

i) Saving ratio is constant and saving equals investment

j) Population grows at constant rate 'n' and capital depreciates at constant rate 'd'.

Sum up various results of Solow model:

- Growth rate of output in steady-state equilibrium is equal to the growth rate of population or labour force and is exogenous of the saving rate, that is, it does not depend upon the rate of saving.
- Although saving rate does not determine the steady-state growth rate in output, it does cause an increase in steady-state level of per capita income (and therefore also total income) though raising capital per head.
- A significant conclusion of neoclassical growth theory is that if the two countries have the same rate of saving and same rate of population growth rate and have access to the same technology (i.e., production function), their levels of per capita income-will eventually converge, that is they will ultimately become equal. In this context it is worthwhile to quote Dornbusch, Fischer and Startz, 'The poor countries are poor because they have a less capital but if they save as the same rate as rich countries, and have access to the same technology, they will eventually catch up'.

Robinson's Model of Capital Accumulation

Robinson's model of capital accumulation, also known as golden age model given by Mrs. John Robinson in 1963 in book "The Accumulation of Capital".

Assumptions :

- Laissez-faire
- Two factors - labour, capital
- Perfect competition
- Constant returns to scale

- Fixed capital - labour ratio
- National income is sum of wages and profits.

Desired rate [Harrodian warranted rate] –

Rate which makes the firm satisfied with the situation in which they find themselves.

Possible rate [Harrodian natural rate] –

Depends on physical conditions i.e., population growth and technical knowledge.

Golden age → Desired rate = Possible rate

In other words, Growth rate of labour = Growth rate of capital

Static state –

Where Growth rate is zero and Profit rate is zero.

State of economic bliss –

When consumption is at maximum level.

Difference

Harrod-Domar Model	Robinson's Model
1) Growth rate is determined by saving income ratio and productivity of capital	1) Growth rate is determined by profit wage relationship and productivity of labour
2) Capital is prime source of capital accumulation.	2) Labour is ultimate source of capital accumulation.

Kaldor's Model

It relates technical progress with capital accumulation. He follows the Keynesian's theory and Harrod's analysis.

Assumptions –

a) Full employment

b) Technical progress depends on the rate of capital accumulation

c) Income = wages + profit

d) Total savings = savings out of wages and profits

e) Constant Returns to scale.

Kaldor gave theory in two respects –

Firstly, when population remain constant. Secondly, when population is expanding.

1) Constant population: Relation between growth in capital and growth in income.

2) Expanding population: Relation between growth in population and growth in income.

Saving Function: Total savings = savings from wages + savings from profits

Investment Function: $I_t = K_{t+1} - K_t$

Investment in period t equals stock of capital in next period minus stock of capital in current period.

Technical Progress Function: T = f(c)

It relates technical progress (T) to growth of capital accumulation (c).

Endogenous Growth Models

A group of growth theorists became increasingly dissatisfied with common accounts of exogenous factors determining long-run growth. Growth in these models is due to indefinite investment in human capital which had a spillover effect on the economy and reduces the diminishing return to capital accumulation.

This group of growth theorists are Arrow (1962), Uzawa (1965), Sidrauski (1967), Romer (1986), Lucas (1988), Rebelo (1991), Santos (1997).

Endogenous growth theory maintains that economic growth is primarily the result of internal forces, rather than external ones. It argues that improvements in productivity can be tied directly to faster innovation and more investments in human capital from governments and private sector institutions. This view contrasts with neoclassical economics.

Assumptions –

a) Increasing returns to scale by investing in human capital through education or training. Doing so, increases quality of labour, which increases productivity.

b) Imperfect competition

c) Long run growth rate on the basis of endogenous factor- Technical progress. It depends on rate of investment, size of capital etc.

d) Assumes constant saving rate/ Savings rate exogenously determined

Romer's Model: Learning by investment. Creation of knowledge is a side product of investment [Ideas are important than Natural sources].

Uzawa–Lucas Model: The Uzawa-Lucas model explains how economic growth, in the long term, is attributed to the accumulation of human capital. In order to produce human capital, education should be used.

Arrow's Learning by Doing Model: Also known as the AK model of economic growth, the arrow model is used to explain economic changes as a result of innovation and technology. The "learning by doing" model is also used in the arrow model to explain how self-practice and innovation result in productivity and improved human capital. It is because learning by doing leads to a decrease in labor required to create a unit of output

Technical Progress: Inventing a new technology or improving existing through innovations.

(1) Neutral technical change: The technical change is neutral if more output can be produced by using the same ratio of inputs, say labour and capital, where with the shift in production function, capital-labour ratio remains the same at a given $MRTS_{LK}$.

(2) Labour-saving technical change: If due to a technical change, the firm produces more output by using relatively less labour per unit of capital; the technological change will be labor-saving, where with the technological change, capital-labour ratio rises at a given $MRTS_{LK}$.

(3) Capital-saving technical change: If as a result of technological change relatively less capital than labour is used to produce a given output so that capital-labour ratio falls, it will be capital-saving technological change, where with the shift in production function capital-labour ratio falls at a given $MRTS_{LK}$.

<u>Hicks Neutral Technical Progress</u>: It is a type of neutral technical progress where output increases without changing the marginal rate of technical substitution (MRTS) between capital and labour. This means that at a constant capital-labour ratio (K/L), the marginal products of both capital and labour increase proportionally.

<u>Harrod's neutral Technical Progress</u>: It is labour-augmenting, meaning it increases the efficiency of labour over time. At a constant capital-output ratio (K/Y), the marginal product of capital remains unchanged.

<u>Hicks Vs Harrod Neutral Technical Progress</u>:

The distinction between Hicks and Harrod neutral technical progress lies in what is held constant during the comparison.

In Harrod's classification, technical progress is considered neutral if, at a constant capital-output ratio (K/Y), the marginal product of capital remains unchanged.

In Hicks's approach, technical progress is neutral if, at a constant capital-labour ratio (K/L), the MRTS remains unchanged.

<u>Hicks vs Harrod (labour saving and capital saving) Technical Progress:</u> Technical progress is said to be labour-saving in Harrod's sense if, at a constant capital-output ratio (K/Y), the ratio of relative factor income shares (rk/wl) is increasing. In other words, this occurs when the Marginal Rate of Technical Substitution ($MRTS_{LK} = MP_L/MP_K$) decreases. Conversely, technical progress is capital-saving in Harrod's sense if, at constant K/Y, the rk/wl ratio is decreasing, and MRTS increases.

In contrast, in Hicks's sense, technical progress is considered labour-saving if, at a constant capital-labour ratio (K/L), the relative income share of capital to labour (rk/wl) is increasing, or equivalently, if MRTS decreases. Similarly, it is capital-saving if, at constant K/L, the rk/wl ratio decreases and MRTS increases.

Thus, both interpretations differ in what ratio is held constant: K/Y in Harrod's case, and K/L in Hicks's.

Embodied Technical Progress: Investing in new equipment to improve technology.

Disembodied Technical Progress: Improved technology from given inputs without investing in new equipment.

Dualism

Social Dualism: Given by H Boeke

Prevalence of East and West economies, Underdeveloped and developed economies, etc.

Technological Dualism: Given by Higgins

Different techniques of production in different parts of world.

Financial Dualism: Given by Myint

Financial dualism refers to the co- existence of different interest rates between the organized and unorganized money markets in the LDCs.

Rostow Stages of Economic Growth (1960)

The theory talks about the five stages of economic growth –

1) The traditional society: Predominance of agriculture, family and caste system, science and technology are unknown.
2) Pre-conditions of take-off: Less dependence on agriculture, enlarged outlook, change in views, decline birth rate, modernization, natural income is invested less than 10%.
3) Take off stage: Rate of investment over 10%, development of leading sectors, technical development, and increase in demand.
4) Self-sustained stage/ Drive to maturity: Investment rate 10 - 20%, Modern techniques, dependence reduced, skilled personal, standard of living raise.
5) Stage of economic affluence /high mass consumption: Spending more on power [military], increase consumption of durable goods i.e., Cars, economy is leading towards welfare state.

Dependency Theory

Given by Frank, Amin, Santos. Main cause of Underdevelopment in UDC is dependency. Frank calls DC's are metropolis and LPC's are satellite.

Two Gap Model

Given by Hollis Chenery and Alan Strout. The idea is that savings gap and foreign exchange gap are two separate and independent constraints on the attainment of a target rate of growth in LDCs. Chenery sees foreign aid as a way of filling these two gaps in order to achieve the target growth rate of the economy.

Myrdal Theory of Circular Causation

Economic development results in circular causation process whereby the rich are awarded more favor. The backwash effects predominate and spread effects dampened. In UDCs, circular and cumulative process (also known as vicious circle of poverty) operates downwards and being unregulated causing increasing inequalities.

Backwash Effects: All relevant adverse changes of economic expansion in a locality. i.e., the locality and regions where economic activity is expanding will attract young and active people from other parts of country. This will tend to favour the developing region and depress economic activity in backward region where from such labour migrates.

Poverty

Poverty Line: The estimated minimum level of income needed to secure the necessities of life.

Poverty Gap Ratio: Measure intensity of poverty

$$Poverty\ Gap\ Ratio = \frac{1}{N}\left[\frac{z-t}{z}\right] + \ldots\ldots\ldots$$

N: total population

Z: Poverty line

T: income of individual

Squared Poverty Gap: Measure severity of poverty

Averaging the square of poverty gap ratio.

Head Count Ratio: HCR Ignores depth of poverty as if poor become poorer, HCR does not change.

$$Head\ Count\ Ratio = \frac{No.of\ people\ below\ poverty\ line}{Total\ Population}$$

Poverty Committee in Ascending Order

→ Dandekar committee (1971)

→ Alagh committee (1977)

→ Lakhadwala committee (1989)

→ Tendulkar committee set up in 2005

→ Rangarajan committee set up in 2012

Tendulkar	Rangarajan
Considers Per capita monthly expenditure	Considers Monthly expenditure of family of 5
Considers only calorific value.	Considers calories + protein +fat intake.

Poverty Estimates by Different Committees

Year	Lakdawala Committee Estimates			Tendulkar Committee Estimates			Rangarajan Committee Estimates		
	Rural	Urban	Total	Rural	Urban	Total	Rural	Urban	Total
1993-94	37.3	32.4	36.0	50.1	31.8	45.3	-	-	-
2004-05	28.3	25.7	27.5	41.8	25.7	37.2	-	-	-
2009-10	-	-	-	33.8	20.9	29.8	39.6	35.1	38.2

2011-12	-	-	-	25.7	13.7	21.9	30.9	26.4	29.5

Inequality

Gini Coefficient

It is a measure of degree of inequality. It varies from 0 (complete equality) and 1 (complete inequality). The changes in the distribution of income as measured by Gini coefficient in relation to increase in per capita income trace out Kuznets inverted U shaped curve.

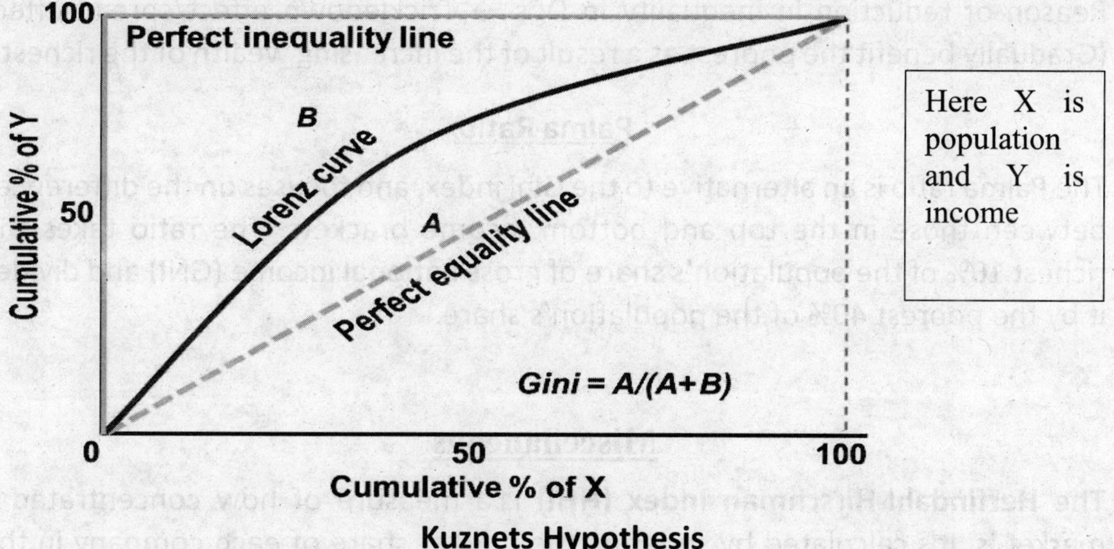

Kuznets Hypothesis

→ Size distribution of income was more unequal in less developed countries (LDC's) than in developed countries (DC's). It was in his 1963 study that Kuznets developed his inverted U-shaped hypothesis. He constructed Lorenz curve for DC's and LDC's and derived their Gini Coefficients. It was 0.37 for DC's and 0.44 for LDC's. It showed that income inequalities were higher in LDC's than in DC's. The greater this ratio, the more unequal distribution of income i.e. The more the Lorenz curve falls below the 45° line.

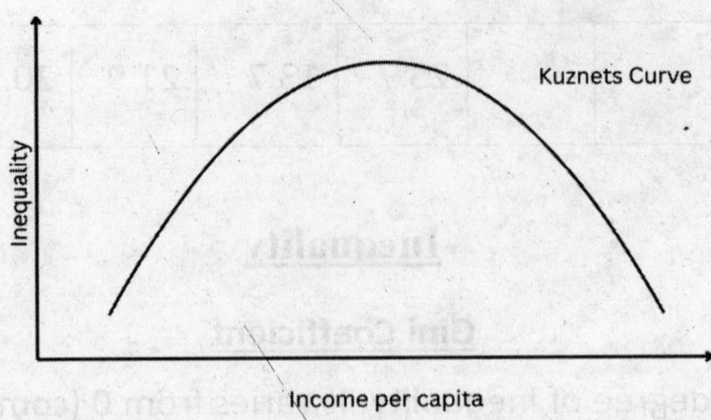

Income inequality falls with an increase in per capita income.

Reason of increase in inequality in LDCs – Dualism

Reason of reduction in inequality in DCs → Trickledown effect/spread effect (Gradually benefit the poorest as a result of the increasing wealth of the richest).

Palma Ratio

The Palma ratio is an alternative to the Gini index, and focuses on the differences between those in the top and bottom income brackets. The ratio takes the richest 10% of the population's share of gross national income (GNI) and divides it by the poorest 40% of the population's share.

Miscellaneous

The Herfindahl-Hirschman Index (HHI) is a measure of how concentrated a market is. It's calculated by squaring the market share of each company in the market and then adding the results together.

Concentration Ratio: A concentration ratio is a percentage that measures how much of an industry's output is controlled by its largest firms. It's used in economics to understand how competitive an industry is. The concentration ratio is the sum of the market shares of the largest firms in an industry.

Health and Education: For health sector, government schemes like National Health Mission (2013), National Health Policy (2017), NFHS-5 have to be covered from video classes. For education sector, new education policy (2020), census data on education related parameters and education related government schemes have to be covered from video lectures.

Shadow Prices: For quantifying the value of benefits and costs, some substitutes of market prices termed shadow prices are used. They are hypothetical prices which are supposed to represent the real social valuation of the costs incurred and benefits received. They are alternate to market prices as some inputs/outputs are not sold in market and having no market price. For example, for a labour surplus economy, shadow prices assign to unskilled labour is low, while shadow prices assign to capital is high.

Investment Criteria: How the resources are allocated in such a way that profits are maximize

1) Capital turnover criteria /Marginal rate of return criteria → Polak and Buchanan
2) Social Marginal productivity criteria → Kahn/ Chenery
3) Reinvestment criteria → Galenson and Leibenstein
4) Time series criterion → AK Sen

Sustainable Development: Amartya Sen was major contributor in the concept of SD. The concept appeared in 1987 in "The Brundtland Report". SD means meeting the needs of present generation without compromising the needs of future generation.

Environment Economics

Note: Market Failure and all types of Goods covered in public economics.

Theories of Population

Malthusian Theory

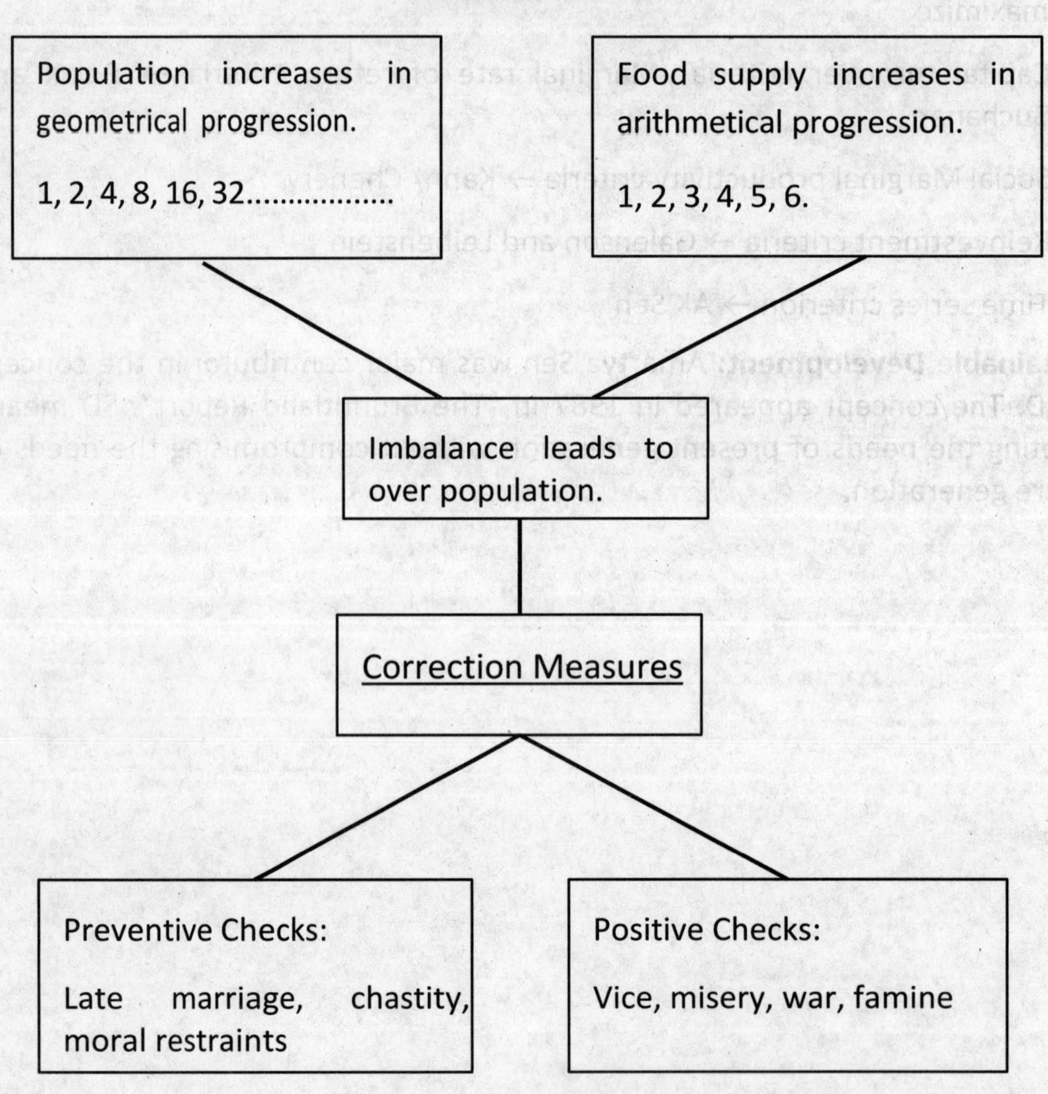

Optimum Theory of Population

Given by Canon, Sedwick, & Dalton. Optimum population is the ideal population which combined with the other available resources of the country will yield maximum returns. Concept of optimum population has been defined by Robbins, Carr-Saunders and Dalton. Any change in the size of population above or below the optimum level will diminish income per head.

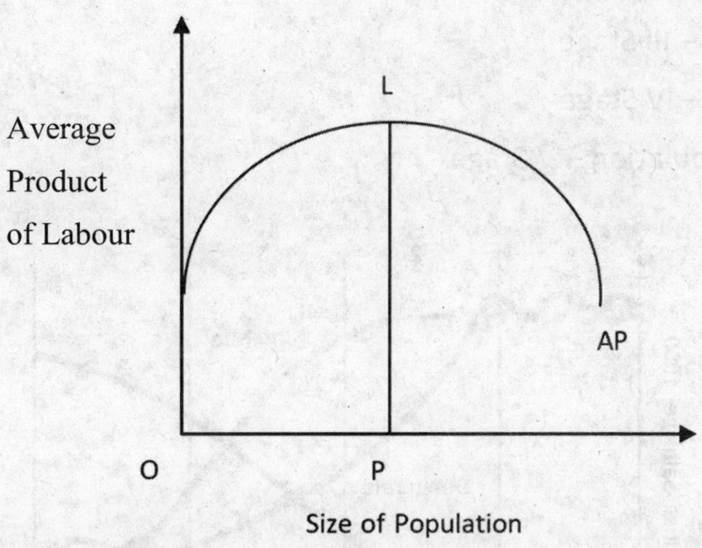

Theory of Demographic Transition

Propounded by Thompson and Notestein with three stages. Later Karl Sax gave 4 stages and famous version given by Blacker with five stages of population growth. It explains the effect of changes in birth rate and death rate, on the growth rate of population.

First Stage : Country is backward. It is characterized by high birth and death rates with the result that the growth rate of population is low.

Second stage : Country enters in the phase of economic growth. Decline in death rate but no change in birth rate leads to population explosion.

Third Stage : Birth rate starts declining accompanied by death rates .

<u>Fourth Stage</u> : Fertility rate declines and tends to equal the death rate so that the growth rate of population is stationary. Growth gains momentum and people's level of income increases. Their standard of living rises.

<u>Fifth Stage</u> : Death rate exceeds birth rates and population growth declines.

High Stationary – I Stage

Early Expanding – II Stage

Late Expanding – III Stage

Low Stationary – IV Stage

Diminishing Population – V Stage

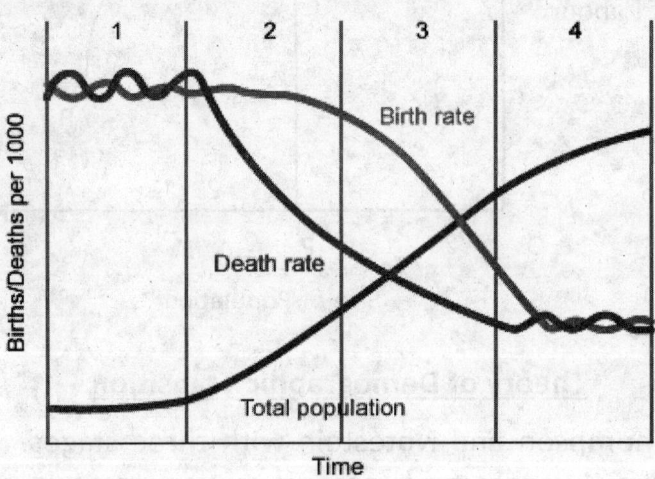

Property Rights and Coase Theorem

If property rights are clearly defined, the affected parties will adopt policies to internalize the externality. In other words, if property rights and liability are properly defined and there is no transaction cost, then people can be held responsible for any negative externalities they impose on others and market transactions will produce an efficient outcome. It is the solution of the problem of externality through private bargaining.

Assumptions:

- Negotiation cost is nil.

- No transaction cost.
- No Govt. interference.

Measures To Internalize the Environmental Externality

Pigouvian taxes, tradable pollution permits, and carbon taxes are all policy instruments that can help reduce pollution and its negative effects on society.

Pigouvian taxes

- A tax on the producer or consumer of goods or services that create negative externalities.
- The tax is set to equal the cost of the damage caused by the externality.
- The tax aims to recoup some of the cost of the externality by adding it to the price of the product.
- Examples include carbon taxes, fuel taxes, and tobacco taxes.

Carbon taxes

- A type of Pigouvian tax that aims to reduce greenhouse gas emissions
- Carbon taxes can create incentives to reduce fossil fuel usage and emissions
- The tax revenue can be used to support investments in new resources and energy efficient infrastructure

Tradable pollution permits

- A system where a regulatory authority allocates permits equal to a determined aggregate quantity of emissions
- The permits are tradable among emitters
- The trading of permits establishes a market-determined price of emissions.

Sustainability

Solow defines sustainability as making sure the next generation is as well off as the current generation and ensuring that this continues for all time.

Weak sustainability: Manmade and natural capital are substitutes. As we deplete energy resources of world, we invent ways of getting along with less energy and build machines that reduce energy use and extract it from sun. In other words, it refers to path of consumption overtime that yields non declining utility level, assuming sustainability between manmade and natural capital.

Strong sustainability: Sustainability with no substitution. No amount of machinery or invention will make up for the loss of wildness or key species.

Valuation of Environment

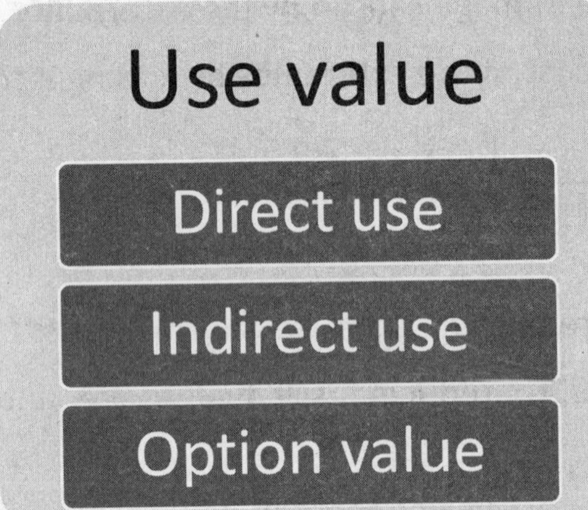

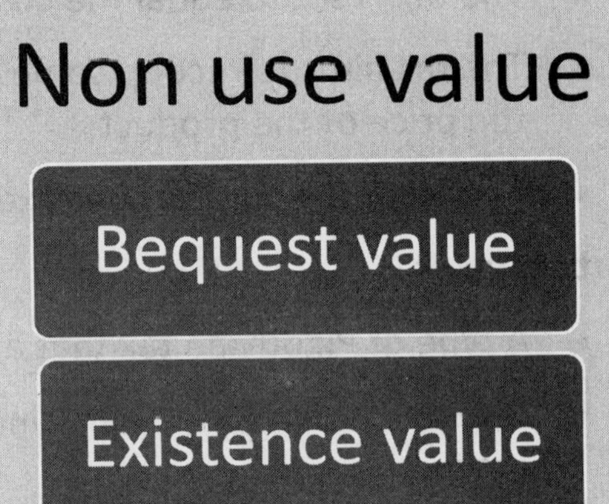

Use Value

Pertains to different uses the environment is subject to.

Direct use: Obtained through removable product in nature i.e.- fish. In other words, output can be consumed directly i.e., using a lake for swimming and fishing.

Indirect use: Obtained through non removable product in nature, i.e., sunset. In other words, benefits accruing indirectly to users, i.e., simply looking at a lake's beauty has aesthetic value.

Option value: Possible use of resources in future. It includes direct and indirect use values. One may be willing to pay to preserve wildlife so that the option of visiting wildlife habitats in future remains open.

Non-use Value

Increase in the individual's utility without actually using the good.

Bequest value: People have a sense of obligation to preserve the environment for future generations. Thus, a person may derive bequest value in passing a beautiful garden to the next generation.

Existence value: Individual assign importance to the existence of natural resources even though it may not be of any economic use to them. i.e., individuals are willing to pay to protect the endangered species of plants and animals.

Willingness to pay (WTP): Maximum willingness to pay for a change in environmental quality. i.e., How much an individual would be willing to pay to reduce CO2 emissions?

Willingness to accept (WTA): Minimum you would accept to go without a change in environmental quality. i.e., How much compensation an individual would be willing to receive to allow C02 emissions to increase?

An individual WTP to avoid flood may not be equal to the WTA compensation after floods. WTA can be more than WTP as WTP is limited by the income of the individual.

Method of Valuation

Contingent valuation method : Most popular method to evaluate non-use value. Though can be used to estimate use value too.

This method puts direct questions to individuals to determine how much they might be willing to pay for environmental resources or how much compensation they would be willing to accept if they were deprived of the same resources. i.e., survey-based techniques. It estimates demand for environmental goods and services that are not traded in the market.

Travel cost method : This approach is used to value the recreational benefits of public parks and other natural areas. This method seeks to determine the demand for recreational site (i.e., number of visits per year to a park) as a function of variables like price, visitor's income and socioeconomic characteristics. The price is sum of entry fees, cost of travel and opportunity cost of time spent. It only estimates use value of an environmental good/service.

Hedonic price method :In this method, price of property is related to stream of benefits derived. Hedonic pricing applies to goods that are sold/traded goods in market. i.e., in housing market where the value of two comparable properties differs depending on environmental amenities of each site.

Other methods:

Opportunity cost method :This method values the benefits of environmental protection in terms of what is being foregone to achieve it.

Replacement cost method : Measure the potential expenditure that would be required to replace or restore a productive asset that would be damaged by some development.

Demography

Stable Population: It implies that the fertility and mortality rate is constant.

Life Expectancy: The average number of additional years a person expects to live, if we assume that the current mortality trends persist. It is also known as life expectancy at birth.

Maternal Mortality Ratio: It is the statistic revealing the number of women who die during pregnancy or child birth per 1,00,000 live births

Crude Birth Rate: Number of live births per 1000 population in a given year.

$$CBR = \frac{Total\ live\ births\ during\ a\ given\ year}{Total\ population\ at\ the\ mid\ of\ same\ year} \times 1000$$

Crude Death Rate: Number of deaths per 1000 population in a given year.

$$CDR = \frac{Total\ registered\ deaths\ in\ a\ year}{Total\ population\ at\ the\ mid\ of\ same\ year} \times 1000$$

Carrying Capacity: It is the maximum sustainable size of a resident population in a given eco system. When there is an increase in the population size above the carrying capacity, there is an overutilization of natural resources such as water, land, etc. Also, there tends to be an increase in pollution-causing many environmental problems.

Cohort: It is the group of people that are sharing a common temporal demographic experience observed through time.

De-population: It implies the decline in population.

Replacement Level Fertility: The level of fertility at which a couple has only enough children to replace themselves. In simple words, it implies two children per couple. It is the average number of births per woman which will lead to zero population growth. If a country's average fertility is less than the replacement level, it implies that the population will decline.

Population Momentum: It refers to the tendency of the population to continue growing beyond the time when replacement level fertility has been achieved because of relatively high level of concentration in child bearing years. Example – imagine a country had a high birth rate in the past, so now it has a large number of young people entering child bearing age. Even if each of these individuals only has 2 children, the total number of births remains high because so many people are having children.

Infant Mortality rate : Death of children of age group 0 to 1

$$IMR = \frac{No.of\ deaths\ among\ infants\ registered\ in\ a\ year}{No.of\ registered\ births\ in\ the\ same\ year} \times 1000$$

Zero Population Growth : Annual number of births = Annual number of deaths.

Life table : Measuring average life expectancy in a country.

Morbidity : The condition of suffering from a disease. The rate of disease in a population.

Total Fertility Rate : It is the sum of the age specific fertility rates of women in all age specific groups.

In simple words, Total number of children, a woman will have during her reproductive lifespan.

Gross Reproduction Rate : Total number of female children, a woman will have during her reproductive life span.

Net Reproduction Rate : Out of total number of female children, a woman will have during her reproductive lifespan; total number of alive female children forms Net Reproduction Rate. The rate takes into account that some females will die before completing their child bearing years.

Human Population Pyramid : When the age structure of population is classified by sex in the form of a histogram, it is allied age- sex pyramid.

Expansive Population Pyramid

Demographic Dividend: As defined by United Nations population fund (UNFPA) means, "the economic growth potential that can result from shifts in population's age structure, mainly when the share of the working age population (15 - 64) is larger than the non- working age share of the population (14 and younger, 65 and older).

Life Table

Life table shows, for each age, what the probability is that a person of that age will die before his or her next birthday (probability of death).

Calculation of Life Table							
Age	l_x	$d_x = l_x - l_x$+1	$q_x = \frac{d_x}{l_x}$	$p_x = 1 - q_x$	$L_x = \frac{l_x + l_x + 1}{2}$	$T_x = L_x + L_x + 1 + L_x + 2$	$e_x^o = \frac{T_x}{l_x}$
0	4	2	$\frac{1}{2}$	$1 - \frac{1}{2} = \frac{1}{2}$	$= \frac{4+2}{2} = 3$		
1	2	1					
2	1	-					

Definitions of Terms

- l_x = Number of persons living at age x year.
- d_x = Number of persons at age x who die before reaching x+1.
- q_x = Mortality rate [probability that a person of age x will die].
- p_x = Survival rate.
- L_x = Average number of persons living between the ages x and x+1.
- T_x = Total number of years lived by the cohort from age x onward.
- e_x^0 = Complete expectation of life [average number of future years to be lived by a person at age x].

Migration

It is the movement of people between regions / countries.

Todaro Migration Model : It explains the relationship of accelerated rural-urban migration in the context of rising urban unemployment.

Important Environmental Conventions/ Protocols

World Heritage Convention (1972) – Identifying and protecting cultural and natural heritage sites of outstanding universal value.

First UN Environment Conference (Stockholm, 1972) – Marked the beginning of global environmental governance and led to the creation of UNEP.

Montreal Protocol (1987) – Protecting the ozone layer by phasing out ozone-depleting substances (ODS) like CFCs.

Basel Convention (1989) – Controlling the transboundary movement of hazardous waste to prevent dumping in developing countries.

Agenda 21 (1992) – A global action plan for sustainable development, adopted at the Rio Earth Summit.

United Nations Framework Convention on Climate Change (UNFCCC) (1992) – Providing a framework for international cooperation on climate change.

Kyoto Protocol (1997) – Legally binding commitments for developed countries to reduce greenhouse gas emissions.

Paris Agreement (2015) – Addressing climate change by limiting global temperature rise to well below 2°C, ideally 1.5°C.

List of important COPs (conference of parties)

COP	Year	Location	Key Outcome
COP 1	1995	Berlin, Germany	Berlin Mandate – Laid the groundwork for future climate agreements.
COP 3	1997	Kyoto, Japan	Kyoto Protocol – Set legally binding targets for developed nations to reduce GHG emissions.

COP 7	2001	Marrakesh, Morocco	Marrakesh Accords – Finalized Kyoto Protocol rulebook.
COP 11	2005	Montreal, Canada	First Meeting of Kyoto Protocol Parties (MOP 1) – Kyoto Protocol entered into force.
COP 12	2006	Nairobi, Kenya	Nairobi Framework launched to support developing countries.
COP 13	2007	Bali, Indonesia	Bali Roadmap – Outlined post-Kyoto climate action.
COP 16	2010	Cancún, Mexico	Cancún Agreements – Established Green Climate Fund (GCF).
COP 18	2012	Doha, Qatar	Doha Amendment – Extended Kyoto Protocol until 2020.
COP 19	2013	Warsaw, Poland	Warsaw International Mechanism – Addressed loss and damage from climate change.
COP 21	2015	Paris, France	Paris Agreement – Historic global deal to limit warming to well below 2°C.
COP 22	2016	Marrakesh, Morocco	Focused on Paris Agreement implementation rules.
COP 24	2018	Katowice, Poland	Katowice Climate Package – Finalized rulebook for Paris Agreement.
COP 26	2021	Glasgow, UK	Glasgow Climate Pact – Strengthened 1.5°C commitment, phased down coal.
COP 27	2022	Sharm El-Sheikh, Egypt	Loss and Damage Fund – Agreement to fund climate-related damages.

Indian Economy

Note: Indian Economy section mostly features factual questions, not conceptual or analytical ones. Specific data and schemes keep changing frequently. Therefore, we have not included time-sensitive factual content. For factual content related to current data—such as reports by PLFS, RBI, NSSO, NFHS, census statistics, government schemes related to agriculture, industry, rural and urban development, budget and Economic Survey highlights, recent trends in foreign trade, the structure of income and employment (i.e., sector-wise contribution of primary, secondary, and tertiary sectors), policy rates, unemployment rates, the latest MSME classification, state-wise sex ratio, and similar dynamic topics—**students are advised to rely on the course classes delivered by Dr. Simranjit Kaur on MS STUDY GURU application**, where such information is regularly updated in line with the latest exam requirements and official sources.

Overview of the Indian Economy

Indian economy is agricultural dependent.

→It is mixed economy [Mixture of capitalistic and socialistic Society].

→It is developing economy.

Structural change refers to dramatic shift in the way a country, industry, or market operates, usually brought on by major economic developments.

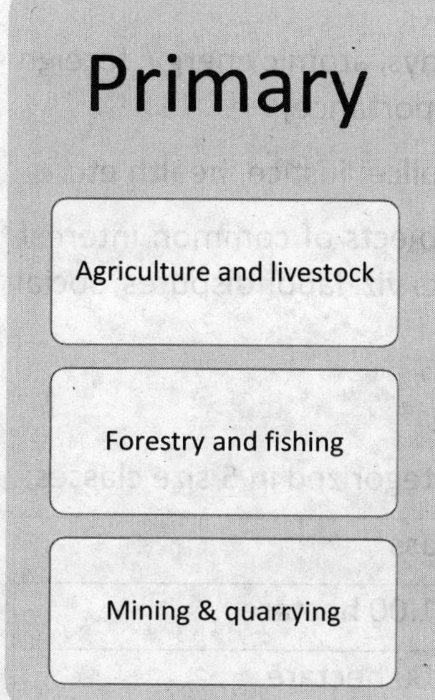

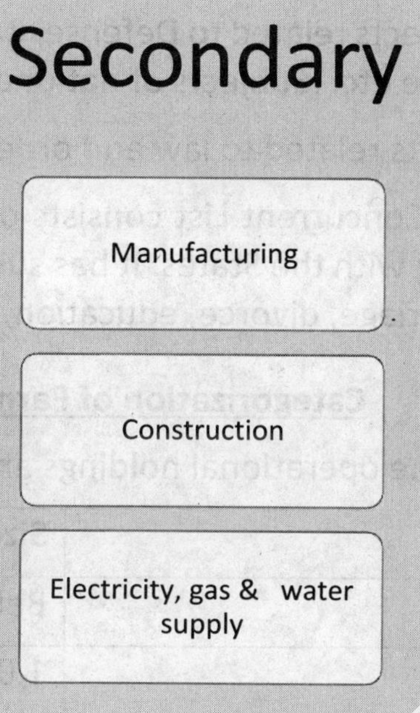

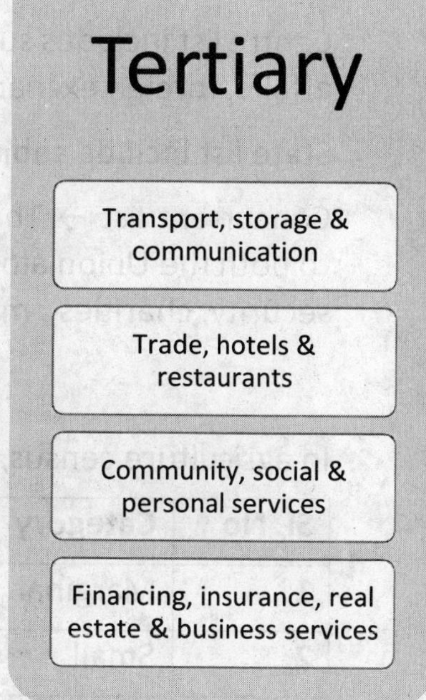

Note: Mining & Quarrying is generally classified under the Primary Sector, but in some government reports, it is grouped under the Industrial Sector. Students should interpret the classification based on context.

Sector wise rankings of GVA and employment in India based on 2019-20

Share in Employment	Share in GVA
1. Agriculture	1. Services
2. Services	2. Industry
3. Industry	3. Agriculture

Inclusive Growth : Term introduced in 11th Five Year Plan. Inclusive growth is economic growth that benefits society as a whole by reducing inequality and creating opportunities for all.

Minimum Support Price : Government announces MSP to prevent fall in prices in case of over-production and to protect the interest of the farmers by ensuring the minimum price of their crop. It is announced on the recommendations of CACP [Commission of agricultural cost and prices].

Centre - State Relations

Centre list includes subjects related to Defense, Railways, atomic energy, foreign affairs, foreign exchange etc. [Subjects of national importance]

State list include subjects related to law and order, police, justice, health etc.

Concurrent list → The Concurrent List consists of subjects of common interest to both the Union along with the States. It has subjects viz. labor disputes, social security, charities , marriage, divorce, education, etc.

Categorization of Farmers

In agriculture census, the operational holdings are categorized in 5 size classes:

Sl. No	Category	Size-Class
1.	Marginal	Below 1.00 hectare
2.	Small	1.00-2.00 hectare
3.	Semi-Medium	2.00-4.00 hectare
4.	Medium	4.00-10.00 hectare
5.	Large	10.00 Hectare and above

Cropping Intensity

Cropping intensity is a measure of how many times a field is cultivated with crops in a year.

$$Cropping\ Intensity = \frac{Gross\ Cropped\ Area}{Net\ Sown\ Area} \times 100$$

Size of an operational holding in agriculture = owned land + leased inland – leased outland

Index of Industrial Production (IIP)

It is an indicator that measures the changes in the volume of production of industrial products during a given period. Base Year- 2011-2012. It is compiled and published monthly by the National Statistical Office, Ministry of Statistics and Programme Implementation.

Index of Eight Core Industries (ICI)

This is an index of the eight most fundamental industrial sectors of the Indian economy and comprises 40.27% of the weight in IIP.

The monthly Index of Eight Core Industries (ICI) measures collective and individual performance of production in eight core industries. The eight core sector industries in decreasing order of their weightage:

Refinery Products > Electricity > Steel > Coal > Crude Oil > Natural Gas > Cement > Fertilizers.

The industry groups that it measures are classified under the following:

- Broad sectors like manufacturing, mining, and electricity.
- Use-based sectors like capital goods, basic goods, intermediate goods, infrastructure goods, consumer durables, and consumer non-durables.

Weights of different sectors under the used based classification – 2011-12 series

Sector	Number of Groups	Weights
Primary Goods	15	34.05
Capital Goods	67	8.22
Intermediate goods	110	17.22
Infrastructure / construction goods	29	12.34
Consumer durables	86	12.84
Consumer nondurables	100	15.33
Total	**407**	**100**

Following are the three sectors of the IIP as per the revision based on 2011-12 series.

(i) Mining,

(ii) Manufacturing and

(iii) Electricity as in the old series.

Sectors, number of item groups and weight as per the 2011-12 IIP series

Sector	Number of item groups	Weight (%)
1. Mining	1	14.373
2. Manufacturing	405	77.633
3. Electricity	1	7.994
Total	**407**	**100**

Industry Weights in the IIP Core Sector (2011–12 Base)

Industry	Weight
Coal	10.33
Crude Oil	8.98
Natural Gas	6.88
Refinery Products	28.04
Fertilizers	2.63
Steel	17.92
Cement	5.37
Electricity	19.85
Total	**100**

NITI Aayog

The Planning Commission was replaced by the National Institution for Transforming India (NITI Aayog) in 2015. The NITI Aayog is a government agency that helps the Indian government formulate policies and strategies. It was established on January 1, 2015. The NITI Aayog's approach is bottom-up, with an emphasis on maximum governance and minimum government.

NITI Aayog VS Planning Commission

NITI Aayog	Planning Commission
NITI Aayog functions as a policy think tank and does not have the power to impose policies on states.	The Planning Commission had the authority to impose policies on states for approved projects.
The power of fund allocation is not vested with NITI Aayog but with the Finance Ministry.	The Planning Commission had the power to allocate funds to state governments and central government ministries for various national and state level programs and projects.
State Governments play a more active role in NITI Aayog.	In the Planning Commission, state governments had a limited role and were mostly involved in National Development Council meetings.

First Five-Year Plan (1951-1956): The first five-year plan was launched in 1951 with the objective of laying the foundation for a self-reliant economy. The plan focused on developing agriculture, irrigation, and industry. **(Harrod Domer Model)**

Second Five-Year Plan (1956-1961): The second five-year plan aimed to achieve a 5% annual growth rate in the economy. The plan focused on heavy industries and public sector-led industrialization. **(Mahalanobis model)**

Third Five Year Plan (1961-1966): The third five-year plan was focused on making India a **"self-reliant and self-generating economy".** The plan aimed to increase agricultural production and develop heavy industries. It failed due to wars (1962 & 1965) and drought (1966).

Fourth Five Year Plan (1969-1974): The fourth five-year plan was interrupted by the Indo- Pakistani war of 1965 and the Bangladesh Liberation War of 1971. The plan focused on stabilizing the economy and reducing poverty. **(Growth with Stability, poverty reduction)**

Fifth Five Year Plan (1974-1979): The fifth five-year plan was focused on achieving a 4.4% annual growth rate in the economy. **(Minimum needs programme, Garibi Hatao)**

Sixth Five Year Plan (1980-1985): The sixth five-year plan was focused on achieving a 5.2% annual growth rate in the economy.

Seventh Five Year Plan (1985-1990): The seventh five-year plan was focused on achieving a 5% annual growth rate in the economy.

Eighth Five Year Plan (1992-1997): The eighth five-year plan was focused on achieving a 5.6% annual growth rate in the economy. **(Human Resource Development)**

Ninth Five Year Plan (1997-2002): The ninth five-year plan was focused on achieving an 6.5% annual growth rate in the economy. The plan focused on **growth with social justice and equity.**

Tenth Five Year Plan (2002-2007): The tenth five-year plan was focused on achieving a 8% annual growth rate in the economy.

Eleventh Five Year Plan (2007-2012): The eleventh five-year plan was focused on achieving a 9% annual growth rate in the economy. The plan focused on faster and more inclusive growth.

Twelfth Five Year Plan (2012-2017): The twelfth five-year plan was focused on achieving 8% annual growth rate in the economy. The plan focused on faster, sustainable and inclusive growth.

Unemployment

Three concepts of unemployment developed by NSSO are:

1. Usual status unemployment: All those who are found "usually" unemployed in the reference year.
2. Current weekly status unemployment: If a person fails to get work for even one hour on any day of a week, he is deemed to be unemployed.
3. Current daily status unemployment: If a person works for 4 hours or more during a day, he is considered as employed for the whole day.

Structural Unemployment : Workers lack the requisite job skills or live too far from regions where jobs are available. Jobs are available but there is mismatch between what companies need and what workers offer.

Frictional Unemployment : When the existing person is looking for a new job or he has quit its previous job and he is yet to join the new organization.

Under Employment : If a person works less than his/ her skill [part time works, or doing less skilled job than his /her skill].

Disguised Unemployment : It occurs when more people are working than are needed for a job, or when people are working but not contributing to production. It's also known as hidden unemployment.

Land Reform Program

1 Elimination of intermediaries: Its aim is to abolish zamindari and other intermediary systems and to establish direct relation between the state and cultivators.

2 Tenancy reforms- Its aim is regulation of rent, security of tenure, provision of ownership rights to tenants.

3 Ceiling of landholdings: Its aim is to determine ceiling of holding and to distribute surplus among landless people.

4 Consolidations of Holdings: its aim is to merge fragmented land holdings into a single plot.

New Agriculture Policy (2000) Features

1) Achieve 4% growth rate for next two decades.

2) Provide land to poor farmers.

3) Consolidation of Holdings.

4) Provide insurance for crops to farmers.

Revolutions

Name	Target

Green Revolution	Food Grains
White Revolution	Milk
Yellow Revolution	Oil seeds
Blue Revolution	Fisheries
Golden Revolution	Fruit- Apples
Round Revolution	Potato

Green Revolution in India 1966 : Dr. M.S. Swaminathan is known as the "Father of the Green Revolution in India". Key highlights:

- ➔ Green Revolution refers to a period of significant agricultural transformation in India during 1960s, which led to a substantial increase in foodgrain production, especially wheat and rice.
- ➔ Introduction of scientifically developed High Yielding Variety (HYV) seeds.
- ➔ Use of chemical fertilizers & pesticides
- ➔ Expansion of irrigation
- ➔ Mechanization of agriculture.
- ➔ Focus regions – mainly benefited states like Punjab, Haryana, Uttar Pradesh.

Merits:

1) Significant increase in wheat & rice production.
2) India became self-sufficient in food grains by 1970s.

Demerits:

1) Benefits concentrated few states.
2) Focus was mostly on wheat & rice.
3) Large farmers benefitted more than small & marginal farmers.
4) Overuse of fertilizers, pesticides & groundwater.

MGNREGA

The Mahatma Gandhi National Rural Employment Guarantee Act (MGNREGA) is a program that guarantees employment to rural households in India. The program was passed in 2005 to improve the livelihoods of people in rural areas. It seeks to provide at least 100 days of guaranteed wage employment in a financial year to at least one member of every rural household.

New Industrial Policy - 1991

(By former PM P.V. Narsimha Rao)

Features :

1. De-reservation of public sector. Public sector Industries reduced to 2.
2. Delicensing: abolished industrial licensing except for five Industries related to security environment.
3. Disinvestment from public sector: Partial dilution of control by the government, i.e., retaining 51% share with the public sector organization.
4. Liberalization of foreign investment.

These reforms are also known as LPG reforms.

Liberalization : Removal or loosening of restrictions. Increase FDI limits; reduce trade barriers etc.

Privatization : Transfer of ownership of public enterprise to private enterprise.

Globalization : Integration of world economy.

Non-Performing Assets

When the borrower stops paying interest or principal on a loan, the lender will lose money. Such a loan is known as Non-Performing Asset (NPA). Indian banking industry is seriously affected by NPAs. In other words, NPA is a loan where interest or principal remain overdue for a period of more than 90 days.

Sub Standard Assets	An asset which remains as NPA& for less than or equal to 12 months.
Doubtful Assets	An asset which remained in the above category for 12 months.

Loss Assets	Asset where loss has been identified by the bank or by the RBI

Twin Balance Sheet Problem : Over leveraged corporate Dept plus High NPA'S of nationalized Bank.

Twin Deficit: It refers to the fiscal and current account deficit. Fiscal deficit means higher expenditure over income. The gap between expenditure and income is bridged through borrowing from market. The term current account deficit is derived from current account balance.

NEP-2020 [National Education Policy]

NEP -2020 paving way for transformational reforms in school and higher education system of country.

→Aims at universalization of education from pre-school to secondary level with 100% GER in school education by 2030.

→This is the first education policy of 21st century and replaces the 34-year-old NEP, 1986.

→The 10+2 structure of school curriculum is to be replaced by 5+3+3+4 circular structure.

→ In higher education, the policy targets a GER of 50% by 2035, promoting multidisciplinary learning, flexibility, and multiple entry-exit options.

→ The Centre and States will work together to increase the public investment in education sector to reach 6% of GDP at the earliest.

Finance Commission of India

Article 280 of the Constitution requires that FC to be constituted. To recommend the distribution of the net proceeds of taxes between the Centre and states and among the states.

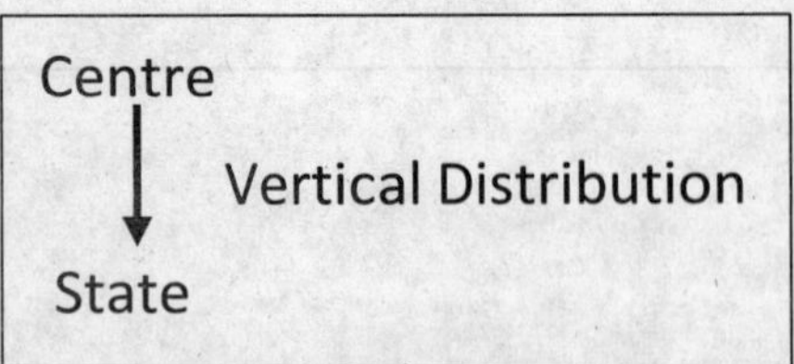

State ⟶ State

Horizontal Distribution

NK Singh →Chairman of 15th FC.

→The formula for sharing revenues is decided by the FC every 5 years.

→ This time, however the 15th FC will decide the formula for six years.

→The 15th FC was required to submit two reports.

First Report

Recommendations for the FY 2020-21 was tabled in Parliament on 1 February, 2020

Final Report

With recommendations for the 2021-26 period

Key Recommendations

Devolution of taxes to states :

The share of taxes to states decreased from 42% to 41% [Vertical Devolution].

Horizontal Devolution	14th FC	15th FC
Income distance [States with higher average in- come will get less share]	50	45
Population 1971	17.5	-
Population 2011	10.0	15.0
Area	15.0	15.0
Forest Cover	7.5	-
Forest and Ecology	-	10

[share of dense forest of each state in the aggregate dense forest of all states]		
Demographic Performance [States with lower fertility ratio will be scored higher]	-	12.5
Tax effort [Reward States with higher tax collection efficiency	-	2.5
Total	100	100

Various Acts and Dates

Competition Act - Replaced MRTP Act	**2002**
MRTP act [Monopolies Restrictive Trade Practices Act] - Prevent Concentration of Economic Power	**1969**
FERA [Foreign Exchange Regulation Act] - Regulating the Foreign Exchange Market	**1973**
FEMA [Foreign Exchange Management Act] - Management of Foreign Exchange	**1999**
First National Commission on Labor	**1966**
Second National Labor Commission	**1999**
RBI Nationalized	**1949**
14 commercial banks nationalization	**1969**
Narsimha Committee establishment	**1991**
RBI establishment	**1935**
SEBI establishment	**1988**
IDBI establishment	**1964**
SIDBI establishment	**1989**

IFCI establishment	**1948**
EXIM establishment	**1982**
UTI establishment	**1964**
LIC establishment	**1956**
RRB establishment	**1975**
ICICI establishment	**1955**
IRBI establishment	**1971**
NABARD establishment	**1982**

Various Indices

Indices	Publisher
Human Development Index	UNDP
Human Capital Index	World Bank
Global Hunger Index	Previously: International Food Policy Research Institute (IFPRI). Published GHI until 2014. Currently (since 2015): Concern Worldwide (Ireland-based NGO) and Welthungerhilfe (German NGO). These two jointly publish the Global Hunger Index each year.
Ease Of Doing Business	World Bank
Global Competitiveness Index, Gender Gap Index	World Economic Forum
World Inequality Index	Oxfam

Global Multidimensional Poverty Index	Oxford Poverty & Human Development Initiative (OPHI) And United Nations Development Programme (UNDP).
Sustainable Development Goal Index (National level)	The National Institution for Transforming India (NITI) Aayog

CPI (Consumer Price Index) (Retail inflation)

Measures changes in price level of market basket of consumer goods and services purchased by households. Four types of CPIs

1. CPI-IW (Consumer Price Index for Industrial Workers)

Measures inflation for industrial workers.

Used to calculate Dearness Allowance (DA) for government employees and industrial workers.

Base year: 2016=100.

2. CPI-AL (Consumer Price Index for Agricultural Labourers)

Tracks inflation for agricultural laborers.

Helps in determining minimum wages and rural welfare policies.

Base year: 2019=100.

3. **CPI-RL (Consumer Price Index for Rural Labourers)**

Similar to CPI-AL but covers all rural laborers, not just agricultural workers.

Base year: 2019=100.

4. **CPI (Consumer Price Index - Combined)**

Represents the general CPI, covering both rural and urban areas.

Published by the National Statistical Office (NSO).

Used for monetary policy decisions by the Reserve Bank of India (RBI).

Base year: 2012=100.

Note: The base year is revised periodically. Students are advised to regularly update themselves with the latest base year information from official sources.

WPI (Wholesale Price Index)

Price of representative basket of wholesale goods. The base year of All-India WPI has been revised from 2004-05 to 2011-12 on 12 May 2017. It is published by the office of Economics Advisor, Ministry of Commerce & Industry. WPI basket includes these major groups:

1) Primary activities
2) Fuel & power
3) Manufactured products

GDP Base Year: The last series has changed the base to 2011-12 from 2004-05. MoSPI has initiated the process of revising the base year of GDP to **2022–23.**

Headline inflation: Includes price of food & fuel, the goods whose prices are fluctuating.

Core inflation: Excludes price rise of food, fuel etc. So, prices of volatile goods are not included in it.

Some famous books and authors

Note: All books and authors mentioned alongside their corresponding theories are also important and should be thoroughly learned.

1. The Theory of Moral Sentiments – Adam Smith (1759)
2. An Inquiry into the Nature and Causes of the Wealth of Nations – Adam Smith (1776)
3. Principles of Political Economy and Taxation – David Ricardo (1817)
4. Principles of Political Economy – John Stuart Mill (1848)

5. Principles of Economics – Alfred Marshall (1890)
6. The Accumulation of Capital – Rosa Luxemburg (1913), Joan Robinson (1956)
7. The Economics of Welfare – A.C. Pigou (1920)
8. Nature and Significance of Economic Science – Lionel Robbins (1932)
9. The General Theory of Employment, Interest, and Money – John Maynard Keynes (1936)
10. Value and Capital – John Hicks (1939)
11. Capitalism, Socialism, and Democracy – Joseph Schumpeter (1942)
12. Foundations of Economic Analysis – Paul Samuelson (1947)
13. A Behavioural Theory of the Firm – Richard Cyert & James March (1963)
14. Interaction between Multiplier and Accelerator – Paul Samuelson (1939)
15. A Revision of Demand Theory – John Hicks (1956)
16. The Affluent Society – John Kenneth Galbraith (1958)
17. Capitalism and Freedom – Milton Friedman (1962)
18. Asian Drama: An Inquiry into the Poverty of Nations – Gunnar Myrdal (1968)
19. Development as Freedom – Amartya Sen (1999)
20. Why Nations Fail – Daron Acemoglu & James Robinson (2012)
21. Capital in the Twenty-First Century – Thomas Piketty (2013)
22. Rise and Fall of Nations – Ruchir Sharma (2016)
23. What the Economy Needs Now – Abhijit Banerjee (2019)
24. I Do What I Do – Raghuram Rajan (2017)

Important Committees

✓ A M Khusro Committee (1989) – Agricultural Credit Review Committee

✓ C R Rangarajan (1991) – Committee on Balance of Payments

- ✓ C Rangarajan Chairman (2008) – Committee on Financial Inclusion
- ✓ Chakravarthy Committee (1985) – on Monetary policy.
- ✓ Choksi Committee (1978) – Direct Tax Laws Committee
- ✓ Dantwala Committee 1970 – Committee in Unemployment Estimates
- ✓ Kaldor Report (1956) – Indian Tax Reform
- ✓ Kelkar Panel (2002) – on Direct and Indirect Taxes
- ✓ Kelkar Taskforce (2004) – on the enforcement of the FRBM Act
- ✓ L K Jha Committee (1976) – Indirect Taxation Enquiry Committee
- ✓ Lakdawala (1993)– Expert Group Report on Poverty Estimation (Planning Commission)
- ✓ Narasimham I (1991) – Committee on Financial System
- ✓ Narasimham II (1998) – Committee on Financial Sector Reforms.
- ✓ Raghuram Ranjan Committee (2008) – Financial Sector Reforms
- ✓ Raj Committee (1972) – Agricultural Taxation.
- ✓ Raja J Chelliah Committee (1992) – Tax Reforms Committee
- ✓ Rangarajan Committee (1992) – Committee on Disinvestment of Public Sector Enterprises
- ✓ Rekhi Committee (1993) – Indirect Taxation
- ✓ Wanchoo committee (1970) – Direct Taxation Enquiry Committee
- ✓ Shivraman Committee (1979) – Establishment of NABARD
- ✓ Tendulkar Committee (2009) – Redefining poverty line and its calculation
- ✓ NK Singh Committee – Review of FRBM act
- ✓ Khusro Committee (1989) – Agricultural credit system -1989

Concepts and Introducers

Accelerator → J.M. Clark

Super multiplier → J.R. Hicks

Social Accounting → J.R. Hicks

Social Marginal Productivity Criteria → Kahn, Chenery

Offer Curve → Marshall, Edge worth

Uncertainty bearing theory of profit → Knight

Learning by doing → Kenneth Arrow

Gross Barter TOT → F.W. Taussig

Income TOT → Dorrance

Single and double factoral TOT → Jacob Viner

Purchasing Power Parity → Gustav Cassel

Theory of Reciprocal Demand → J.S. Mill

Modern Theory of International Trade → Heckshen Ohlin

Factor Price Equalization Theorem → Samuelson

Immiserizing Growth → Jagdish Bhagwati

Absorption approach → Alexander

Vent for Surplus → Adam Smith

Protectionism supporter → Friedrich List

Free trade supporter → Jagdish Bhagwati, Lipsey

Absolute Advantage Theory → Adam Smith

Theory of Value and Theory of Rent → Ricardo

Theory of Circular Causation → Myrdal

Principles of Public Finance → Dalton & Pigou

Public Choice Theory → James Buchanan

Benefit Theory→ Lindahl

Principles of Taxes →Adam Smith

Canon of Budget → Harrod. D. Smith

Ability to Pay → Seligman

Time Series Criteria → AK Sen

Reinvestment Criteria → Galenson/Lebenstein

LPP → Dantzig

Social Dualism → Boeke

Technical Dualism → Higgins

Two Gap Model → Chenery and Strout

Golden Rule of Accumulation → Phelps

Golden Age → Robinson

Low level equilibrium trap → Nelson

Demonstration effect → Duesenberry

Permanent Income Hypothesis → Friedman

Relative Income Hypothesis → Duesenberry

Absolute Income Hypothesis → J.M. Keynes

Life Cycle Income Hypothesis → Modigliani and Brumberg

Wealth Effect → Pigou

Real Balance Effect → Patinkin

Financial Dualism → Myint

Comparative Cost Theory → Ricardo

Opportunity Cost Theory → Haberler

Real Cost Theory → Marshall, Bastable

X-inefficiency → Lebenstein

Efficiency Wage Theory → Yelen and Stiglitz

Supply Side of International Trade → Ricardo

Demand Side of International Trade → Marshall, Edgeworth

Principles of Public Expenditure: George Findlay Shirras

Note: The book is just revision notes. For detailed explanations, kindly rely on course classes of MS Study Guru by Dr. Simranjit Kaur.

References/ Further Readings

Ahuja, H. L. (2017). Modern Microeconomics. S. Chand Publishing.

Bhatia, H. L. (2022). Public Finance. Vikas Publishing House.

Froyen, R. T. (2013). Macroeconomics: Theories and Policies. Pearson (3rd ed.).

Gujarati, D. N., & Porter, D. C. (2008). Basic Econometrics (5th ed.). McGraw-Hill.

Gupta, S. C. (2021). Fundamentals of Statistics. Himalaya Publishing House.

Jain, T. R., et al. (2007). Development Economics. VK Publications.

Jhingan, M. L. (2017). Macroeconomic Theory. Vrinda Publications.

Koutsoyiannis, A. (1977). Theory of Econometrics: An Introductory. Macmillan.

Koutsoyiannis, A. (1975). Modern Microeconomics (2nd ed.). Macmillan.

Mishra, S. K., & Puri, V. K. (2022). Indian Economy. Himalaya Publishing House.

National Council of Educational Research and Training (NCERT). (2023). Mathematics – Class XII (Parts 1 & 2). NCERT.

Salvatore, D. (2016). International Economics (11th ed.). Wiley.